Ecotourism Book Series

General Editor: David B. Weaver, Professor of Tourism Management, George Mason University, Virginia, USA.

Ecotourism, or nature-based tourism that is managed to be learning-orientated as environmentally and socioculturally sustainable, has emerged in the past 20 years as one of the most important sectors within the global tourism industry. The purpose of this series is to provide diverse stakeholders (e.g. academics, graduate and senior undergraduate students, practitioners, protected area managers, government and non-governmental organizations) with state-of-the-art and scientifically sound strategic knowledge about all the facets of ecotourism, including external environments that influence its development. Contributions adopt a holistic, critical and interdisciplinary approach that combines relevant theory and practice while placing case studies from specific destinations into an international context. The series supports the development and diffusion of financially viable ecotourism that fulfils the objective of environmental, socio-cultural and economic sustainability at both the local and global scale.

Titles available
1. *Nature-based Tourism, Environment and Land Management*
        Edited by R. Buckley, C. Pickering and D.B. Weaver

Nature-based Tourism, Environment and Land Management

Edited by

R. Buckley

International Centre for Ecotourism Research
Griffith University
Queensland
Australia

C. Pickering

International Centre for Ecotourism Research
Griffith University
Queensland
Australia

and

D.B. Weaver

Department of Health, Fitness
and Recreation Resources
George Mason University
Manassas
USA

CABI Publishing

CABI Publishing is a division of CAB International

CABI Publishing
CAB International
Wallingford
Oxon OX10 8DE
UK

CABI Publishing
44 Brattle Street
4th Floor
Cambridge, MA 02138
USA

Tel: +44 (0)1491 832111
Fax: +44 (0)1491 833508
E-mail: cabi@cabi.org
Website: www.cabi-publishing.org

Tel: +1 617 395 4056
Fax: +1 617 354 6875
E-mail: cabi-nao@cabi.org

A catalogue record for this book is available from the British Library, London, UK.

Library of Congress Cataloging-in-Publication Data
Fenner Conference on Nature Tourism and the Environment (2001 : Canberra, A.C.T.)
    Nature-based tourism, environment, and land management / edited by R. Buckley, C. Pickering, and D. Weaver.
        p. cm. -- (Ecotourism book series)
Papers presented at the Fenner Conference on Nature Tourism and the Environment, held in Canberra, Australia, 2001.
Includes bibliographical references and index.
    ISBN 0-85199-732-5 (alk. paper)
    1. Ecotourism--Congresses. 2. Ecotourism--Australia--Congresses. 3. Land use--Congresses. 4. Land use--Australia--Congresses. I. Buckley, Ralf. II. Pickering, C. (Catherine) III. Weaver, David B. (David Bruce) IV. Title. V. Series.
    G156.5.E26F47 2001
    338.4'791--dc21
                        2003004153

ISBN 0 85199 732 5

Typeset by Wyvern 21 Ltd, Bristol
Printed and bound in the UK by Biddles Ltd, King's Lynn.

Contents

Contributors

C. **Arrowsmith**, *Department of Geospatial Science, RMIT University, GPO Box 2476V, Melbourne, Vic 3001, Australia.* colin.arrowsmith@rmit.edu.au

R. **Aspinall**, *Department of Earth Science, Montana State University, Bozeman, Montana, USA.*

R. **Booth**, *School of Animal Studies, University of Queensland, Gatton, Qld 4343, Australia.*

W.T. **Borrie**, *University of Montana, Missoula, Montana, USA.*

R. **Buckley**, *International Centre for Ecotourism Research, Griffith University, PMB 50, Gold Coast Mail Centre, Qld 9726, Australia.* r.buckley@griffith.edu.au

R. **Bushell**, *School of Environment and Agriculture, University of Western Sydney, Locked Bag 1797, Penrith South DC, NSW 1797, Australia.* r.bushell@uws.edu.au

T. **Byrnes**, *School of Environmental and Applied Sciences, Griffith University, PMB 50, Gold Coast Mail Centre, Qld 9726, Australia.* t.byrnes@griffith.edu.au

L. **Carlisle**, *Conservation Corporation Africa, PO Box 966, White River, 1240 South Africa.* l.carlisle@ccafrica.com

N. **Chilcott**, *Department of Primary Industries, Water and Environment, GPO Box 44A, Hobart, Tas. 7001, Australia.*

G. **Enders**, *New South Wales National Parks Service, Snowy Mountains Region, PO Box 2228, Jindabyne, NSW 2627, Australia.*

K. **Green**, *New South Wales National Parks Service, Snowy Mountains Region, PO Box 2228, Jindabyne, NSW 2627, Australia.*

M. **Guest**, *School of Environmental and Applied Sciences, Griffith University, PMB 50, Gold Coast Mail Centre, Qld 9726, Australia.* m.guest@griffith.edu.au

K. **Higginbottom**, *School of Environmental and Applied Sciences, Griffith University, PMB 50, Gold Coast Mail Centre, Qld 9726, Australia.* k.higginbottom@griffith.edu.au

W. **Hill**, *School of Environmental and Applied Sciences, Griffith University, PMB 50, Gold Coast Mail Centre, Qld 9726, Australia.*

J. **Johnson**, *Department of Political Science, Montana State University, Wilson Hall 2-438, Bozeman, MT 69717, USA.* jdj@montana.edu

S. **Johnston**, *School of Resources, Environment and Society, Australian National University, Canberra, ACT 0200, Australia.*

N. **King**, *International Centre for Ecotourism Research, Griffith University, PMB 50, Gold Coast Mail Centre, Qld 9726, Australia.*

R. **Ling**, *Department of Primary Industries, Water and Environment, GPO Box 44A, Hobart, Tas. 7001, Australia.*

J. **McDonald**, *School of Law, Griffith University, PMB 50, Gold Coast Mail Centre, Qld 9726, Australia.* jan.mcdonald@griffith.edu.au

B. Maxwell, *Land Resources and Environmental Science, Montana State University, Bozeman, Montana, USA.*

C. Pickering, *School of Environmental and Applied Sciences, Griffith University, PMB 50, Gold Coast Mail Centre, Qld 9726, Australia.* c.pickering@griffith.edu.au

A. Tribe, *School of Animal Studies, University of Queensland, Gatton, Qld 4343, Australia.*

J. Ward, *Australian School of Environmental Studies, Griffith University, Kessels Road, Nathan, Qld 4111, Australia.* john.ward@griffith.edu.au

J. Warnken, *School of Environmental and Applied Sciences, Griffith University, PMB 50, Gold Coast Mail Centre, Qld 9726, Australia.* j.warnken@griffith.edu.au

A.E. Watson, *Aldo Leopold Wilderness Research Institute, Departments of The Interior and Agriculture, Box 8089, Missoula, Montana, USA.* awatson@fs.fed.us

D.B. Weaver, Tourism and Events Management, *Department of Health, Fitness and Recreation Resources, George Mason University, 10900 University Blvd, M5-4E5 Manassas, VA 20110-2203, USA.* dweaver3@gmu.edu

J. Whinam, *Department of Primary Industries, Water and Environment, GPO Box 44A, Hobart, Tas. 7001, Australia.* jennie.whinam@dpiwe.tas.gov.au

N. Witting, *School of Environmental Studies, Griffith University, Kessels Road, Nathan, Qld 4111, Australia.* n.witting@griffith.edu.au

P. Wyatt, *Department of Primary Industries, Water and Environment, GPO Box 44A, Hobart, Tas. 7001, Australia.*

E. Yunis, *Sustainable Development of Tourism, World Tourism Organization, Capitan Haya 42, 28020 Madrid, Spain.* eyunis@world-tourism.org

Preface

The nature-tourism industry needs access to land with scenery, native plants and wildlife. Land managers need money to maintain their land, its natural resources and built infrastructure. For private lands and public lands managed for economic production, landholders also expect an economic return over and above operating costs. In national parks and other public lands allocated for conservation, management agencies face increasing costs from growing visitor numbers, demands and sometimes litigation, and severe shortfalls in government funding.

Links, partnerships and conflicts between commercial tourism interests and land-management agencies are hence assuming increasing importance worldwide; and similar issues are faced repeatedly in different places, jurisdictions and nations. It is therefore in the interests of land managers and tour operators alike to exchange information on approaches attempted and lessons learned, whether within the same country or between different continents. Neighbouring states can learn from each others' experiences, and developed countries have as much to learn from developing nations as vice versa.

With these considerations in mind, the International Centre for Ecotourism Research convened the 2001 Fenner Conference on Nature Tourism and the Environment, with major support from the Australian Academy of Science and Griffith University, and additional sponsorship from parks agencies and tourism interests throughout Australia and elsewhere (Buckley, 2001). That conference provided the catalyst for this volume. From 72 presentations, this book has distilled 15 technical chapters, plus introductory chapters by the editors and Mr Eugenio Yunis of the World Tourism Organization. Contributions to the conference were screened for international relevance, refereed for academic content and significance, revised repeatedly by the authors and modified more or less extensively by the editors of this volume.

We trust these chapters will be of broad contemporary interest worldwide. In particular, we take pleasure in presenting a number of Australian case studies which can provide valuable counterparts to the more extensive literature from Europe and North America.

Reference

Buckley, R.C. (ed.) (2001) *Abstracts 2001 Fenner Conference on Nature Tourism and the Environment.* Australian Academy of Science, Canberra, and Griffith University, Gold Coast.

1

The Practice and Politics of Tourism and Land Management

Ralf Buckley

International Centre for Ecotourism Research, Griffith University, Queensland, Australia

Tourism based on natural environments is a huge international industry with major economic, social and environmental consequences at both local and global scales. Just how big it is depends on what we include. For example, how far do we attempt to disaggregate or unbundle the motivations and expenditure of tourists, and the packaging of tour products, so as to distinguish built, cultural and natural attractions? How much of the indirect economic activity associated with tourism do we include, such as recreational equipment manufacturing, or recreational use of private vehicles and personal time? In very broad terms, it seems that the attractions of natural areas and their closely associated local cultures, and the various associated tourist, recreational and leisure activities, contribute around half the total economic activity attributable to the travel and tourism sector (Stueve *et al.*, 2002). Global nature tourism, in other words, is worth at least US$250 billion a year. Indeed, one past estimate (J. Mallett, 1998, unpublished) suggests that the US adventure-tourism sector alone is almost this large, if recreational equipment is included; and a more recent estimate suggests that US and Canadian national parks inject around US$250 billion a year into the North American economy, through various mechanisms including nature tourism (Eagles, 2002).

As tourism in natural areas continues to grow, it has an increasing influence on land managers in those areas. Many private, public and community landholders are turning to nature tourism as a profitable adjunct or replacement for farming, forestry or fisheries; and management agencies for public conservation, heritage, wilderness and recreation areas are facing more and more clamorous and conflicting demands from increasing numbers of visitors and users, commercial tour operators as well as individual recreational users and non-profit groups.

The precise patterns and trends differ among continents, countries and regions, but many of the issues are very similar. For example, private wildlife reserves have a rather different history in North America and sub-Saharan Africa, but in either case they have to fund their entire land and wildlife management costs through various commercial ventures, which may include sport hunting as well as photo safaris and game lodges. The politics of tourism in public forests differs enormously between Australia and the USA, but

© CAB International 2003. *Nature-based Tourism, Environment and Land Management*
(eds R. Buckley, C. Pickering and D.B. Weaver)

the techniques used to compare the economic value of tourism with that of logging are the same. Entrance, camping fees and commercial tour-operator permit fees are different from country to country and indeed park to park, but the issues are very similar worldwide. The list is long.

Historically, landholders and land-management agencies around the world have tended to address such issues rather independently. Information exchanges have been largely informal, through personal contacts, exchanges of agency reports and occasional conferences. While this provides opportunities for innovation and creativity, it can also be inefficient – and, given the chronic underfunding of many of the world's protected area management agencies, inefficiency is not something they can easily afford. Fortunately, the World Wide Web has provided much easier international access to major agency reports than in the past. Commonly, however, material available is at either a policy or an operational level, with little indication of the data, analysis and rationale used to devise either.

As a small contribution to land management for nature tourism, therefore, we have compiled the 19 contributions presented here, addressing a wide range of relevant issues. Australian voices are prevalent but by no means dominant, and many of the approaches to nature tourism and land management in Australia are as relevant for other continents as vice versa.

In the world's developed nations, in all continents and languages, there seem to be two very large-scale social trends that are affecting the interactions between nature tourism and land managers. The first of these is the growth of the adventure-tourism sector and its increasing connections with the fashion, clothing and entertainment industries. I have argued elsewhere (Buckley, 1998) that the growth of packaged commercial outdoor recreation, in the form of adventure tourism, is a consequence of the increased urbanization of most developed nations. Likewise, I have argued (WTO, 2000) that, in terms of its financial and corporate structure, adventure tourism is increasingly becoming a subsidiary of the clothing industry. The latter, however, is driven by fashion rather than large-scale social change, and is therefore likely to be a more temporary phenomenon.

In any event, there is an increasing demand for commercial outdoor adventure activities worldwide. Forest lodges that formerly offered nature walks as their sole visitor activity have now installed canopy cables, and national parks are under pressure to host multi-sport endurance races. Private landholders can make more money by charging four-wheel-drive owners to use their paddocks as an obstacle course than by running cattle. And, as visitor numbers increase, occasional encounters between hikers and horseback riders can escalate into major conflicts between different user groups. At the same time, questions of legal liability (McDonald, Chapter 6, this volume) and of recreational capacity (Haas, 2002) have assumed increasing importance.

The other major global trend is so-called amenity migration, where rich people from large cities build big houses in scenic rural areas, often adjacent to national parks, and continue to conduct business through high-speed cable communications. The financial scale of associated land and property sales commonly dwarfs that of tourism, to the point where Johnson et al. (Chapter 9, this volume) have referred to tourism as a transitional economy. Links between tourism and residential developments are long-standing, but the pattern has changed. Historically, it was beach towns and similar destinations that attracted amenity migrants, and this is still the case in cities such as Australia's Gold Coast, where hotels, tourist apartments and permanent residents are inextricably intertwined and there is a continuing influx of permanent migrants from larger cities, such as Sydney and Melbourne. This, however, is very much an urban migration, unrelated to nature tourism. A more recent trend is that greenfield tourist resorts, whether featuring ocean-front marinas, rural golf courses or mountain ski fields, have relied on residential subdivisions as their major financial engine, with the retail tourism operations acting principally as a base for property investment. Such developments, though sometimes in areas of considerable conservation significance, are commonly large enough to trigger legal requirements for formal environmental-impact assessment (EIA) as a component of development approval processes. Where such developments are likely to have impacts on national parks or heritage areas, in principle the EIA process should take such impacts into account, though this does not always happen in practice.

Construction of holiday homes in scenic rural areas, often with a view to continuous occupation during retirement, is also a long-standing phenomenon in many of the world's holiday-destination areas. What seems to be new is the migration of active, wealthy, mid-career professional and business people to upmarket-acreage residential communities in areas famous for outdoor recreation opportunities, often adjacent to national parks. This is occurring particularly in the Rocky Mountains states and provinces of north-west USA and south-west Canada, where tiny rural towns have recently attracted a rush of land speculation. A similar effect is occurring on a much smaller scale in the Australian snow country, and in South Africa it is now possible to buy residential land inside private game reserves, with appropriate covenants on building design and management.

This growth of residential development around the borders of protected areas introduces new challenges for protected-area managers. Residential land divisions are commonly much smaller than farms, and more often fenced, so residential estates provide more of a barrier to wildlife movement than farms or forests. Straying livestock may become less common, but feral cats and dogs much more so, as well as other exotic species kept as pets. A new suite of garden weeds may be added to introduced pasture grasses and other farm weeds. Ranchers' concerns over livestock losses to native predators may be replaced by residents' lobbies for greater recreational access. Residential areas not only increase fire sources enormously, but also restrict fire-management options and increase the financial and human risks from wildfires that escape from the borders of protected areas.

Pressure around the borders of protected areas is certainly not restricted to developed nations. In much of east and South-East Asia, for example, areas nominally allocated as buffer zones around core conservation areas are in fact occupied by subsistence landholders right up to the last metre, and sometimes beyond. Incursions into protected areas, whether for wildlife poaching or subsistence hunting, are commonplace. In many parts of Africa and South America, there is constant pressure for protected areas to be made available for subsistence settlement. In parts of Zimbabwe, this has in fact already happened. Private game reserves, in consequence, must continually demonstrate their economic support for neighbouring communities (Carlisle, Chapter 4, this volume). Similarly, the economic success of nature tourism in the Galapagos Islands has attracted a large number of migrants from mainland Ecuador, who are now lobbying to be given land inside the national park (Weaver, 2000).

National Parks in North America and Australia may not be under quite such immediate threat as those in Africa, but there are none the less considerable similarities. In the USA, for example, the Bush government recently opened Alaska's Arctic National Wildlife Refuge for oil exploration, despite major concerns from conservation interests. In Yellowstone National Park, lobbying by recreational-equipment manufacturers led the Bush government to overturn plans to curb off-track winter use by snowmobiles, despite the major noise and disturbance impacts on wildlife as well as other users.

Increasingly, parks agencies can no longer rely on the legal mandate of their own establishing legislation to carry out their primary conservation function. Facing politically powerful and experienced lobby groups who want to use parks for their own purposes, conservation-management agencies are being forced to mobilize their own political support. Historically, this has come directly from voters with conservation interests, such as members of voluntary conservation groups. In countries with right-wing national governments, such as the USA and Australia in 2002, however, these groups have little political power, since their members are in any event unlikely to vote for the incumbent government. Instead, therefore, land-management agencies have to turn to their low-impact users, those whose primary interest is in the peaceful contemplation of nature, to provide a political force for the future.

In the USA, this has led the National Parks Service to turn to the concepts of relationship marketing (Watson and Borrie, Chapter 5, this volume). In Australia, however, these pressures seem to be leading instead to a kind of political fire-sale of public protected areas to commercial tourism interests. While the various parks agencies certainly recognize the importance of maintaining political support for future public funding, this is a long-term exercise. In the meantime, they are faced with rapidly increasing visitor numbers and demands. They do not have the political capital to obtain a corresponding increase in public funding in the short term, or even to impose limits on visitor numbers except in the most obvious cases of major environmental degradation. Nor do they have the political capital to charge entrance and activity fees that are large enough to cover a significant proportion of their operating costs.

Under these circumstances, protected-area management agencies may be forced into bargains with commercial interests that are prepared to provide cash in return for preferential rights, typically the exclusive privilege to build and operate tourist infrastructure of various types. Such ventures are commonly carried out under the rhetoric of partnership. In principle, the primary purpose of a partnership is to provide benefits for all partners. The critical issue for protected-area management agencies is that, if they are forced into arrangements where they have weak negotiating leverage, the costs and benefits of these partnerships are likely to be highly asymmetric. Tourism interests can obtain commercial access to publicly owned natural attractions far more cheaply than if they had to buy private land; and in addition they obtain the benefits of publicly funded roads, tracks, visitor facilities, land management, rangers and even marketing.

Economic analyses such as those by Ward (Chapter 8, this volume) indicate conclusively that nature tourism can provide major economic benefits from public lands, such as national or state forests; and, indeed, the US Forestry Service has now recognized for some years that its primary business is in providing recreation opportunities rather than timber. In the very few instances in Australia where public forest-management agencies have turned their hands to tourism, notably the Tree Top Walk in Western Australia and the Tahune Airwalk in Tasmania, the economic returns have far exceeded expectations (Buckley, 2003). Similarly, examples from around the world indicate that, in many circumstances, nature tourism can be more profitable than farming, and private landholders are modifying their land-use mix accordingly. If commercial tour operators can get free or cheap access to public national parks with all their associated facilities, however, clearly their costs are far less than if they have to install their own infrastructure elsewhere. In addition, existing visitors to national parks effectively provide a ready-made and semi-captive market for commercial enterprises with concession rights.

As the area of wilderness worldwide continues to decrease, particularly in regions with easy access from major urban centres, national parks and other protected areas become increasingly valuable. It seems that tourism interests, government as well as commercial, recognize this value and its future growth, and are trying to capture them. One approach is to buy adjacent land that is similar but unprotected; as in the case of amenity migration, many private lodges and a number of major tourist resorts. In countries such as Australia, however, tourism interests are currently pursuing political approaches that would allow them to reap most of the potential profits available from public demand to visit protected areas, while paying only a small fraction of management costs and none of the capital costs.

Tourism interests, principally government rather than private, sometimes argue that other industry sectors such as forestry have free or even subsidized access to public natural resources, so why not tourism? This argument, however, misses the fundamental point that some public lands are allocated for production and others for protection. If tourism can generate greater economic benefits from publicly owned forest or farmland than logging or livestock respectively, or greater benefit from publicly owned rivers and oceans from boating, diving and angling than from commercial fisheries, that does indeed provide a strong argument to change land- or water-use allocation in those areas from primary industries to tourism. It does not, however, provide an argument to provide access to protected areas as a public subsidy for the tourism sector, at the same time continuing to subsidize forestry, farming and fisheries in other areas.

The political behaviour of landholders and land-management agencies has been mixed. Private landholders, not surprisingly, have taken advantage of commercial opportunities in nature tourism where these have arisen. In most cases, these landholders are farmers and ranchers, and they have added tourism to their land-use mix in the same way that they would add any other new crop or livestock species: cautiously at first, and without abandoning other crops or stock. Tourists are seen as an exotic, slightly speculative but potentially profitable venture, akin to planting vines or starting an alpaca stud or an ostrich farm. And why not?

Management agencies for public land such as state and national forests have effectively taken a similar approach, but much more slowly, because their principal currency is political support rather than market returns. If a forestry agency relies on logging contractors, sawmills and timber towns for political support, simply knowing that nature tourism is a far more productive use of public forest assets than timber production (Ward, Chapter 8, this volume) does not in itself lead to a change in land use. Unless the change is forced upon it from above by larger-scale political events, a forestry agency can only add tourism to its land-use mix gradually and in such a way as to maintain its political capital and currency from timber interests. Only once residents in local communities begin to feel the economic benefit of nature tourism can forestry agencies increase the scope of their tourist activities.

In national-parks and protected-area management agencies, there seems to be a perception that agencies should retain responsibility for resource- and conservation-management activities, which is what their staff are commonly trained in, and hive off vis-

itor services as quickly as possible to commercial tourism interests. There does not seem to be a general perception that these revenue streams may be essential in future to fund primary conservation activities. As noted by Coggins and Glicksman (1997), however, there is no obligation for parks agencies to fulfil only the unprofitable components of their mandates.

How these various political debates pan out in different countries remains to be seen. Meanwhile, however, at a global scale the interactions between the nature-tourism industry and conservation land management, both positive and negative, are becoming more and more significant for both, and a shared and solid information base in both the natural and social sciences is equally important for both. We trust that this compilation will provide a small addition to previous contributions, such as those of Lime (1990), Cole *et al.* (1999), Manning (1999), Eagles and McCool (2002), Hendee and Dawson (2002) and Newsome *et al.* (2002), and that it may provide a catalyst for more detailed information exchange in future.

References

Buckley, R.C. (1998) Ecotourism megatrends. *Australian International Business Review* 1998, 52–54.

Buckley, R.C. (2003) *Case Studies in Ecotourism.* CAB International, Wallingford.

Coggins, G.C. and Glicksman, R.L. (1997) Concessions law and policy in the national parks system. *Denver University Law Review* 74, 729–778.

Cole, D.N., McCool, S.F., Borrie, W.T. and O'Loughlin, J. (eds) (1999) *Wilderness Science in Time of Change*, Vols 4 and 5. USDA Forest Service, Ogden, Utah.

Eagles, P.F.J. (2002) Trends in park tourism: economics, finance and management. *Journal of Sustainable Tourism* 10, 132–153.

Eagles, P.F.J. and McCool, S. (2002) *Tourism in National Parks and Protected Areas.* CAB International, Wallingford.

Haas, G. (2002) *Visitor Capacity on Public Land and Waters.* NRPA, Ashburn, Virginia.

Hendee, J. and Dawson, C. (eds) (2002) *Wilderness Management,* 3rd edn. WILD Foundation and Fulcrum Publishing, Golden, Colorado.

Lime, D.W. (ed.) (1990) *Managing America's Enduring Wilderness Resource.* University of Minnesota, St Paul.

Manning, R. (1999) *Studies in Outdoor Recreation,* 2nd edn. Oregon University Press, Corvallis.

Newsome, D., Moore, S.A. and Dowling, R.K. (2002) *Natural Area Tourism: Ecology Impacts and Management.* Channel View, Clevedon.

Stueve, A.M., Cock, S.D. and Drew, D. (2002) *The Geotourism Study: Phase 1 Executive Summary.* www.tia.org/pubs/geotourismphase-final.pdf Last viewed 12 June 2002.

Weaver, D. (2000) Tourism and national parks in ecologically vulnerable areas. In: Butler, R.V. and Boyd, S.W. (eds) *Tourism and National Parks: Issues and Implications.* John Wiley & Sons, Chichester, pp. 107–124.

World Tourism Organization (WTO) (2000) *Island Tourism in Asia and the Pacific.* World Tourism Organization, Madrid.

2

Nature-based Tourism and Sustainability: Issues and Approaches

Catherine Pickering[1] and David Bruce Weaver[2]

[1]School of Environmental and Applied Sciences, Griffith University, Queensland, Australia; [2]Tourism and Events Management, Department of Health, Fitness and Recreation Resources, George Mason University, Manassas, Virginia, USA

What can we say with authority about nature-based tourism? First, it accounts for a large proportion of the global tourism industry (Eagles *et al.*, 2002; Newsome *et al.*, 2002; Buckley, Chapter 1, this volume). Secondly, this proportion is increasing as nature-based tourism continues to grow faster than the tourism sector overall (Newsome *et al.*, 2002; Watson and Borrie, Chapter 5, this volume). Thirdly, nature-based tourism occurs in both public and private spaces and hence is managed by public agencies as well as private industry and non-governmental organizations (Buckley, Chapter 1, Carlisle, Chapter 4, Watson and Borrie, Chapter 5, and Yunis Chapter 3, this volume). Fourthly, nature-based tourism is an extremely diverse sector that encompasses such potentially incompatible activities as wildlife viewing (i.e. ecotourism) (Carlisle, Chapter 4, and Higginbottom *et al.*, Chapter 17, this volume), boating (Byrnes and Warnken, Chapter 12, and Warnken and Byrnes, Chapter 11, this volume) and skiing and walking in alpine areas (Pickering and Hill, Chapter 14, and Pickering *et al.*, Chapter 13, this volume). Fifthly, there is a complex array of potential economic, sociocultural and environmental costs and benefits associated with nature-based tourism, as illustrated by most of the chapters in this volume.

As with all forms of tourism, the planning and management of nature-based tourism is increasingly mediated by the paradigm of sustainability. In the third chapter of this book, Yunis outlines the current state of play in the formulation of policies and practices that ensure environmentally, economically and socioculturally sustainable outcomes for the tourism sector, especially as they have evolved since the seminal Rio Earth Summit in 1992. Given the size, growth rate, ubiquity, diversity and variable impacts cited above, it can be argued that the goal of sustainability is especially imperative in the nature-based tourism sector. Indeed, the attempt to operate in a sustainable manner is universally acknowledged as one of the core criteria of ecotourism (Blamey, 2001).

The chapters in this volume all provide insights into the complex relationships that are evolving between nature-based tourism and the paradigm of sustainability. For example,

Carlisle's discussion of the Conservation Corporation Africa (CCA) in Chapter 4 illustrates how the private sector can employ nature-based tourism to protect indigenous wildlife populations while simultaneously producing economic and sociocultural benefits for local communities that would otherwise continue to degrade their surroundings while failing to move beyond a marginal subsistence-based economy. Profit-motivated efforts such as these are often looked upon with suspicion by social scientists, and yet they seem to be both increasingly viable and vital in destinations where a financially constrained public sector cannot by itself maintain a protected-area system that effectively preserves the integrity of native ecosystems.

Constrained public sectors are not confined to the less developed world. As described by Watson and Borrie in Chapter 5, protected-area authorities in the USA are struggling to fulfil the dual mandates of environmental preservation and the provision of services to an ever-growing nature-based tourism clientele. In response, the US Forestry Service is experimenting with a 'businesslike' marketing approach that packages tourism 'products' for 'customers' whose needs must be satisfied. The authors point out that such an approach must combine commercial impulses with a focus on relationships, trust, commitment and social responsibility in order to be successful within a broader sustainability model.

An additional consideration that can profoundly influence the viability of public protected areas, especially in the more developed world, is the issue of liability. In Chapter 6, McDonald examines the competing policy considerations posed for park managers of conserving natural environments and providing an array of nature-based experiences while protecting visitors to the park from injury. She examines the common-law principles of negligence, nuisance and breach of statutory duty, and how these relate to providing warning signs, the obviousness of a danger and visitor carelessness. Alternative approaches, such as statutory immunities and statutory compensation schemes, are also described.

Whether liability is a pressing issue or not, park agencies must always pay heed to the financial bottom line in their quest to remain effective and viable. Tourists clearly pose a potential liability threat, but they also offer lucrative opportunities for revenue generation through the levying of visitor user fees and activity permits. Buckley, Witting and Guest review the use of fees and permits in Australian protected areas in Chapter 7. They find considerable variation among the states and territories in terms of types of fees and licences and the amounts charged. The potential for linking fees to sustainability is considerable, not just in the revenues that are generated to facilitate sustainable management in protected areas, but also through such developments as the expanding practice of giving preferential access to tour operators and tour guides accredited under the Nature and Ecotourism Accreditation Program (NEAP). This Australian trend will, hopefully, encourage other countries to pursue a NEAP-type accreditation scheme.

The previous four chapters all demonstrate the link between environmental, economic and sociocultural sustainability on the one hand and financial sustainability on the other. If protected areas cannot generate sufficient revenues from tourism and other activities, they are unlikely to be effective in preserving ecosystems while providing high-quality visitor experiences. It is therefore reassuring to read Ward's comparison in Chapter 8 between the revenue-generating potential of tourism and logging in the Australian state of New South Wales. His modelling finds that the promotion of nature tourism in the native forests of national parks can maximize economic benefits more than timber production for the same forest types and locations. This benefit occurred without including additional potential economic benefits from non-consumptive use of the forest such as ecosystems services and options values.

Ward's study reminds us that the environmental, economic and sociocultural sustainability of tourism is also crucially influenced, both directly and indirectly, by the sustainability of other resource stakeholders. A model ecotourism operation in an Australian native forest, for example, is of little consequence if a local timber company is unsustainably logging those same or adjacent forests or if extensive strip mining is occurring in the vicinity. External influences of a different sort are evident in the case study of amenity migration provided by Johnson, Maxwell and Aspinall in Chapter 9. Their examination of the Greater Yellowstone Region in the western USA shows that private lands adjacent to public protected areas are an increasingly popular migration destination of choice for urban exiles and others desiring proximity to a relatively undisturbed natural environment. Yet the scope of this so-called amenity migration (triggered in most instances by one's own experience as a visitor to the area) is such that it threatens to undermine the very qualities that induced the flow in the first place. The authors describe land-use change models that can assist local communities in managing population growth so that the basic integrity of the region and its public protected areas is not undermined.

Because external influences are often more difficult to identify and control, it is not surprising that more attention has been paid to the impacts of tourism itself. However, as Buckley and King emphasize in Chapter 10, our knowledge of nature-based tourism impacts is itself still rudimentary in some respects. The authors find that the direct and obvious impacts of tourism and recreation are widely recognized (for example, the effects of off-road vehicles), but that for more complex and less obvious direct and indirect impacts, such as weed and pathogen diffusion, there is limited knowledge. Their review of knowledge regarding the relationship between nature-based tourism and the dieback pathogen *Phytophthora cinnamomi*, moreover, illustrates that even the most ostensibly benign tourism activity, such as wildlife viewing, can lead to inadvertent negative environmental impacts. They highlight the need for more local and high-quality ecological research for the management of tourism and recreation in areas of high conservation value.

Subsequent chapters in this book pursue the theme of environmental impacts related to nature-based tourism. In Chapter 11, Warnken and Byrnes follow on from Buckley and King by examining the impacts associated with small recreational and tourist boats using inshore coastal areas, an activity that is becoming increasingly popular. They examine the impact of anti-fouling agents and sewage discharge, particularly on mooring sites, and find that, while there is evidence of impacts, there is a clear need for better sampling technology and design to identify the extent of marine pollution from small boats. The follow-up chapter by the same authors examines the effectiveness of legislation and regulation aimed at reducing the environmental impacts of the tour-boat industry. Using Australia as a case study, they find that a major impediment to self-regulation in this sector is a lack of recognition by stakeholders that they are part of an industry sector and that they do have negative impacts. This chapter indicates that the identification of negative impacts within the nature-based tourism sector does not automatically result in their timely alleviation, due to the intervention of various political, cultural, psychological and other 'human' factors.

The high conservation environment of the Australian snow country is the subject of Pickering and her colleagues in the following two chapters. In Chapter 13, Pickering, Johnston, Green and Enders describe the known impacts of tourism in the high mountain ecosystems surrounding Australia's highest peak. Adventurous activities such as cross-country skiing and ice climbing occur in the winter while wildflower appreciation and other forms of ecotourism tend to occur in the summer. As with Chapter 10, this research emphasizes the potentially harmful environmental effects that 'passive' activities such as walking can have on fragile habitats. More obvious are the deleterious effects of snow manipulation (snow making, grooming, etc.) at ski resorts, as described by Pickering and Hill in Chapter 14. This study highlights the fact that changed snow conditions can cause a cascade of effects on the ecology of this fragile ecosystem. Again, however, the impacts of such manipulations may be dwarfed by the influence of macro-external forces such as climate change, which could eliminate Australia's alpine ecosystems entirely within the next few decades (Green, 1998).

The issue of walking-related environmental impacts is pursued further in Chapter 15 within the context of the Tasmanian Wilderness World Heritage Area. Whinam,

Chilcott, Ling and Wyatt examine how walking carrying capacities have been calculated for this area. The methods that have been used for the walking track-management strategy emphasizes the ways in which impacts can be modelled and therefore more effectively managed using a combination of experimentation and geographical information systems mapping. The implications of these findings clearly extend well beyond the isolated confines of the Tasmanian wilderness.

Also internationally relevant is Arrowsmith's demonstration as to how models of environmental resilience can be combined with tourism-attractiveness models to produce a 'tourism-potential model'. Using a case study from a high-use protected area in south-eastern Australia (Grampians National Park), Arrowsmith in Chapter 16 shows how this tourism-potential model can assist in planning for nature-based tourism by identifying areas that have clusters of sites which are attractive to tourists as well as environmentally resilient. They can also identify, for management attention, existing hot spots where high attractiveness and use are resulting in negative impacts.

In Chapter 17, Higginbottom, Tribe and Booth move from a landscape level of management to an examination of the contributions of non-consumptive wildlife tourism to conservation. They compare the viewing of animals in captive settings such as zoos with wildlife viewing in free-range settings, and find that both ends of the non-consumptive nature-based tourism spectrum (i.e. captive to free-ranging) can produce significant positive environmental benefits. While more attention has been paid in the literature to the ethical problems of captive wildlife settings (Croke, 1997), these in fact are associated with important captive breeding programmes and serve to educate large numbers of people who may go on to develop a stronger environmental ethic. It is still unclear, however, whether the provision of mass-market wildlife viewing opportunities within captive settings serves to relieve or create tourism-related pressure on protected areas and other free-range environments.

Bushell, in Chapter 18, amalgamates many of the issues addressed in the earlier chapters in highlighting the global extent of nature-based tourism and its robust growth.

Cash-strapped protected-area agencies have an ambivalent relationship with tourism in that the latter is probably the best vehicle for alleviating the financial situation, but the increased visitation levels required to generate sufficient cash also pose a direct and indirect threat to the environmental integrity of those same protected areas. Bushell emphasizes that increased visitation therefore requires better but more costly management to limit negative environmental impacts from tourism. How cash-strapped park agencies obtain funds to operate sustainably is a paramount issue. Associated issues include the equitable levying of fees and the equitable distribution of economic benefits associated with nature-based tourism. Also, park managers must balance their competencies in conservation and nature-resource management with the ability to manage visitor flows in a way that both preserves the integrity of the natural environment and allows for high-quality and satisfying visitor experiences. It is fair to say that nature-based tourism is now a permanent fixture in most of the world's high-order protected areas, and the ability to balance and, hopefully, synergize the twin mandates of tourism and environmental preservation is perhaps the greatest challenge faced by protected-area managers.

References

Blamey, R. (2001) Principles of ecotourism. In: Weaver, D. (ed.) *The Encyclopedia of Ecotourism.* CAB International, Wallingford, UK, pp. 5–22.

Croke, V. (1997) *The Modern Ark: the Story of Zoos Past, Present and Future.* Scribner, New York.

Eagles, P.F.J., McCool, S.F. and Haynes, C.D. (2002) *Sustainable Tourism in Protected Areas: Guidelines for Planning and Management.* Best Practice Protected Area Guideline Series No. 8. World Commission on Protected Areas, Cambridge.

Green, K. (1998) *Snow, a Natural History: an Uncertain Future.* Australian Alps Liaison Committee, Canberra.

Newsome, D., Moore, S.A. and Dowling, R.K. (2002) *Natural Area Tourism: Ecology Impacts and Management.* Channel View, Clevedon, UK.

3

Sustainable Tourism: World Trends and Challenges Ahead

Eugenio Yunis

Sustainable Development of Tourism, World Tourism Organization, Madrid, Spain

Abstract

Sustainability has undoubtedly become the central issue in tourism development policies throughout the world. The chapter summarizes the role played and type of actions taken, since the Rio Earth Summit, by different stakeholders in tourism, including central and local governments, the tourism industry, the academic community, international agencies with special reference to the World Tourism Organization (WTO), and non-governmental organizations with a view to raising the level of sustainability of tourism.

A critical assessment of the actual progress made since Rio reveals that the road ahead now seems longer than it was in 1992, due to two main factors: the rapid growth in tourist movements, actual and forecast; and the absence of public regulation and public control of tourism activities, associated with the liberal economic-development policies currently in vogue. Though the level of sustainability awareness and the techniques and technologies have made substantial progress, the level of actual application in tourism is still limited to a few market segments, a few destinations and, a few operators. The tourism community cannot feel satisfied with the progress towards sustainable development until existing sustainable practices in tourism are capable of expanding beyond a few niche markets while the rest of the tourism industry keeps its priority clearly on profit rather than sustainability.

The WTO is a catalyst for efforts by a large number of international and national actors. The main elements of WTO's current work are: in the development and use of sustainable-tourism indicators; in providing local authorities with planning and management tools for the sustainable development of tourism; in providing new and exchanging successful management tools for handling congestion at mature tourism destinations; in giving higher credibility to certification schemes and ecolabels in tourism; and in the follow-up from the International Year of Ecotourism in 2002.

Introduction

Since the Rio Earth Summit, sustainability has undoubtedly become the central issue in tourism development policies throughout the world, almost without exception. The World Tourism Organization (WTO) has been promoting environmentally friendly and culturally sensitive tourism policies since the mid-1980s. This has included the adoption of a number of global declarations and associated methodological approaches for implementing the principles they contain, as well as the formulation of a number of national tourism master plans and similar tools through its technical cooperation activities. Similarly, since the 1970s a small but significant number of tourism companies, especially those offering nature-related services, have been promoting and adopting a more sustainable approach in their overall conception and operations, with what can be considered a pioneering attitude. However, the Rio Earth Summit was clearly a turning-point in the level of awareness about the need to ensure a more sustainable development of tourism among central and local governments, the tourism industry at large, academic institutions and other groups assembled around non-governmental organizations (NGOs).

Progress in Sustainable Tourism

In general terms, the need for a systematic planning approach in tourism has now become widely accepted. Tourism policies and strategies stressing the sustainability imperative have been recommended by a wide range of international organizations: WTO, the United Nations Environment Programme (UNEP), the Convention on Biological Diversity, the UN Educational, Scientific and Cultural Organisation (UNESCO), the regional UN commissions, the European Union, the international banks and, most recently, the UN Commission on Sustainable Development (UN-CSD). This sustainability imperative has generally been embraced by national, regional and local government authorities and, to some extent, by the tourism and travel trade: all such stakeholders have increasingly addressed environmental, economic and social sustainability issues in tourism.

The tourism academic community has also embraced sustainability as a research topic. It generated an impressive amount of literature on the subject during the 1990s, some based on empirical experience and some of a more theoretical nature. Multidisciplinary approaches to sustainability have added richness to the study of tourism. The academic research outcome, added to publications by international organizations and NGOs, consultants and other professionals, has created an abundant and widely available body of knowledge in the field of sustainability in tourism.

NGOs have played an important role in furthering awareness about sustainability issues in tourism among governments, the tourism trade and tourists. Many NGOs have taken significant steps not only in warning the authorities about the dangers of excessive and unplanned tourism growth or in campaigning against some of the negative impacts of tourism in developing countries, such as sexual exploitation of children, but also in educating consumers and tourism companies on how to better contribute to a sustainable development of the destinations they visit, including the welfare of local host communities.

Among other progress made over the last 10 years, we should also mention the increased adoption of voluntary initiatives related to sustainability in tourism, such as ecolabels, certification schemes, environmental awards and similar programmes. These have been created mainly by the tourism industry and occasionally by local or even central government agencies, and they reflect the growing concern of tourists and tourism companies vis-à-vis the environmental and social sustainability of tourism.

Can we then say that tourism is now operating in a sustainable manner throughout the world? Can we state that tourism destinations are generating economic, environmental and social benefits out of tourism, and that such benefits are evenly distributed among all those involved or affected by tourism activities? Is it realistic to say that massive tourism flows are no longer having a negative impact upon the natural environment, especially in small islands and coastal areas, or that such flows are not impinging on the cultural and social values of traditional societies? Can we be assured that a large majority of hotels and other tourism companies have adopted environmental management systems in their operations, minimizing the use of non-renewable resources and their untreated effluents? Finally, can we give assurances that the several hundred million tourists travelling around the world are aware of the likely impacts of their consumption patterns or their behaviour upon the places and countries they visit?

It would certainly be naive to pretend to give a purely positive answer to all these questions. Though the level of awareness and the techniques and technologies have made substantial progress, the level of actual application is still limited to a few market segments, a few destinations and a few operators. Progress towards sustainable development of tourism is hardly satisfactory while sustainable practices are restricted to a few niche markets, with the rest of the tourism industry keeping its priorities clearly on profit rather than sustainability.

higher level of sustainability in tourism, since tourism is, by definition, an international activity and an international business. Neither can the public sector alone, given its increasingly reduced involvement in economic activities, be made fully responsible for ensuring a sustainable tourism industry. The private sector has to adopt a more decisive attitude *vis-à-vis* sustainability, while the non-governmental sector and community organizations need to continue their vigilant role and contribute more positively to finding realistic solutions.

Challenges Ahead

In spite of the progress made since Rio, I personally have the impression that the road ahead of us is much longer than it was in 1992, given the continued and unstoppable growth of tourism around the world and the more liberal attitude that most governments and peoples have adopted towards its development and management.

According to data collected by WTO, the number of international tourist arrivals reached nearly 700 million in 2000, well over 10% of the world population. This represents a growth of 7.4% since 1999, much higher than expected and over twice the 1998/99 rate of 3.8%. These international movements generated receipts for a value of US$476 billion, plus an estimated US$100 billion in international transport fare receipts. The industry is expanding at a tremendous speed. International arrivals have grown steeply, from 25 million in 1950 to 166 million in 1970 and 700 million in 2000. Measured over the period 1975–2000, international tourist arrivals grew at an average rate of 4.8% a year.

Our forecasting studies, rigorously prepared and regularly updated to take into account changing factors, indicate that international tourist arrivals are expected to reach 1 billion by the year 2010 and almost 1.6 billion by the year 2020.

The challenge we have in front of us is, therefore, enormous. And it is a challenge that must be faced by all types of stakeholder, by all types of institution, public and private, in all countries, and with a cooperative spirit. No single country on its own can advance to a

The Role of WTO

What is the WTO doing towards achieving sustainability in tourism? I have already mentioned our pioneering role in generating awareness on some issues related to sustainability, as well as the generation of a substantial body of knowledge and its dissemination worldwide. Furthermore, the sustainability issues have been aggregated together with other ethical concerns into the *Global Code of Ethics for Tourism*, approved by consensus at our last General Assembly and subsequently endorsed by the UN General Assembly.

These efforts and their results would not have been possible without the cooperation of WTO's member states, among which Australia was one of our leading and most active members in the 1979–1990 period, but regrettably absent today.

At a more particular level, one major focus of our activity in this field over the last few years has been the local-authority sector. In most countries, it is at the local level that the main decisions concerning the extent, type and quality of tourism development are taken. Local authorities are normally in an institutional position to make key decisions in a number of public policy areas – related to physical, economic, cultural and social aspects – and it is these decisions that will determine whether tourism is harmoniously developed or whether it just grows, eating public and private spaces, allowing local traditions and value systems to disappear in a false attempt to replace most, if not all, traditional economic activities, instead of becoming integrated with them.

Local authorities can serve as the focal point for community participation in tourism policy decisions, in tourism management and in tourism monitoring. They are also well placed to generate the necessary links between key institutions, public and private, that must be involved in the tourism process to ensure its sustainability and its contribution to sustainable development in general.

We have produced methodological and planning guidelines for ensuring a sustainable development and public management of tourism specifically addressed to local authorities. These guidelines, in the form of practical manuals, have been disseminated via publications, with special volumes to cater for the regional differences in Africa, the Americas and Asia-Pacific, but also via training seminars in which over 1000 mayors and councillors have participated in the last couple of years.

Our work on indicators of sustainability in tourism has been equally critical, providing tourism stakeholders with practical instruments to evaluate performance and measure progress towards sustainability. The concept of sustainability is relatively new, although its three dimensions – social, environmental and economic – have a long history. The difficulty that many destinations and companies face is how to assess the degree to which their tourism operations are sustainable and whether they are making progress or not. The identification of a battery of environmental, economic and social indicators is fundamental to this process, as is the establishment of composite indicators that combine these three dimensions. Following recommendations ensuing from Agenda 21, WTO set up a task force in the early 1990s to study this matter, and a first publication was issued in 1996 proposing a methodology for the identification and development of sustainability indicators in tourism. Over the last 3 years we have been conducting practical-application workshops in various parts of the world and for different types of destinations to promote the use of indicators and teach stakeholders how to adapt them to their local conditions.

We are now reaching the stage where further methodological progress is needed in this area. A new international task force has been set up to exchange experiences with other organizations that have been involved with such indicators, and particularly with countries that have effectively applied sustainability indicators in tourism, such as Canada, France, Germany and Spain. A new handbook on sustainable tourism indicators is due for publication at the end of 2003.

A third area of WTO activity in the field of sustainable tourism relates to certification processes. Increased concern about the environmental and sociocultural impacts of tourism has led to the appearance of a number of labels, awards and certification schemes, usually of a voluntary nature. Such schemes have proliferated over the last 3–4 years to such an extent that it is difficult for the various tourism stakeholders, let alone for the tourist, to understand the real meaning of each of them and to use them as guidelines in their choice of tourism destinations and suppliers.

It was at WTO's instigation that the UN-CSD at its seventh session in April 1999 recommended 'an evaluation of the effectiveness of voluntary initiatives in tourism'. In 2000 we started our work in this field with a compilation of all such schemes, identifying nearly 500 of them around the world. In 2001 we completed a second stage with a selection of around 100 schemes to identify their operational features and the factors that make some of them more effective and credible than others. In the third stage, in 2002, we examined the need for and the feasibility of an accreditation body to guarantee that sustainability certificates, ecolabels and other such voluntary schemes are really fulfilling their declared purpose. In this phase we worked jointly with a number of other institutions and a large number of key stakeholders.

In the meantime, the public sector has a special and urgent role in ensuring that privately run certification schemes, ecolabels and similar voluntary initiatives currently being applied in tourism are not merely paying lip-service to sustainability, and that they do in fact respond to stringent and verifiable sustainability requirements and achieve a higher level of credibility among consumers.

WTO is also initiating a study on the management of congestion at mature tourism destinations, especially beach destinations that tend to attract mass tourist movements. It is sometimes mistakenly considered that sustainability concerns apply only to nature-based tourism or to other special forms of tourism. This mistake sometimes extends to the belief that mass tourism will always be unsustainable and should therefore be replaced by other forms of tourism. We believe that this is the wrong approach. Whether we like it or not, beach tourism will continue to be the largest segment of the tourism market, and it is our obligation to ensure that it is developed and managed in the most sustainable fashion.

Many coastal destinations have already succeeded in making substantive improvements in some areas related to sustainability. Our project is structured around a network of destinations with different degrees of success and failure, so that a rich exchange of experiences can benefit all those participating in the work, while WTO will extract the lessons that can also assist other destinations, especially in the developing world (WTO, 2003).

Finally, let me refer to the International Year of Ecotourism (IYE), 2002, as designated by the UN. Following this designation and the specific request that the UN-CSD made to the WTO, we decided to undertake a number of activities at the international level with a view to achieving the following objectives:

1. Generate greater awareness among public authorities, the private sector, civil society and consumers regarding ecotourism's capacity to contribute to conservation of the natural and cultural heritage in natural and rural areas and the improvement of standards of living in those areas.
2. Disseminate methods and techniques for the planning, management, regulation and monitoring of ecotourism to guarantee its long-term sustainability.
3. Promote exchanges of successful experiences in the field of ecotourism.
4. Increase opportunities for the efficient marketing and promotion of ecotourism destinations and products on international markets.

The WTO has also encouraged all its member states and affiliate members to undertake activities at the national and local levels, as a means of disseminating the above objectives as widely as possible. Indeed, WTO considers that activities at the national and local levels are likely to be more significant and have longer-lasting effects than those at the international level. This is because ecotourism activities are generally small-scale, as are the related services and infrastructure provided by small and medium-sized enterprises (SMEs). Similarly, monitoring, regulation and supervision of such services is carried out principally by local authorities or local institutions. It is therefore crucial to reach this type of audience if the long-term objectives of the IYE are to be achieved in any substantive manner. In fact, many nations in all continents have set up national multi-stakeholder committees for IYE, many of which have continued beyond 2002 and can serve as coordinating or monitoring bodies to promote the long-term sustainability of ecotourism operations.

At the international level, WTO joined with UNEP to convene the World Ecotourism Summit in Quebec, Canada, from 19 to 22 May 2002, with the support of the Canadian Tourism Commission and Quebec Tourism. The Summit was the largest ever gathering of all stakeholders involved in or affected by ecotourism, including national and local governments, private-sector organizations, NGOs, academic institutions, etc. It considered four main subjects:

1. Ecotourism planning and product development: the sustainability challenge.
2. Monitoring and regulation of ecotourism: evaluating progress towards sustainability.
3. Marketing and promotion of ecotourism: reaching sustainable consumers.
4. Costs and benefits of ecotourism: a sustainable distribution among all stakeholders.

Throughout the four themes, two main issues were addressed, namely:

• The sustainability of ecotourism from the environmental, economic and sociocultural points of view.
• The involvement of local communities in the ecotourism development process, in management and monitoring of ecotourism activities and in the sharing of profits resulting from it.

The Summit was the culmination of a

process of regional conferences through which a more detailed and in-depth analysis of the above issues was made, focusing on the specificities of each region and each type of ecotourism destination. At these conferences a high level of participation was encouraged from all parties, including tourism public officials, local authorities, representatives of the local communities, the local private-tourism sector, academic institutions, etc.

The results, conclusions and recommendations of all these meetings were reported to the World Ecotourism Summit in May 2002. The Summit provided a wide forum for a rich exchange of experiences, and concluded with recommendations addressed to all types of stakeholders:

- to governments, on how to improve their ecotourism policy-making, planning and monitoring processes with ample stakeholder participation;
- to local communities, on how to enhance their involvement in such processes and maximize the benefits they derive from ecotourism;
- to the private sector, on how to better serve the sustainability objectives while ensuring profitable and long-lasting ecotourism operations;
- to international organizations, on how to improve the support they provide for individual countries to develop a sustainable ecotourism industry.

The road towards a more sustainable tourism industry is a lengthy one, but a possible one. The WTO is not alone on this road, but it is certainly playing a leading, catalyst role. We wish more and more people to join us on this road, particularly those who have already understood that this is the only way to achieve a more human, environmentally and socially sustainable development of our societies.

Reference

World Tourism Organizations (WTO) (2003) http://www.world-tourism.org/sustainable/coastalnetwork

4

Private Reserves: the Conservation Corporation Africa Model

Les Carlisle
Conservation Corporation Africa, White River, South Africa

Abstract

The Conservation Corporation Africa (CCA) model attempts to address threats to Africa's land and wildlife resources from burgeoning populations and reduced budgets. CCA recognizes that much of Africa's wildlife heritage and real estate is influenced or owned by local communities. Maintenance of biodiversity is crucial to our local economies, and local economic development is crucial to the maintenance of our biodiversity.

The CCA model is to link international tourists to these communities, taking a commercial approach to conservation. This is an African problem and we use an African solution, modelled on the three-legged African cooking pot. If the pot had four legs it would need a level surface to stand on. If it had only two legs, the food would be in the fire. Our approach relies on partnerships between: (i) the private sector; (ii) the local community; and (iii) the state conservation agency.

We aim to adopt best-value use for any given area, which is not always the current use. We have large tracts of fallow land all over Africa, far from infrastructure and water. We also have communal land neighbouring some of the world's great parks, currently used for subsistence agriculture. We have shown that, in marginal-rainfall areas of Africa, the best form of land use is conservation. Cattle farming produces R150 (US$16) per ha annually, gross. Conservation on the same land is currently producing R1500 (US$160) per ha per annum. Where cattle farming employed 60 people, wildlife conservation and tourism employs 300 on the same area of land. In some areas Africa's current poverty cycle need not continue if commercial conservation land use is practised.

Introduction

Africa's lands and wildlife resources are under threat. The two greatest threats are lack of money to manage the parks and the pressure of population growth outside the parks, encroaching on park boundaries and creating areas of conflict. The tools exist to manage the parks and wildlife, but they are not always applied, for a variety of reasons. The international community may be partly responsible for these problems, despite good intentions. This is illustrated, for example, by current elephant management in Botswana.

To address these problems, therefore, an approach is needed which can both: (i) gen-

© CAB International 2003. *Nature-based Tourism, Environment and Land Management*
(eds R. Buckley, C. Pickering and D.B. Weaver)

erate the funds for land and wildlife management; and (ii) contribute to local communities in a way that leads them to protect wildlife and reserve areas. This is the mission for Conservation Corporation Africa (CCA): care of the land, care of the wildlife, care of the people. CCA's approach is to buy or lease land, restore and restock if required, establish tourism operations to provide ongoing funding, and reinvest in communities and conservation as well as providing a return to shareholders. CCA was established in 1990, but many of its individual lodges and reserves had been operating for many decades previously. Aspects of CCA's approach have also been used as models by many other companies and government agencies throughout sub-Saharan Africa. It is therefore well tried and tested and has proved eminently successful.

CCA's overall approach is based on the conviction that maintaining biodiversity and developing the local economy are both essential, and that they are totally interdependent: neither is possible without the other. If we can successfully link international tourist markets to local rural communities, we have a potential mechanism to conserve wildlife and habitat. From a marketing perspective, the principal selling-point for CCA's tourism products is Africa's wild and dangerous animals. Our local people own some of the best wildlife real estate in the world, but we have to integrate land use for wildlife into broader regional economic and infrastructure planning. In sub-Saharan Africa, the social, financial and ecological aspects of sustainability are very closely connected at a very short and immediate time-scale, and CCA has to address each aspect together and equally.

Six-point Conservation Strategy

During the past few years CCA has expanded considerably, taking on new land and lodges and merging with other enterprises, such as the tour company Afro Ventures. We have also come to appreciate that our experience is valuable beyond the company itself, as a model for other corporations – which may be our partners in sustainability even while they remain our competitors in commercial tourism. We have therefore taken steps to formalize what we were doing already in the shape of a six-point conservation strategy, as set out below. In addition, the practical techniques we have developed for the successful capture, relocation and reintroduction of different wildlife species, notably the big cats, have been adopted by government agencies as well as private landholders and are now the industry standard.

The six-point strategy is as follows:

- Continually improve environmental management at individual operations.
- Develop cooperative ventures with neighbouring communities.
- Continually improve technical and interpretative skills of guides and trackers.
- Encourage individual efforts to care for land, wildlife and people.
- Support reputable voluntary conservation groups and government agencies.
- Use profits from savannah areas to support conservation in other ecosystems.

To improve environmental management and reduce the impacts of individual camps, lodges and safari operations, we have commenced a company-wide environmental audit programme under a corporate conservation team. Stringent but practical environmental-management guidelines are being developed for each lodge. The conservation team provides lodge managers with expertise, incentives and workable and cost-effective solutions. 'Green teams' composed of volunteer staff members are also being established at each lodge or camp, to investigate on-site problems and implement solutions. Key issues include: wise use of energy and water; disposal of waste, including litter; control of alien plants; and habitat management aspects, such as the siting of roads and dams, bush clearing, burning and animal relocation. Sensitivity towards wildlife and landscapes is paramount in all that we do, and game drives and walks should never compromise animals or their habitats.

Historically, CCA lodges have provided a significant return to local communities through direct employment and training, provision of entrepreneurial opportunities and establishment of community facilities, such as schools and clinics. To enhance our role in community development further, we are now investigating opportunities to establish new lodges and activities as cooperative ventures, to expand local economies and improve people's lives. This involves the development of trusting relationships with our neighbours. Such lodges need to meet criteria both for CCA's portfolio and for community aspirations. They will generally be funded by loan capital. They will make use of the rural development expertise established by the Africa Foundation, formerly CCA's Rural Investment Fund. Monitoring and evaluation are a critical component of such initiatives. CCA staff involved in such joint ventures will need a particular understanding of the initiatives and processes involved in local development and the ability to convey these to guests. It is essential that we relate to and work with our neighbours in a manner that is in no way patronizing, paternalistic or expedient.

CCA provides guests with exciting encounters and accurate information on wildlife, local culture and ecosystems. CCA's publications distribute this knowledge more broadly. As part of our corporate conservation strategy, therefore, it is critical that we continue to improve and develop skills among all guides and trackers through advanced training, continual knowledge acquisition, grading and specialization. In addition to providing enthralling encounters with wildlife, our guides strive to ensure that guests absorb an appreciation of the ecological processes on which different animals and plants are interdependent. CCA also publishes an annual high-quality and informative record of wildlife and ecosystem observations, the *Ecological Journal*. Data are also posted on Wildwatch.com. All CCA staff and others can contribute to these publications, which demonstrate our long-term commitment to Africa's wild places. In addition, our quarterly newsletter *The Bateleur* promotes CCA's philosophy and endeavours to staff, guests, the industry and the outside world. We also plan to diversify our wildlife experience by introducing specialist 'EcoStudy Encounters' linked to field lodges, together with secluded observation hides, interpretative centres and libraries at the lodges.

CCA encourages all its staff and guests to make individual and collective contributions to environmental conservation by adopting eco-friendly lifestyles and promoting the ethics of the company. 'Care of the wildlife, care of the land, care of the people' is not just a catch-phrase but a creed that we should all adopt and live by. To provide ideas and incentives to reduce impacts, we are producing a booklet, *Guidelines for EcoLiving*, covering aspects such as recycling waste in your own home, planting indigenous trees or taking underprivileged children on nature outings. CCA intends to offer awards to individuals who demonstrate outstanding commitment towards environmental conservation.

In addition to our own conservation activities, CCA will make annual contributions to respected conservation organizations such as the Endangered Wildlife Trust, East African Wildlife Society and BirdLife South Africa, with which we also undertake cooperative commercial ventures. We shall foster and maintain positive relations with government agencies, such as KwaZulu-Natal Parks, Tanzania National Parks (TANAPA) and South Africa National Parks.

Most of CCA's lodges are situated within Africa's savannah biome, since this is where the large mammals are most common and easily viewed. Except for species such as African wild dog, black rhino and saddle-billed stork, however, most savannah species are reasonably well conserved in large public reserves and are not currently threatened. There are other biomes with many threatened species, which are less attractive for tourism and have received less attention. CCA is therefore exploring ways to use profits generated in the savannah-based operations to help protect threatened ecosystems elsewhere. These include the grasslands of the South African high veld, the Kakamega forest in Kenya and the Usambara forest in Tanzania. Expertise and training will eventually be provided for communities in or adjacent to areas rich in biodiversity so as to facilitate the development of small-scale ecotourism enterprises.

Phinda Case Study

The reserve and lodges

When CCA was established in 1990 to develop destinations for discerning ecotourists around southern Africa, our aim was to consolidate degraded and undervalued land under wildlife, and generate long-term financial returns through ecotourism. The CCA mission is to apply a balanced approach to tourism, conservation and local community involvement which promotes ecological sustainability while providing guests with a quality wildlife experience and investors with attractive returns. The Phinda Resource Reserve in the centre of the vast, ecologically rich area of Maputaland fitted these objectives perfectly and has become the prime test case and demonstration model for the CCA approach. At Phinda, CCA has been able to: consolidate degraded and undervalued land assets; rehabilitate and restock the land; create rural wealth; and generate financial returns through ecotourism.

The project initially involved the consolidation of 7500 ha of farmland between Mkuzi Game Reserve and Sodwana State Forest Reserve, just north of Lake St Lucia. This land had long been recognized by conservation bodies as a key addition to the Greater St Lucia Wetland Park World Heritage Area, the first in South Africa. In 1991 CCA bought and added a further 6000 ha, including frontage along the Mzinene River, which flows into Lake St Lucia.

In October 1991 the 44-bed Phinda Mountain Lodge was opened, accompanied by one of the largest game-restocking exercises on private land in South Africa. In November 1993, Phinda Resource Reserve opened a second lodge, the 32-bed Forest Lodge, built within an area of dry sand forest, one of the world's rarest forest types. In 1997 two smaller 12-bed lodges were added, Rock and Vlei Lodges. These two lodges have individual plunge pools in each room, and each room is individually custom-designed to blend into its surroundings. Phinda now boasts 96 world-class beds, and these form the economic engine for the CCA model. The Phinda project was funded with venture capital, 60% offshore in the initial stages. As subsequent

opportunities presented themselves across Africa, new rights issues were used to fund further acquisitions. CCA's recent merger with Afro Ventures has reduced the overall offshore holdings to 50%. The company is an unlisted public company, or private placement funded company.

Wildlife and environment

Phinda supports an enormous range of animal, bird and plant life within a relatively compact area. It lies at the boundary between tropical and subtropical climate zones and includes seven distinct habitat types: ilala palm savannah, montane woodlands, riverine forest, acacia thorn veld, sand forest, open grassland and natural pan systems. One of the major attributes of the reserve is 800 ha of dry sand forest, representing 90% of the total remaining area of this rare vegetation type on private conservation land in South Africa. The Mzinene River on Phinda's southern boundary is a major source of fresh water for Lake St Lucia and a haven for water-birds. Phinda Reserve has contributed to conserving this vital water source for Lake St Lucia and protecting its river-banks from further degradation. Guests at Phinda can also combine big-game viewing and bird-watching with scuba-diving on the coral reefs of the Maputaland coastline, a short flight away.

Much of the land consolidated within Phinda has been scarred by decades of inappropriate farming of cattle, banana, cotton and sisal. Decaying farm infrastructure, internal fences and power lines had to be removed and an extensive rehabilitation programme implemented. Clearing of invasive species and exotics is conducted continually, so as to reinstate the water balances disturbed by bush encroachment. Erosion gullies are filled with the brush tops of trees that have been cleared, and a proper road network along contour lines is currently being established.

Historically, wildlife in this region had been wiped out ruthlessly during the infamous nagana campaign of the 1920s. In recent years, predators such as leopard, hyena and jackal, as well as baboons, were shot off the land by farmers. Gradually these predators are returning, many from the adjoining Mkuzi Game Reserve, and predator interactions are now a common feature of the reserve. Since March 1991, an extensive game-restocking programme has been undertaken on Phinda: the biggest game restocking on private land in South Africa at the time. The initial restocking included over 1000 head of game, including 25 white rhinos, 50 elephants, 13 cheetahs and 12 lions, as well as giraffe, zebra, wildebeest and numerous antelope species.

Phinda has also established itself as a research base for predator introduction programmes. Dr Luke Hunter of Pretoria University's Mammal Research Institute used Phinda Reserve to investigate predator adaptation in confined areas surrounded by dense populations of people. Bophutatswana Parks Board officials and neighbouring chiefs visited Phinda to study its predator reintroduction techniques before giving the go-ahead for a lion reintroduction programme at Pilanesberg National Park. Such cooperation with neighbours has become part of the national standard for all predator reintroductions. The lion reintroduction programme included techniques for mixing individuals from different prides, using sedation in confined areas to create the required familiarity. This technique is now widely use in reintroduction programmes to establish prides in new reserves.

In February 1993, an association of landowners, including Phinda, combined forces to create a greater conservation area, the Mun-ya-wana Game Reserve, all operating under one constitution, which commits them to wildlife conservation. It is expected that the Mun-ya-wana Game Reserve will continue to grow, with Phinda as its core, to a potential size of 30,000 ha. The proclamation of the Greater St Lucia World Heritage Area (GSLWHA) and the establishment of the management authority have opened the door to include private land in the World Heritage Area; and Mun-ya-wana Game Reserve is ideally positioned to participate. The GSLWHA management authority has approached the Mun-ya-wana Game Reserve to negotiate the dropping of the fences. Consolidation of the Mun-ya-wana Reserve under common management has established a structure to conserve the area under wildlife in perpetuity.

Community involvement

Surrounding Phinda are four KwaZulu tribal areas, with a population of 22,500 people living within 15 km of the Reserve's boundaries. Over the next 20 years, this population is expected to increase, resulting in ever-increasing land pressure on limited natural resources. A major danger facing Phinda, as with many other African wildlife reserves, is the prospect of becoming an island of conserved habitat in a sea of rural poverty. In 1991, therefore, CCA established a *Framework for Community Participation*, based on the premise that local people are a cornerstone of the region's natural environment and are entitled to sustained benefits from its natural resources. 'Island' reserves that do not take cognizance of the socio-economic aspirations of surrounding communities foster resentment and antagonism, which eventually lead to interference in the wildlife areas. To survive, the private-enterprise initiative at Phinda must therefore play a significant role in regional rural development beyond its boundaries. And, indeed, Phinda has become a vehicle for socio-economic advancement and enhanced sustainable resource utilization, rather than a source of tension in the region.

In 1992, Phinda established community development committees (CDCs) at Mnqobokazi, Mduku and Nibela. These CDCs included representatives from the traditional tribal authorities, the school authorities and the CCA staff at Phinda. Through weekly meetings and project-site meetings, the CDCs are responsible for defining community development needs and town-planning aspects, overseeing the construction of the facilities and identifying areas of cooperation and concern. The CDCs have formal constitutions that allow them to act as official recipients of funds and project managers. The CDCs are democratic, representative, regionally integrated and development oriented. Informal consultations have thus been replaced by established organizations, and the CDCs are now serving as major channels for other developments and the upliftment in the region.

Of the 22,500 people who live within 15 km of the Reserve, 250 are employed at Phinda. In this region, one employed person supports eight to ten dependants, so the Phinda Reserve provides direct benefits to 10% of its neighbouring population. Of the R$5.5 million (currently US$600,000) spent on building Phinda Mountain Lodge, R$2.5 million (US$270,000) was channelled directly into surrounding communities in the form of local wages. When Forest Lodge was built in 1993, CCA broke away from first-world building techniques and established a community construction team so as to upgrade local skills, provide job opportunities and complete construction with far less environmental impact than by first-world techniques. Of the R$7 million (US$750,000) spent on the construction of Forest Lodge, some R$3.2 million (US$345,000) reached the local economy through wages and materials purchases.

In total, 110 local unskilled people were employed, effectively providing economic support for more than 1000 people. Local artisans were trained in simplified building techniques, which were thereby transferred to neighbouring communities. A prime example is that of Zibane Mazibuko, who was caught with a nyala he had poached from Phinda in mid-1992. In line with CCA's philosophy, Mr Mazibuko's own community imposed a penalty of 3 months' work manufacturing bricks at Phinda. At the end of this term, Mr Mazibuko was given the opportunity of going into business as a brick-maker in partnership with the Reserve. Funded by a company loan, Zibane today operates two brick-making machines, which together manufacture 2000 bricks a day. Zibane is now able to bring in more than four times the average regional per capita income for his family and he employs five to ten locals to assist with production.

A charcoal-manufacturing operation was also set up on Phinda, in partnership with 40 local-community people, using wood derived from the bush-clearing programme. Using the traditional earth-kiln method, the business produces about 1000 bags of charcoal a week, which are sold to markets in the local and urban areas. Resource utilization, such as ilala palm-wine harvesting and, wood, thatch and medicinal-plant collection, is practised on a sustainable-yield basis at Phinda. Revenue generated from the sale of these natural resources is ploughed into a community fund,

with proceeds used for the purchase of recreational equipment for community members.

In September 1992, CCA's Rural Investment Fund, now the Africa Foundation, received R$650,000 (US$70,000) from an overseas donor for a substantial community development project surrounding Phinda. Through this support, Phinda has funded additional school classrooms for the Mnqobokazi, Nibela and Mduku community areas adjacent to Phinda's boundaries, plus a skills training centre, which provides training in carpentry, adult literacy, building techniques, community health and permaculture. In conjunction with the Independent Development Trust, the Rural Investment Fund also assisted in the construction of a R$650,000 (US$70,000) residential clinic at Mduku village. Throughout the region, 40 classrooms have been constructed at 20 different schools, providing space for 1200 pre-primary children with trained teachers. This has generated 60 permanent jobs, supporting about 600 dependants. In total, 3200 children have educational facilities because of the Phinda project. The Africa Foundation has also established a bursary system, which has educated between 15 and 20 people each year for the last 3 years. In the last 10 years, almost R$10 million (over US$1 million) in development assistance has been provided for these local communities.

Environmental education and leadership are essential if communities are to make informed decisions about conservation and land use, to forge successful partnerships with conservation bodies or to contribute to conservation policies. CCA Phinda has therefore taken several steps to promote community environmental awareness. In 1995 CCA established a Community Leaders Education (CLE) Fund, which offers bursaries for academic study on the condition that recipients later return to their community to share their newly acquired skills. The CLE Fund committee has received an overwhelming number of applications, particularly for teaching diplomas. Most schools in the surrounding areas are short of qualified teachers, and some schools have over 100 pupils per class. Dozens of university and college education bursaries have been awarded to rural youngsters, destined to become leaders in their local communities and/or provide services for a marginalized local economy. Since starting operations, Phinda has also hosted visits by 20 teachers and 320 students. The impact of these visits is immense, as many of these local African people have never seen their own wildlife heritage or view it only as a source of protein.

Through the programme *Footprints Across Africa*, CCA brings children from other countries to learn about human values, adventure, wilderness, the environment, cultures, history and themselves in a bush setting. If children are the future of conservation, then they need opportunities to explore the natural world. *Footprints* also plans to embark on safaris across Africa, allowing rural children to interact with children from other countries and cultures. Interest in the environment among secondary-school students is also promoted through CCA's environmental debate bursaries. These involve cash prizes for students who present the best research debate on current environmental topics and equipment awards for their schools.

Conclusions

The CCA approach has demonstrated that, in the marginal subsistence-agriculture areas of Africa, wildlife is the best form of land use on economic, social and environmental grounds alike. Our approach is being copied extensively elsewhere and we are glad that it should be so. As CCA and the Africa Foundation continue to grow with revenues and donations from our guests, we should be able to keep increasing the size of our natural areas and supporting more local economic development. Bigger systems need less management and are more resilient to outside influences. As recognition of the CCA model becomes more widespread, it becomes increasingly attractive to communities and areas that are contemplating a change from subsistence agriculture to wildlife conservation. This in turn gradually secures Africa's ability to stand on its own feet. There are no quick fixes in sustainable development, but, after 12 years of replicating and testing the CCA approach, we are confident that it works.

5

Applying Public-purpose Marketing in the USA to Protect Relationships with Public Lands

Alan E. Watson[1] and William T. Borrie[2]

[1]Aldo Leopold Wilderness Research Institute, Departments of the Interior and Agriculture, Missoula, Montana, USA; [2]University of Montana, Missoula, Montana, USA

Abstract

As domestic and international recreation demands on federal lands in the USA continue to increase, there is a growing need for commitment of revenue to provide services and meet stewardship mandates. With increasing demand and testing of methods to provide needed resources, the relationships between the public and public lands are changing. One force of that change has been a tendency towards more business-like approaches to managing public lands in the USA, including the use of marketing and customer fees. A recent test for applying marketing principles to the establishment of fee policies for Forest Service lands entailed active engagement by scientists, managers and planners, marketing consultants and key members of the public. A proposal has emerged to blend marketing activities with protection of public land resources through a focus on relationships, trust, commitment and social responsibility.

Outdoor recreation Trends on Public Land in the USA

The US Department of Agriculture (USDA) sponsors efforts to assess trends in outdoor recreation demand and supply in the USA. The most recent report (Cordell, 1999) provides a summary of recent knowledge about current participation levels and anticipated trends. These national trend data are produced from surveys of households in all regions of the USA and have been ongoing since 1960. A brief summary of the findings is useful in setting the stage for examining the importance of public-lands marketing in the USA.

Current participation levels

Cordell (1999) found that 95% of the US population reported active involvement in some type of outdoor recreation activity over the past year. The most common activities reported for that part of the US population over the age of 16 were viewing and learning activities (e.g. walking – 67%, viewing a beach or waterside – 62%); trail, street and road activities (e.g., sightseeing – 57%, biking – 29%); and social activities (e.g. family gatherings outside – 62%). These activities do not occur solely on federal or even public lands, but public lands are popular for these activities, though availability is widely variable across the country, with much greater access to public lands in most parts of the West and in Alaska.

Some activity levels that are of particular interest to public-lands managers and of greater potential impact on public lands include 29% of the population aged 16 or over who fished over the past year, 26% who camped overnight (9% in recreation vehicles, 15% in tents on developed sites and 14% in primitive conditions), 48 million people (23% of the population) hiked and 9% hunted. Only 8% backpacked, 8% downhill skied and 4% rode snowmobiles.

Projected trends to 2050

The activities that are projected to grow at the fastest rate (number of participants) between now and the year 2050 are cross-country skiing (95% increase), downhill skiing (93% increase), visiting historic places (66% increase), sightseeing (71% increase) and biking (70% increase). Those that are projected to grow at the slowest rates are rafting (26% increase), backpacking (26% increase), off-road driving (16% increase), primitive camping (10% increase) and hunting (projected to decrease by 11%). These lower rates of increase are near the projected population-increase rates, though some regional differences are anticipated. Among the factors believed to be contributing to these shifting trends is a general ageing of the population of the USA, a continuing shift to a metropolitan population base and changes in ethnic and racial background (Johnson, 1999). Eighty per cent of the population growth over the next 25 years is expected to be from within current minority groups. The US population is currently 75% white, 12% African American, 10% Hispanic, 3% Asian and less than 1% American Indian (Johnson, 1999).

International visitation trends

O'Leary (1999) describes tourism as the third largest industry in the USA and in a constant state of growth, despite fluctuations in relationship to exchange rates and other economic factors in various countries of tourist origin. Over the last decade the growth in numbers of international visitors to the USA has been about 66%, to nearly 46 million visitors in 1997. These visitors are contributing nearly US$100 billion dollars to the economy of the USA currently. Visitors have come predominantly from Canada, Mexico, Japan, the UK and Germany (listed in order of decreasing dominance). Visitation is expected to continue to grow at a rate of 3–4% annually over the short term, though this increase will come increasingly from Asia and South America. O'Leary (1999) describes US public land-management agencies as uncertain how to approach international visitation. These agencies have seemed to oscillate between marketing of opportunities to the international visitors and keeping them at a distance to protect the resource.

Major challenges in meeting demands

Pandolfi (1999), Chief Operations Officer of the USDA Forest Service at the time, suggested that finding financial resources to meet this growth in demand for domestic outdoor recreation activities and international tourism will become a critical issue in the future. To meet these needs, Pandolfi (1999) suggests that the Forest Service apply the principles of sound, private-sector marketing to provide satisfying outdoor recreation products and services for the public and charging fees to recover the costs of these services. Packaging recreation activities on public lands as 'products' for 'customers' has been proposed as the way of the future to obtain acceptance of charging fees and, therefore, meeting the demand for increasing recreation services. Pandolfi suggests acceleration of research aimed at understanding what recreation visitors want and how satisfied they are with what they experience. These comments typify current public-agency tendencies in the USA to try to address recreation demands through the application of the fundamental concept in the commercial world of building brand loyalty as a reflection of satisfied customers (Pandolfi, 1999).

One of the most significant changes in land-management policy in the USA, aimed at trying to meet this anticipated increase in outdoor recreation demand, has been the introduction of recreation fees on a broad scale on federal lands. In 1996, the *Omnibus Consolidated Rescissions Act* established the Recreational Fee Demonstration Program. The USDA Forest Service, the US Department of the Interior (USDI) National Park Service, Fish and Wildlife Service and the Bureau of Land Management were authorized to test recreation user-fee programmes on a temporary basis, with at least 80% of proceeds staying at the individual projects where the money is collected. Past fee-collection authorization has generally only allowed fees to be charged for developed recreation areas and the revenues have generally been transferred to the general treasury of the US Government, not used specifically for providing services at the place where the fee was charged. Fees have not previously been charged for dispersed recreation participation. Extending this programme to include wilderness, picnicking and many of the more casual, non-consumptive recreation uses of public lands has also introduced a major change in delivery of services to the majority of visitors.

In a review of recent recreation-fee research, Watson and Herath (1999) highlighted seven major barriers to agencies taking more businesslike approaches to providing the financial resources needed to meet increasing demands:

1. There is concern that taking a purely consumer-economics, business point of view in pricing and administering fee programmes is counter to the collective movement that has established an extensive system of outdoor recreation opportunities on public lands in the USA. If revenue generation and efficiency dominate our public land-management decisions, we are not acknowledging people as stakeholders in the intended purpose of these lands and the societal values associated with access to these places.

2. Taking a businesslike approach may substantially alter the perception of stewardship responsibilities that many agencies have worked hard to create within the public. Intentionally changing roles to buyer and seller, versus those of stakeholder and stewards, raises concern that there may be severe impacts on benefits intended from public lands. Agencies have worked for decades to foster the development of a land ethic among the public. Stewardship implies personal acceptance of responsibility, a commitment to the resource, a commitment to other users and a commitment to future generations who will benefit from our actions.

3. It seems that the public is most supportive of charging fees to accomplish the stated purpose of public lands. Sometimes fees are supported to recover the costs associated with the development of facilities, if facilities are an integral part of that place (e.g. boat ramps in order to enjoy the benefits of boating on a lake), and sometimes they are not (e.g. bathrooms in association with wilderness access). Vogt and Williams (1999) found that visitors often supported maintenance of current conditions in compliance with the purpose of the public place over development and improvements that increased capacity for uses or use levels not compatible with the intended purpose.

4. A tendency to ask visitors who have paid the fee if they find the experience worth the price they paid for it provides a false sense of public response to the fees. Findings of displaced visitors (Schneider and Budruk, 1999) due to fees when studying visitors to non-fee sites, indications of lack of trust and support by non-participants in community studies (Winter *et al.*, 1999) and national surveys that show more support for using taxes to meet increasing demands for some recreation activities than for charging fees (Bowker *et al.*, 1999) are often in stark contrast to manager reports from interaction with satisfied customers who have paid the fee and receive the benefits of a specific visit.

5. It remains unclear who is most affected by fees on public lands. The fear of exclusion of low-income people is partly resolved by examination of the sociodemographics of public-lands visitors. There are many obstacles to accessing much of the public-domain land besides the fee. Therefore, More (1999) concentrates more on those on the income margins within our current societal structure. Those most affected by fees may be within the dominant user group, not the minority group with low incomes. With the very low income currently under-represented on public lands, however, policies that further reduce their access seem irresponsible.

6. There has been a lack of systematic evaluation to adequately judge the effects of fee policies on visitors (Absher et al., 1999). An alarming lack of rigorous scientific investigation has created a situation with conflicting sources being commonly referenced in debates over recreation fees. The amount of revenue generation can hardly be discounted, but the cost of producing those revenues is seldom considered. In one exception, Richer and Christensen (1999) demonstrate that the dominant pricing and fee policy implementation procedures do have costs involved, but forgoing some of the potential for revenue generation can provide societal benefits.

7. A more exact role needs to be defined for research in establishing and testing policies aimed at meeting the anticipated shifts in recreation demand. If fees are necessary to meet these demands, adequate review of existing research should be an integral part of making the decision about how fee policies will be implemented. In addition, since knowledge is not perfect, science must be involved in establishing monitoring and evaluation processes to determine if policies achieve the stated objectives. Scientists must be involved in setting objectives, obtaining public input and consideration of alternative management solutions. Without close relationships between science and management, science will remain reactive to policy shifts, with a resultant negative public opinion and pleas for help in solving problems after they have been created (Watson, 2001).

Blending Marketing with Protecting Public Lands

In 1998, the USDA Forest Service convened a national team of scientists, managers and plan-

ners to test the principles of marketing to enhance management of current programmes of the agency and prepare for future demands on natural-resource programmes. This team agreed that a marketing approach would also meet public-purpose mandates if it: (i) helped identify and address the public's needs and expectations; (ii) yielded additional financial and other resources to accomplish the agency's work; (iii) facilitated achievement of quality standards for work accomplished; (iv) enhanced the efficiency of the Forest Service in accomplishing work and making decisions; (v) supported efforts of the agency to accomplish its mandated public purpose with respect to the lands they manage; and (vi) maintained or increased public support for the agency and its programmes. These criteria for success flow largely out of an examination of the marketing literature and an effort to integrate private-sector marketing applications with the mandated public purposes attached to public lands. A case study application of 'public-purpose recreation marketing', described more fully in Borrie et al. (2002), illustrates application of a market-segmentation method that is compatible with public-land stewardship. A description of the underlying proposed framework for public-purpose marketing follows.

Marketing in the Public Sector

Crompton and Lamb (1986) suggested that marketing is an appropriate approach for government and social-service agencies to analyse public needs and gain support for their programmes. They acknowledged that many public agencies were beginning to experiment with marketing and they stated their intent to increase acceptance of marketing tools and concepts through the 'marketing of marketing itself' (p. 33). Recent literature offers a foundation for a marketing approach to meet the criteria listed above, focusing on relationships (not transactions), trust, commitment and social responsibility.

Relational marketing

In the past, marketing has largely focused on methods to generate revenue-producing transactions between customers and providers of products or services. For most of the history of marketing, creating or increasing customer satisfaction with this transaction has been the primary emphasis (Morgan and Hunt, 1994; Garbarino and Johnson, 1999), with repeat purchases being the primary measure of success. But Webster (1992), Kotler (1995) and others have described a fundamental shift towards relationship marketing, which acknowledges the importance of relationships to long-term business success. Morgan and Hunt (1994) discussed the importance of paying attention to all relationships that a business has, including those with suppliers, buyers and both lateral and internal partnerships. For the purposes of marketing in the public sector, and particularly for providing guidance for market segmentation, a focus on relationships between the managing agency and the public as primary stakeholders (both customers and partners) is a feasible and appropriate conceptual framework to guide data collection about the public and guide other aspects of marketing and policy development.

A discrete transaction with a customer is said to have a distinct beginning, short duration and sharp ending by performance (Dwyer *et al.*, 1987). A relational exchange, on the other hand, builds from previous agreements, is longer in duration and reflects an ongoing process. When providing services for the public through the development of programmes on public lands, the more appropriate view of 'customer service' would probably be as the development or fostering of a relationship between the members of the public and the places that have been established on their behalf as public lands. The role of the public-land management agency is as stewards of that relationship, and that relationship should be the focus of any marketing effort undertaken by the public agency.

Several definitions of relational marketing exist (see Berry, 1983; Jackson, 1985; Paul, 1988; Berry and Parasuraman, 1991; Doyle and Roth, 1992), orientated towards desirable relations with different types of groups (i.e. suppliers, buyers, partners, etc.). Most recently, Morgan and Hunt (1994) defined relational marketing as 'all marketing activities directed toward establishing, developing, and main-

taining successful relational exchanges' (p. 22). Morgan and Hunt (1994) emphasize theoretical and empirical research on commitment and trust as the primary influences on successful relational marketing. Support for public-agency actions also depends on confidence in efforts that recognize responsibility to current and future generations and efforts to meet the public purpose (legislation or policy mandates), versus vested-interest demands.

Trust and commitment

Anderson and Narus (1991) acknowledge that not all customers desire the same relationship with a producer of goods or services. They suggest that an organization may need to pursue both transactional and relational marketing simultaneously, and that customers may exist on a continuum of transactional to collaborative exchanges. In the public sector, however, members of the public are, by definition, involved in a collaborative relationship, with the stewardship agency taking responsibility for implementation of public policy. While we are suggesting that a collaborative relationship exists for all people, we do acknowledge that the level of commitment or involvement with the services provided by an agency and the level of trust instilled among members of the public may vary substantially. Relational marketing suggests that a focus on understanding variation in commitment and trust will be paramount in developing and implementing public policy to meet the mandates or purpose of public lands (Moorman *et al.*, 1993; Morgan and Hunt, 1994; Garbarino and Johnson, 1999).

Trust is widely viewed as an essential ingredient for successful marketing relationships (Dwyer et al., 1987; Berry, 1995). Trust is indicated by a willingness to rely on an exchange partner. While much of the research reported has investigated factors that influence trust in a single salesperson, some recent marketing research has specifically examined a customer's trust in the organization providing the product or service for the consumer (Garbarino and Johnson, 1999). As of 1993, Moorman et al. (1993) reported that very little research had attempted to understand the factors that affect trust in marketing relationships. Emphasis has been primarily on measuring associated factors, such as perceptions of sincerity, effort in establishing a relationship, goal congruence and expectations for cooperation.

Until very recently, studies of trust in organizations or institutions were virtually unknown (Earle and Cvetkovich, 1995). Historically, trust and studies of trust were limited to the interpersonal dimension. Only in the modern era has social trust become a topic of interest, accompanying our movement towards a more complex society. Two dominant views of trust held by an individual for a social institution have emerged. The more traditional view is that trust is based on confidence in competence, objectivity, fairness, consistency or predictability and caring, or the perception of goodwill (Earle and Cvetkovich, 1995). Based upon the belief that the level of knowledge necessary to make that traditional view of trust judgements accurate is generally not attainable due to the increasing complexity of social systems, Earle and Cvetkovich (1995) suggest an alternative view. In their view, people judge the similarity of values they hold to those expressed by an agency. Trust is then quantified in terms of perceptions of shared values, direction, goals, views, actions and thoughts (Winter *et al.*, 1999).

Commitment, also a strong influence on relationships between providers and customers, has been defined by Gundlach et al. (1995) as having three components: (i) an instrumental component or investment; (ii) an attitudinal component or psychological attachment; and (iii) a temporal dimension, indicating that the relationship exists over time. A relationship commitment requires that an exchange partner believes that an ongoing relationship with another is so important as to warrant maximum efforts at maintaining it (Morgan and Hunt, 1994). Cook and Emerson (1978) characterized commitment as a central factor in distinguishing social from economic exchange. Even the concept of brand loyalty, which was initially thought to be indicated only by repeat purchases (Morgan and Hunt, 1994), is now more likely to be defined as commitment to a particular brand, and is

sometimes sought by establishing perceived commonality in values between the purchaser and the providing organization (Morgan and Hunt, 1994).

Social responsibility

Even in corporate-America marketing, the concept of social responsibility has taken on a new emphasis in the development of products and in research on customer attitudes (Drumwright, 1994). The adoption of non-economic criteria in customer decision making (criteria other than price or relationship between price and quality) has led to greater understanding of how some purchase decisions pose social dilemmas and prompt moral reasoning (Drumwright, 1994). Samli (1992) focuses entirely on the private sector and those who want to make a positive profit picture but who also care. In the public sector, it is mandated that the public agency care. It must care about the stakeholders and it must care about the public purpose of the places and resources it manages. Gaski's (1985) position, that marketing with social responsibility was undemocratic, certainly did not adequately consider the growing energy aimed at marketing in the public sector at the time. In recent years, Smith and Alcorn (1991) and Smith (1994) have heralded a tendency towards acknowledgement of social responsibility in marketing as marketing's greatest contribution to society. While Drumwright (1994) indicates that there are some questions about the motives for businesses to adopt an element of social responsibility in their marketing strategies, in the public sector social responsibility is required in the delivery of services and mandated by the legislation and policy that guide a public agency.

Public-purpose marketing

The use of marketing principles by public-recreation land-management agencies poses both a threat and a promise to the people who depend on them for pleasurable outdoor experiences and protection of the public-land base. The most serious threat comes in the form of a focus on these experiences as a transaction and the temptation to focus too much on measures of on-site satisfaction and repeat visitation as indicators of success. Although it has been previously suggested that 'the goal of government ... service agencies is to provide satisfaction to their client groups, which is exactly the same goal pursued by private sector organizations' (Crompton and Lamb, 1986, p. 37), we suggest that marketing focused on a simple transaction with the public as a customer is too limited. Instead, promise more probably lies in a positive focus on the purpose of these land-management agencies that have been assigned the relatively weighty responsibility of representing the values of society in making policy decisions. Focus on the relationship between the public and these public-recreation land-management agencies, with emphasis on trust, commitment and social responsibility, should be a guiding principle when employing marketing principles in the public sector.

Discussion

The use of trust, commitment, social responsibility and support for public purpose as segmenting variables in marketing studies successfully yields distinct and valid market segments (Borrie *et al.*, 2002). Using trust, commitment, social responsibility and support for public purpose to develop market segments means that managers can ensure appropriate communications with the general public and a focus on long-term relationships: that is, public-purpose marketing, as described in this chapter, can help in the development of messages that foster, not undermine, the relationship between the public and the public-recreation manager. The tailoring of messages to different public audiences is an important expression of the responsiveness of the agency. Public-land management agencies have been entrusted not only with the stewardship of the land but also the public purpose and mandate for that land. Marketing methods should reflect not only the values of the public but also the trust that has been placed with the agency. Public-purpose marketing is well suited to help recreation managers be good

stewards of the relationships they have with the public.

It is worth highlighting how public-purpose marketing for recreation emphasizes an appropriate relationship with the public. First, it should be noted that all publics should be included in these procedures, not just the currently recreating public. The management of recreation lands serves many off-site and symbolic values in addition to the benefits gained by visitors. Managers also have obligations to recognize and preserve both bequest and option values: that is, not only should marketing efforts be tailored and communicated to all constituencies, but they should also be reflective of the opinions of both supportive and non-supportive publics and of recreating and non-recreating publics. Public-purpose marketing also resolves the dilemma that managers face regarding international tourists. Rather than a focus on satisfying visits, a focus on building relationships between foreign visitors and the natural resources of the USA can have a positive international influence to the benefit of all people. A lofty goal of using our interpretative, educational and experiential programmes to create and improve the relationship between people and natural resources in all countries is compatible with other US international programmes.

Furthermore, public-purpose marketing is aimed at accomplishing objectives by treating all members of the public more like owners and stakeholders than as clients and customers. In emphasizing the long-term relationship between the public and the recreation manager, rather than the provision of individual satisfying recreation experiences, managers avoid the dangers of building inappropriate expectations. Public-land management agencies probably cannot, and should not, compete with private entrepreneurs, and the use of marketing terminology certainly runs the risk of triggering that association. Instead, public-purpose marketing intrinsically endorses notions of duty, service and a continuing presence. The maintenance of a public constituency for public-recreation management will require an approach to marketing that does not send messages (both literal and implied) that confuse the relationship between the public and the agency. The more the agency looks and sounds like a private operator, the more the agency will be expected to focus on extremely high standards and approaches to providing short-term satisfaction, such as those used by companies such as Disney, possibly at the risk of failing in long-term resource-management mandates. Public-recreation managers should carefully compare the appropriateness of Disney's approach to designing and prescribing the visitor experience (Borrie, 1999) with the mandate of public-land management.

Public-purpose marketing endorses an approach to judging and monitoring the quality of the recreation experience that focuses less on immediate satisfaction and more on long-term relationships to the place and the managing agency. Success is more defined by the development or fostering of the relationship and less by the matching of short-term outcomes with preferences. This reflects a trend in recreation research away from a multi-attribute, commodity view and towards a more meanings-based view (Williams et al., 1992). Measuring the success of public-recreation management entails more than counting the number of satisfying experiences, if not only because there are many factors beyond the control of managers that influence the achievement of those experiences. Research and management performance goals may soon become more focused on measuring these relationships and understanding communications, land-management practices and collaborative planning procedures that influence these relationships.

Conclusions

The purpose of this chapter was to present a feasible and appropriate framework for the application of marketing principles and approaches to public-recreation management in response to the need to balance increasing demands with mandates to protect the resource. In doing so, it has presented a logical and valid approach to marketing and fostering relationships that can be adopted and applied in further situations. The collection and analysis of marketing data can have a profound influence on planning and management

decisions and this chapter lays the groundwork for an approach that reflects both public demands for services and public-policy mandates.

References

Absher, J.D., McCollum, D.W. and Bowker, J.M. (1999) The value of research in recreation fee project implementation. *Journal of Park and Recreation Administration* 17(3), 116–120.

Anderson, J.C. and Narus, J.A. (1991) Partnering as a focused market strategy. *California Management Review* 33(spring), 95–113.

Berry, L.L. (1983) Relationship marketing. In: Berry, L., Shostack, G.L. and Upah, G.D. (eds) *Emerging Perspectives on Services Marketing.* American Marketing Association, Chicago, pp. 25–28.

Berry, L.L. (1995) Relationship marketing of services – growing interest, emerging perspectives. *Journal of the Academy of Marketing Science* 23(autumn), 236–245.

Berry, L.L. and Parasuraman, A. (1991) *Marketing Services.* The Free Press, New York.

Borrie, W.T. (1999) Disneyland and Disney World: designing and prescribing the recreational experience. *Loisir et Société/Society and Leisure* 22(1), 71–82.

Borrie, W.T., Christensen, N., Watson, A.E., Miller, T.A. and McCollum, D.W. (2002) Public purpose marketing: a focus on the relationships between the public and public lands. *Journal of Parks and Recreation Administration* 20(2), 49–68.

Bowker, J.M., Cordell, H.K. and Johnson, C.Y. (1999) User fees for recreation services on public lands: a national assessment. *Journal of Park and Recreation Administration* 17(3), 1–14.

Cook, K.S. and Emerson, R.M. (1978) Power, equity and commitment in exchange networks. *American Sociological Review* 43(October), 721–739.

Cordell, H.K. (1999) *Outdoor Recreation in American Life: a National Assessment of Demand and Supply Trends.* Sagamore Publishing, Champaign, Illinois, 449 pp.

Crompton, J.L. and Lamb, C.W., Jr (1986) *Marketing Government and Social Services.* John Wiley & Sons, New York, 485 pp.

Doyle, S.X. and Roth, G.T. (1992) Selling and sales management in action: the use of insight coaching to improve relationship selling. *Journal of Personal Selling and Sales Management* 12(Winter), 59–64.

Drumwright, M.E. (1994) Socially responsible organizational buying: environmental concern as a non-economic buying criterion. *Journal of Marketing* 58(July), 1–19.

Dwyer, R.F., Schurr, P.H. and Oh, S. (1987) Developing buyer–seller relationships. *Journal of Marketing* 51(April), 11–27.

Earle, T.C. and Cvetkovich, G.T. (1995) *Social Trust: Toward a Cosmopolitan Society.* Praeger Publishers, Westport, Connecticut.

Garbarino, E. and Johnson, M.S. (1999) The different roles of satisfaction, trust and commitment in customer relationships. *Journal of Marketing* 63(April), 70–87.

Gaski, J.F. (1985) Dangerous territory: the societal marketing concept revisited. *Business Horizons* July–August, 42–47.

Gundlach, G.T., Achrol, R.S. and Mentzer, J.T. (1995) The structure of commitment in exchange. *Journal of Marketing* 59(January), 78–92.

Jackson, B.A. (1985) *Winning and Keeping Industrial Customers: the Dynamics of Customer Relationships.* D.C. Heath and Company, Lexington, Massachusetts.

Johnson, C. (1999) Participation differences among social groups. In: Cordell, H.K. (Principal Investigator) (ed.) *Outdoor Recreation in American Life: a National Assessment of Demand and Supply Trends.* Sagamore Publishing, Champaign, Illinois, pp. 248–268.

Kotler, P. (1995) *Strategic Marketing for Non-profit Organizations.* Prentice Hall, Upper Saddle River, New Jersey.

Moorman, C., Deshpande, R. and Zaltman, G. (1993) Factors affecting trust in market research relationships. *Journal of Marketing* 57(January), 81–101.

More, T.A. (1999) A functionalist approach to user fees. *Journal of Leisure Research* 31(3), 227–244.

Morgan, R.M. and Hunt, S.D. (1994) The commitment–trust theory of relationship marketing. *Journal of Marketing* 58(July), 20–38.

O'Leary, J. (1999) International tourism in the United States. In: Cordell, H.K. (Principal Investigator) (ed.) *Outdoor Recreation in American Life: a National Assessment of Demand and Supply Trends.* Sagamore Publishing, Champaign, Illinois, pp. 294–298.

Pandolfi, F. (1999) Perpetual motion, unicorns, and marketing in outdoor recreation. In: Cordell, H.K. (Principal Investigator) (ed.) *Outdoor Recreation in American Life: a National*

Assessment of Demand and Supply Trends. Sagamore Publishing, Champaign, Illinois, pp. ix–xii.

Paul, T. (1988) Relationship marketing for health-care providers. *Journal of Health Care Marketing* 8(September), 20–25.

Richer, J.R. and Christensen, N.A. (1999) Appropriate fees for wilderness day use: pricing decisions for recreation on public land. *Journal of Leisure Research* 31(3), 269–280.

Samli, A.C. (1992) *Social Responsibility in Marketing: a Proactive and Profitable Marketing Management Strategy.* Quorum Books, Westport, Connecticut, 198 pp.

Schneider, I.E. and Budruk, M. (1999) Displacement as a response to the federal recreation fee program. *Journal of Park and Recreation Administration* 17(3), 76–84.

Smith, C. (1994) The new corporate philanthropy. *Harvard Business Review* 72, 105–116.

Smith, S.M. and Alcorn, D.S. (1991) Cause marketing: a new direction in the marketing of corporate responsibility. *Journal of Consumer Marketing* 8, 19–35.

Vogt, C.A. and Williams, D.R. (1999) Support for wilderness recreation fees: the influence of fee purpose and day versus overnight use. *Journal of Park and Recreation Administration* 17(3), 85–99.

Watson, A.E. (2001) Recreation fee issues: an emphasis on science involvement. In: Järviluoma, J. and Saarinen, J. (eds) *Luonnon Matkailu-ja Virkistyskäyttö Tutkimuskohteena. Metsäntutkimuslaitoksen Tiedonantoja* 796, 7–18.

Watson, A.E. and Herath, G. (1999) Research implications of the theme issues 'recreation fees and pricing issues in the public sector' and 'societal response to recreation fees on public lands.' *Journal of Leisure Research* 31(3), 325–334.

Webster, F.E., Jr (1992) The changing role of marketing in the corporation. *Journal of Marketing* 56(October), 1–17.

Williams, D.R., Patterson, M.E., Roggenbuck, J.W. and Watson, A.E. (1992) Beyond the commodity metaphor: examining the emotional and symbolic attachment to place. *Leisure Sciences* 14(1), 29–46.

Winter, P.L., Palucki, L.J. and Burkhardt, R.L. (1999) Anticipated response to a fee program: the key is trust. *Journal of Leisure Research* 31(3), 207–226.

6

The Financial Liability of Park Managers for Visitor Injuries

Jan McDonald
School of Law, Griffith University, Queensland, Australia

Abstract

Protected-area management agencies are sometimes sued by visitors injured during recreational activities. The legal context for such actions and hence the likely outcomes differ considerably between countries and jurisdictions. A review of litigation in Australia suggests that it is currently impossible to predict precisely how a claim will be resolved. Recent case-law seems to recognize the dilemma facing park managers in fulfilling their broad-ranging statutory functions. There may be a modest shift away from the 'land manager as quasi-insurer' approach of the early 1990s, with several decisions recognizing the need for greater personal responsibility on the part of visitors. These trends cannot be relied upon, however, in an uncertain legal environment, where no-win/no-fee arrangements drive speculative litigation. Alternative approaches include the enactment of statutory immunities or the establishment of statutory compensation schemes that replace common-law avenues.

Introduction

Park managers face financial constraints. Limited resources must be divided between conservation activities and the provision and maintenance of visitor facilities. In the provision of such facilities, a tension exists between maintaining the natural experience for which an area has attracted conservation status and protecting visitors from danger. This chapter examines the legal framework within which this tension is resolved when a park visitor is killed or injured. It briefly surveys the relevant basis of liability, focusing on the common-law principles of negligence. It considers how Australian courts have grappled with the competing policy considerations of protecting the natural and scenic values of a place while protecting visitors. The importance of warning signs, the visitor's own carelessness and the obviousness of the danger are all considered. Where possible, emphasis is placed upon cases arising from incidents in nature reserves, national parks and state-forest recreation areas. Cases arising in urban environments are also considered in so far as they provide useful points of reference for understanding the modern law.

© CAB International 2003. *Nature-based Tourism, Environment and Land Management*
(eds R. Buckley, C. Pickering and D.B. Weaver)

The Basis of Liability – Overview

There are several avenues by which a park manager may be fixed with liability for injury to a visitor. The statute under which the agency operates may impose upon it a duty to protect park visitors. The statute might provide some means by which private individuals may recover for breach of such duty, although this is generally unlikely. For the most part, authorizing statutes impose upon park managers only a general duty to manage conservation areas, by reference to a set of management principles. They also confer the powers necessary to discharge that broad statutory obligation. The most common basis of liability in such circumstances is a common-law claim in negligence.

A negligence action rests upon the plaintiff visitor establishing that the land manager owed the plaintiff a duty of care and that the manager breached that duty by failing to act in the manner of a reasonable agency in its position. These issues are considered in detail below.

A claim in public nuisance might also be available. Any substantial and unreasonable interference with the use and enjoyment of public land, such as pollution of a navigable watercourse or the emission of wide-ranging air pollutants, might be actionable as a public nuisance.[1] In practice, however, visitor injury cases are never argued as nuisance actions. This is probably because the basis of a nuisance claim rests on the creation of an interference, whereas most visitor injuries occur because of something that the agency has failed or omitted to do. Far from creating a situation constituting a nuisance, therefore, claims are argued on the basis that the agency failed to act to protect visitors from the dangers of the natural area. The emphasis of the following examination, therefore, is on the principles of negligence law and their application to accidents occurring in parks, reserves and other public recreation areas.

Park Managers Owe Visitors a Duty of Care

Park managers who provide access and recreational facilities owe a duty to take reasonable care to avoid foreseeable risks of injury to lawful visitors.[2] The source of the duty in such a case is the statutory powers conferred on the agency and the statutory duty of 'care, control and management'.[3] The duty extends to averting foreseeable risks present at the area to which visitors have been encouraged, or warning visitors thereof.[4]

In *Nagle* v. *Rottnest Island Authority*, the High Court held that the provision of toilets, picnic and changing facilities at 'The Basin' on Rottnest Island gave rise to a duty to warn swimmers of the dangers of diving on to submerged rocks. In *Prast* v. *Town of Cottesloe*,[5] the plaintiff sued the Town of Cottesloe alleging that a failure to warn of the dangers of body-surfing caused him to be dumped by a wave and to suffer severe injury. Justice Ipp was satisfied, applying the principles set out in *Nagle*, that the Council promoted Cottesloe Beach as a venue for swimming and encouraged the public to use it by installing, maintaining and servicing various facilities.[6] It therefore owed beach goers a duty of care. The question in that case then became whether it had discharged or breached that duty to visitors, an issue considered in detail in the next section.

Typically, a land manager's duty of care only arises in relation to the normal uses to which the area or place should be put. If it can be argued that a visitor's behaviour took him/her outside the range of persons to whom or circumstances in which a duty of care is owed, claims will fail automatically. Since the High Court's decision in *Nagle*, this approach has been far harder to satisfy. A duty may be extended where the authority knows of additional higher-risk activities taking place. For example, in *Scarf* v. *State of Queensland & Gold Coast City Council*, Justice White held that the Queensland Commissioner for Main Roads owed a duty of care to people using Tallebudgera Bridge to dive into the waters of Tallebudgera Creek. In ordinary circumstances, her Honour would have limited the duty to keeping the footpath free of hazards and the guard-rail in good repair. In her view, the plaintiff, 'literally, stepped outside this relationship when he climbed the fence and dived from it'.[7] Since the Commissioner had not encouraged this activity, no duty of care would have arisen if this had been a single occurrence. A duty was found to arise on the facts, however, because the Commissioner had been well aware that it was common practice for young people to jump from the bridge into the creek below.[8]

The capacity to control the relevant park or reserve is central to a duty of care arising. Where the park manager has no control over the relevant site or risk, no duty arises. Local authorities in Queensland and Western Australia, for example, have been held to owe no duty to warn of the risks of jumping from bridges or jetties that are located beyond their jurisdiction.[9] Where land is owned by one agency, but managed by another, responsibility for that area may be shared between the two. For example, the management of Katherine Hotsprings was considered in *NT* v. *Shoesmith*.[10] The Hotsprings were owned by the Northern Territory (NT) government and under the supervision of the NT Conservation Commission (NTCC), as part of its functions to 'promote the conservation and protection of the natural environment of the Territory'.[11] The area was routinely maintained by the Katherine Council, however, and the Council received Territory funding for works around the springs to improve their recreational value. The Council owed a duty of care because it had assumed control of the area.[12] Even though the day-to-day management and maintenance of the area was the responsibility of Katherine Council, the NT Supreme Court also held that the Conservation Commission owed a duty of care because it supervised the site and knew, or should have known, of the works that had been undertaken.[13]

What Must Park Managers do to Discharge Their Duty?

The duty to visitors is to take reasonable measures to guard against a foreseeable risk of injury. This requires measures against all risks – even those that are quite unlikely to occur, provided that they are not far-fetched or fanciful.[14] It does not require elimination of risk, however. Managers are not public insurers and their duty is only to take those measures that

are reasonable in light of the risk presented.[15] In *Romeo* v. *Northern Territory Conservation Commission*, the High Court had to determine what measures the NTCC should have taken to prevent the risk of people falling off Dripstone Cliffs, a popular scenic area in Darwin. In concluding that a reasonable authority would neither fence nor erect signs warning of what was an obvious danger, Justice Kirby commented:

> Insufficient attention has been paid in some of the cases, and by some of the critics, to the practical considerations which must be 'balanced out' before a breach of the duty of care may be found. It is here, in my view, that courts have both the authority and responsibility to introduce practical and sensible notions of reasonableness that will put a break on the more extreme and unrealistic claims sometimes referred to by judicial and academic critics of this area of the law. Thus, under the consideration of the magnitude of the risk, an occupier would be entitled, in a proper case, to accept that the risk of a mishap such as occurred was so remote that 'a reasonable man, careful of the safety of his neighbour, would think it right to neglect it'. It is quite wrong to read past authority as requiring that any reasonably foreseeable risk, however remote, must in every case be guarded against.[16]

In all cases, the powers and responsibilities conferred on the park manager will be the starting-point for determining what it was reasonable to expect the authority to do.[17] If the statute under which a reserve is managed does not confer the powers necessary to avoid, mitigate or warn of a risk, it will be difficult to argue that a duty to take such action arises. Attention must therefore be paid to the relevant statutory instruments under which the agency is operating. These include those specific to park managers, but may also cover more general statutes dealing with civil liability. For example, in *Secretary to the Department of Natural Resource and Energy* v. *Harper*,[18] the plaintiff's action was considered pursuant to the *Wrongs Act* 1958 (Vic). The *Wrongs Act* specifically provides that, where the Crown is an occupier, it shall owe the same duty to persons on the premises as it would owe if it were a private individual.[19] Section 14B provides:

> (3) An occupier of premises owes a duty to take such care as in all the circumstances of the case is reasonable to see that any person on the premises will not be injured or damaged by reason of the state of the premises or of things done or omitted to be done in relation to the state of the premises.

What measures are reasonable is a case-specific inquiry, considering all of the circumstances. In *Harper*, the *Wrongs Act 1958* (Vic) provided guidance on what factors would be relevant in determining whether the duty of care had been breached. These large-ly reflect the position at common law. Section 14B(4) provides that:

> (4) in determining whether the duty of care under subsection (3) has been discharged consideration shall be given to –
> (a) the gravity and likelihood of the probable injury;
> (b) the circumstances of the entry on to the premises;
> (c) the nature of the premises;
> (d) the knowledge which the occupier has or ought to have of the likelihood of persons or property being on the premises;
> (e) the age of the person entering the premises;
> (f) the ability of the person entering the premises to appreciate the danger;
> (g) the burden on the occupier of eliminating the danger or protecting the person entering the premises from the danger as compared to the risk of the danger to the person.

At common law, the obviousness of the risk, the seriousness of any injury that might be suffered and the difficulty and cost of avert-ing the danger are obvious factors. These are to be assessed in light of the possibility that visitors might not take reasonable care for their own safety, although no breach will be estab-lished if an agency fails to warn of a risk that 'existed only in the case of someone ignoring the obvious'.[20] Although a court must consid-er the land manager's conduct in the context of the case before it, it must also bear in mind the resource implications of finding that the agency acted unreasonably. The authority's

ability to insure against liability will also be relevant.[21]

Courts may also take into account more subtle considerations, such as the managers' inability to bar access to public reserves, their conservation obligations and the 'wildness' or otherwise of the reserve:

> In the case of a public authority which manages public lands, it may or may not be able to control entry on the land in the same way that a private owner may; it may have responsibility for an area of wilderness far removed from the nearest town or village or an area of carefully manicured park in the middle of a capital city; it may positively encourage, or at least know of, use of the land only by the fit and the adventurous, or by those of all ages and conditions. All of these matters may bear upon what the reasonable response of the authority may be to the fact that injury is reasonably foreseeable. Similarly, it may be necessary, in a particular case, to consider whether the danger was hidden or obvious, or to consider whether it could be avoided by the exercise of the degree of care ordinarily exercised by a member of the public or to consider whether the danger is one created by the action of the authority or is naturally occurring. But all of these matters (and I am not to be taken as giving some exhaustive list) are no more than particular factors which may go towards judging what reasonable care on the part of a particular defendant required.[22]

The types of precautions to be taken fall into two general categories: those designed to avert or eliminate the risk, including fencing, restricting access or modifying a structure or area; and those aimed at warning of the risk. The approach that Australian courts have taken to these precautions in recent cases is explored below.

Fence off or prohibit access to dangerous areas

It might be simple in individual cases for a plaintiff to argue that fencing a dangerous area was a cheap and efficacious precaution. Yet courts have generally been reluctant to expect national park and other land managers to adopt such precautions, because of the cost implications for other areas under the management of the agency. In *Romeo*, Justice Kirby emphasized that:

> in considering whether the scope of the duty extends . . . to the provision of fencing or a wire barrier, it is not sufficient to evaluate that claim by reference only to the area of the Dripstone Cliffs. An accident of the kind which occurred to the appellant might have occurred at any other elevated promontory in every similar reserve under the control of the Commission to which members of the public had access. The projected scope of the duty must therefore be tested, not solely with the hindsight gained from the happening of the accident to the particular plaintiff but by reference to what it was reasonable to have expected the Commission to have done to respond to foreseeable risks of injury to members of the public generally coming upon any part of the lands under its control which presented similar risks arising out of equivalent conduct.[23]

In recent decisions, several justices have referred to the preservation of natural values and environmental amenity as relevant to the duty to fence. In *Romeo*, for example, Justice Kirby recognized the need to make choices about the allocation of resources and the impact of fencing on the visual amenity:

> regard may be had to considerations such as the preservation of the aesthetics of a natural environment and the avoidance of measures which would significantly alter the character of a natural setting at substantial cost and for an improvement in safety of negligible utility.[24]

Justices Toohey and Gummow also concluded that the taking of steps to prevent persons entering the reserve from suffering injury 'do not extend to fencing off an area of natural beauty where the presence of a cliff was obvious'.[25] A corollary of the cases dealing with obviousness is that there might not be an obligation to warn of dangers if they only arise once a visitor has stepped outside the ordinary visitor experience, for example by leaving a walking track or engaging in hazardous activities like abseiling. In such cases, the visitor's status is perhaps more analogous to a trespasser, to whom a duty of care may not be as rigorous or demanding.[26]

What do these comments mean for recent cliff accidents? There were three incidents in late 2001 in which visitors to national parks in south-east Queensland fell from cliffs, so the issues surrounding such hazards merit closer scrutiny. In the third of these, a young man slipped while taking a photograph at a waterfall, falling approximately 10–15 metres. He survived with only soft-tissue damage and is therefore unlikely to pursue any claim. The other two cases resulted in death. The first incident occurred in a remote part of the Main Range in south-east Queensland. The circumstances of the fall are unclear since the walker was alone and was able only to alert emergency services of his situation by mobile phone. The massive search that ensued only located the man's body some time after he had died. No evidence suggested any 'fault' on the part of park managers, although some questions have arisen about the handling of the emergency call.

In the second case, an elderly woman stepped off the main walking track at Springbrook National Park to be photographed with her grandchildren beside a stream as it flowed over the edge of the cliff. She died when she slipped and plunged over 30 metres to the rocks below. Plaintiffs' law firms were quoted in the local press immediately following the fall, urging the woman's family to sue National Parks for their failure to either fence off an obviously dangerous area or to warn people of the dangers of approaching the edge. The comments in *Romeo*, quoted above, are relevant to the appropriateness of fencing the Springbrook escarpment. A court would have to consider the fact that this person chose to leave a well-marked track in order to get a better photographic opportunity. In such cases, where a track already runs a safe distance from a clearly dangerous cliff, one might reasonably question the reasonableness of a requirement that the site be fenced. This is especially so when one considers further the flow-on implications of such a conclusion, namely that access to the whole escarpment and every other cliff or promontory in a Queensland park would have to be similarly restricted. The issue of whether warning signs should have been erected for visitors will be considered in more detail below.

Render hazardous objects or areas safe

Similar considerations to those outlined above apply in weighing up whether other positive steps should have been taken to avert a danger. To demonstrate a breach of duty in failing to render an area safe, a plaintiff must do more than show that she was injured. She must produce evidence of poor original design of a structure, a history of accidents or complaints that have been ignored or manifestly dangerous deterioration.[27]

Only where the risk is especially great or peculiar to an area of visitor access, such as a walking track, will a Court entertain an obligation to render a natural area 'safe'. In *Schiller* v. *Mulgrave Shire Council*,[28] a case predating its decision in *Romeo* by more than two decades, the High Court found the Mulgrave Council liable for failing to remove a dead tree that stood within falling distance of a walking track. Justice Walsh noted that the case was concerned 'only with a strip of forest adjacent to the track and not with the whole area of the reserve and not, of course, with the forest outside the reserve'.[29]

The less natural and the more manicured the state in which an area is maintained, the more likely it is that managers will be expected to neutralize danger.[30] In finding that the Victorian Department of Natural Resources and Energy (DNRE) owed no duty to warn of the dangers of falling branches in a forest reserve, the Victorian Supreme Court in *Harper* noted that, as part of the Australian bush, much of the reserve was virgin forest, and that

> Forests are a hazard by the very nature of them
> . . . An area such as that in question is not to be
> compared, for example, with a metropolitan
> park, a municipal playground or an ordered
> picnic spot, much less with some sculptured
> woodland glade.[31]

In *Shire of Manjimup* v. *Bill*,[32] the neat and manicured nature of a council park made it foreseeable that people would walk through it at night and gave rise to an obligation to protect such visitors from dangers that could not be detected in the dark. The plaintiff, having fallen into a disused, empty and open septic tank, was therefore entitled to recover. The Shire should have covered the tank or fenced it off.

Risks that have been created or exacerbated by the park manager might also have to be removed altogether. Katherine Shire Council and the NTCC were held liable in 1996 for failing to remove a fallen tree that projected over Katherine Hotsprings swimming hole and which provided an attractive diving point for visitors.[33] The plaintiff, a junior army officer, slipped from the log while eluding friends who were attempting to drag him into the pool during horseplay. He struck his head on a shallow rock ledge that had been constructed by the Katherine Council at the edge of the swimming hole. Katherine Council had removed one fallen tree altogether, but merely pruned the branches from another that had fallen across the pool. The removal of the entire tree would have been simple and inexpensive, but removal only of excess branches made it 'an obvious and enticing means of entering the water by diving and jumping from it'.[34] Katherine Council and the NTCC were both found to have breached their duty in failing to remove the log, since the risk of a slip, fall or dangerous dive was obvious and the difficulty and expense of removing the log were low.[35] Liability was apportioned 20% to the Conservation Commission and 80% to Katherine Council.

This case also predates *Romeo*. It is possible but unlikely that it might be decided differently today. The fact that the Shire had modified the fallen tree would probably be said to have triggered an obligation to avert any dangers it posed to visitors. Justice Tadgell in *Harper* noted that the area in which the accident occurred was not a designated cleared campsite, but it is unclear whether this might have made a difference to his conclusion. He said that the fact that the tree fell in an area frequented by visitors was merely 'coincidental or adventitious'; the Department was not more liable in those circumstances than if the accident had occurred a considerable distance downstream or along a walking track.

The cost implications for all of the

agency's activities will also be important. In *Scarf* v. *State of Queensland & City of Gold Coast*,[36] the plaintiff was seriously injured when he struck his head on the shallow bottom of Tallebudgera Creek, having dived from the top of the guard-rail on the four-lane bridge crossing the creek. Scarf argued that the defendant Council and Commissioner for Main Roads had failed to warn against or prohibit diving from the top of the guard-rail. He also argued that the guard-rail was too low to deter or prevent persons from climbing on to its horizontal top; and that the top rail was so designed that it provided a natural platform from which to dive. On the facts, Justice White rejected the claim that the top of the guard-rail constituted a natural platform.[37] On the question of whether Main Roads should have modified the design of the guard-rail to increase its height, the Court took into account that the agency was responsible for 2559 bridges with a total length exceeding 140 kilometres. An expectation that the Tallebudgera Bridge be modified necessarily gave rise to an expectation that other similar bridges would also be modified, a costly proposition.[38] Moreover, since the only real deterrent would be a cage-like, climb-proof fence, such a construction would adversely affect the amenity of the bridge to other pedestrians and motorists.[39]

The *Scarf* decision must be contrasted with the conclusion of the New South Wales (NSW) Court of Appeal in *Lettice* v. *Council of the Shire of Muswellbrook & Others*.[40] The plaintiff in *Lettice* fell over a bridge while vomiting, landing head-first in the empty creek bed below. He sued the NSW Department of Public Works, alleging faulty design of the bridge railing, since it lacked any useful handhold for persons leaning over the bridge. He also sued the Shire of Muswellbrook for poor bridge design and failure to warn of the dangerous design. It is worth noting that, in deciding what a reasonable authority would do, the Court held that compliance with engineering standards for the bridge was irrelevant, because the standard of care must necessarily depend upon the particular circumstances of each case.[41] Accordingly, the Court had regard to the location of the bridge adjacent to clubs and other licensed recreational facilities, con-

cluding that this increased the likelihood of intoxicated people leaning over the bridge to vomit. The estimated cost of altering the bridge was only Aus$10,000–20,000, which the Court considered not to be excessive.[42] The Council therefore breached its duty to maintain the pedestrian bridge crossing in a safe way by failing to erect a proper handrail at an appropriate height and to erect warning notices.[43] The State as constructor of the bridge was held one-sixth liable for the poor design and construction.[44] In comparable cases, authorities have been found liable for failing to erect a guard-rail around public jetties.[45]

Scarf and *Lettice* might, at first glance, appear to be irreconcilable. The significant difference between the two lies in the fact that the Muswellbrook bridge lacked any useful handrail at all, thus making it potentially unsafe for any pedestrian. The guard-rail of the Tallebudgera Bridge, in contrast, was an appropriate height and of suitable design. It only became dangerous once pedestrians chose to use it as a diving platform.

Erect Signs or Otherwise Warn of Hazards

Once land managers become aware of the existence of some risk or danger that cannot easily be averted, it may be necessary for them to warn of the risk. The requirement that park agencies must warn visitors of the gamut of potential risks associated with visiting natural areas is controversial, especially because the duty to warn is imposed with the benefit of hindsight, only once an accident has occurred. In *City of Rockingham* v. *Curley & Fremantle Port Authority*, the Port Authority was held liable to the injured Curley for failing to warn of the hazards of diving from its jetty, even though no diving accident had occurred previously. It was enough that it was aware that diving was commonplace and that a dive could not be executed safely in shallow water.[46]

The case-law on the duty to warn highlights a range of relevant considerations. An obligation to erect warning signs will be influenced by the obviousness of the danger, the cost of requiring signage, the likely efficacy of warnings and the impact of such a require-ment on the amenity of the area. It will be recalled, for example, that the High Court held in *Nagle* v. *Rottnest Island Authority* that the authority should have warned swimmers at The Basin of the dangers of diving because the sunlight obscured the shallowness of sub-merged rocks, making them a hidden danger.

The obviousness or otherwise of a hazard has been highlighted in numerous subsequent cases as a basis for determining the duty to warn.[47] In *Romeo*, Justice Kirby held that:

> While account must be taken of the possibility of inadvertence or negligent conduct on the part of entrants, the occupier is generally entitled to assume that most entrants will take reasonable care for their own safety ... Where a risk is obvious to a person exercising reasonable care for his or her own safety, the notion that the occupier must warn the entrant about that risk is neither reasonable nor just.[48]

In *Franklins Selfserve Pty Ltd* v. *Bozinovska*[49] (a case arising from an injury in a supermarket), Mason P echoed Justice Kirby's views on the relevance of the obvi-ousness of danger:

> It is foreseeable that if a person jumps off a cliff he or she will be injured or killed. It does not follow that every cliff face must be smattered with warning signs. In some circumstances the danger is so obvious that, when coupled with the likelihood that persons will exercise reasonable care for their own safety, their duty is satisfied by letting the blindingly obvious speak for itself.

The Victorian Supreme Court in *Harper* held that the Victorian Department of Natural Resources and Energy did not breach its duty to visitors to Toorongo Falls Reserve – a for-est reserve within the Yarra Ranges National Park – in not warning them of the dangers of falling trees and branches. Justice Batt empha-sized the obviousness and endemic nature of the danger to be guarded against, especially in high winds:

> To enter a forest or its immediate surrounds, like entering the surf, is to take a risk of injury, albeit a remote risk. The risk is 'endemic' or part and parcel of the recreation of camping,

walking and indeed living outdoors in the Australian bush and in particular in forest reserves.

Similarly, in *Prast* v. *Town of Cottesloe*,[50] the Court held that the danger of being dumped by a wave was obvious and inherent in body-surfing. It distinguished the 'diving cases' of *Nagle* v. *Rottnest Island Authority*, *Inverell Municipal Council* v. *Pennington*[51] and *City of Rockingham* v. *Curley*,[52] all of which involved the materialization of 'hidden dangers'.[53] According to Justice Ipp,

> the risk facing all body-surfers . . . of being hurled on to the seabed, out of control, by a wave that turns out to be dumper . . . is inherent in body-surfing itself, cannot be avoided and is well-known.[54]

An interesting aspect of Justice Ipp's judgement and a key element of his conclu-sion that the risks were obvious is his reference to body-surfing as part of the unique Australian experience. He comments that:

> There must be few who have never thrown themselves upon a wave in the hope of being carried by the rush of water to the shore, and there must be few who do not know (from hearsay at least, if not personal experience) what a 'dumper' is, and how it can throw a helpless surfer about. *This knowledge is generally learned relatively early in childhood and, in any event, is commonsense.*[55]

Justice Ipp accepted that special warnings may be required for dangerous currents or rips or surges or rocks, or the possibility of occa-sional 'king' waves, but rejected as 'absurd' the suggestion that every beach in the coun-try should have to warn of the dangers of body-surfing.[56] While the evidence in *Prast* supported this view in relation to the particu-lar plaintiff in question, it seems hard to conclude that the same could be said of for-eign visitors to Australian coastal resorts. The high representation of Asian tourists in the Gold Coast's drowning statistics certainly sug-gests that surf-sense is by no means common to those who have had minimal exposure to the ocean. The idea that a beach or other land manager owes a duty to some tourists, because of their ignorance of conditions, but not others, will not assist the simplification of this area of the law.[57]

What of the incident described above, in which a woman fell to her death at Springbrook National Park in early 2001? Applying *Romeo*, this should be a case where the cliff was an obvious risk that did not require a warning sign. Imaginative lawyers might argue that the relevant risk was not the obvious cliff but the slick and slippery rocks that the woman stepped on to. These rocks appeared safe, it might be argued, but were actually a 'hidden danger', akin to the cases of *Nagle* and *Curley*. In the face of such an argument, one might invoke the reasoning of Justice Ipp in *Prast*, noted above, to suggest that it is common sense and part of the 'Australian experience' that rocks beside a rainforest stream are likely to be slippery and that the uneven ground of a national park must always be trodden with care. This more robust view is supported by a decision of the High Court of May 2001, dealing with a pedestrian fall from a city footpath.[58] There, Justices Gaudron, McHugh and Gummow noted that, pedestrians' ability to examine carefully the surfaces upon which they stepped was far greater than that of a motorist examining the road. Pedestrians should therefore be assumed capable of taking that level of care for their own safety.[59] Justice Callinan noted that there was no concealment of the difference in height that was said to constitute the hazard, adding:

> The world is not a level playing field. It is not unreasonable to expect that people will see in broad daylight what lies ahead of them in the ordinary course as they walk along.[60]

The cost of requiring warnings is also a major consideration. If a single catch-all warning at the vehicular entrance to a park would be effective in alerting visitors to relevant risks, its cost will not be unduly burdensome. But, in *Harper*, the Victorian Supreme Court recognized the large number of sites within the forest reserve at which signs would have to be posted, as well as the large number of other reserves under the care, control and management of the DNRE. A requirement that warnings be posted therefore imposed an unreasonable burden, in terms of cost, time and trouble. Justice Batt said that this burden

was out of proportion to the remote, albeit eventuating, risk of danger to visitors. Justice Tadgell held that the duty to warn was 'unrealistic'. He accepted that there was a real risk that during a high wind in the reserve a tall tree might topple on to an innocent visitor, but he ventured that the same might be said of any comparable tract of Crown land.

The likely efficacy of a warning sign also affects the question of whether it is reasonable to expect signs to be posted. In *Harper*, the wide range of possible hazards to be warned against made it difficult to conclude what the text of an appropriate sign should be, or whether the text should vary according to where the sign might be placed in order to afford an adequate warning of a particular hazard:

> If the appellant's duty of care to a member of the public who roams in a forest in a National Park requires a written warning of the hazard of injury by any undifferentiated tree, it would seem to require also a written warning of any other undifferentiated natural or endemic hazard – animal, vegetable or mineral. In the absence of evidence to warrant it, I could not accept that as a proposition.[61]

The expectation that every natural area will be littered with unsightly warning signs has also figured in judicial reasoning. Justice Batt in *Harper* acknowledged that the amenity of nature reserves would be adversely affected by signs. Justice Tadgell took this issue further by suggesting that signage would undermine the statutory objectives of national-park designation. He said that it was reasonable to infer from the preamble and s.17 of the *National Parks Act* 1975 (Vic) that bush-walking and other enjoyment of the natural environment was officially authorized, if not positively encouraged, in parks and reserves. From this, he inferred that:

> one of the justifications of a National Park under the Act is that it enables those of the public who wish to do so to get away from suburban orderliness and to commune with nature in her elemental simplicity, roaming (within reason) where they will.[62]

It will be recalled that Justice Wallwork suggested in *Prast* that signs warning of the dangers of body-surfing might be beneficial even if not actually required. But, in a reference to either cost or visual amenity, he added that this did not require that 'the whole beach front needs to be littered with signs'.[63] Instead, a sign in an obvious place, such as a walkway down to the beach, would suffice.

If warning signs are erected, care must me taken to ensure their adequacy. A failure to provide a proper warning of risks is as likely to result in liability as a failure to warn at all. Expert evidence in *Scarf* identified the following factors as key to the effectiveness of a warning sign:

- Signal word (e.g. DANGER).
- Hazard statement (e.g. High Voltage Wires).
- Consequences (e.g. Can Kill).
- Instruction (e.g. Stay away).[64]

The evidence in that case also suggested that people are more likely to comply with a warning if compliance requires minimal effort. The salience or flamboyance of a sign adds to its effectiveness and the more serious the hazard or risk identified, the more likely people are to comply.

Accidents on park roads

Brief mention should be made of the principles governing liability for road accidents that occur on roads under the control and maintenance of park managers. This issue is of far greater importance to local councils than to park managers: in NSW, at least, claims made by pedestrians who have sustained injuries in a fall on a council footpath comprise the majority of claims against local councils and are the single most expensive basis of public liability.[65] While local authorities are most exposed to liability for unsafe roads, this is none the less potentially relevant to park managers as well. It is easy to envisage cases of branches falling across roads, subsidence or poor grading creating hazards for park visitors.

Until 2001, Australian courts applied a historical exception to the general rules governing an authority's duty to exercise its statutory powers that have already been explained in this section. In essence, the

exception conferred on authorities with responsibility for the maintenance of roads an immunity for accidents that arose from their failure to repair or maintain a roadway, known as nonfeasance. Liability only arose in cases where repairs had been undertaken but had been performed carelessly, known as cases of misfeasance. This 'highway immunity' was abolished in a recent decision of the High Court, thereby bringing this area of the law into line with broader negligence principles.[66]

The High Court decision considered two cases together. In *Brodie* v. *Singleton Shire Council*, the plaintiff/appellant sustained back injuries when a bridge maintained by the defendant/respondent, Singleton Council, collapsed as he drove his truck over it. The bridge was adapted to take loads of up to 15 tonnes. The plaintiff's truck was 22 tonnes. The NSW Court of Appeal had applied the highway immunity, found this to be a case of non-repair and dismissed the claims against Council. *Ghantous* v. *Hawkesbury City Council* involved a claim by an elderly woman against the Hawkesbury Council for injuries sustained when she fell on a public footpath. The relevant statutory definition of 'road' included footpath, and the Court again found this to be a case of nonfeasance that attracted the immunity.

A 4 : 3 majority of the High Court held that the traditional immunity for nonfeasance either never constituted the common law or was no longer good law in Australia.[67] It held that the general principles of negligence provide the criterion of liability. The question of breach will therefore be determined by what would be expected of a reasonable authority, taking into account the expectation that footpath and road users will exercise care for their own safety[68] and considering the competing or conflicting responsibilities of the authority.[69] According to Gaudron, McHugh and Gummow JJ:

> the discharge of the duty involves the taking by the authority of reasonable steps to prevent there remaining a source of risk which gives rise to a foreseeable risk of harm. Such a risk of harm may arise from a failure to repair a road or its surface, from the creation of conditions during or as a result of repairs or works, from a

failure to remove unsafe items in or near a road, or from the placing of items upon a road which create a danger, or the removal of items which protect against danger.[70]

In *Ghantous*, the Court could find nothing in the Council's conduct that suggested a want of reasonable care. The uneven surface of the footpath was plainly visible and the plaintiff's fall could have been prevented by simply watching where she was placing her feet. The *Brodie* case was referred back to the NSW Court of Appeal to determine whether Singleton Council had been negligent in the circumstances. Evidence suggested that there had been substantial deterioration of the girders supporting the bridge and that this damage had already been repaired by Council, albeit ineffectually. It seems highly likely that a breach of duty will be established on the facts in *Brodie*.[71] The Council will undoubtedly argue that the fact that the plaintiff disregarded a recommended load-limit warning broke the chain of causation, but Council's knowledge that the bridge was routinely used by heavier vehicles will probably operate against them on this point.

Can it be Said that the Accident would have Occurred in Any Event?

The plaintiff bears the burden of proving on the balance of probabilities that the failure to avert or warn of a hazard caused the accident or injury. The causation issue is especially critical to a case based upon alleged failure to warn of dangers. The plaintiff must be able to prove that it was more probable than not that he would have heeded a warning and, thus warned, could have avoided injury.

Two things may prevent plaintiffs from establishing this element. The first is where the evidence suggests that the plaintiff would not or could not have heeded the warning. Even if a warning is salient, informative and concise, it will not necessarily be effective. The expert evidence adduced in *Scarf* concluded that no sign used in the experiments on warning design had been 100% effective, because there will always be those who read but ignore them.[72] Whether the plaintiff would have

heeded a warning is a difficult issue because it is necessarily hypothetical. It requires the Court to evaluate whether events would have been different if something that was not done had been done.

A plaintiff will sometimes testify that he/she would have read and followed whatever warning had been given. In other cases, the Court is left to draw inferences from the surrounding facts.[73] In *Harper*, for example, no evidence was adduced at trial bearing directly upon what the injured woman would have done had a notice been erected. Justice Batt therefore concluded that it was not open on the evidence to infer that, if she had been warned, she would have taken notice.

Evidence of intoxication at the time of the accident or a history of disregarding authority and engaging in risk-taking behaviour could all be raised to undermine a causal connection. In *Scarf*, the plaintiff testified that he would not have jumped had he seen warning signs, but Justice White concluded that this evidence must be assessed against the kind of individual the plaintiff was at the time of the accident.[74] Justice White adopted an approach advocated by Justice McHugh and Justice Kirby in *Chappel* v. *Hart*.[75] In that case, Justice McHugh said:

> Human nature being what it is, most plaintiffs will genuinely believe that, if he or she had been given an option that would or might have avoided the injury, the option would have been taken . . . [G]iven that most plaintiffs will genuinely believe that they would have taken another option, if presented to them, the reliability of their evidence can only be determined by reference to objective factors, particularly the attitude and conduct of the plaintiff at or about the time when the breach of duty occurred.[76]

The plaintiff in *Scarf* had routinely engaged in risk-taking behaviour and defied authority prior to the accident. He also conceded in testimony that he would not have jumped had his mother been there to see him. Justice White therefore concluded that, on balance, it was more probable than not that the plaintiff would have disregarded warning signs had they been posted.[77] In contrast, the erection of a higher guard-rail would have prevented the accident, had the Court found that the defendants' duty of care extended to such measures.[78]

The second thing that might prevent a plaintiff from proving the causal connection is where the sudden nature of the event meant that no amount of warning could have been effective. In such cases, the plaintiff must instead argue that the park manager should have neutralized the risk altogether. In *Schiller*,[79] for example, Justice Gibbs concluded that it would have served no good purpose merely to warn persons using the walking track on to which the dead tree fell. The accident showed that a tree might come down so suddenly that a person on the track could not escape it.[80]

A park manager will not be able to point to the plaintiff's own careless conduct as 'breaking the chain of causation' if that type of foolhardiness or inadvertence is the very kind of thing that was likely to happen in the ordinary course of things.[81] In such cases, once it is established that managers owe a duty to protect against a visitor's inadvertence, that carelessness will not be considered to be the cause of the incident unless it was gross, extreme or outside the ordinary course of events.

Should Liability be Reduced Because of the Plaintiff's Own Carelessness?

In some cases, the carelessness of the plaintiff is taken into account in ruling that the park manager did not breach its duty of care to visitors. If visitors are only likely to be injured if they fail to exercise care for their own well-being or safety, it may be reasonable for park managers to take no precautions to protect them.[82] In these cases, the park manager will not be liable at all, because it will have discharged its duty to visitors.

On the other hand, the very nature of some reserves and parks will bring with it a risk that some visitors will act carelessly.[83] In cases where the plaintiff has managed to show that a reasonable park manager would have acted differently – by fencing, redesigning or warning against dangers – the quantum of damages may none the less be reduced where the Court concludes that some account should be taken of the plaintiff's own carelessness.

A claim of contributory negligence will require more than proof of mere inadvertence or carelessness on the plaintiff's part. The park manager must establish a negligent want of care for one's own safety.[84] In *City of Rockingham* v. *Curley and Fremantle Port Authority*, the plaintiff successfully claimed against the Fremantle Port Authority (FPA) for failing to warn of the dangers of diving off an FPA-managed jetty, but had his award of damages reduced. Curley had dived from the jetty on other occasions without incident, but on the day of the accident struck his head on the shallow bottom. At trial, damages were reduced by 20% for Curley's own carelessness, but this proportion was increased to 33.3% on appeal.[85] The Court distinguished earlier cases where there had been no finding of contribution. In those cases, evidence suggested that the diver had attempted to check the bottom before diving. In *Lettice*, the Court took account of the plaintiff's above-average height in concluding that he should have exercised greater care for his own safety when deciding to become intoxicated and vomit over the side of a dangerously low bridge.[86] His higher centre of gravity meant that he should have been more vigilant than a shorter pedestrian leaning over the bridge. The Court apportioned 25% of liability to the plaintiff's contributory negligence.[87]

It was unnecessary for the Court in *Scarf* to decide the issue of contributory negligence, because it was satisfied that the plaintiff would have disregarded any warning that might have been given. Justice White none the less indicated that, had her conclusions been different, she would have reduced liability for the plaintiff's own careless by 35%. Scarf had testified that he deliberately angled his dive towards the shallow creek bank (in order to make a hasty escape from the water to avoid sharks) and because he was probably still affected by alcohol and drugs when he undertook the dive.[88]

NT v. *Shoesmith* provides a somewhat surprising contrast. The NT Supreme Court upheld a finding that the plaintiff was not contributorily negligent when he slipped and fell from a log as he rushed to escape from his friends during horseplay at Katherine Hotsprings. The Court concluded that the fact that he slipped and hit his head, rather than intentionally diving into the shallow water, militated against a finding of contributory negligence. The Court held that the horseplay itself was not careless, because that was the very type of activity the defendants should have anticipated at the recreation area.[89] Justice Angel, dissenting on this issue, would have found Shoesmith 15% liable. In Justice Angel's view, the alleged contributory negligence was not the fact that Shoesmith slipped, but that he jumped too hastily to escape his friends, knowing of the wetness of the log and the submerged rock ledge.[90] He held that the fact that the Shire and NTCC should have considered the risks of horseplay did not relieve those engaging in such behaviour from all personal responsibility. Justice Angel's approach is supported by the High Court in *Nagle* v. *Rottnest Island Authority*. In *Nagle*, the High Court held that the Authority should have anticipated that some visitors would act carelessly and that its duty was to protect even inadvertent visitors against foreseeable risks. It none the less remitted the case back to the Western Australian (WA) Supreme Court for determination of whether liability should be reduced for contributory negligence. Had the *Shoesmith* decision been taken further, a different conclusion might well have been reached on this issue.

Liability will not be apportioned where there were not precautions a plaintiff could reasonably be expected to have taken. In *Shire of Manjimup* v. *Bill*, for example, the WA Supreme Court overturned the trial judge's finding of contributory negligence. Bill had fallen into an open disused septic tank while walking off the path in a public park late at night. At trial, the court had found that she had failed to take care for her own safety when she strayed from the path to relieve herself in nearby bushes. On appeal, this conclusion was overturned, the Court being satisfied that the buried tank constituted a hidden trap against which risk the plaintiff could not have been expected to take precautions.[91]

Does a Separate Action Lie for Breach of Statutory Duty?

The foregoing analysis has considered the common-law principles of negligence as they apply to visitor injuries. These principles concern breach of a common-law duty of care. There may be circumstances in which the statute creating or empowering the park manager also imposes separate statutory duties. It is thus sometimes possible for plaintiffs to bring a separate action for the tort of breach of statutory duty, instead of, or in addition to, the common-law claim.

In order to bring a discrete claim for breach of statutory duty, the plaintiff must show that the statute intended to confer upon persons like him a private right to sue for damages if the duty is breached.[92] It seems unlikely that a class of persons as potentially broad as 'all park visitors' would satisfy this requirement. The wider the class of persons in the community who may derive benefit from the performance of a statutory duty, the less likely is it that the statute can be construed as conferring an individual right of action for damages for its breach. It will be difficult to say that a national-parks statute that imposes on the agency a duty to maintain parks for recreational and other uses confers on visitors a private right to sue.

Statutory Immunity an Appropriate Solution?

This chapter has attempted to highlight the considerable uncertainty surrounding the liability of park managers. Agencies are already struggling to balance scarce resources between the provision of visitor access and recreational facilities and the maintenance of conservation and environmental values. While liability principles remain creatures of the common law, there will always be the potential for an injured visitor to argue an agency's want of reasonable care. The claim should fail if the factors set out above are properly considered and weighed. Rather than engaging in costly litigation, however, it might be preferable to remove such cases from the courts altogether. For example, it is open to parliament to enact statutory immunities for certain acts or omissions of park managers. Such immunity would have to be carefully worded, however, since Courts will construe them very narrowly.[93] Protection from failing to exercise powers would restore some protection; agencies could only be held liable if they undertake works but perform them in a negligent fashion. Where a policy decision has been taken, for example, to allocate a majority of resources to weed or pest eradication, to enhance the conservation values of an area, the failure to repair a walking track or remove a fallen branch should not be actionable.

An alternative might be the establishment of a statutory compensation scheme, administered through non-judicial channels. There are various precedents for statutory schemes, including no-fault workers' compensation and dust-diseases tribunals, and the compulsory insurance schemes. The scope and operation of any statutory compensation scheme would require a great deal of careful consideration. Thought would have to be given to whether it should encompass all statutory entities, not just land managers, or whether it should relate to 'occupiers' liability' in its most general sense. The basis for recovery and the source of funds for the scheme would also require resolution. One option here is the imposition of a specific visitor fee that would go into an insurance fund, similar to third-party car insurance. Those who object to a user-pays philosophy for national-park funding because of its anthropocentric view of the value of conservation areas could not hold this against a specific-purpose insurance levy. Visitors are the only people who would claim against a scheme established to deal with visitor injuries, so, on any analysis, they are the 'users' of compensation. The main concern then is whether it is equitable to require careful visitors to subsidize the careless or foolhardy, but this concern is hardly unique to accidents in natural areas.

Conclusions

Expansion of liability carries considerable risks. It risks distracting park managers' attention from their conservation priorities and diverting resources into identifying myriad potential dangers and rendering them safe. It also risks sanitizing the visitor experience, thus undermining a park's attraction and conservation values.

In recent cases, the courts have tried to 'introduce practical and sensible notions of reasonableness that would put a brake on the more extreme and unrealistic claims'.[94] They have done so in a variety of ways. In particular, they will not expect land managers to warn visitors of obvious dangers. They will also consider the implications for a land manager's entire jurisdiction of requiring preventive measures in one place. The negative impacts of fencing and signage on areas of natural beauty will also militate against their being required. No court has yet ruled that a preventive measure is unreasonable because it would interfere with the conservation values, as distinct from the scenic or amenity values, but nor has it been necessary to do so.

While uncertainty over the scope of liability remains, park agencies may direct resources away from valuable conservation activities. Some alternative scheme may be required. Options include a statutory immunity, a no-fault compensation scheme and a visitor insurance scheme, funded from a hypothecated visitor fee. None of these options is likely to attract wide support unless it is part of broad reform of negligence law, aimed at curbing the trend towards speculative litigation. In the absence of legislative solutions, it may be hoped that the courts will themselves establish a more predictable legal environment, in which the natural and wilderness values of protected areas are respected and visitors are expected to take personal responsibility for their own safety:

> As a matter of law, there is a point at which those who indulge in pleasurable but risky pastimes must take personal responsibility for what they do. That point is reached when the risks are so well-known and obvious that it can reasonably be assumed that the individuals concerned will take reasonable care for their own safety.[95]

Notes

1 *A-G* v. *PYA Quarries Ltd* [1957] 2 QB 169.

2 *Nagle* v. *Rottnest Island Authority* (1993) 177 CLR 423 at 429–430; *Romeo* v. *Conservation Commission (NT)* (1998) 192 CLR 431 at 460, 477.

3 *Schiller* v. *Mulgrave Shire Council* (1972) 129 CLR. 116 at 120; *Romeo*, above n. 2, at 439–440, 451, 472 and 487–488.

4 *Nagle*, above n. 2, at 430, per Mason CJ, Deane, Dawson & Gaudron JJ. This approach has since been applied in numerous cases. See, for example, *City of Rockingham* v. *Curley & Fremantle Port Authority* Unreported [2000] WASCA 202, Ipp & Wallwork JJ, Anderson J dissenting, available at: www.austlii.edu.au; and *Brodie* v. *Singleton Shire Council*; *Ghantous* v. *Hawkesbury City Council* (2001) 180 ALR 145, at 174, ¶102 per Gaudron, McHugh & Gummow JJ.

5 (1999–2000) 22 WAR 474, Ipp, Wallwork & Parker JJ.

6 Ibid., at 478, ¶12.

7 Unreported, Supreme Court of Queensland, 30 October 1998, White J, at ¶68.

8 Ibid.

9 Ibid., at ¶65. The Supreme Court of Queensland held that the Gold Coast City Council owed no duty to visitors of Tallebudgera Creek reserve to warn of the dangers associated with diving into the creek from a road bridge adjacent to the reserve controlled by Queensland Transport.

10 *NT & Katherine Town Council* v. *Shoesmith* (1996) 5 NTLR 155, Kearney, Angel & Mildren JJ.

11 *Conservation Commission Act* 1980 NT, s19(a).

12 *Shoesmith*, above n. 10, at 165.

13 Ibid., at 163–164.

14 *Wyong Shire Council* v. *Shirt* (1980) 146 CLR 40, at 48; *Nagle*, above n. 2, at 431.

15 *Romeo*, above n. 2, at 454–456 per Toohey & Gummow JJ; 478 per Kirby J; 488 per Hayne J.

16 *Romeo*, above n. 2, at 480–481, ¶¶128–130.

17 *Brodie/Ghantous*, above n. 5, at 185, ¶139, per Gaudron, Gummow & McHugh.

18 [2000] 1 VR 133, Tadgell, Callaway & Batt JJA.

19 *Wrongs Act* 1958 (Vic) s14C.

20 *Romeo*, above n. 2, at 455 per Toohey & Gummow JJ. Hayne J (at 489) and Brennan CJ (at 443–444, dissenting on other grounds) also referred to obviousness as a relevant factor.

21 *Brodie/Ghantous*, above n. 5, at 174–175, ¶¶104–105, per Gaudron, Gummow & McHugh JJ; *Schiller*, above n. 3, at 136, per Gibbs J.

22 *Romeo*, above n. 2, at 488, per Hayne J.

23 *Romeo*, above n. 2, at 478–479, ¶123–124, per Kirby J. Hayne J expressed a similar view at 490, ¶163.

24 *Romeo*, Ibid., at 481, ¶130.

25 Ibid., at 456.

26 *Critchley* v. *Cross* [2000] NSWSC 6, 8 February 2000, Studdert J, at ¶¶57–59.

27 *Brodie/Ghantous*, above n. 5, at 212, ¶246, per Kirby J.

28 Above n. 3.

29 Ibid., at 132.

30 *Romeo*, above n. 2, at 477 per Kirby J; *Australian Capital Territory* v. *Badcock* [2000] FCA 142, 18 February 2000, at ¶24 per Einfeld J (with whom Hill, Drummond, Tamberlin, & Hely JJ agreed).

31 Above n18, at 135 per Tadgell JA.

32 Unreported [2000] WASCA 256, 14 August 2000, Ipp, Parker & Miller JJ.

33 *Shoesmith*, above n. 10.

34 Ibid., at 161.

35 Ibid., at 165–166.

36 Above n. 7.

37 Ibid., at ¶54.

38 Ibid., at ¶52.

39 Ibid., at ¶77.

40 Unreported [2000] NSWSC 81, 24 February 2000, Dowd J.

41 Ibid., at ¶¶73–75.

42 Ibid., at ¶80.

43 Ibid., at 76–81.

44 Ibid., at ¶99.

45 *Ansett Transport Industries (Operations) P/L* v. *Lennard*, Unreported, Queensland C of A, 16 June 1998, Pincus JA, McPherson JA, Fryberg J; *Kemp & Kemp* v. *District Council of Yankalilla*, Unreported [2000] SADC 45, David J.

46 *Curley*, above n. 4, at ¶158.

47 *Mountain Cattlemen's Association of Victoria Inc.* v. *Barron*[1998] 3 V.R. 302; [1997] A Torts Rep. 81–426. Brooking JA (with whom Phillips JA agreed) said (at 64,136):

> The danger to be guarded against here was the obvious one that a person leading a horse over small and slippery rocks, in the partly dried up bed of a river, would be injured as a result of the horse's slipping and falling. The danger that a horse would slip when walking in such a place must have been apparent to anyone with any real experience as a horse rider to say the least. . . That there was a danger cannot be gainsaid, but it was of a kind and degree which in my view the organiser could reasonably have expected participants to take, as it were, in their stride, using their own common sense, skill and experience to guard against it.

48 *Romeo*, above n. 2, at 478–479, ¶¶123–124; and at 453–454, per Toohey & Gummow JJ.

49 Unreported, Court of Appeal, Supreme Court of NSW, 14 October 1998.

50 Above n. 5.

51 [1993] A. Torts Rep. 62,397.

[52] Above n. 4. Other 'diving' cases have reached similar conclusions. See, for example, *Western Australia* v. *Dale & Anor* (1996) 15 WAR 464 at 477, Kennedy J.

[53] *Curley*, above n. 4, at ¶¶30–32, per Ipp J. But note the strong dissent of Anderson J in *Curley*, where, at ¶206, his Honour concluded, 'I cannot subscribe to the view that there is a common law duty upon every municipality or public authority who has a jetty or groyne under its management or control to put up signs prohibiting diving because someone may ignore the obvious risk of diving head first into shallow water.'

[54] *Prast*, above n. 5, at 482, ¶32.

[55] Ibid., at ¶33 (emphasis added).

[56] Ibid., at 485, ¶43.

[57] Wallwork J generally agreed with Ipp J in *Prast*. But he did conclude, at 488, ¶57, that although there is no legal duty to do so, in the light of the injuries suffered by Prast, it would be beneficial to post signs at popular beaches warning of the dangers of body-surfing.

[58] *Brodie/Ghantous*, above n. 5.

[59] Ibid., at 192, ¶163

[60] Ibid., at 240, ¶355.

[61] *Harper*, above n18, 136, ¶6, per Tadgell J.

[62] Ibid.

[63] *Prast*, above n. 5, at 488, ¶57.

[64] *Scarf*, above n. 7, discussed at ¶38 of the judgment.

[65] *Brodie/Ghantous*, above n. 5, at 157–158, ¶51, per Gaudron, McHugh & Gummow.

[66] Ibid.

[67] Ibid. See the joint judgment of Gaudron, McHugh & Gummow JJ at 159, ¶55 and 185, ¶¶137–138; and the judgment of Kirby J at 208–211, ¶¶226–238, Gleeson CJ and Hayne & Callinan JJ dissenting on the issue of the highway immunity. Gaudron, McHugh & Gummow JJ also held that the tort of public nuisance in highway cases has been subsumed by the law of negligence.

[68] Ibid., at 191, ¶160 per Gaudron, McHugh & Gummow JJ.

[69] Ibid., at 192, ¶162.

[70] Ibid., at 191, ¶159, footnotes omitted.

[71] Ibid., at 185–186, ¶139.

[72] *Scarf*, above n. 7, at ¶38.

[73] *Chappel* v. *Hart* (1998) 195 CLR 232 at 246, per McHugh J (dissenting) and at 272–273, per Kirby J.

[74] *Scarf*, above n. 7, at ¶39.

[75] Above n. 73, at 247.

[76] *Chappel*, above n. 73, at 246, n. 64 per McHugh J.

[77] *Scarf*, above n. 7, at ¶43.

[78] Ibid., at ¶¶52–53, 77.

[79] Above n. 3, at 133.

[80] Ibid., at 135.

[81] *March* v. *Stramare* (1991) 171 CLR 506, at 518, 519–520, 536–537; *Nagle*, above n. 2, at 431.

[82] *Romeo*, above n. 2, at 489 per Hayne J.

[83] *Shoesmith*, above n. 10, at 158, per Angel J, citing *Inverell Municipal Council* v. *Pennington* (1993) A Torts Rep 62,397.

[84] *Podrebersek* v. *Australian Iron & Steel Pty Ltd* (1985) 59 ALJR 492, at 493–494.

[85] *Curley*, above n. 4, at ¶162.

[86] *Lettice*, above n. 40, at ¶90.

[87] Ibid., at ¶92.

[88] *Scarf*, above n. 7, at ¶79.

[89] *Shoesmith*, above n. 10, at 167–168.

[90] Ibid., per Angel J dissenting on this point, at 158–159.

[91] *Bill*, above n. 32, at ¶29.

[92] *Sovar* v. *Henry Lane Pty Ltd* (1967) 116 CLR 397.

[93] *Brodie/Ghantous*, above n. 5, at 199, ¶¶197 and 207, ¶223 per Kirby J.

[94] *Romeo*, above n. 2, at 480, ¶128, per Kirby J.

[95] *Prast*, above n. 5, at 485, ¶44, per Ipp J.

7

Visitor Fees, Tour Permits and Asset and Risk Management by Parks Agencies: Australian Case Study

Ralf Buckley,[1] Natasha Witting[2] and Michaela Guest[3]

[1]*International Centre for Ecotourism Research;* [2]*School of Environmental Studies;* [3]*School of Environmental and Applied Sciences, Griffith University, Queensland, Australia*

Abstract

During 2000/01 we reviewed the current practices of each Australian terrestrial protected-area agency in regard to visitor and user fees, tour and activity permits, risk and asset management and visitor monitoring and education programmes. Current practices differ widely between, and in some cases also within, individual State, Territory and Commonwealth protected-area agencies. Most require commercial tour operators to be licensed, and most charge licence application and annual fees. Most parks also charge visitor entrance and camping fees, whether visitors arrive independently or with commercial tours. Tour operators may receive discounts. There are concessions for children, seniors, community groups and local residents, and season passes as well as daily entrance fees. Most States and Territories charge different camping fees, depending on infrastructure and facilities and sometimes also on season and demand. Different parks charge fees either per person, per vehicle, per site or various combinations of these. Proportions of fees retained at individual parks, in individual regions, within the overall parks agency, or within the state government treasury differ between states, as do the budget procedures, which may offset any fees collected. Fees are relatively low and unlikely to influence behaviour for most tourists. Overall, fees contribute a small but still significant proportion of total parks operating funds. All States and Territories have risk- and asset-management systems in place, but these differ considerably in sophistication, integration and practical application. Recent changeovers by many State governments from cash-flow to accrual accounting systems have introduced a number of practical problems in park budgeting. The introduction of the Commonwealth Government's Goods and Services Tax (GST) also forced parks agencies to review fees and revise fee-collection mechanisms.

Introduction and Methods

Parks worldwide are used for public recreation and commercial tourism as well as conservation. Protected-area agencies have to manage people, infrastructure and equipment as well as plants, animals and landscapes. For this they need money, tools and information. As visitor numbers continue to outstrip government funding in most countries, protected-area management agencies have introduced visitor fees as a contribution to visitor management costs. To control commercial tourism and some types of public recreation they use permit systems. As their infrastructure and equipment inventories continue to grow they have introduced asset databases for systematic maintenance and accounting. And, as the number of injury claims against landholders has risen, they have adopted risk-management frameworks to assess and limit potential legal and financial liabilities.

Australia provides a good test bed to examine these systems. It has a combination of federal and state jurisdictions, with most national parks under the latter. It has only eight subsidiary States and Territories, which have faced the same issues in regard to visitors and tourism in parks, but have responded independently. Some Australian parks agencies have charged fees for years or decades, whereas others still do not. Permit systems for commercial tour operators and asset- and risk-management frameworks have evolved independently, with limited information exchange via a former ministerial council, the Australian and New Zealand Environment Conservation Council (ANZECC). Information on current practices in regard to fees, permits and asset and risk management by Australian protected-area agencies is not available from any single source nationally or indeed even within individual States and Territories. During 2000/01, therefore, we compiled and compared this information from each of the state jurisdictions and also the federal agency. Data were derived from all available sources, including agency reports and websites, publications and consultancies, and, most importantly, directly from relevant staff in each of the agencies concerned.

Fees

Global issues

User charges for recreation in parks and other public lands are well established and widespread, but still contentious (WCPA, 2000; Buckley, 2001). Fees are used both to raise revenue and as a visitor-management tool. Other tools include site hardening, regulation (including zoning) and education (Buckley, 1998, 2000; Newsome et al., 2002). Larger fees raise more money and have more influence on visitor behaviour, but are more likely to be inequitable. User fees may include charges for: entry to the park or particular areas; overnight camping; specific recreational or educational activities; and use of park transport, accommodation, facilities or equipment.

The term 'user fees' is generally applied to public rather than private parks, and excludes prices for retail sales and rentals. It includes licence and per capita fees paid to the park by commercial tour operators but excludes prices paid to operators by clients. These distinctions are somewhat arbitrary. In particular, fees that are readily distinguishable in a legal sense may act identically in an economic sense, or vice versa.

The significance and acceptance of user fees depend on their social, political, legal and economic context and on the characteristics of the fees themselves, including their size and type, how they are set and collected and what the money is spent on. The Recreation Fee Demonstration Program in the USA has been studied in particular detail (Watson, 1999). User fees have also been examined in Canadian parks (van Sickle and Eagles, 1998) and US forests (Harris et al., 1987).

Parks charge fees because visitor numbers and management costs have increased, but government budget allocations have not kept pace. The highest value of parks to human economies is in conservation of biodiversity and land and water quality. These benefits, however, accrue at larger scales in space and time than individual governments. Governments therefore under-invest in protecting conservation values. Recreation benefits are localized and more easily captured, so governments expect parks to charge for them.

Many people object on
ing to use parks. Some cou
historical public rights of way
a strong traditional right of acce
vate land (e.g. in Scandinavia).
also argue that taxpayers have alrea
parks, or that user fees are an ineffi
of funding a public good. Wheth
accept fees also depends on what the f
used for (Vogt and Williams, 1999).

In countries with ineffective, *laissez-f*
or decentralized governments, parks or res
dents may levy visitors at a very local scale
legally or otherwise. In countries with strongly centralized control and enforcement, user
fees are collected on behalf of central treasuries. In countries with elected governments,
especially federated systems, fees are subject
to a wide range of political constraints. People
who did not pay in the past do not want to
pay in the future. People who think themselves
disadvantaged want discounts. People who
think taxes should pay for parks object to fees
on principle.

User fees may be subject to legal constraints on the actions of the land-management
agency. They may have legal consequences,
e.g. in increasing the duties of care or the contractual obligations of that agency. They may
also increase the expectations of visitors and
tour operators, particularly in regard to park
infrastructure.

Many parks charge differential fees for foreign nationals, for multiple visits, for
commercial tours as compared with independent visitors, for visitors travelling by different
means, for local residents or for educational
groups and senior citizens. Heavily used parks
may charge different fees from less visited
parks in the same region. Elected governments
may use parks and user fees as a political tool
for regional development, to gain regional
votes.

The most critical economic characteristic
for any kind of user charge is how the money
is used and who controls it. Fees may be used
to manage the specific activity in the park
where they were collected, or be paid into a
central government treasury, or any intermediate level of control, or shared between
several levels. In addition, fees retained by a
park or region may be offset by a corre-

53

Stoeckl, 1995; Lindbe g
Lindberg, 2001). A small fee may have a large
effect on some users in some parks (Schneider
and Budruk, 1999; Buckley *et al.*, 2001a);
whereas elsewhere a large fee may have little
influence.

Most public-land management agencies
have to ensure that recreational user fees are
equitable. This is difficult. Equity in legal principle does not guarantee equity of opportunity
in practice between different socio-economic
groups. Additionally, should fees be the same
for foreigners as for citizens; for local residents
as for those living far away; for multiple visits
as for single; for visitors in groups as for those
visiting alone; for visitors using different forms
of transport; for commercial-tour clients as for
independent visitors; and for people with different recreational preferences?

Which takes higher priority, a park's
needs for management funds or its public
obligations? Should parks charge higher fees
for visitors likely to create higher social and
environmental impacts or claim compensation, like an insurance company? Should they
restrict access to increase demand, like diamond cartels? Should they offer services at
market rates in competition with commercial
tour operators? If they form partnerships with

arks

of government.
are under federal
g nearly all nation-
e jurisdiction. Limited
formerly provided by
er reviewed user fees in
update in 2000 (ANZECC,
agencies have since revised fees
to a federal goods and services tax,
d in July 2000.

uring 2000/01 we reviewed entrance
camping fees for individual visitors and
ermits and fees for commercial tour operators and other commercial users. We also
reviewed agency practices in regard to risk management, asset management, visitor education programmes and visitor monitoring (Buckley *et al.*, 2001b). We obtained data from printed materials, websites, surveys and interviews, and circulated two draft reports to check accuracy and completeness.

Most Australian parks charge entrance and camping fees for all visitors, whether travelling individually or on commercial tours. Fees are calculated per person, per vehicle, per campsite, or some combination of these. Various concessions are available. Except in the Australian Capital Territory (ACT), commercial tour operators have to be licensed, and licence fees include an application fee, an annual fee and per capita fees for clients. Commercial permits may contain a range of general, site-specific and activity-specific conditions.

Depending on the park, fees may be paid: in advance to park offices and agencies; on entry, at road booths or visitor centres; to rangers or by self-registration at campsites. Fees are reviewed every few years.

In Western Australia, Queensland (Qld), New South Wales (NSW), ACT and federal parks, fees are retained either in individual parks or within a district or region. In South Australia and Tasmania, they are collected by the parks-service headquarters. In the Northern Territory (NT) and Victoria, they are paid into the State government treasury. Parks Australia (PA), South Australian Parks and Wildlife Service and Queensland Parks and Wildlife Service also make use of trusts to hold part of the fees collected for specific purposes, e.g. for use in particular land tenures (Queensland), or for Aboriginal traditional owners (PA).

Different States and Territories charge entrance fees either per person, per vehicle or both (Table 7.1). Broadly, NT and Queensland do not charge individual members of the public for entry to national parks, except for federally managed or co-managed parks in the NT and parks under the *Recreation Areas Management* Act in Queensland.

Agencies in other States and Territories commonly charge daily vehicle entrance fees, mostly around US$5 per vehicle, at specific parks. They also offer season passes for all or most parks as an alternative, mostly in the range of US$25–75. Fees are generally highest in heavily used parks, such as those in alpine areas or near cities (Buckley, 2001). A

Table 7.1. Simplified summary of maximum vehicle entrance fees (Aus$) in Australian national parks in 2001/02. Figures are rounded to nearest dollar. Currently, US$1 is about Aus$2. Fees may apply to some parks only. Concessions may also be available. (Details in Buckley *et al.*, 2001b.)

Period of validity	WA	NT	SA	QLD	NSW	ACT	VIC	TAS	PA
Day	9	0	36	0	15	9	13	10	n/a
Month	23	0	18	40	n/a	n/a	n/a	17	33
Year	51	0	170	150	80	11	63	46	65

WA, Western Australia; NT, Northern Territory; SA, South Australia; QLD, Queensland; NSW, New South Wales; ACT, Australian Capital Territory; VIC, Victoria; TAS, Tasmania; PA, Parks Australia, the federal agency.

variety of 1-week, 2-week, 1-month and 2-month passes are offered for particular parks, and some offer concessional rates for local residents. Most parks agencies also charge entrance fees per person for individuals on buses or bicycles. These are typically around US$1.50–2.00 per person per day, but range up to US$7.50 in some parks, with the highest fees in NSW. Season passes specifically for visitors without vehicles are not generally available.

For comparison, an annual all-parks pass in the USA costs about US$50 (USDI and USDA, 2001). In Costa Rica's Monteverde Cloud Forest Reserve, daily entrance fees applicable since 1995 are US$1.50 for residents, US$8.00 for foreign independent travellers and US$16.00 for foreigners on package tours (Fennell, 1999, p.166). National parks in Costa Rica have charged an entrance fee of US$6.00 per person per day since 1996 (Honey, 1999, p.141). In Kenya, fees for foreign visitors to enter national parks have been charged at US$20 per person since 1993 (Honey, 1999, p.175).

Camping fees in Australian parks

All Australian parks agencies, including NT and Queensland, charge fees for camping overnight in national parks. Different States and Territories charge camping fees per person, per vehicle, per site or some combination. Some agencies charge identical fees for all parks under their jurisdiction; others charge different fees at different parks. Several have tiered fee structures, with higher fees for camp-sites that have more facilities or heavier use. Some charge higher fees during peak seasons. Most offer concessional rates for children, school groups, pensioners and/or families. Age and size limits for these categories are defined differently in each State and Territory. A highly simplified summary is shown in Table 7.2.

Permits

Commercial tour operators need permits in all Australian parks. The ACT is currently an exception, but is in the process of introducing a permit system. All parks agencies impose a set of general conditions that apply to all permitted tour operators. Most also impose activity-specific conditions and some set site-specific conditions. Some have two or more tiers or categories of tour-operator permits. Operators may be prosecuted, fined and/or lose their licences for breaches of permit conditions, though this rarely happens in practice.

Generic conditions typically fall into two main categories, related to safety and environmental management, respectively. For example, permits may require operators to ensure that vehicles are properly maintained, that guides are appropriately skilled and qualified and that emergency response and evacuation procedures are in place. They may also require operators to keep to roads, tracks and areas open to the public; to remove waste; to bring and use specified minimal-impact equipment and practices; and to instruct clients in minimal-impact behaviour. Generic conditions may also include quotas on the maximum number of clients an operator may

Table 7.2. Simplified summary of camping fee structures (Aus$) in Australian national parks, 2001/02. Fees rounded to nearest whole dollar. Fees may apply for some parks only. Group sites excluded. (Details in Buckley et al., 2001b.)

Unit	WA	NT	SA	QLD	NSW	ACT	VIC	TAS	PA
Structure	S+A	P	V	P	V+P	P	S+A	P	PorS
Person	9(A)	7	–	4	5(P)	–	4(A)	6	5
Car	–	–	18	–	6	–	–	–	–
Site	13	–	–	–	–	11	18	–	16

WA, Western Australia; NT, Northern Territory; SA, South Australia; QLD, Queensland; NSW, New South Wales; ACT, Australian Capital Territory; VIC, Victoria; TAS, Tasmania; PA, Parks Australia. Structures: S, per site; V, per vehicle; P, per person; A, per person additional to a predefined site or vehicle quota.

carry. All Australian parks agencies also require licensed tour operators to carry $10 million public liability insurance that indemnifies the parks agency as well as the operator.

Different parks agencies apply particular permit conditions to various specific activities – up to 28 different activities in Victoria. Common examples include guided walks and camping, mountain biking, caving, vehicle-based and four-wheel-drive tours, abseiling and rock-climbing, boating and boat cruises, rafting and kayaking, ski touring, hang-gliding and parapenting, horse riding, wildlife watching and spotlighting. Activity-specific conditions may cover, for example, equipment, guide qualifications, client-to-guide ratios, group sizes and timing, etc.

Site-specific conditions are less common. The most common are site quotas, setting maximum numbers of people at a given site at a given time, either in total or engaged in a particular activity. Some sites are also subject to seasonal closures or other restrictions. Site-specific conditions are often applied to cultural-heritage sites.

Most Australian parks agencies issue licences to commercial tour operators for 1 year in the first instance. Short-term licences may also be available for special events such as orienteering events. Commercial tour-operator licences may be issued for longer periods in some States and Territories: up to 3 years in Queensland and Victoria, and 5 years in Western Australia and NT. Accreditation with the Ecotourism Association of Australia (EAA), Nature and Ecotourism Accreditation Program (NEAP II) and/or other national or State accreditation programmes is a significant consideration in granting longer licence terms, in addition to past environmental performance.

Charges for commercial-tour permits may include an application fee, an annual fee and daily user fees calculated per client (Table 7.3). These per capita fees are generally the same as for individual public visitors, but in some States and Territories there are significant discounts for commercial-tour clients, and in some there are public land-use fees that apply only to commercial operators.

In Tasmania, the parks service has the right to levy additional fees for commercial operations that require exclusive use of a particular site, have a high environmental impact or a high risk that rehabilitation or restoration works may be needed or require special infrastructure or monitoring. These additional fees may be levied as an additional daily per capita fee of Aus$1.50 for day tours or Aus$3.00 (US$1.50) for overnight tours, and/or a flat fee, a percentage of gross takings or a site rental.

Assets

Australia's parks agencies manage a very significant proportion of Australia's natural and cultural assets. Parks Victoria, for example, manages 16% of that State (Stone, 2001). Asset-management programmes by Australian parks agencies, however, focus principally on infrastructure, buildings and equipment. Park services in Western Australia, South Australia, and Victoria all have established strategic asset-management frameworks, and those in Queensland and Tasmania are currently under development. In NT, NSW and ACT, parks services have specific policies, plans and manuals that address different aspects of asset-management, rather than integrated asset management frameworks. Each national park

Table 7.3. Simplified summary of commercial tour permit fees (Aus$) in Australian parks, 2001/02. Standard camping fees generally also apply. (Details in Buckley et al., 2001b.)

Component	WA	NT	SA	QLD	NSW	ACT	VIC	TAS	PA
Applications	50	300	300	200	var.	n/a	165	55	–
Annual	250	250–2000	125	160	var.	n/a	55	275	50–500
Per client entrance	sdd	var.	sdd	2.30	var.	n/a	1.10+ sdd	sdd	sdd

WA, Western Australia; NT, Northern Territory; SA, South Australia; QLD, Queensland; NSW, New South Wales; ACT, Australian Capital Territory; VIC, Victoria; TAS, Tasmania; PA, Parks Australia; var., variable; n/a, not available; sdd, standard fees for individual public visitors.

under the administration of PA includes guidelines for asset management in its individual park-management plans.

All of the agencies use computerized asset registers or databases, but these differ in sophistication and integration. In Western Australia, South Australia, Queensland and Victoria, asset-management systems form one module of integrated management databases, which also contain data on other aspects of financial operations. Asset databases for most agencies classify assets into fixed and movable items, with various subsidiary categories. The system in Parks Victoria, for example, recognizes over 45 different types of fixed asset. Asset-management systems generally record location, category, condition and value. The last may be recorded as initial, replacement or depreciated value. Parks agencies in Western Australia, South Australia, Queensland, Victoria and the Commonwealth have recently changed from cash-flow to accrual accounting systems, which routinely use depreciated values for assets. This is not necessarily the most useful approach for managing maintenance or insurance. Most agencies therefore also record replacement values, as well as the age and condition of some or all assets.

Risks

Risk management is an increasingly significant aspect of management for protected areas and other land-management agencies throughout Australia (McDonald, 2001). All Australian parks agencies refer to written risk-management policies, but these differ considerably between States and Territories. Parks Victoria refers directly to the *Australia/New Zealand Standard on Risk Management AS/NZS4360*, in conjunction with its own policies. Parks services in Western Australia, NT, South Australia and NSW have their own internal risk-management strategies. In Queensland there is a strategy for the entire Queensland Environment Protection Agency, including the Queensland Parks and Wildlife Service; and in the ACT there is a strategy for the entire ACT government, including Environment ACT.

All of the Australian parks agencies have risk-management strategies, which generally include:

- formal incident response and reporting procedures;
- formal or *ad hoc* risk identification and inspection framework;
- staff-training requirements or opportunities, in-house or external.

Parks agencies in the NT, NSW and Victoria rely principally on private legal advice in regard to visitor risk, injury and public liability, whereas the other six agencies rely principally on the Crown Solicitor. Western Australia Conservation and Land Management uses both. All agencies require tour operators to carry Aus$10 million (approx. US$5 million) public liability insurance, which specifically indemnifies the landholder and land manager as well as the tour operators. This requirement can also be applied to the organizers of events such as foot races across parkland.

In several countries there are statutory limitations on the liability of landowners and occupiers for injury to visitors on the land concerned. The best known of these are national legislation in New Zealand and State laws, such as the *Colorado Skier Safety Act*, in the USA. Several other American States have similar legislation, covering a range of potentially hazardous recreational activities, such as horse-riding. This approach has not yet been adopted by parks agencies in Australia. There have, however, been recent legislative moves to limit liability on Crown Land in some States. In South Australia, a recent amendment to the *Crown Lands Act* 1929 limits Crown liability on unoccupied Crown Land. In Western Australia, the *Land Administration Act* 1997 aims to remove liability associated with public-access routes over Crown Land.

Conclusions

User fees for visitors in parks are not always efficient, effective or equitable, but they are widespread and likely to continue and increase as recreation in parks continues to grow far faster than government funding for park management. There are innumerable different mechanisms and models, and optimal fee structures, rates, collection mechanisms and allocation depend on the political, legal, economic and social context in which each park management agency operates. Currently, fees are generally used more to raise revenue than to influence visitors. Where parks want to restrict visitor numbers or activities for environmental or social reasons, they generally use non-economic mechanisms rather than raise fees, for reasons of social equity. While many parks are coming to rely on user fees, these fees generally make up only a small proportion of their total budget, and the costs of collecting the fees are relatively high. In some cases there may well be a place for paying to play in parks, but, as a means of funding the primary conservation function of protected areas, user fees are probably not the most efficient option.

Currently, permit fees for commercial tour operators in Australian protected areas are low. Essentially, they reflect only the marginal administrative costs of processing an application. Tour clients generally have to pay entrance and camping fees in the same way as individual members of the public, but even these are discounted in many cases. Permit fees do not begin to reflect the cost of increased infrastructure to meet the demands of commercial tour operators and their clients, let alone the costs of conservation management for the primary environmental assets.

Parks agencies throughout Australia have begun to design and implement permit systems that incorporate screening and accreditation systems, recreational capacities and site quotas, environmental performance guarantees and differential fees for high-impact activities. We can anticipate that these will become more widespread, along with specific permit conditions for specific sites and activities.

Asset-management systems in Australian parks are evolving rapidly. The changeover to accrual accounting systems and the introduction of the GST have caused significant complications. Because of general underfunding by governments, most parks agencies are running down their assets. Parks cannot operate as businesses, because they cannot exclude consumption of their most valuable assets, namely biodiversity and ecosystem functions. Asset-management systems, which pool the depreciated value of infrastructure and equipment with operating cash reserves, do not reflect the state of park resources accurately.

Parks agencies throughout Australia have noted an increase in public-liability claims, though to some degree this may be due to improved incident-reporting systems. Most claims are settled out of court, so we cannot judge how valid they may or may not have been or how a court might have assessed them. The sums involved are relatively small but certainly not negligible. Parks agencies seem to be taking more cautious steps to ensure that they are not exposed to potential liability, e.g. by closing tracks or lookouts assessed as potentially risky, and by requiring engineering and geotechnical inspections of new or repaired structures. If these approaches prove inadequate, Australian governments may have to consider statutory limitations on landholder liabilities, as overseas. Note that this is distinct from statutes that limit operator liability, which also exist in some jurisdictions.

Acknowledgements

Data were kindly provided by staff of the protected-area management agencies from each State and Territory and the Commonwealth. This project was funded in part by Cooperative Research Centre Tourism.

References

Australian and New Zealand Environment and Conservation Council (ANZECC) (2000) *Benchmarking and Best Practice Program: User-Pays Revenue.* ANZECC Working Group on National Parks and Protected Area Management, Canberra.

Buckley, R.C. (1998) Tools and indicators for managing tourism in parks. *Annals of Tourism Research* 26, 207–210.

Buckley, R.C. (2000) Tourism in the most fragile environments. *Tourism and Recreation Research* 25, 31–40.

Buckley, R.C. (2001) Pay to play in parks: global issues and Australian case study. In: Taylor, L. (ed.) *Human Use Management in Mountain Areas.* The Banff Centre, Banff, pp. 99–105.

Many people object on principle to paying to use parks. Some countries have strong historical public rights of way (e.g. the UK) or a strong traditional right of access, even to private land (e.g. in Scandinavia). Many people also argue that taxpayers have already paid for parks, or that user fees are an inefficient way of funding a public good. Whether users accept fees also depends on what the fees are used for (Vogt and Williams, 1999).

In countries with ineffective, *laissez-faire* or decentralized governments, parks or residents may levy visitors at a very local scale, legally or otherwise. In countries with strongly centralized control and enforcement, user fees are collected on behalf of central treasuries. In countries with elected governments, especially federated systems, fees are subject to a wide range of political constraints. People who did not pay in the past do not want to pay in the future. People who think themselves disadvantaged want discounts. People who think taxes should pay for parks object to fees on principle.

User fees may be subject to legal constraints on the actions of the land-management agency. They may have legal consequences, e.g. in increasing the duties of care or the contractual obligations of that agency. They may also increase the expectations of visitors and tour operators, particularly in regard to park infrastructure.

Many parks charge differential fees for foreign nationals, for multiple visits, for commercial tours as compared with independent visitors, for visitors travelling by different means, for local residents or for educational groups and senior citizens. Heavily used parks may charge different fees from less visited parks in the same region. Elected governments may use parks and user fees as a political tool for regional development, to gain regional votes.

The most critical economic characteristic for any kind of user charge is how the money is used and who controls it. Fees may be used to manage the specific activity in the park where they were collected, or be paid into a central government treasury, or any intermediate level of control, or shared between several levels. In addition, fees retained by a park or region may be offset by a corresponding or proportional reduction in budget allocations from a higher level.

Collecting user fees costs money, not only for collection booths and counters and people to staff them, but for repairs; cash transfers and audits; higher costs because of increased expectations from visitors and tour operators; and potentially also from increased liabilities. Direct collection costs for the US Recreation Fee Demonstration Project are around 20% of revenue (USDI and USDA, 2001).

As a management tool, user fees are only effective if they change visitor behaviour in a way the agency wants: e.g. reducing visitor numbers; relocating a particular activity; or reducing per capita impacts. Behavioural responses to user fees depend on: the size of the fee; visitors' personal convictions; their investment to reach that destination; how the fee is packaged; the point at which visitors become aware of the fee; the availability and cost of alternative sites; and the time of year and degree of crowding (Knapman and Stoeckl, 1995; Lindberg and Aylward, 1999; Lindberg, 2001). A small fee may have a large effect on some users in some parks (Schneider and Budruk, 1999; Buckley *et al.*, 2001a); whereas elsewhere a large fee may have little influence.

Most public-land management agencies have to ensure that recreational user fees are equitable. This is difficult. Equity in legal principle does not guarantee equity of opportunity in practice between different socio-economic groups. Additionally, should fees be the same for foreigners as for citizens; for local residents as for those living far away; for multiple visits as for single; for visitors in groups as for those visiting alone; for visitors using different forms of transport; for commercial-tour clients as for independent visitors; and for people with different recreational preferences?

Which takes higher priority, a park's needs for management funds or its public obligations? Should parks charge higher fees for visitors likely to create higher social and environmental impacts or claim compensation, like an insurance company? Should they restrict access to increase demand, like diamond cartels? Should they offer services at market rates in competition with commercial tour operators? If they form partnerships with

the private sector, how can they assure a reasonable return while insulating themselves
from potential private-business collapse?

Entrance fees in Australian parks

Australia has a federal system of government.
Some of its protected areas are under federal
control, but most, including nearly all national parks, are under state jurisdiction. Limited
coordination was formerly provided by
ANZECC. The latter reviewed user fees in
1996 with an update in 2000 (ANZECC,
2000), but all agencies have since revised fees
in response to a federal goods and services tax,
introduced in July 2000.

During 2000/01 we reviewed entrance
and camping fees for individual visitors and
permits and fees for commercial tour operators and other commercial users. We also
reviewed agency practices in regard to risk
management, asset management, visitor education programmes and visitor monitoring
(Buckley et al., 2001b). We obtained data from
printed materials, websites, surveys and interviews, and circulated two draft reports to
check accuracy and completeness.

Most Australian parks charge entrance
and camping fees for all visitors, whether travelling individually or on commercial tours.
Fees are calculated per person, per vehicle,
per campsite, or some combination of these.
Various concessions are available. Except in
the Australian Capital Territory (ACT), commercial tour operators have to be licensed, and
licence fees include an application fee, an
annual fee and per capita fees for clients.
Commercial permits may contain a range of

general, site-specific and activity-specific
conditions.

Depending on the park, fees may be paid:
in advance to park offices and agencies; on
entry, at road booths or visitor centres; to
rangers or by self-registration at campsites.
Fees are reviewed every few years.

In Western Australia, Queensland (Qld),
New South Wales (NSW), ACT and federal
parks, fees are retained either in individual
parks or within a district or region. In South
Australia and Tasmania, they are collected by
the parks-service headquarters. In the
Northern Territory (NT) and Victoria, they are
paid into the State government treasury. Parks
Australia (PA), South Australian Parks and
Wildlife Service and Queensland Parks and
Wildlife Service also make use of trusts to hold
part of the fees collected for specific purposes, e.g. for use in particular land tenures
(Queensland), or for Aboriginal traditional
owners (PA).

Different States and Territories charge
entrance fees either per person, per vehicle
or both (Table 7.1). Broadly, NT and
Queensland do not charge individual members of the public for entry to national parks,
except for federally managed or co-managed
parks in the NT and parks under the
Recreation Areas Management Act in
Queensland.

Agencies in other States and Territories
commonly charge daily vehicle entrance fees,
mostly around US$5 per vehicle, at specific
parks. They also offer season passes for all or
most parks as an alternative, mostly in the
range of US$25–75. Fees are generally high-
est in heavily used parks, such as those in
alpine areas or near cities (Buckley, 2001). A

Table 7.1. Simplified summary of maximum vehicle entrance fees (Aus$) in Australian national parks
in 2001/02. Figures are rounded to nearest dollar. Currently, US$1 is about Aus$2. Fees may apply
to some parks only. Concessions may also be available. (Details in Buckley *et al.*, 2001b.)

Period of validity	WA	NT	SA	QLD	NSW	ACT	VIC	TAS	PA
Day	9	0	36	0	15	9	13	10	n/a
Month	23	0	18	40	n/a	n/a	n/a	17	33
Year	51	0	170	150	80	11	63	46	65

WA, Western Australia; NT, Northern Territory; SA, South Australia; QLD, Queensland;
NSW, New South Wales; ACT, Australian Capital Territory; VIC, Victoria; TAS, Tasmania;
PA, Parks Australia, the federal agency.

variety of 1-week, 2-week, 1-month and 2-month passes are offered for particular parks, and some offer concessional rates for local residents. Most parks agencies also charge entrance fees per person for individuals on buses or bicycles. These are typically around US$1.50–2.00 per person per day, but range up to US$7.50 in some parks, with the highest fees in NSW. Season passes specifically for visitors without vehicles are not generally available.

For comparison, an annual all-parks pass in the USA costs about US$50 (USDI and USDA, 2001). In Costa Rica's Monteverde Cloud Forest Reserve, daily entrance fees applicable since 1995 are US$1.50 for residents, US$8.00 for foreign independent travellers and US$16.00 for foreigners on package tours (Fennell, 1999, p.166). National parks in Costa Rica have charged an entrance fee of US$6.00 per person per day since 1996 (Honey, 1999, p.141). In Kenya, fees for foreign visitors to enter national parks have been charged at US$20 per person since 1993 (Honey, 1999, p.175).

Camping fees in Australian parks

All Australian parks agencies, including NT and Queensland, charge fees for camping overnight in national parks. Different States and Territories charge camping fees per person, per vehicle, per site or some combination. Some agencies charge identical fees for all parks under their jurisdiction; others charge different fees at different parks. Several have tiered fee structures, with higher fees for camp-

sites that have more facilities or heavier use. Some charge higher fees during peak seasons. Most offer concessional rates for children, school groups, pensioners and/or families. Age and size limits for these categories are defined differently in each State and Territory. A highly simplified summary is shown in Table 7.2.

Permits

Commercial tour operators need permits in all Australian parks. The ACT is currently an exception, but is in the process of introducing a permit system. All parks agencies impose a set of general conditions that apply to all permitted tour operators. Most also impose activity-specific conditions and some set site-specific conditions. Some have two or more tiers or categories of tour-operator permits. Operators may be prosecuted, fined and/or lose their licences for breaches of permit conditions, though this rarely happens in practice.

Generic conditions typically fall into two main categories, related to safety and environmental management, respectively. For example, permits may require operators to ensure that vehicles are properly maintained, that guides are appropriately skilled and qualified and that emergency response and evacuation procedures are in place. They may also require operators to keep to roads, tracks and areas open to the public; to remove waste; to bring and use specified minimal-impact equipment and practices; and to instruct clients in minimal-impact behaviour. Generic conditions may also include quotas on the maximum number of clients an operator may

Table 7.2. Simplified summary of camping fee structures (Aus$) in Australian national parks, 2001/02. Fees rounded to nearest whole dollar. Fees may apply for some parks only. Group sites excluded. (Details in Buckley *et al.*, 2001b.)

Unit	WA	NT	SA	QLD	NSW	ACT	VIC	TAS	PA
Structure	S+A	P	V	P	V+P	P	S+A	P	PorS
Person	9(A)	7	–	4	5(P)	–	4(A)	6	5
Car	–	–	18	–	6	–	–	–	–
Site	13	–	–	–	–	11	18	–	16

WA, Western Australia; NT, Northern Territory; SA, South Australia; QLD, Queensland; NSW, New South Wales; ACT, Australian Capital Territory; VIC, Victoria; TAS, Tasmania; PA, Parks Australia. Structures: S, per site; V, per vehicle; P, per person; A, per person additional to a predefined site or vehicle quota.

carry. All Australian parks agencies also require licensed tour operators to carry $10 million public liability insurance that indemnifies the parks agency as well as the operator.

Different parks agencies apply particular permit conditions to various specific activities – up to 28 different activities in Victoria. Common examples include guided walks and camping, mountain biking, caving, vehicle-based and four-wheel-drive tours, abseiling and rock-climbing, boating and boat cruises, rafting and kayaking, ski touring, hang-gliding and parapenting, horse riding, wildlife watching and spotlighting. Activity-specific conditions may cover, for example, equipment, guide qualifications, client-to-guide ratios, group sizes and timing, etc.

Site-specific conditions are less common. The most common are site quotas, setting maximum numbers of people at a given site at a given time, either in total or engaged in a particular activity. Some sites are also subject to seasonal closures or other restrictions. Site-specific conditions are often applied to cultural-heritage sites.

Most Australian parks agencies issue licences to commercial tour operators for 1 year in the first instance. Short-term licences may also be available for special events such as orienteering events. Commercial tour-operator licences may be issued for longer periods in some States and Territories: up to 3 years in Queensland and Victoria, and 5 years in Western Australia and NT. Accreditation with the Ecotourism Association of Australia (EAA), Nature and Ecotourism Accreditation Program (NEAP II) and/or other national or State accreditation programmes is a significant consideration in granting longer licence terms, in addition to past environmental performance.

Charges for commercial-tour permits may include an application fee, an annual fee and daily user fees calculated per client (Table 7.3). These per capita fees are generally the same as for individual public visitors, but in some States and Territories there are significant discounts for commercial-tour clients, and in some there are public land-use fees that apply only to commercial operators.

In Tasmania, the parks service has the right to levy additional fees for commercial operations that require exclusive use of a particular site, have a high environmental impact or a high risk that rehabilitation or restoration works may be needed or require special infrastructure or monitoring. These additional fees may be levied as an additional daily per capita fee of Aus$1.50 for day tours or Aus$3.00 (US$1.50) for overnight tours, and/or a flat fee, a percentage of gross takings or a site rental.

Assets

Australia's parks agencies manage a very significant proportion of Australia's natural and cultural assets. Parks Victoria, for example, manages 16% of that State (Stone, 2001). Asset-management programmes by Australian parks agencies, however, focus principally on infrastructure, buildings and equipment. Park services in Western Australia, South Australia, and Victoria all have established strategic asset-management frameworks, and those in Queensland and Tasmania are currently under development. In NT, NSW and ACT, parks services have specific policies, plans and manuals that address different aspects of asset-management, rather than integrated asset management frameworks. Each national park

Table 7.3. Simplified summary of commercial tour permit fees (Aus$) in Australian parks, 2001/02. Standard camping fees generally also apply. (Details in Buckley *et al.*, 2001b.)

Component	WA	NT	SA	QLD	NSW	ACT	VIC	TAS	PA
Applications	50	300	300	200	var.	n/a	165	55	–
Annual	250	250–2000	125	160	var.	n/a	55	275	50–500
Per client entrance	sdd	var.	sdd	2.30	var.	n/a	1.10+ sdd	sdd	sdd

WA, Western Australia; NT, Northern Territory; SA, South Australia; QLD, Queensland; NSW, New South Wales; ACT, Australian Capital Territory; VIC, Victoria; TAS, Tasmania; PA, Parks Australia; var., variable; n/a, not available; sdd, standard fees for individual public visitors.

under the administration of PA includes guidelines for asset management in its individual park-management plans.

All of the agencies use computerized asset registers or databases, but these differ in sophistication and integration. In Western Australia, South Australia, Queensland and Victoria, asset-management systems form one module of integrated management databases, which also contain data on other aspects of financial operations. Asset databases for most agencies classify assets into fixed and movable items, with various subsidiary categories. The system in Parks Victoria, for example, recognizes over 45 different types of fixed asset. Asset-management systems generally record location, category, condition and value. The last may be recorded as initial, replacement or depreciated value. Parks agencies in Western Australia, South Australia, Queensland, Victoria and the Commonwealth have recently changed from cash-flow to accrual accounting systems, which routinely use depreciated values for assets. This is not necessarily the most useful approach for managing maintenance or insurance. Most agencies therefore also record replacement values, as well as the age and condition of some or all assets.

Risks

Risk management is an increasingly significant aspect of management for protected areas and other land-management agencies throughout Australia (McDonald, 2001). All Australian parks agencies refer to written risk-management policies, but these differ considerably between States and Territories. Parks Victoria refers directly to the *Australia/New Zealand Standard on Risk Management AS/NZS4360*, in conjunction with its own policies. Parks services in Western Australia, NT, South Australia and NSW have their own internal risk-management strategies. In Queensland there is a strategy for the entire Queensland Environment Protection Agency, including the Queensland Parks and Wildlife Service; and in the ACT there is a strategy for the entire ACT government, including Environment ACT.

All of the Australian parks agencies have risk-management strategies, which generally include:

- formal incident response and reporting procedures;
- formal or *ad hoc* risk identification and inspection framework;
- staff-training requirements or opportunities, in-house or external.

Parks agencies in the NT, NSW and Victoria rely principally on private legal advice in regard to visitor risk, injury and public liability, whereas the other six agencies rely principally on the Crown Solicitor. Western Australia Conservation and Land Management uses both. All agencies require tour operators to carry Aus$10 million (approx. US$5 million) public liability insurance, which specifically indemnifies the landholder and land manager as well as the tour operators. This requirement can also be applied to the organizers of events such as foot races across parkland.

In several countries there are statutory limitations on the liability of landowners and occupiers for injury to visitors on the land concerned. The best known of these are national legislation in New Zealand and State laws, such as the *Colorado Skier Safety Act*, in the USA. Several other American States have similar legislation, covering a range of potentially hazardous recreational activities, such as horse-riding. This approach has not yet been adopted by parks agencies in Australia. There have, however, been recent legislative moves to limit liability on Crown Land in some States. In South Australia, a recent amendment to the *Crown Lands Act* 1929 limits Crown liability on unoccupied Crown Land. In Western Australia, the *Land Administration Act* 1997 aims to remove liability associated with public-access routes over Crown Land.

Conclusions

User fees for visitors in parks are not always efficient, effective or equitable, but they are widespread and likely to continue and increase as recreation in parks continues to grow far faster than government funding for park management. There are innumerable different mechanisms and models, and optimal fee structures, rates, collection mechanisms and allocation depend on the political, legal, economic and social context in which each park management agency operates. Currently, fees are generally used more to raise revenue than to influence visitors. Where parks want to restrict visitor numbers or activities for environmental or social reasons, they generally use non-economic mechanisms rather than raise fees, for reasons of social equity. While many parks are coming to rely on user fees, these fees generally make up only a small proportion of their total budget, and the costs of collecting the fees are relatively high. In some cases there may well be a place for paying to play in parks, but, as a means of funding the primary conservation function of protected areas, user fees are probably not the most efficient option.

Currently, permit fees for commercial tour operators in Australian protected areas are low. Essentially, they reflect only the marginal administrative costs of processing an application. Tour clients generally have to pay entrance and camping fees in the same way as individual members of the public, but even these are discounted in many cases. Permit fees do not begin to reflect the cost of increased infrastructure to meet the demands of commercial tour operators and their clients, let alone the costs of conservation management for the primary environmental assets.

Parks agencies throughout Australia have begun to design and implement permit systems that incorporate screening and accreditation systems, recreational capacities and site quotas, environmental performance guarantees and differential fees for high-impact activities. We can anticipate that these will become more widespread, along with specific permit conditions for specific sites and activities.

Asset-management systems in Australian parks are evolving rapidly. The changeover to accrual accounting systems and the introduction of the GST have caused significant complications. Because of general underfunding by governments, most parks agencies are running down their assets. Parks cannot operate as businesses, because they cannot exclude consumption of their most valuable assets, namely biodiversity and ecosystem functions. Asset-management systems, which pool the depreciated value of infrastructure and equipment with operating cash reserves, do not reflect the state of park resources accurately.

Parks agencies throughout Australia have noted an increase in public-liability claims, though to some degree this may be due to improved incident-reporting systems. Most claims are settled out of court, so we cannot judge how valid they may or may not have been or how a court might have assessed them. The sums involved are relatively small but certainly not negligible. Parks agencies seem to be taking more cautious steps to ensure that they are not exposed to potential liability, e.g. by closing tracks or lookouts assessed as potentially risky, and by requiring engineering and geotechnical inspections of new or repaired structures. If these approaches prove inadequate, Australian governments may have to consider statutory limitations on landholder liabilities, as overseas. Note that this is distinct from statutes that limit operator liability, which also exist in some jurisdictions.

Acknowledgements

Data were kindly provided by staff of the protected-area management agencies from each State and Territory and the Commonwealth. This project was funded in part by Cooperative Research Centre Tourism.

References

Australian and New Zealand Environment and Conservation Council (ANZECC) (2000) *Benchmarking and Best Practice Program: User-Pays Revenue.* ANZECC Working Group on National Parks and Protected Area Management, Canberra.

Buckley, R.C. (1998) Tools and indicators for managing tourism in parks. *Annals of Tourism Research* 26, 207–210.

Buckley, R.C. (2000) Tourism in the most fragile environments. *Tourism and Recreation Research* 25, 31–40.

Buckley, R.C. (2001) Pay to play in parks: global issues and Australian case study. In: Taylor, L. (ed.) *Human Use Management in Mountain Areas.* The Banff Centre, Banff, pp. 99–105.

Buckley, R.C., Ward, J. and Warnken, W. (2001a) Tourism and World Heritage in the central eastern rainforests of Australia. *Tourism and Recreation Research* 26, 106–108.

Buckley, R.C., Witting, N. and Guest, M. (2001b) *Managing People in Australian Parks*, 6 vols. CRC Tourism, Griffith University, Gold Coast.

Fennell, D. (1999) *Ecotourism: an Introduction.* Routledge, London, 314 pp.

Harris, C.C., Driver, B.L., Binkley, C.S. and Mendelsohn, R.O. (1987) Recreation user fees: pros and cons, an economic analysis. *Journal of Forestry* 85(5), 25–40.

Honey, M. (1999) *Ecotourism and Sustainable Development: Who Owns Paradise?* Island Press, Washington, DC, 405 pp.

Knapman, B. and Stoeckl, N. (1995) Recreation user fees: an Australian empirical investigation. *Tourism Economics* 1, 5–15.

Lindberg, K. (2001) Economic impacts of ecotourism. In: Weaver, D. (ed.) *The Encyclopaedia of Ecotourism.* CAB International, Wallingford, pp. 363–378.

Lindberg, K. and Aylward, B. (1999) Price responsiveness in the developing country nature tourism context: review and Costa Rican case study. *Journal of Leisure Research* 31(3), 281–299.

McDonald, J. (2001) Financial liability of park managers for visitor injuries. In: Buckley, R.C. (ed.) *Abstracts, Nature Tourism and the Environment.* Australian Academy of Science, CRC Tourism and Griffith University, Gold Coast, p. 15.

Newsome, D., Moore, S. and Dowling, R. (2002) *Natural Areas Tourism: Ecology, Impacts and Management.* Channel View, Clevedon, UK.

Schneider, I.E. and Budruk, M. (1999) Displacement as a response to the federal recreation fee program. *Journal of Park and Recreation Administration* 17(3), 76–84.

Stone, M. (2001) Managing visitors in the national parks of Victoria. In: Buckley, R.C. (ed.) *Abstracts, Nature Tourism and the Environment.* Australian Academy of Science, CRC Tourism and Griffith University, Gold Coast, p. 13.

US Department of Interior and US Department of Agriculture (USDI and USDA) (2001) *Recreation Fee Demonstration Program: Progress Report to Congress Fiscal Year 2000.* USDI and USDA, Washington, DC.

van Sickle, K. and Eagles, P.F. (1998) Budgets, pricing policies and user fees in Canadian parks tourism. *Tourism Management* 19, 225–235.

Vogt, C.A. and Williams, D.R. (1999) Support for wilderness recreation fees: the influence of fee purpose and day versus overnight use. *Journal of Park and Recreation Administration* 17(3), 85–99.

Watson, A.E. (1999) Recreation fees and pricing issues in the public sector. *Journal of Park and Recreation Administration* 17(3), 1–20.

World Commission on Protected Areas (WCPA) (2000) *Financing Protected Areas: Guidelines for Protected Area Managers.* IUCN, Gland.

8

The Net Economic Benefits of Recreation and Timber Production in Selected New South Wales Native Forests

John Ward
Australian School of Environmental Studies, Griffith University, Queensland, Australia

---

Abstract

The National Forest Policy Statement recognized that forests provide a multiplicity of jointly produced goods and services. The resulting Regional Forest Agreements (RFA), as a joint Commonwealth and State compliance initiative, attempt to resolve contentious and protracted debate regarding the allocation and conservation of forest resources. Proposed outcomes are designed to ensure conservation of forest diversity in concert with industry resource security.

Net economic returns of the two main direct-use economic activities of forestry and tourism in selected New South Wales (NSW) native forests for the 1997/98 financial year are compared. The research analysis is based on 11 distinct sites of paired, contiguous or proximate native forests, under the management of either NSW State Forests or the National Parks and Wildlife Service. The sites are located in the three RFA regions in NSW and provide a geographically dispersed sample of native forests situated on the eastern seaboard of Australia. The logging revenue and management costs derived from selected native forests were calculated from disaggregated raw data supplied by State Forests of NSW. The economic value of recreation at selected national parks was determined by the analysis of on-site survey results, using the travel-cost method.

For six of the 11 research sites, recreation confers higher economic benefits than timber production, inclusive of estimated error statistics. For the remaining sites, the magnitude of estimated variance in net economic values precludes the conclusive determination of site differentials. It is of note that there is a negative net value of logging at 12 of 17 state-forest sites. The magnitude of the estimated values for native-forest recreation established by this research challenges the conventional wisdom of the economic primacy of logging compared with alternative non-wood outputs. Modelling based on the research results indicates that the promotion of recreation in native state forests will maximize both the economic values of individual state forests and, in aggregate, the economic benefits accruing to society. In contrast, the failure to incorporate and account for the substantial value of native-forest recreation into the decision-making process breaches the codified National Forest Policy Statement of maximizing the economic benefits of native forests within an ecologically sustainable framework.

Introduction

Native forests provide an extensive suite of goods and services, which contribute an important source of wealth and well-being. Historically, timber has been seen as the main economic contribution from native Australian forests. The environmental and economic importance of non-wood, non-market values of forests is increasingly subject to more formal institutional recognition and assessment, potentially informing contemporary forest policy and management. These values include, but are not limited to, biodiversity, flood and soil-loss mitigation, climate stabilization, maintenance of water catchments, carbon sequestering and other ecosystem services and recreational amenities. The scope and extent of these values are testimony to the expectations and dependence society places on forests, which, in concert with a depleted forest estate, have led to a contentious and, at times, hostile conflict between stakeholders regarding the allocation and conservation of forest resources and services. The conflict has been protracted and highly polarized and extends through all levels of politics. As a large proportion of native forests are publicly tenured, this conflict has been focused upon the government agencies and departments responsible for their management (Dargavel, 1998; National Forest Inventory, 1998).

Recent trends have exacerbated the pressures placed on native forests and the expectations of responsible land-management agencies. These include increasing levels of demand on forest resources, more rigorous environmental regulations, market constraints, agency imperatives of commercial self-sufficiency and a change in the hierarchy of societal values.

Amid an amalgam of industry, union and conservation interests, Australian forest policy has in part been shaped and directed by a number of international forums, conventions and treaties (*inter alia*, WCED, 1987). As a signatory, the Australian government has committed both State and Commonwealth forest-managing agencies to a number of in-principle policies and non-binding compliance initiatives (Commonwealth of Australia, 1992a; Resource Assessment Commission, 1992). The commitment to meet these international and legislated obligations, in concert with the political pressure exerted by stakeholder groups, has led to the National Forest Policy Statement (Commonwealth of Australia, 1992b) and the genesis and ratification of the Regional Forest Agreements (RFA) in 1995. The process is iterative and still evolving (Dargavel, 1998).

The identification and compilation of a systemic set of forest values into the RFA procedure have been an important outcome (Commonwealth of Australia, 1997, 1998). The policy changes highlight the institutional recognition of a broader suite of forest values than those associated with past forest management and commissions. As an initiative, the comprehensive and multilateral approach to data collation, in conjunction with independent, open and thorough analysis, stands in contrast to the reactive, *ad hoc* and expedient rationale associated with the 79 forest-resource inquiries and commissions held since 1940 (Mercer, 1995). However, the limited collation of field data and the subsequent estimation of the economic values of alternative non-wood forest uses have hampered a more comprehensive implementation. The primary rationale of the RFA, negotiated between the States and the Commonwealth, has been to ratify the conservation of forest ecosystems and to secure resources for the timber industry, without the risk of attenuation based on environmental grounds.

Many of the values of native forests are intangible and remain largely unpriced (Bowes and Krutilla, 1989; Adger *et al.*, 1995). They are measured by value-specific parameters and scales, making direct comparison of value measures extremely complex and their interpretation generally ambiguous. The rapid increase in demand for non-market forest resources and the services and experiences associated with them has necessitated the determination of a common metric to enable meaningful comparison. Applying the appropriate econometric methodology to value individual forest outputs provides a suitable comparative metric, particularly as the synthesis and mutual reinforcement of economic instruments and environmental policy are a central tenet in the RFA process. The recognition and eventual economic valuation of all forest outputs and services, the reliance on market mechanisms to determine the extent and allocation of forest products and the preservation of the functional and spatial integrity of forest ecosystems are integral components of forest-policy formulation. In articulating these precepts, the National Forest Policy Statement (Commonwealth of Australia, 1992b) states that, within a sustainable framework, forests are to be managed to maximize the economic benefits to society.

The prevailing institutional convention that forestry values substantially outweigh those of recreation is not surprising. There is a historical precedence and a substantial political, industry and agency inertia to conserve the status quo. While the comparative economic techniques also have an extensive international pedigree, their institutional recognition and application to measure the non-wood economic benefits of Australian native forests are limited. Non-wood economic benefits are not always translated as financial cash flows. This, in concert with the financial self-sufficiency imperative imposed on forest-management agencies, has led to an operational impedance and agency reluctance to adopt management strategies and accounting conventions that incorporate the economic values of non-wood forest outputs.

A number of factors have therefore led to the formulation of this research project:

1. The mandatory inclusion of a systemic set of forest values in the RFA process is rhetorically persuasive; however, there is no protocol for their estimation, analysis or comparison.[1]
2. The pivotal National Forest Policy Statement recommendation that, within the government regulatory and appraisal framework, commercial market forces will determine the use, extent and allocation of forest resources has not eventuated in two key areas. First, the prerequisites to ensure efficient market allocation have not been satisfied. The heterogeneous outputs of native forests are jointly produced and physically interdependent and the attributes are often empirically indivisible, confounding the accurate measurement of attribute scarcity (Randall, 1978, 1987; Bromley, 1991). The simultaneous provision of the multiple benefits conferred by native forests precludes the determination of relative scarcity described by a single marginal-benefit estimate. The consumption of each benefit attributable to forests is described by a specific demand schedule, indicative of perceived relative scarcity. The demand schedule and the elasticity of demand are similarly benefit-specific. The total economic value of native forests represents the aggregate of the partial marginal-benefit estimates and is not simply a function of a scalar and an 'average' partial benefit. The difficulty in imputing a reliable metric of scarcity for many of the attributes of native forests complicates the unambiguous partial and hence total determination of economic benefits and costs (Toman, 1993; MacDonald *et al.*, 1999; Adger and Luttrell, 2000). Secondly, the term 'forest resources' appears to apply only to wood production and excludes other, non-wood, values, particularly recreation. Given these failings, the chances of market forces efficiently allocating all forest outputs are remote.
3. The failure to rigorously determine recreational uses by Australian forestry agencies reflects their apparent belief that wood production is the most economically beneficial utilization of native forests. Evidence suggests that this may not be the case and contrasts with appraisals of the US Forest Service (Bowes and Krutilla, 1989; USDA, 1995; Hanson, 1999) and the public forest estate of

[1] The JANIS criteria refer to the nationally agreed criteria for the establishment of a comprehensive, adequate and representative reserve system for forests in Australia, prepared by the Joint Australian and New Zealand Environment and Conservation Council (ANZECC)/Ministerial Council on Forestry, Fisheries and Aquaculture (MCFFA) National Forest Policy Statement Implementation Subcommittee (JANIS) (Commonwealth of Australia, 1997). The Montreal criteria refer to a set of internationally agreed, non-binding criteria and indicators to monitor and assess the sustainable management of boreal forests, originally drafted in 1993. An addendum agreement, consisting of seven criteria and 67 indicators, was ratified by 12 countries in Santiago, Chile, 1995.

British Columbia (Eagles, 1999; Eagles *et al.*, 1999; Gallon, 1999). Driml and Common (1995, 1996) and Carlsen (1997) suggest similar results in the wet tropics in north Queensland and northern New South Wales (NSW), respectively. In these instances, the economic value of forest recreation, both explicit and implicit, is greater than that of logging.

The aims of this study may be summarized as follows:

1. To compile data on and determine the net economic values of the two main direct uses of representative NSW native forest reserves, namely timber production and tourism, respectively. The annual net value is determined as the gross value minus the relevant management cost and compared for the period 1997/98.
2. To establish the sensitivities of revenues, costs and net benefits to the relevant scale and management regime for each use in different forest types, and hence the potential range of net economic returns from each use.
3. To establish and model the circumstances under which both forestry and recreation activities may be implemented concurrently in the same forest reserve and meet the stipulations of current forest policy.

In seeking to resolve these issues, a number of methodologies are deployed and discussed. The chapter reports the level of native forest-site concordance, measured as the correlation of forest ecosystems at 11 pairs of contiguous or proximate national parks and state forests. A summary of the methodology employed to estimate the level of recreational demand at 11 national parks and the determination of net logging revenues at 17 state forests follows. The chapter reports on the determination of decision criteria to account for variable levels of uncertainty in the economic-value estimates. Finally, modelled scenarios are presented, based on the ranked net economic values of the research sites, enabling state-forest managing agencies to meet the criteria stipulated in Commonwealth and State forest policies.

Methods

The working hypothesis developed for this research is that the net economic value of recreation in native forests in NSW is less than that of logging. To test the research hypothesis, the net economic returns of the two main direct-use economic activities within selected areas of the NSW native forest estate, namely forestry in state forests and recreation in national parks, are estimated and compared for the 1997/98 financial year (Ward, 2000). The logging revenue and management costs derived from native forests are calculated from disaggregated data supplied by State Forests of New South Wales (SFNSW). The recreational value of national parks is determined by the analysis of on-site survey results, using the travel-cost method. A research site's net economic benefits are estimated as gross economic values less infrastructure and management costs. The comparative temporal unit is set as an accounting period of one financial year and the hectare is employed as the unit for spatial comparisons.

Specific econometric techniques measure specific values and therefore only represent partial valuations of the total economic value of native forests. The difference in the measured, direct-use values and the total economic value equates to those values associated with the critical natural capital of native forests. For empirical purposes, the current natural capital of native forests under public tenure is assumed as non-depreciating and conserved through legislation, irrespective of management. Agency compliance with the *Forestry and National Park Estate Act* 1998 provides a control for the economic values of forests that are not traded in the market-place. These non-wood, non-use values are not included in the estimation of a site's net economic value. As a corollary, the research estimates of the direct-use value of recreation and logging constitute only a partial component of the total economic benefits of environmental commodities from selected native forests. Bateman *et al.* (1996) note that direct-use values are recognized as exerting considerable influence on the decision-making process.

Table 8.1. Proximate state forests and national parks at each research site.

National park	State forest	National park	State forest
Bald Rock	Boorook	Nightcap	Whian Whian
Ben Boyd	Yurramie	Toonumbar	Beaury, Yabbra, Toonumbar
Border Ranges	Mebbin, Toonumbar	Wadbilliga	Badja, Wandella
Bournda	Yurramie	Washpool	Ewingar, Washpool
Deua	Dampier, Badja	Werrikimbe	Mt Boss
Mt Warning	Mebbin, Wollumbin		

Location of the Research Sites

The research analysis is based on 11 distinct sites of paired, contiguous or proximate native forests, used principally for logging (state forests) and tourism (national parks) respectively. The sites are located in three of the four RFA regions in NSW and provide a spatially dispersed sample of native forests situated on the eastern seaboard of Australia. For those national parks characterized by several contiguous or proximate state forests, a composite state-forest value is determined, consisting of the mean value of logging, standardized to account for spatial differences and expressed as dollars per hectare. The economic comparison for six of the research sites is made between a national park and up to three state forests, summarized in Table 8.1.

The correlation of forest ecosystems observed at each research site is deployed as a measure of site concordance. In accord with the RFA forest ecosystem research (NSW NPWS, 1999), ecosystem concordance provides a surrogate spatial control of a raft of biogeographical and abiotic variables. The attributes are a composite index of variables that potentially influence commercial timber management, visitor perception of forest characteristics and the subsequent level of recreational demand. These variables include: mean annual rainfall, slope, soil depth, mean temperature, solar-radiation index, soil fertility, minimum temperature of coldest month, topographic wetness index, geological classes, ruggedness indices, soil-moisture index, topographic position, topographic indices and rainfall in the driest quarter (NSW NPWS, 1999).

All paired sites, except Washpool National Park and Ewingar State Forest, are correlated ($P < 0.05$) and treated as having statistically similar forest composition, measured by the forest-ecosystem classification index (Ward, 2000). As a corollary, the majority of observed variation in site-specific economic value is ascribed to the primary variable of the dominant forest use, independent of variations in biogeographical, abiotic or demographic attributes. The correlation of ecological and biogeographical attributes at each site indicates that the primary management focus of recreation or logging is theoretically transposable between management regimes and constitutes a site-specific appraisal of the economic opportunity cost of each forest output.

The estimation of the economic value of recreational demand

Apart from entrance fees to some national parks, the use of these parks and the consequent values placed on the recreational experience are not transacted in the market-place and a direct valuation of revenues (as is the case with forestry and log royalties) is not possible. The travel-cost method assumes that the value of forest recreation is more than the entrance fee and individuals' preferences and evaluations of recreation can be revealed by their purchase of goods associated with the consumption of the environmental asset – in this case national parks located throughout NSW: that is, the value placed on associated goods (and the transactions that occur in the market-place) acts as a surrogate or proxy for the value of recreation. The goods consumed in the production of the recreational experience include the monetary and time costs of travelling to the site, specialized equipment and accommodation.

Visitor information is obtained by means of a questionnaire to ascertain place of residence, demographics, means of travel, frequency of visits, substitute sites, length of travel and travel costs. A non-compensated demand curve can be described relating visits per capita as a function of travel and visit costs. Total recreational value can be estimated from the demand curve. Total value is partitioned into on-site and residual components by the imposition of incremental hypothetical entrance fees as a means of simulating increased travel costs. A second demand schedule is estimated which describes visits against entrance fees. The welfare measure equates to the non-priced value of recreational participation at a national park.

The survey instrument is based on a questionnaire developed by Bennett (1995) for the National Parks and Wildlife Service (NPWS), ensuring compatibility of the research data set and those from previous studies. Reference to questionnaires prepared by Wilman (1980), Connolly and Price (1991) and Bateman et al. (1996), as well as respondent reaction to instrument testing, enabled refinement of the questions specific to the research.

A total of 1518 questionnaires were distributed to respondents from 2/10/1997 to 14/4/1998. Of these, 845 were self-completed by respondents on site and 673 were supplied with postage-paid envelopes. A total of 1201 usable questionnaires (representing 4081 visitors) are incorporated into the research analysis, pooled from the on-site completions and the mail-back responses. This represents a response rate of 81.5%. According to results of the chi-squared test, there is no statistical difference in the methods of questionnaire administration at all sites ($P < 0.05$). The site-specific sample size and expected error are reported in Table 8.2.

Despite a long and extensive pedigree, the travel-cost method is characterized by methodological and theoretical issues that are yet to be fully resolved and require further refinement and calibration (Bateman, 1993; Loomis and Walsh, 1997; Ward and Beal, 2000). The estimated values are treated by some analysts as ordinal rather than cardinal and reflect criticisms that the estimates of recreational demand remain an artefact of the travel-cost accounting convention employed (Randall, 1994; Common et al., 1999). Several sensitivity analyses were carried out to mitigate these criticisms, to ensure that the results best reflect extant levels of recreational consumption and to minimize the degree of uncertainty in the error parameters (Ward, 2000).

The zonal travel-cost method was determined as the appropriate travel-cost model. The failure to describe a relationship between the number of annual visits reported by individuals and the distance travelled precludes the individual travel-cost model. Geographical information system software was used to mea-

Table 8.2. Survey sample sizes and expected error used in the analysis of 11 NSW national parks, 1997/98.

National park	Sample	Sample visits	Confidence interval at 95% confidence level
Bald Rock	278	1036	±3.1%
Ben Boyd	139	470	±4.6%
Border Ranges	108	335	±5.5%
Bournda	118	452	±4.7%
Deua	56	163	±7.8%
Mt Warning	317	973	±3.2%
Nightcap	59	234	±6.5%
Toonumbar	20	82	±11.0%
Wadbilliga	29	106	±9.7%
Washpool	55	155	±8.0%
Werrikimbe	22	75	±11.5%

Note: Sample = number of completed questionnaires at each site; sample visits = total number of visitors reported in completed questionnaires.

sure visitors' travel distance accurately, and weighted according to the population distribution of a postcode. The analysis accounted for the effects of multiple-site visitors, perceived site substitution, site-specific costs of travel time and on-site congestion. In all cases the double-log functional form was statistically the most appropriate functional form and best describes the recreational-demand schedule. At all sites the variation in the single independent variable of travel costs significantly explains the variation in visit rates (all B_1 coefficients are significant, $P = 0.05$; R^2 values range from 0.394 for Washpool National Park to 0.966 for Bald Rock National Park). The effect of aggregation of visitor's travel origin into zones of differing sizes was also quantified. Derived consumer surplus values are found to be sensitive to zone resolution and to be site-specific. An optimal zone resolution of 5 km is employed for the analysis of the Ben Boyd, Bournda, Deua, Nightcap, Toonumbar, Washpool and Werrikimbe National Parks. The 10 km zone is used for Wadbilliga, the 50 km resolution for the Border Ranges and Mt Warning and the 100 km resolution for Bald Rock National Park.

A hypothetical entrance fee schedule ranging from Aus$0.01 to Aus$500, in increments of Aus$5 to Aus$25, was used to predict the number of visits at each site, from the trip-generating function specified for each site. The predicted consumer surplus was calculated as the definite integral of the on-site demand equation between the limits of Aus$0.01 and a cut-off price calculated from the reported maximum travel costs from the on-site survey data. Total consumer surplus was calculated for a proposed site-specific entrance fee that predicts the number of visits to equal one. In all cases, a polynomial equation best describes the predicted number of visits (log-transformed) as a function of proposed fees.

The determination of logging revenues

The provision of and access to data from the SFNSW central database enabled the collation and compilation of timber yields, compartment harvest volumes and product stratification and the computation of actual royalty revenues for 17 forest sites used in the research. The timber-harvest details for the period 1978/98 represent the economic value of logging in state forests of the paired sites employed in this research. Observed variation in total annual revenue indicates that, for all sites, the value from a specific year cannot be taken as a representative revenue period (Ward, 2000).

The main source of revenue for all state forest sites was from quota log sales (SFNSW, 1998). The relative stability of royalty prices for quota log sales implies that the observed variation in annual revenue is a function of harvesting volumes, not price fluctuations. This is hardly surprising considering that the 20-year period approximates an average forest-cutting cycle (SFNSW, 1995, 1996; National Forest Inventory, 1998), inclusive of the normal logging oscillations of silvicultural management. The current management strategy allows for years of both intense and minimal logging activity as a means of dispersing and mitigating log-harvesting impacts and as a function of the availability of merchantable logs. The level of logging is subject to a range of operational guidelines, many of which are related to rainfall levels and may be simply an outcome of prevailing weather conditions.

The 20-year period in question has arguably been one of the most volatile in Australian forestry history in terms of jurisdictional changes in tenure, forest quota allocations and political and agency changes in the definition, codification and practice of sustainable forestry. The period is epitomized by conflict and acrimonious debate in establishing a set of operational principles, guidelines and prescriptions to ensure minimum acceptable standards for harvesting and multiple-use forest management at both State and Commonwealth levels.

Year-by-year comparisons can therefore reflect a changing regime of quota allocations, negotiated and enforced deferments and dispersal strategies superimposed on the established cutting and rotation cycle for compartments and forests. Harvesting levels over this time horizon can also reflect the evolution in the hierarchy of agency priorities of alternative forest uses and services, such as

Table 8.3. Consumer surplus (CS) estimated for 11 national parks for 1997/98.

National-park research site	CS per visit (Aus$)	Total CS (Aus$ million)	Gross value (Aus$ per ha)	Cost (Aus$ per ha)	Net value (Aus$ per ha)
Bald Rock	15.66	0.782	171	16.10	154.90
Ben Boyd	36.00	1.909	199	20.30	178.70
Border Ranges	33.22	2.751	86	38.80	47.20
Bournda	36.00	1.693	661	20.30	640.70
Deua	58.60	1.663	40	14.20	25.80
Mt Warning	29.00	2.999	1260	38.80	1212.0
Nightcap	10.60	0.648	132	38.80	93.20
Toonumbar	9.65	0.048	8	38.80	−30.80
Wadbilliga	18.15	0.245	6	14.20	−8.20
Washpool	45.40	0.665	13	16.90	−3.90
Werrikimbe	46.00	0.253	9	16.90	−7.90

water catchment, habitat preservation, maintenance of riparian-zone integrity, socio-economic effects, soil maintenance, fire management and the preservation of amenity values.

In establishing the state-forest logging values, the revenues from forest products are consumer price index (CPI)-adjusted. They do not, however, provide an index of prevailing forest-management practices. There is no extant prescription to nominate a specific year as being a representative value of the research period without calibration to a composite of temporal and spatial factors, such as the duration of the cutting cycle, prevailing operational guidelines, localized conditions and the political milieu that these values are dependent on.

To establish a logging value that accounts for the forestry guidelines and regulations of 1997/98, adjusts for the cutting cycle and allows for site productivity, two methods are employed and compared. They are the CPI-adjusted mean 20-year value (1978–1998) and the site's *pro rata* value based on the regional quota allocations and total loggable area for the financial period 1997/98.

The 20-year CPI-adjusted mean annual revenue is representative of a typical cutting cycle and accounts for site productivity, despite its non-calibration to the prevailing management regime: that is, the model assumes that regional quota allocation, land tenure, operational guidelines, deferments and the overarching forestry legislation are constant throughout the 20-year period. The

regional *pro rata* value calibrates for the prevailing management regime but does not account for specific site productivity, topographical characteristics or variability in forest access, infrastructure and haulage distance. Analysis indicates that, while the *pro rata* values accurately reflect management prescriptions at the regional scale, the averaged yields do not account for the observable individual site variance (Ward, 2000). They are unable to provide sufficient detail to accurately estimate revenues at the individual forest scale. It is assumed for this analysis that the estimation of annual revenue is more sensitive to the composite of variables that constitute site productivity, measured over an approximation of a 20-year cutting cycle, than those constituting regional management regimes.

Results

The estimated consumer surplus per visit at the 11 national-park sites ranges from Aus$9.65 to Aus$59 at an imputed cost of travel time equivalent to 33% of the mean respondent wage rate, site-specific travel speeds and NPWS estimates of annual number of visitors. The values are consistent with recent Australian estimates of native-forest recreational demand (Knapman and Stanley, 1993; Stoeckl, 1994; Bennett, 1995; Driml, 1996; Lockwood and Lindberg, 1996; Gillespie, 1997). Table 8.3 summarizes the results and indicates that four national park sites are char-

Table 8.4. The net timber revenues for the 1997/98 financial year of 17 native forests in NSW.

State forest	Annual revenue (Aus$ per ha per year)	Direct costs (Aus$ per ha per year)	Net revenue (Aus$ per ha per year)
Badja	11.25	15.60	−4.35
Beaury	14.49	16.00	−1.51
Boorook	63.83	16.00	47.83
Dampier	5.13	15.60	−10.47
Eboyd	0.11	17.80	−17.69
Ewingar	16.20	16.00	0.20
Mebbin	74.33	16.00	58.33
Mt Boss	6.88	14.60	−7.72
Nadjee	1.19	17.80	−16.61
Nullica	3.52	17.80	−14.28
Toonumbar	12.56	16.00	−3.44
Wandella	7.79	15.60	−7.81
Washpool	62.38	16.00	46.38
Whian Whian	49.27	16.00	33.27
Wollumbin	9.59	16.00	−6.41
Yabbra	13.14	16.00	−2.86
Yurramie	11.64	17.80	−6.16

acterized by negative net economic values of recreational consumption, namely Toonumbar, Wadbilliga, Washpool and Werrikimbe. Costs represent the amortized per-hectare value of regional operational and infrastructure costs, provided by the regional offices of NPWS responsible for the management of the research sites (Ward, 2000).

Logging revenues are derived from disaggregated state-forest data and calculated as the mean CPI-adjusted value determined for 1978–1998. The results are presented in Table 8.4. Direct costs represent the amortized per-hectare value of regional operational and infrastructure costs, provided by the regional offices of state forests responsible for the management of the research sites (Ward, 2000). Twelve state-forest sites are characterized by negative net present values of logging.

Intra-site comparisons of economic value

Meaningful comparisons of economic value at each site are contingent on the efficacy of error estimates and the accounting convention employed to incorporate them into the decision criteria. There is no theoretical formula or protocol currently established, *ex ante* or *ex post*, to account for the array of permutations

of variance in the economic values observed for this research (Ward, 2000). The research strategy relies on the sensitivity analysis of calculated values for the range of input variables. A primary outcome for the research is the determination of specified differences, inclusive of variance, in the economic value of logging and recreation in biogeographically paired sites.

To account for observed variation in the economic value of recreation and logging in native forests, intra-site difference is predicated on discrete value sets specific to state-forest logging revenues and national-park recreational consumer surpluses. The evaluation protocol specifies the range of values imputed for logging at specific sites as the minimum and maximum royalty revenues for the period 1978–1998. The variance in the consumer surplus of the recreational use of specific national parks is calculated as a function of the imputed value of travel time (25%, 30%, 50% and 100% of median respondent wage rates) and the variance in estimated annual visits (Ward, 2000). The results are presented in Fig. 8.1. The intra-site comparisons are made according to paired sites noted in Table 8.1: that is, the economic value of Bald Rock National Park is compared with the economic value of Boorook State Forest, Ben Boyd is compared with Yurramie and so on. Where a

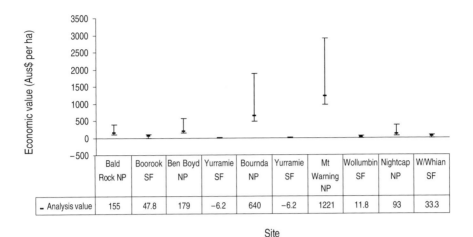

	Bald Rock NP	Boorook SF	Ben Boyd NP	Yurramie SF	Bournda NP	Yurramie SF	Mt Warning NP	Wollumbin SF	Nightcap NP	W/Whian SF
Analysis value	155	47.8	179	−6.2	640	−6.2	1221	11.8	93	33.3

Site

	Border Ranges NP	Mebbin SF	Deua NP	Badja SF	T/numbar NP	Yabbra SF	W/billiga NP	Wandella SF	W/pool NP	Ewingar SF	W/ikimbe NP	Mt Boss SF
Analysis value	47	18	26	−4.4	−30.4	−2.9	−8	−7.8	−4	8	−8	−7.7

Site

Fig. 8.1. The variance in the net economic value of state forest (SF) logging and national park (NP) recreation during 1997/98 at 11 research sites in NSW. The lower bound of NP sites represents the site-specific minimum value of net recreational consumer surplus per hectare; the upper bound represents the site-specific maximum value; the lower bound of SF sites represents the site-specific minimum value of logging per hectare; the upper bound represents the site-specific maximum value. Analysis value is the mean NP net recreational consumer surplus per-hectare value at an imputed 33% of respondent wage rate, and SF is the mean 20-year per-hectare net value of logging.

national park is abutted by more than one state-forest, the imputed state forest value represents the mean economic value of logging per hectare of state forests.

Applying these methodological constraints, the ranked net value of recreation at five of the 11 national parks, estimated over a range of values specified for the significant ($P < 0.05$) explanatory variables of recreation-

al demand, is greater than the net present value of logging in correlated and proximate state forests. These national-park sites are Bald Rock, Ben Boyd, Bournda, Mt Warning, Nightcap and Deua. Intra-site equivalence of economic value is observed for Nightcap, Border Ranges, Toonumbar, Wadbilliga, Washpool and Werrikimbe. There are no state forests characterized by positive logging values greater than the value of recreational demand observed at a paired national park.

In view of the research results, a number of applications and strategies for the optimal use of forests are articulated as possible solutions in fulfilling the National Forest Policy Statement requirement of maximizing the economic benefits of native forests.

A Model to Optimize the Net Benefit of State Forests

The *NSW Forest and National Park Estate Act 1998* and the Commonwealth *National Forest Policy Statement 1992* stipulate the economic optimization of native forests within an ecologically sustainable framework as a primary management objective. Modelled scenarios are presented, based on the ranked net economic values of the research sites, enabling state forests to meet the criteria of national and State forest policy. As a prescriptive index of an optimal economic solution, the highest-ranked net value (NV) confers the greatest benefit to society. With no political constraints, the forest use characterized by the highest-ranked NV would be the appropriate pattern of intervention to optimize economic benefits. The results do not imply that a native forest managed by State Forests or NPWS and analysed in isolation is a net economic cost to society. The computed net values are for logging and recreation only and do not purport to be an estimate of the total economic value of a native forest.

The aim of the model is to reveal possible state-forest management regimes and prescriptions, comprising recreational and logging strategies based on the research results, to fulfil the economic-optimization criteria. Currently, there is no quantifiable standard prescribed in the legislation against which the extant levels of economic optimization in native forests can be reconciled or calibrated. Therefore, the adequate compensation of the opportunity cost of alternative non-wood economic services provided by publicly tenured native forests is employed as the minimum benchmark for state-forest economic outputs. The primary alternative

non-wood use of recreation in state forests is poorly defined and quantified and the estimated value of recreational consumption in proximate and paired national parks is employed as a surrogate index of evaluation. The established intra-site correlation of bio-geographical characteristics, which concurrently influence levels of logging activity and recreational participation, indicates a comparable spectrum of recreational opportunity at both state-forest and national-park sites (Stankey *et al.*, 1985). Combinations of the state-forest economic outputs of logging and recreational participation are modelled to determine:

1. As a prerequisite, the minimum levels of state-forest logging revenues and recreation to establish a positive net value of state forests (NV_{sf});
2. The potential of individual state forests, managed under the aegis of a multiple-use regime, to generate an economic benefit at least equivalent to those estimated at adjacent national parks (NV_{np}).

State forests are included in the model if:

$$NV_{sf} < NV_{np} \text{ and } NV_{np} > 0 \text{ or}$$
$$NV_{sf} \equiv NV_{np} \text{ and } NV_{sf} < 0$$

The model inputs for Yurramie State Forest represent estimates for the proximate East Boyd, Nullica and Nadjee State Forests. The derived values for the latter are substantially less than those calculated for Yurramie and are excluded from the model. Based on a similar rationale, the modelled estimates for Badja State Forest substitute for and exclude Dampier State Forest. Ewingar, Mebbin and Washpool State forests are not included in the model as $NV_{sf} \equiv NV_{np}$ and $NV_{sf} > 0$, which satisfies the optimizing criteria. Whian Whian State Forest is characterized by a substantial and identified existing recreational value and is excluded as a modelled site.

The model is limited by the following assumptions and constraints:

1. Logging volumes are not included as a model variable. The assessment and establishment of current harvesting volumes is assumed to equate to a sustained, maximized yield calibrated to growth rates and site productivity, and not subject to change.

2. Annual State Forests and NPWS infrastructure and management costs are assumed to be constant.

3. The management strategy is predicated on the principles of multiple-use forestry, the primary agency charter of State Forests.

4. The number of annual national-park visits is assumed to be constant and independent of additional annual visits at an adjoining state forest.

5. There is a potential spillover of visitors from national parks approaching carrying capacity to adjoining state forests. In accord with Toman (1993), Seidl and Tisdell (1999) propose that carrying capacity is a complex and symbiotic construct, responsive to institutional settings, ecological dynamics, human values and norms and prevailing management regimes. Quantifying site-specific ecological carrying capacity, sensitive to the type and magnitude of recreational activity, is the focus of ongoing research (Brown *et al.*, 1995; Tisdell, 1997; Buckley, 1999; Seidel and Tisdell, 1999). The level of recreational participation in national parks is potentially conditioned by the imposition of visitation limits, a corollary of identified breaches in ecological carrying capacity.

6. State Forests allows a broader range of recreational activities, such as four-wheel driving, mountain-bike riding, horse riding and motor-cycle riding. An increase in the number of visits to state forests may occur as a result of recruitment from non-national park sites that facilitate these 'harder' recreational activities.

7. The receipts from logging royalties are imputed as the mean 20-year value (the current rate) and the current rate plus an increment of 30%, 50% and 100%.

The number of annual recreational visits is estimated at a range of incremental additions to royalty values, such that the net revenue per hectare of the state forest equals zero or the net revenue of the adjoining national park, whichever is the greater. The model outputs are estimated such that $N_{sf} = N_{np}$ or 0 if $N_{np} < 0$.

The model variables are:

$$N_{sf} = (LO_{sf} - MIC_{sf}) + CS_{sf}V$$

where:

N_{sf} is the net economic value of a state forest;
LO_{sf} is the 1997/98 revenue received by state forests in the form of log royalties (Aus\$ m³) and estimated as the mean 20-year value (Aus\$ m³ per ha);
MIC_{sf} is the 1997/98 management costs of the specific state forest (Aus\$ per ha);
CS_{sf} is the consumer surplus per visit in state forests for 1997/98 (Aus\$ per ha);
V is the number of annual visits;
N_{np} is the 1997/98 net value of the adjacent national park (Aus\$ per ha),

where:

N_{np} = annual consumer surplus per hectare (CS/V at 33% of the median respondent wage rate × NPWS 1998 estimate of the number of visits) – NPWS management costs.

The value of recreational consumption at a specific state forest is estimated assuming three values of consumer surplus. CS_{10} is the estimated consumer surplus per visit of recreation at Toonumbar National Park and employed as a proxy of the economic value of current state-forest recreational consumption. CS_{np} is the consumer surplus value of the adjoining national park and CS_{59} is the consumer surplus per visit (\$59) of recreational demand at Deua National Park. Wadbilliga and Deua National Parks are contiguous and characterized by similar areas and biogeographical attributes, the existence of wilderness zones and concordant forest ecosystems. In contrast to Deua, recreational demand at Wadbilliga is valued at \$18 consumer surplus per visit. Deua is the only national park where four-wheel driving is authorized. For the purposes of the model, CS_{59} is imputed as an estimate of the value of 'harder' recreational activities in native forests.

Mt Boss, Toonumbar and Wandella are associated with national parks characterized by a negative N_{np} and modelled such that $N_{sf} = 0$. Badja, Beaury, Boorook, Wollumbin, Yabbra and Yurramie are modelled such that $N_{sf} = N_{np}$.

Table 8.5. Calculated ratio of visit numbers at NSW state forests required to optimize economic benefits.

| State forest | Ratio at R = +0% | | | Ratio at R = +30% | | | Ratio at R = +50% | | | Ratio at R = +100% | | |
	CS_{10}	CS_{np}	CS_{59}	CS_{10}	CS_{np}	CS_{59}	CS_{10}	CS_{np}	CS_{59}	CS_{10}	CS_{np}	CS_{59}
Badja	1.76	0.30	0.30	1.58	0.27	0.27	1.29	0.22	0.22	0.94	**0.16**	**0.16**
Beaury	0.57	**0.17**	**0.10**	0.52	0.16	0.09	0.49	0.15	0.08	0.40	0.12	0.07
Boorook	0.94	0.58	**0.16**	0.76	0.47	0.13	0.65	0.41	0.11	0.35	0.22	0.06
Mt Boss	4.29	0.93	0.73	2.79	0.61	0.47	2.23	0.48	0.38	0.56	**0.12**	**0.09**
Toonumbar	0.38	**0.11**	**0.06**	0.35	0.11	0.06	0.31	0.09	0.05	0.23	0.07	0.04
Wandella	0.64	0.36	**0.11**	0.45	0.25	0.08	0.32	**0.18**	0.05	**0.08**	0.05	0.01
Wollumbin	2.78	0.96	0.47	2.77	0.96	0.47	2.76	0.95	0.47	2.76	0.95	0.47
Yabbra	1.13	0.34	**0.19**	1.04	0.31	0.18	0.99	0.30	0.17	0.83	0.25	0.14
Yurramie	1.41	0.39	0.24	1.39	0.39	0.24	1.37	0.38	0.23	1.32	0.37	0.22

Note: R = royalty at nominated % increase on current rates. CS_{10} is the consumer surplus per visit value of Aus\$10. CS_{np} is the state forest's consumer surplus per visit derived from the proximate national park. CS_{59} is the consumer surplus per visit of recreational consumption at Deua National Park, assumed to represent the perceived recreational benefits accruing from four-wheel driving in native forests.

The results for individual state forests are assessed using the modelling parameters and policy constraints of optimized economic benefits. The feasibility of a state forest complying with the policy objectives is determined by the ratio of predicted state-forest visit numbers compared with observed annual visits at the proximate national park (called the output ratio).

The National Forest Inventory (1998) estimates that state-wide, total annual levels of recreation in forests managed by State Forests approximate 0.2 of the current number of annual visits to NSW national parks. Initial combinations of modelled increases to royalty and consumer surplus per visit resulting in an output ratio of less than 0.2 are highlighted in bold in Table 8.5. Subsequent proposed royalty increases combined with the same consumer surplus value are not highlighted. The results are presented in Table 8.5.

The model outcomes indicate that, when recreational demand is imputed at CS_{59}, the optimizing criteria of a positive economic benefit and national-park equivalence are satisfied at five sites with current annual state-forest visitor numbers and royalty levels. For the remaining state forests, there exists a suite of combinations of timber royalty increases and increments of recreational consumer surplus that satisfy the model objectives. Output ratios equal to or less than 0.2 indicate positive

model combinations associated with the number of state-forest annual visits held constant (or reduced) to 1997/98 levels. Ratios of greater than 0.2 quantify the increase in the annual state-forest recreational visits required to satisfy a positive model outcome, in conjunction with the modelled increases to royalties and consumer surplus. The model indicates that, at constant current state-forest annual visits and imputing CS_{10}, variable royalty increases are needed to satisfy the optimization criteria. The mean royalty increase to existing levels for the nine state-forest sites is estimated at a factor of 17.95. Excluding Wollumbin State Forest (defined as a statistical outlier) reduces the mean royalty increase to a factor of 4.44 for the remaining eight forest sites.

Conclusion

The opportunity costs of the management at each site are the revenues or values forgone as a result of exclusion of a particular forest use. Traditionally, this has been considered as the opportunity cost of logging due to a change in forest management from a state forest to a national park. The results from this research challenge that assumption. The calculated net value of logging at 12 of 17 state forests are negatively signed or are less than the value determined for an adjacent national park. The negatively signed values do not confer an economic benefit and therefore do not constitute an opportunity cost if logging were to cease. Boorook, Mebbin, Ewingar, Washpool and Whian Whian state forests would incur a loss of economic benefits if there were to be a cessation of logging. The value of logging at those sites is equivalent to or less than the estimated recreational demand at the proximate, correlated national park.

The research results also challenge the conventional wisdom of the economic primacy of timber production in native forests at the 11 research sites. *Ceteris paribus*, the derived values of recreation confer the greatest economic benefits. The pivotal National Forest Policy Statement recommendation that, within a government regulatory framework, commercial market forces will be relied on to determine the use, scale and allocation of forest outputs is similarly challenged by the research results. The failure to incorporate adequate price signals regarding the substantial economic benefits of recreation, in concert with the lack of a conventional market where transactions may occur, breaches one of the primary conditions of efficient markets. The results of that market failure may include suboptimal royalty prices, overexploitation of timber resources and inappropriate rotation cycles. If multiple-use forestry is not to be considered a pejorative term, associated with the subordination of non-wood forest outputs, the substantive economic value of forest recreation, established by this research, needs to be recognized and incorporated at the policy-making and operational constituencies.

Possible strategies for the optimal use of state forests were simulated as part of this research, with variable inputs of royalty revenue, total recreational visits and consumer surplus per visit. In lieu of a cross-jurisdictional industry standard, the modelling strategy optimized state-forest economic benefits by calibrating state-forest revenues to associated national-park values of recreational demand. The model indicates that there is no one solution to optimising state-forest economic benefits such that values are positive and equivalent to paired national parks. The model

outcomes indicate that, to satisfy the optimizing criteria, a recreational demand of the magnitude of CS_{59} (representing 'hard' recreational activities) is necessary at five state forests if current annual visitor numbers and royalty levels are held constant. For the remaining state-forest sites, a combination of increased consumer surplus per visit, increased annual visit numbers and variable increases in royalties are necessary. In the absence of increases to recreational values or the number of annual visits, the royalty increases must be increased by (up to) two orders of magnitude. In the absence of statistical outliers, existing royalty revenues need to be increased by a mean factor of 4.44 to equate to the economic value of recreation at paired national parks.

The selection and implementation of a specific set of model variables are conditioned by an amalgam of localized biogeographical, physical and social factors affecting both recreational participation rates and regional forest-management regimes and strategies. Tension between potential forest uses and the regional determination of management regimes is played out within an institutional and political milieu that has historically been subject to intransigence and bureaucratic inertia (Mercer, 1995; Dargavel, 1998). The successful implementation of increasingly stringent economic and environmental objectives is conditioned by institutional settings geared to objectives of single-resource development and expansion rather than the optimal allocation of a raft of jointly produced forest outputs. The research results provide cogent reasons for designing and implementing management regimes and strategies that focus on recreational demand and participation in native forests with at least the same degree of vigour and efficiency of execution as those ascribed to timber extraction.

Acknowledgements

The chapter is a synopsis of an unpublished PhD thesis entitled 'The net economic benefits of recreation and timber production in selected New South Wales native forests',

School of Environmental and Applied Sciences, Griffith University (Ward, 2000). For further elaboration, methodological detail or clarification please contact the author.

References

Adger, N. and Luttrell, C. (2000) Property rights and the utilisation of wetlands. *Ecological Economics* 35, 75–89.

Adger, W., Brown, K., Cervigni, R. and Moran, D. (1995) Total economic value of forests in Mexico. *Ambio* 24(5), 286–296.

Bateman, I. (1993) Valuation of the environment, methods and techniques: revealed preference methods. In: Turner, R.K. (ed.) *Sustainable Environmental Economics and Management.* Belhaven Press, London, pp. 192–265.

Bateman, I., Brainard, J., Garrod, G. and Lovett, A. (1996) Measurement issues in the travel cost method: a geographical information systems approach. *Journal of Agricultural Economics* 47(2), 191–205.

Bennett, J. (1995) *Economic Value of Recreational Use: Gibraltar Range and Dorrigo National Parks.* NPWS Environmental Economics Series, NSW Government, Sydney.

Bowes, M. and Krutilla, J. (1989) *Multiple Use Management: the Economics of Public Forestlands.* Resources for the Future, Washington, DC.

Bromley, D. (1991) *Environment and Economy: Property Rights and Public Policy.* Blackwell, Massachusetts.

Brown, K., Turner, R.K., Mameed, H. and Bateman, I. (1995) *Tourism and Sustainability in Environmentally Fragile Areas: Case Studies from the Maldives and Nepal.* CSERGE Working Paper GEC 95–30, CSERGE, University of East Anglia, Norwich.

Buckley, R. (1999) An ecological perspective on carrying capacity. *Annals of Tourism Research* 26(3), 705–708.

Carlsen, J. (1997) Economic valuation of recreation and tourism in natural areas: a case study in New South Wales, Australia. *Tourism Economics* 3(3), 227–239.

Common, M., Bull, T. and Stoeckl, N. (1999) The travel cost method: an empirical investigation of Randall's difficulty. *Australian Journal of Agricultural and Resource Economics* 43(4), 457–477.

Commonwealth of Australia (1992a) *National Strategy for Ecologically Sustainable Development.* AGPS, Canberra.

Commonwealth of Australia (1992b) *National Forest Policy Statement.* AGPS, Canberra.

Commonwealth of Australia (1997) *Proposed Nationally Agreed Criteria for the Establishment of a Comprehensive, Adequate and Representative Reserve System for Forests in Australia. A Report by the Joint ANZECC/MCFFA National Forest Policy Statement Implementation Subcommittee.* AGPS, Canberra.

Commonwealth of Australia (1998) *A Framework of Regional (Sub-national) Level Criteria and Indicators of Sustainable Forest Management in Australia.* Department of Primary Industries, Canberra.

Connolly, D. and Price, C. (1991) The Clawson method and site substitution: hypothesis and model. Manuscript, University College of North Wales, Bangor (cited in Bateman, 1993).

Dargavel, J. (1998) Politics, policy and process in the forest. *Australian Journal of Environmental Management* 5, 25–30.

Driml, S. (1996) Sustainable tourism in protected areas? Unpublished PhD dissertation, ANU.

Driml, S. and Common, M. (1995) Economic and financial benefits of tourism in major protected areas. *Australian Journal of Environmental Management* 2, 19–29.

Driml, S. and Common, M. (1996) Ecological economics criteria for sustainable tourism: applications to the Great Barrier Reef and Wet Tropics World Heritage Areas, Australia. *Journal of Sustainable Tourism* 4(1), 3–16.

Eagles, P. (1999) International trends in park tourism. In: *Conference Proceedings: the 1999 International Symposium on Society and Resource Management: Application of Social Science to Resource Management in the Asia Pacific Region, 7–10 July, University of Queensland, Brisbane.*

Eagles, P., Mclean, D. and Stabler, M.J. (1999) Estimating the tourism volume and value in parks and protected areas in Canada and the USA. *George Wright Forum* 17(3), 62–76.

Gallon, G. (1999) British Columbia forestry and environment. *The Gallon Environment Letter* 3(20) www.gallon.elogik.com

Gillespie, R. (1997) *Economic Value and Regional Impact: Minnamurra Rainforest Centre, Budderoo National Park.* Economics and Regulatory Reform Policy Unit, NSW National Parks and Wildlife, Sydney.

Hanson, C. (1999) *Ending Logging on National Forests: the Facts.* The John Muir Project, Pasadena, California.

Knapman, B. and Stanley, O. (1993) Measuring environmental benefits: a travel cost analysis of

Kakadu National Park. In: *Building a Research Base in Tourism: Proceedings from the National Conference on Tourism Research.* Bureau of Tourism Research, Canberra, pp. 183–191.

Lockwood, M. and Lindberg, K. (1996) *Non-market Economic Value of Recreation in Eurobodalla National Park.* Albury Report No. 67, Johnstone Centre of Parks, Recreation and Heritage, Charles Sturt University, Perth.

Loomis, J. and Walsh, R. (1997) *Recreation Economic Decisions: Comparing Costs and Benefits.* Venture Publishing, Pennsylvania.

MacDonald, D., Hanley, N. and Moffatt, I. (1999) Applying the concept of natural capital criticality to regional resource management. *Ecological Economics* 29, 73–87.

Mercer, D. (1995) *A Question of Balance: Natural Resources Conflicts and Issues in Australia.* Federation Press, Sydney.

National Forest Inventory (1998) *Australia's State of the Forests Report: 1998.* Bureau of Regional Sciences, Canberra.

New South Wales, National Parks and Wildlife Service (NSW NPWS) (1999) *Derived Forest Ecosystems: an Evaluation of Surrogacy Value and Internal Biological Variation.* Project No. NA44/EH, Forests Taskforce, Commonwealth of Australia, Canberra.

Randall, A. (1978) Property institutions and economic behaviour. *Journal of Economic Issues* 12, 1–21.

Randall, A. (1987) *Property Rights, Efficiency and the Distribution of Income.* John Wiley & Sons, New York.

Randall, A. (1994) A difficulty with the travel cost method. *Land Economics* 70(1), 88–96.

Resource Assessment Commission (1992) *Forest and Timber Inquiry, Final Report,* Vol. 2b. AGPS, Canberra.

Seidel, M. and Tisdell, C. (1999) Carrying capacity reconsidered: from Malthus' population theory to cultural carrying capacity. *Ecological Economics* 31, 395–408.

Stankey, G.H., Cole, D.N., Lucas, R.C., Oetersen,

M.E. and Frissel, S.S. (1985) *The Limits of Acceptable Change (LAC) System for Wilderness Planning.* Forest Service, USDA, Ogden, Utah.

State Forest of New South Wales (SFNSW) (1995) *Environmental Impact Statement for the Urbenville Management Area.* SFNSW, Sydney.

State Forest of New South Wales (SFNSW) (1996) *Murwillumbah Management Area: EIS Main Report.* SFNSW, Sydney.

State Forest of New South Wales (SFNSW) (1998) *Annual Report 1997–1998.* SFNSW, Sydney.

Stoeckl, N. (1994) A travel cost analysis of Hinchinbrook Island National Park. In: Faulkner, B. (ed.) *Tourism Research and Education in Australia.* Bureau of Tourism Research, Canberra, pp. 187–201.

Tisdell, C. (1997) *Ecotourism: Aspects of its Sustainability and Compatibility.* Economics, Ecology and the Environment: Working Paper No. 20, University of Queensland, Brisbane.

Toman, M. (1993) Defining an economics of sustainable forestry: general concepts. In: Aplet, G.H., Johnson, N., Olson, J.T. and Sample, V.A. (eds) *Defining Sustainable Forestry.* Island Press, Washington, DC.

USDA (1995) *The Forest Service Program for Forest and Rangeland Resources: a Longterm Strategic Plan.* Forest Service, Washington, DC.

Ward, F. and Beal, D. (2000) *Valuing Nature with Travel Cost Models: a Manual.* Edward Elgar, Cheltenham.

Ward, J. (2000) The net economic benefits of recreation and timber production in selected New South Wales native forests. Unpublished PhD dissertation, Griffith University, Queensland.

WCED (1987) *Our Common Future (The Brundtland Report).* World Commission on Environment and Development, Oxford University Press, Oxford.

Wilman, E. (1980) The value of time in recreation benefit studies. *Journal of Environmental Economics and Management* 7, 272–286.

9

Moving Nearer to Heaven: Growth and Change in the Greater Yellowstone Region, USA

Jerry Johnson,[1] Bruce Maxwell[2] and Richard Aspinall[3]

[1]Department of Political Science; [2]Land Resources and Environmental Science; [3]Department of Earth Science, Montana State University, Bozeman, Montana, USA

Abstract

The recent population growth in the rural counties of the American West promises to surpass the impact of the first western migrations. Much of this growth is associated with tourism and recreation and the desire to live in amenity-rich rural areas such as the Greater Yellowstone Ecosystem. Of concern are changes to the social and geographical landscape resulting from rapid settlement of the rural landscape in the region. Scenic vistas are compromised and there may be impacts on ecological processes as increasing numbers of people settle on productive agricultural lands. This chapter characterizes the social and economic changes to the region, and presents research in land-use change detection and prediction aimed at engaging the local citizenry in land-use decisions. In addition to managing the effects of rapid population growth in the Greater Yellowstone Ecosystem, these models may also be applicable in other amenity-rich tourist destinations.

Greater Yellowstone and a New Western Reality

Rural areas in the American West are in the midst of a demographic and economic shift unlike any in the past. Between 1990 and the recent 2000 census, the West was the fastest-growing region of the USA at 19.7% while the national average was 13.2%. During that period the population of the region grew by over 10 million. Most growth occurred in the coastal urban centres of the nation. But in the rural countryside of the interior West many counties are experiencing a population surge. This new growth promises to surpass the impact of the first western migrations, where 67% of the counties in the Rocky Mountain axis grew at rates faster than the national average (Beyers and Nelson 2000; US Bureau of the Census 1999). The Rocky Mountain states include Idaho, Montana, Wyoming, Utah, Colorado, New Mexico and Arizona. Much of this recent growth is associated with tourism and recreation as visitors return to live in

© CAB International 2003. *Nature-based Tourism, Environment and Land Management* (eds R. Buckley, C. Pickering and D.B. Weaver)

amenity-rich rural areas such as the Greater Yellowstone Ecosystem (GYE) (Johnson and Snepenger, 1992; Johnson, and Rasker, 1995; Snepenger *et al.*, 1995, 1998).

Historically the source of the nation's natural-resource base, the lands west of the 100th meridian were characterized by low human population densities and vast tracts of undeveloped public and private lands (Stegner, 1954; Power, 1996; Johnson and Beale, 1999). Today, the geographical features that provide natural resources are powerful attractants to those who would live near mountains, rivers, forests and protected areas (Power, 1996; Aspinall, 2000). The increases have been primarily in mid-size cities like Boise and Coeur D'Alene, Idaho; Bozeman and Missoula, Montana; and Sheridan and Jackson, Wyoming. Concurrent growth rates are taking place in satellite communities and rural areas around these small cities. Of particular concern are changes to the landscape as a result of rapid population growth. Scenic vistas are compromised and there may be impacts on ecological processes as increasing numbers of people settle on productive agricultural lands. Models that can depict future landscape changes and can engage the local citizenry in land-use decisions are particularly useful for managing the effects of rapid population growth.

Study-area Description

The more than 6 million ha that make up the GYE are but one destination for in-migrants to the Rockies. However, given the high level of international attention as the world's first national park, the GYE is an ideal laboratory for monitoring changes brought on by shifts in rural economies and population growth. The region exhibits all of the features inherent in other rapidly growing areas for similar reasons and with similar outcomes. In addition, a rich history of social and ecological research exists for the area (Williams and Jobes, 1990; Johnson and Snepenger, 1992; Johnson and Rasker, 1995; Snepenger *et al.*, 1995; Johnson and Maxwell, 1996, 2001; Jobes, 2000).

The GYE was originally adopted as a formal management concept as early as 1971 by the National Park Service and was defined as the range of the Yellowstone grizzly bear by Craighead (1984). The region comprises the two national parks (Yellowstone and Grand Teton), seven national forests and numerous other federal and state jurisdictions (Clark *et al.*, 1991; Fig. 9.1). Of particular interest are the private lands that are targets of population growth and resultant land-use change.

The public lands in the region act as ecological and recreational refuges for the 355,000 residents and 3.5 million yearly visitors to the area. These lands are home to key predator species (grizzly bear and grey wolf), prey species (elk, deer, moose) and a host of birds and smaller mammals, as well as a mosaic of vegetation, including coniferous forests, arid shrublands and grasslands. Several major river systems originate in the region and elevational gradients range from lowland river valleys (< 1800 m above sea level) to the Grand Teton at over 4165 m. In the GYE over 40 peaks exceed 3000 m.

Most of the spectacular vistas and recreational possibilities are found on public land, while the remaining 20% of the land base is privately owned. Public land managers are increasingly consumed with recreation and its impacts (e.g. off-road vehicles, snowmobiles, wilderness boundary enforcement). But it is the human settlement on the private lands that is the focus of this chapter.

Like many rural areas in the interior West, the social and economic landscape is undergoing rapid change. The traditional resource-extraction economy is being augmented and in many cases overwhelmed by a new economy based on services, especially tourism, a retirement economy, a declining agricultural economy and urban refugees fleeing the crime and social problems of urban centres. These four social features are inexorably linked. Tourism visitation acts as a catalyst for relocation to rural communities and new business opportunities emerge with more people, all in an era of declining agricultural profitability. New residents inevitably bring with them a dichotomous mix of values, talents and ideas, which may differ from those of long-time residents.

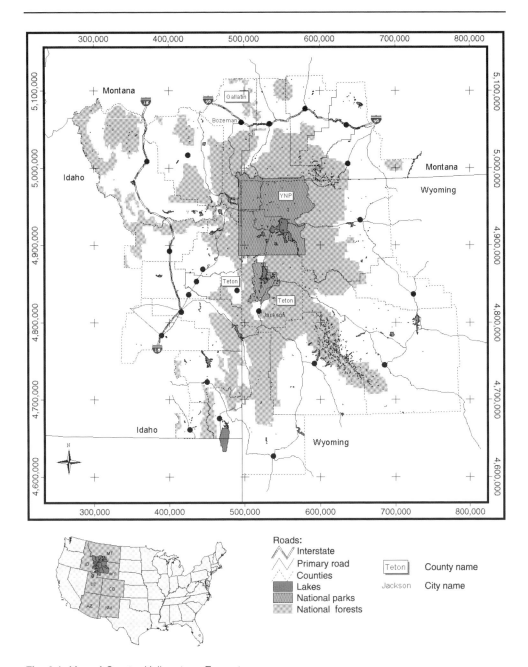

Fig. 9.1. Map of Greater Yellowstone Ecosystem.

A New Socio-economic Reality in the West

The economy of the GYE, like much of the West, is diversifying away from a reliance on resource extraction and agriculture (Johnson and Snepenger, 1992; Beyers and Lindahl, 1996; Power, 1996). Mining, oil, gas, timber, farming and ranching activities collectively accounted for 19% of total personal income in the region in 1970; by 1995 they accounted for 6%. Over 99% of the net growth in personal income from 1970 to 1995, in real terms, was in industries other than the historical economic base of the region (Rasker and Hansen, 2000). They include business, engineering and health services and account for 26% of net new income growth. Non-labour income sources of income account for another 51% of the growth. Main-street businesses today include traditional retail outlets but also include tourist services, several high-tech firms, software development and financial-service offices. Ubiquitous in the area are numerous real-estate brokers and home-construction firms and the services they require, such as architects, interior-design professionals and building-materials suppliers.

Some like to point to the ability of firms to move easily from one location to another as a driving factor behind the character of the communities of the 'New West'. This so-called 'footloose' ability, it is argued, is facilitated by modern telecommunications technology and a willingness of owners to move operations to a lower-cost or a more desirable rural setting. However, Beyers and Lindahl (1996) find little evidence of such widespread migration of firms and, in any case, most are so small (usually one- or two-person operations) as to be unimportant to the community economy. Rather, a more common scenario is that recent arrivals quit old jobs and relocate to small towns to start a small business or simply work for an existing firm. Indeed, small businesses account for over 50% of employment in the West (Shepard, 1993).

One aspect of job growth that is underreported is the high level of competitiveness in the small towns of the Greater Yellowstone Ecosystem. The level of educational attainment in high-amenity communities is significantly higher for recent arrivals than for their old-timer counterparts (Jobes, 2000; Leistritz et al., 2000) and, as a result, they enjoy a competitive advantage in the local job market. The nature of work for even the low- and medium-wage jobs available in rural towns has changed. Jonathan Rauch suggests there is a new/old economy where technology has been integrated into even traditional blue-collar jobs (Rauch, 2001). Architectural plans, for example, are no longer drawn with pen and paper, but are done routinely with digital pens and CAD/CAM programs. Exploration for natural resources is now done electronically via remote-sensed data and a laptop computer. Even the most mundane job now has some high-technology component to it. One result is that those who come from backward-looking schools that seek to preserve the old economy will not be able to compete for the jobs available in their home town.

Tourism, as an industry, is notoriously difficult to measure. The standardized industrial classification (SIC) system used in the USA does not measure tourism as a discrete industry. Further, each state and community in the GYE collects a slightly different tax on tourists or business travel, making comparisons and summations problematic. However, given the large number of out-of-state visitors to the region and the number of businesses associated with tourism, it is not unrealistic to believe that tourism increasingly accounts for a large percentage of employment and investment in the region. In one study of tourism in the GYE, growth rates of tourist revenues approached 40% during the 1990s (Johnson and Snepenger, 1992). Tourism activity provides indirect economic activity by serving as an attractant for business creation. In a study conducted in 1995, four out of ten business owners surveyed first experienced the GYE as a tourist (Snepenger et al., 1995). These 'travel-stimulated entrepreneurs' either moved or started a business in the region subsequent to their tourist experience.

Many of the jobs, in the old and new economy, are filled by people simply looking for work and following the burgeoning job market. They are looking for a place to raise their children in safe, clean towns with decent schools. However, two demographic niches are found in the GYE and other high-amenity regions that create special problems for communities.

Retirees (and the semi-retired) make up the largest age cohort of in-migrants to the region. This is partially a function of the economic boom of the 1980s–1990s and partially a function of the post-Second World War 'baby-boom' generation, which is now of retirement age. Life expectancy is not only longer for this generation, but they are also healthier and wealthier. Power (1996) states that the rural communities of the region are desirable locations for retirees and they tend to spend more of their income locally. They demand financial planning, health care, recreation amenities (e.g. developed ski areas, golf, tennis) and homes – all high-value, labour intensive activities. As a result, he points out, they support almost twice as many jobs in an economy as others. Unfortunately, probably as a result of fixed incomes and having less family in the area, retirees tend not to support tax and bond levies for schools, parks and other public infrastructure at the same rate as the community as a whole.

Others moving to the region include 'lifestyle migrants'. Jobes (2000) describes these residents as people who came to the region hoping to ski, fish or find the ideal rural community. Most are gone within 5 years of their arrival. They are young, idealistic and recreation-orientated. However, they are also less financially secure than retirees, for example, and tend not to be as invested in the community either socially or economically. The high turnover of the lifestyle migrant is problematic for communities who seek to preserve some collective memory of the community history, such as local-land use patterns.

Finally, one group of residents is on the decline – the agricultural producer. Faced with declining agricultural prices and their children's inability or reluctance to remain in agriculture (Stauber *et al.,* 1995), owners of farms and ranches often sell the land to developers or farm and ranch brokers. In rapidly growing counties, the potential wealth from selling to developers serves as a lucrative retirement. Many of the new buyers of rural land will not continue the agrarian tradition or will shift from intensive agricultural production to a less utilitarian form of land management, such as 'hobby ranching' or owning the land for its recreational potential. In many cases, developers purchase agricultural land, subdivide it and build 'ranchette' properties of small acreages and thereby permanently remove land from agricultural production. While a market-based economic model might suggest that greater efficiencies are attained by moving the land from produc-

tion agriculture to rural housing, there is an abundance of evidence that current landowners, as well as residents of rural communities, increasingly value the cultural and scenic attributes provided by a productive agricultural landscape (American Farmland Trust, 1998; Johnson and Maxwell, 2000).

The population of the GYE increased 55% between 1970 and 1997, a rate of growth exceeding that of 78.2% of counties in the USA. What is attracting these people and businesses to the region? Two views prevail (Johnson and Rasker, 1995). The quality-of-life argument states that choices by would-be residents to move to a specific region are a function of a mix of amenities acting as pull factors. Examples include a move to a small town in part because of the scenic beauty of the area, the low crime rate, a desirable climate, the recreation opportunity or to be close to family and friends. The demand model asserts that in-migration of population to rural areas is a function of wages and employment. This model of rural migration suggests that increases in the demand for labour will create migration to the community – jobs first, then migration. An example of such migration would be to relocate for a higher wage. In fact, both models have explanatory power and both are probably simultaneously acting to change the social demographic character of the GYE.

The Nature of the Problem

The effects of rapid in-migration to the recreation and retirement communities of the GYE are basically twofold. First, development pressure may result in significant impacts on the ecological quality of the area. These include threats to habitat (e.g. fragmentation, loss), geographical features (e.g. irrigation water supply and quality, diminished soil quality) and native species and ecosystem processes (e.g. weed invasion, biodiversity loss, changes to natural fire regimes). The conversion of native and agricultural lands to residential subdivisions or small ranches is of particular concern because such development will probably never revert to undeveloped land (Riebsame *et al.,* 1996). Hansen *et al.* (2000) and Maxwell *et al.* (2000) document the ecological changes resulting from rural residential development. The other effect is on the people and where they live. Understanding changes to the many communities of the region is a challenge compared with the ecological elements because the rate of change makes it very difficult to assess the impacts across the wide variation of sociodemographic groups and spatial locations. In addition, funding for socio-economic research is not the priority of foundations and agencies to the same degree as ecological study.

The notion of rural western communities is of a close-knit social and economic structure where employment, social and consumer functions are carried out in a self-sufficient socio-economic system. In the New West and the GYE, rural land adjacent to small towns serves primarily as residential rather than social locations (Williams, 1982; Johansen and Fuguitt, 1990), and some have observed that recently arrived rural residents are less attached to the nearby community and have less need of it to meet their social and economic needs (Brown, 1993). One effect is that main-street shopping functions move to regional shopping centres and small-town business districts erode. In the process, the social function of 'downtown' is also affected (Snepenger et al., 1998). The community also loses its sense of place and solidarity (Huang and Stewart, 1996). This may be compounded given the high turnover of new residents, as documented by Jobes (2000). On the other hand, shopping and entertainment possibilities are expanded for residents.

A major effect of rapid in-migration is the inflationary pressure on homes and cost of living. Communities that are good places to live, work and raise a family in are increasingly unaffordable for many would-be residents. In several communities in the region, the average cost of a home is over US$1 million (e.g. Jackson, Wyoming, Big Sky and Yellowstone Club, Montana). Adjacent to these are service communities requiring long commuter journeys for little pay and high housing costs. This pressure, coupled with a limited amount of private land, has resulted in sky-rocketing land prices. In 1977, the average cost of a suburban acre in Gallatin County, Montana, for example, was US$150. In 1981 that same acre

cost about US$600. The same tract near Bozeman may now be priced at over US$10,000. As a result, not only are service workers faced with housing shortages at the resort destination, but there is also a lack of affordable housing for those who work in the retail and service sectors in town. Most measures of economic well-being are on the decline as fewer workers are able to save for a home and more and more people qualify for subsidized school lunches and welfare payments (http://www.nwafdev.org/). Montana, Wyoming and Idaho rank among the highest of the 50 states whose population works multiple jobs and whose pay is among the lowest in the nation. All of these attributes contribute to the rapid turnover of population.

Using voter data from 1970–2000, L. Schell (2000, unpublished) has documented significant changes in the political (re)alignment of high-growth counties in Montana, including those in the GYE. She finds a new 'ecoconservative' voter inhabiting the West. They exhibit pro-environment values but express an anti-government culture. The ecoconservative voter supports legislation for clean water and air but opposes the taxes and programmes needed to ensure them. The ecoconservative vote is growing at a faster rate in the high-growth counties of Montana than in the state as a whole. The effect may be that, in the long run, there will be less political will to elect leaders who would preserve the environmental quality and emergent economy that attracts investment and new residents and supports a thriving tourism industry.

Another part of the social/political realignment is the growing conservative Christian movement in rural areas. Although largely anecdotal, there seems to be a considerable social movement of fundamentalist religious zealots to the many small communities of the region. Much of this behaviour is related to the liberal 'home schooling' laws prevalent in the western states. These laws make it very easy for families to teach children at home while disengaging from the traditional curriculum of the local education system.

Others identify a general loss of the sense of community and place (Jobes, 1988; Carroll and Lee, 1990; Kemmis, 1990; Brown, 1993).

They point out that, as communities change and adapt to new social values and design policy to accommodate them, the small town loses its cultural roots. Patricia Stokowski speaks eloquently of the romanticism and reality of the changes created by new population growth in the West's small towns:

> Newcomers move to Gilpin County (Colorado) in search of expansive personal freedoms and to escape urban congestion and big-city problems, but they complain that development levels and services are inadequate in the county, and desire an economic stability that is unlikely to be provided without broader governmental financing and coordination. Long-standing antagonisms (between newcomers and old-timers) remain unresolved, though few community members lived during the times that gave rise to the confrontations (Stokowski 1996).

Finally, there is a growing concern that rural in-migration is damaging some of the qualities that attract new arrivals to the region. The views and open spaces produced by large tracts of agricultural land are compromised by rural subdivisions and homes on the skylines, lights from rural homes overwhelm night skies and favourite recreational spots are overcrowded.

Changes to the Lands of the GYE and the Rural West

The land is, in large part, why the communities of the West are experiencing a population boom. Compared with urban centres, land in the Rocky Mountain states is inexpensive, clean, safe, a ready source of recreation opportunity and scenically spectacular. But local governments must grapple with uncontrolled growth and loss of agricultural open spaces. Environmental and community planners are concerned about community integrity and the ecological impacts discussed earlier and all concerns eventually focus on the land. Of particular interest are the pace and likely effects of population growth in the agriculturally fertile river valleys of the region. They are home to the mix of social and ecological amenities that attract in-migrants to rural towns and the

surrounding countryside and they constitute the majority of the small amount of private land in the GYE.

Agriculture is the dominant use of rural private lands, with crops ranging from seed potatoes in eastern Idaho to sugar beets in north-west Wyoming; most of the cultivated acreage is devoted to livestock forage. Within the 20 counties, 57% of the private land is range, 20% is in crops, 7% is pasture, 6% is forested and 10% is developed (Greater Yellowstone Coalition, 2001).

Even as they help to define the character of the region, agricultural lands and associated open spaces are highly valued even by those residents who are not involved in agriculture and do not live in the countryside. At present, there is a direct conflict between efforts to maintain this character and the phenomenon of rural residential development. The public is of two minds: wanting to preserve rural character and yet wanting to own rural land in small and agriculturally unproductive parcels. Between 1974 and 1997, the 20 counties in the GYE lost, on average, 18% of farmland – most to rural development. In the last decade, over half a million hectares have been subdivided into parcels of 80 ha or less in the 20-county area. The real amount of developed acreage is underestimated because these figures consider only subdivision that is documented by local governments. The rate of growth is such that in some counties formal record-keeping cannot keep pace.

Research Efforts to Model Land-use Change

The land is central to the people that inhabit the region, and change in land use can readily affect the qualities of the natural ecosystem. We have responded by building an interdisciplinary team to focus research efforts aimed at modelling social, economic and ecological changes taking place across the rural West and the GYE. The overall objective is to assess and predict the rate, nature and impact of land-use change in rural areas and to use the best available technology to do so. A second objective is to develop modelling tools that meet the criteria of being user-friendly (for community employees, volunteers, secondary-school students, etc.), relatively low-cost and applicable to rural communities. Finally, they are designed to be compatible with each other, thereby making multidisciplinary investigation and policy analysis feasible.

The specific design outcomes for the suite of tools are as follows:

- Create awareness of urbanization and other significant land-use changes in rural landscapes.
- Bring objective data and analysis to the planning process.
- Identify the major factors that influence land-use change at multiple scales.
- Determine the socio-economic and ecological impacts of land use change.

Table 9.1 identifies specific tools and delineates the scale to which they are most appropriate.

The Countywide Land-use Change Model (Aspinall 2000) utilizes existing spatial data to assess overall growth and to model large-scale land-use change and residential development. The model is able to predict > 90% of rural residential development in the GYE using two data layers: distance from roads and distance from major regional centres as measured by travel time. These inputs were also found to be important in a study of growth in five counties in the Appalachians between 1950 and 1990 (Wear and Flamm, 1993). Such a simple but effective model demonstrates that straightforward prediction and interpretation are possible with little investment in time and data.

The Public-input Land-use Prioritization Model (PILUM) utilizes a recent addition to the ARCVIEW suite of geographical information system (GIS) tools – Model Builder. Users can weight different landscape attributes to identify lands for conservation and development using virtually any factor they deem important. Output in the form of a land-use map is instantaneous and serves the public with immediate feedback on their choices of priority values. The method works well with focus groups and promotes an awareness of how human values can be used

Table 9.1. Land-use planning and forecasting tools for the GYE.

Tool	Scale
GIS-based tools	
Countywide Land-use Change Model	Large County/multi-county/ecosystem/ watershed
Public-input Land-use Prioritization Model	Medium County/small watershed
GIS-linked LUC Model	Small (approx. 250 km^2) Rural community/countryside Rural growth 'hot spot'
Cost-of-services, Build-out Tool	Small to medium
Visualization tools	
Visual Build-out Analysis	Small
Resident Visual-preference Survey	Medium–small
Socio-economic tools	
Community-attitude Survey	Medium–small
Measuring Change in Rural Communities: A Workbook for Determining Demographic, Economic and Fiscal Trends	Large–small
Landowner-attitude Survey	Medium–small
Ecosystem-response tools	
Wildlife Habitat I D (Gap analysis)	Large
Biodiversity Hot-spot Detection and Response	Medium
Terrestrial Ecosystem-integrity Index	Small

to influence future land-use policy. The model has been used successfully to help rewrite the countywide land-use plan in Gallatin County, Montana (Gallatin County, 2001).

The Land-use/Land-cover Change Prediction System (LUCCPS) (Maxwell *et al.*, 2000) was designed to create a visualization (map) of future land use based on historical changes. The model is based on the history of past land-use change, natural features, human-made infrastructure and land-use decisions. Each layer of information is used as an independent driving variable to calculate the transition probabilities for landscapes in private ownership. LUCCPS currently allows up to 30 secondary influencing layers.

The Cost of Services (COS) (S. Mitchel, 2000, unpublished) build-out tool utilizes another ARCVIEW add-in: Smart Places. This system inventories all the capital costs and tax revenues of subdivision development and then provides for reconfiguration of the mix of homes/commercial property, lot sizes, road layout, etc. to allow developers and citizens to design the most cost-effective land-development plan.

A Visual Build-out has been designed to provide for the aesthetic configuration of rural development where home placement, open-space conversion or the visual impact of development can be assessed and discussed. When combined with the COS model, the visual and economic impacts of rural land development will be integrated into a single tool.

The Resident Visual Preference (RVP) survey is an existing tool in widespread use for urban planning. Briefly, RVP helps residents to quantify the perceptional responses they may hold for an environmental setting or experience by allowing the respondent to take photographs that reflect their feelings about a range of management outcomes. RVP has been used as a method of enquiry to investigate feelings of scenic beauty (Daniel and Boster, 1976) and recreational impact (Cherem and Traweek, 1977), for the management of natural resources in a national park (Taylor *et al.*, 1995) and for community planning. We have used it to assess values residents hold for different types of land use and will integrate those findings into the PILUM.

The workbook *Measuring Change in Rural Communities* (Rasker *et al.*, 1998) is a step-by-step guide designed to help rural residents and community leaders gain a better understanding of the demographic, economic and fiscal features of their communities. Exercises in the workbook focus on trend analysis, using easily accessible federal data to determine how the local population, economy and tax base have changed over the last 25 years. The workbook is intended for non-experts. Other helpful features include suggestions about presenting findings, tracking tourism and listings for other resources (Sonoran Institute, 2002).

Standard social science research methods are used to assess Community Attitudes. These surveys can investigate a well-defined population for attributes such as community attachment, economic security, level of government services, etc. They can be combined with workbook exercises and visual surveys.

As part of the LUCCPS model, Landowner Attitude Survey results indicate that agricultural landowners operate on a continuum from profit maximization to value-driven decision-making (Oglethorpe, 1995). The qualitative semi-structured interviews explore the range of landowner decision-making criteria. The findings confirm those of Dent *et al.* (1995), who describe the management of farm systems as a complex mix of elements contained within two broad categories. The first includes economic factors, such as profit-maximizing behaviour, commodity prices, relative value of land and product mix. The second includes social factors, such as personal values, lifestyle pursuits, family considerations and past experience. The mix of these elements is included in the LUCCPS model through a land-use behaviour index used as a dimension in the probability transition matrices. Including the behaviour index significantly improves predictions, indicating the vital connection between social factors and land-use change. As a discrete project, the survey is a useful depiction of land-management orientations for those who own large tracts of agricultural land in the region.

Wildlife Habitat Identification (Garrot *et al.*, 2000) is carried out at a large scale, using two broad sources of data: national and state databases depicting known fish and wildlife habitat and geographical features. Data sources are primarily federal agency resource inventories for fisheries, birds and wildlife. The other source of data is a series of expert interviews of resource managers and university researchers. Habitat delineations are placed on a land-use data layer (Classified Landsat Images) and draped over a Digital Elevation Model (DEM) at 30 m resolution. The output can be used as a discrete depiction of habitat or in conjunction with the PILUM.

Biodiversity Hot-spot Detection research has been conducted for the western half of the GYE. Using a combination of fieldwork and modelling, population source and sink locations have been developed for several bird species. 'Hot spots' for population source are dominated by deciduous forests (aspen, cottonwood and willow) at low elevation. Private lands in these areas are also desirable for rural residential development and often result in the potentially rich area breeding parasitic birds that have converted the area into a population sink (Hansen *et al.*, 1999).

Finally, a Terrestrial Ecosystem Integrity (EI) Index has been designed to work within several land-use change models. The EI is composed of 14 variables for upland and 13 variables for valley-bottom areas. They include vegetation, animal and soil measures. EI scores are referenced to those areas, predicted to change land use over time, allowing for a dynamic view of how ecosystem function may be affected by rural development (Johnson and Maxwell, 2001).

When coupled with the ability to predict future land use, the methodologies described above that quantify land-use and ecological change in rural communities have application in other amenity-rich locations globally. Data needs are universally available and the field-specific work can be accomplished using students or other university researchers. The land-use prediction systems should be useful to land-use planners concerned with maintaining the integrity of rural communities wherever rapid population growth and its effects are found to be a policy concern. The ability to produce visualization of future land-use scenarios is of value to citizens dis-

turbed by aesthetic changes associated with residential development.

Conclusion

The 6 million ha that make up the GYE are a premier destination for tourists, recreationists and permanent residents seeking a rural lifestyle. As such, the GYE is an ideal location for the study of amenity-driven in-migration. The region is undergoing significant social, economic, political and potentially ecological change as a result of two decades of > 20% population growth. Much of the settlement is a function of the very active tourism and outdoor-recreation activity in close proximity to national parks and forests, large river systems and spectacular natural beauty. Combined with the many small rural communities scattered throughout the region that offer employment and a quality of life not found in larger urban centres, the region continues to attract retirees, lifestyle refugees and those looking for a good place to live and raise a family. The GYE is only one such case study globally.

Concurrent with the population boom is an ongoing transition of land use from traditional natural-resource extraction and agricultural operations to a land use based on rural subdivisions and loss of agricultural production and open space. The results are a conflict between efforts to maintain the rural agricultural character of the region and wanting to own rural land for private home sites and a fragmentation of ownership into small and agriculturally unproductive parcels. The new pattern of ownership and land management may have unfortunate ecological effects for resident herds of ungulates and for fisheries, and it certainly compromises the scenic vista of the mountains and surrounding public lands.

A variety of tools are in development or have been developed to aid in land-use planning, community collaboration and ecological monitoring processes. The tools exist across scales and are intended to deliver objective data and analysis to the planning process, to create awareness of urbanization and other significant land-use changes in rural landscapes and to identify the major factors that influence land-use change. They reside on a GIS platform for ease of visualization and data management.

The problems and possibilities related to tourism and related population growth in the GYE and other amenity-rich areas will persist. Rapid in-migration will inevitably lead to change in the social and economic condition of rural communities. Much of this will be beyond the control of local governments or residents with respect to the rate of growth and its effects. Land-use policy within the GYE, like most western states, is a tenuous and politically charged process and private property rights prevail when it comes to land-use policy. However, the erosion of scenic vistas, overcrowding due to tourists and residents, increasing traffic congestion and other changes to the regional quality of life are providing incentives for residents and decision-makers to engage in local conversations about the effects of population growth and land-use change.

Acknowledgements

Thanks to sociologist Patrick Jobes for the title based on his book *Moving Nearer to Heaven: The Illusions and Disillusions of Migrants to Scenic Rural Places* (Jobes, 2000).

References

American Farmland Trust (1998) Living on the Edge: the Costs and Risks of Scatter Development. http://farm.fic.niu.edu/cae/scatter/e-loe.htm

Aspinall, R. (2000) *Baysean Model for Land Use Change in the Greater Yellowstone*. Society for Human Ecology, Jackson, Wyoming.

Beyers, W.B. and Lindahl, D.P. (1996) Lone eagles and high fliers in rural producers services. *Rural Development Perspectives* 11, 2–10.

Beyers, W.B. and Nelson, P.B. (2000) Contemporary development forces in the nonmetropolitan west: new insights from rapidly growing communities. *Journal of Rural Studies* 16, 459–474.

Brown, R. (1993) Rural community satisfaction and attachment in mass consumer society. *Rural Sociology* 58(3), 387–403.

Carroll, M.S. and Lee, R.G. (1990) Occupational community and identity among pacific northwestern loggers: implications for adapting to economic changes. In: Field, A. and Lees, B. (eds) *Community and Forestry: Continuities in the Sociology of Natural Resources*. Westview Press, Boulder, Colorado.

Cherem, G.J. and Traweek, D.E. (1977) Visitor employed photography: a tool for interpretive planning on river environments. In: *Proceeding on River Recreation Management and Research*. GTR NC-28, USDA Forest Service, St Paul, Minnesota, pp. 236–244.

Clark, T.W., Amato, E.D., Wittemore, D.G. and Harvey, A.H. (1991) Policy and programs for ecosystem management in the Greater Yellowstone Ecosystem: an analysis. *Conservation Biology* 5(2), 412–422.

Craighead, J. (1984) *The Ecocenter*. Audubon Society, Casper, Wyoming.

Daniel, T.C. and Boster, R.S. (1976) *Measuring Landscape Esthetics: the Scenic Beauty Evaluation Method*. GENERIC 76, USDA Forest Service, Fort Collins, Colorado.

Dent, J.B., Edwards-Jones, G. and Mcgregor, M.J. (1995) Simulation of ecological, social and economic factors in agricultural systems. *Agricultural Systems* 49, 337–351.

Gallatin County (2001) Planning Department. http://www.co.gallatin.mt.us/planning Last viewed 5 December 2002.

Garrot, B., Carlson, J., Craighead, A., Harmata, P., Koons, D., Oechsli, L., Ouren, D., Stackhouse, E. and Wilmer, B. (2000) Gallatin County Fish and Wildlife Habitat. http://www.montana.edu/wwwbi/staff/garrott/gallatin/

Greater Yellowstone Coalition (2001) http://www.greateryellowstone.org/lands_private.html

Hansen, A.J., Rotella, J.J., Kraska, M.L. and Brown, D. (1999) Dynamic habitat and population analysis: an approach to resolve the biodiversity manager's dilemma. *Ecological Applications* 9, 1459–1476.

Huang, Y. and Stewart, W.P. (1996) Rural tourism development: shifting basis of community solidarity. *Journal of Travel Research* 34(4), 26.

Jobes, P.C. (1988) Nominalism, realism and planning in a changing community. *International Journal of Environmental Studies* 31, 279–290.

Jobes, P. (2000) *Moving Nearer to Heaven: the Illusions and Disillusions of Migrants to Scenic Rural Places*. Praeger, Westport, Connecticut.

Johansen, H.E. and Fuguitt, G.V. (1990) The changing rural village. *Rural Development Perspectives* 2(6), 2–6.

Johnson, J.D. and Maxwell, B.M. (1996) Community sustainability through ecosystem management and planning. *Montana Policy Review* 6(1), 22–31.

Johnson, J.D. and Maxwell, B.M. (2001) The role of the conservation reserve program in controlling rural residential development. *Journal of Rural Studies* 17(3), 323–332.

Johnson, J.D. and Rasker, R. (1995) The role of economic and quality of life values in rural business locations. *Journal of Rural Studies* 11(4), 405–416.

Johnson, J. and Snepenger, D. (1992) Application of the tourism lifecycle concept in the Greater Yellowstone region. *Society and Natural Resources* 6, 127–148.

Johnson, K.M. and Beale, C.L. (1999) Recreational counties in nonmetropolitan America. http://www.luc.edu/depts/sociology/johnson/p99webr.html

Kemmis, D. (1990) *Community and the Politics of Place.* University of Oklahoma Press, Norman, Oklahoma.

Leistritz, F.L., Cordes, S. and Snell, R. (2000) Inmigrants to the Northern Great Plains: survey results from Nebraska and North Dakota. *Rural Development Perspectives* 15(3), 8–15.

Maxwell, B., Johnson, J. and Montagne, C. (2000) Predicting land use change in and around a rural community. In: Hill, M.J. and Aspinall, R.J. (eds) *Spatial Information For Land Use Management.* Gordon and Breach, Amsterdam, The Netherlands, pp. 173–187.

Oglethorpe, D.R. (1995) Sensitivity of farm plans under risk averse behavior: a note on the environmental implications. *Journal of Agricultural Economics* 46(2), 227–232.

Power, T.M. (1996) *Lost Landscapes and Failed Economies: the Search for a value of Place.* Island Press, Washington, DC.

Rasker, R. and Hansen, A. (2000) Natural amenities and population growth in the Greater Yellowstone Region. *Research in Human Ecology* 7(2), 30–40.

Rasker, R., Johnson, J. and York, V. (1998) *Measuring Change in Rural Communities: a Workbook for Determining Demographic, Economic and Fiscal Trends.* Sonoran Institute, Tucson, Arizona.

Rauch, J. (2001) The new old economy: oil, computers, and the reinvention of the earth. *Atlantic Monthly* 287, 35–49.

Riebsame, W.E., Gosnell, W. and Theobald, D.M. (1996) Land use and landscape change in the Colorado Mountains I: theory, scale and pattern. *Mountain Research and Development* 16(4), 395–405.

Shepard, J.C. (1993) The new economy of the Great Plains: implications for economic development. *Economic Development Quarterly* 7(4), 403–410.

Snepenger, D.J., Johnson, J.D. and Rasker, R. (1995) Travel stimulated entrepreneurial migration. *Journal of Travel Research* (summer) 34(1).

Snepenger, D.J., Reiman, S., Johnson, J.D. and Snepenger, M. (1998) Is downtown mainly for tourists? *Journal of Travel Research* 36(winter), 5–12.

Sonoran Institute (2002) http://www.sonoran.org/library/measure.html Last viewed 5 November 2002.

Stauber, K.N., Hassebrock, C., Bird, E.A.R., Bultena, G.L., Hoiberg, E.O., MacCormack, H. and Menanteau-Horta, D. (1995) The promise of sustainable agriculture. In: Bird, E., Bultena, G.L. and Gardner, J.C. (eds) *Planting the Future: Developing an Agriculture that Sustains Land and Community.* Iowa University Press, Ames.

Stegner, W. (1954) *Beyond the Hundredth Meridian: John Wesley Powell and the Second Opening of the West.* Houghton Mifflin, Houghton.

Stokowski, P.A. (1996) *Riches and Regrets: Betting on Gambling in Two Colorado Mountain Towns.* University Press of Colorado, Niwot, Colorado.

Taylor, J.G., Czarnowski, K.J., Sexton, N.R. and Flick, S. (1995) The importance of water to Rocky Mountain National Park visitors: an adaptation of visitor-employed photography to natural resources. *Journal of Applied Recreation Research* 20(1), 61–85.

US Bureau of the Census (1999) Mountain states show biggest increases in housing; Nevada leads the way, Census Bureau Reports. http://www.census.gov/PressRelease/www/1999/cb99-232.html

Wear, D.N. and Flamm, R.O. (1993) Public and private disturbance regimes in the Southern Appalachians. *Natural Resource Modeling* 7, 379–397.

Williams, A.S. and Jobes, P.C. (1990) Economic and quality of life considerations in urban–rural migration. *Journal of Rural Studies* 6(2), 187–94.

Williams, J.D. (1982) Turnaround migration: grubby economics or delightful indulgence in ruralism? *Rural Sociologist* 2, 104–108.

10

Visitor-impact Data in a Land-management Context

Ralf Buckley and Narelle King

International Centre for Ecotourism Research, Griffith University, Queensland, Australia

---

Abstract

Land managers need to know the impacts of different recreational activities in different environments. Different impacts are critical in different ecosystems. Localized, direct, lasting impacts, which are cheap and easy to measure, such as trampling, have been studied much more than diffuse, indirect, intermittent impacts, which are difficult and expensive to measure, such as water-borne pathogens, noise disturbance to rare fauna or interference with plant-pollination ecology. The latter are more critical for conservation, but relevant research is uncommon and underfunded. The quantitative relationships between the type and intensity of recreational activity and the types and intensity of ecosystem response across a full range of global environments are not known for any type of impact, even pedestrian trampling. Managers must typically rely on summaries of studies of similar impacts in similar environments. For different management issues it may be more useful to review impacts by: (i) type of activity or equipment, e.g. off-road vehicles; (ii) type of impacts, e.g. weeds and pathogens; or (iii) ecosystem components affected, e.g. wildlife or water quality. We have recently reviewed each of these. Different sampling designs are required: (i) to differentiate impacts of tourism from other natural or anthropogenic changes; (ii) to track changes in environmental quality or conservation value over time; or (iii) to test impact mechanisms, e.g. possible increased predation by feral cats on small native mammals along little-used recreational hiking trails. Without much better knowledge of impacts, and management tools to minimize them, increasing tourism (including ecotourism) will damage parks in ways that are not predicted or detected until they become irreversible. Such knowledge needs both long-term skilled observation by rangers and professionally competent scientific studies by appropriately qualified parks staff or others. If parks are to be used for recreation and tourism as well as conservation, parks services will need funds for this work – from either taxpayers, visitors or commercial users.

Management Needs for Impact Data

As tourism and recreation in protected areas continue to increase, an accurate knowledge of their ecological impacts and ways to reduce them becomes increasingly important for conservation and visitor management. We need quantitative information on the effects of particular numbers of people engaged in particular activities with particular equipment in particular ecosystems at particular seasons with particular frequencies under particular management regimes, on particular environmental parameters, components and functions (Buckley, 1994). Without such data, managers cannot predict how more visitors or new activities will affect primary conservation values, or select visitor- and resource-management tools that minimize both degradation of the natural environment and intrusion on visitor experiences. Without such information, land managers can only respond to visitor impacts once they have become obvious; and by then they may be irreversible either for ecological reasons, e.g. introduction of a weed or pathogen; economic reasons, if there are insufficient funds for rehabilitation; legal reasons, if land managers have granted rights to tour operators or other users; or political reasons, once users have become accustomed to access in a particular area.

Detailed stress–response–recovery studies, however, are currently available for only very few ecosystems, recreational activities and environmental parameters. In some other industry sectors, such as mining and manufacturing, information on impact prediction has been built up through large-scale industry-funded environmental-impact assessment (EIA) and monitoring programmes over several decades. This is not the case for nature tourism, for several reasons: (i) EIA and monitoring in the tourism industry are generally of low scientific quality (Warnken and Buckley, 1998, 2000); (ii) most nature tourism and commercial outdoor recreation operations are too small to trigger EIA requirements individually, even though their cumulative economic and environmental significance is large (Buckley, 1998; Buckley and Warnken, 1998); (iii) commercial nature-tourism operations often take place at the same time and place as individual public outdoor recreation, and their impacts are typically similar in type and scale and difficult to distinguish (Manning, 1999; Newsome et al., 2002); and (iv) nature tourism and outdoor recreation commonly take place in protected areas and other areas of high conservation significance, where much smaller and more subtle impacts than those of mining or manufacturing may still be highly significant ecologically (Buckley, 2000).

Most of the information available on the impacts of nature tourism is from independent scientific studies, largely related to public recreation in parks and to a lesser extent other land tenures. Different countries have emphasized different issues, reflecting their different ecosystems and types of recreational use. Globally, some types of impact have received a great deal more research effort than others. Easily studied, localized and direct impacts have been studied far more intensively than impacts which are inconspicuous, diffuse and indirect or require long-term studies, complex sampling designs or expensive equipment to measure (Manning, 1999; Buckley, 2001a; Newsome et al., 2002).

The most-studied indicators are not necessarily those which are most critical, either for ecological integrity or for visitor management. Additionally, impacts that are highly significant for ecological integrity in one ecosystem may be relatively insignificant in another, and vice versa. Worldwide, the effects of pedestrian trampling on soil and ground-cover plants have been studied in far more detail than any other impact, presumably since they are cheap and easy to measure (Cole, 1993; Liddle, 1997). The bulk of this research has been in North America, and the results are indeed useful in advising back-country hikers whether to fan out or hike single-file when travelling off track, and whether to camp in alpine meadows or subalpine forests. The recovery of vegetation if trampling ceases has also been examined in some detail, and the results are useful in determining whether it is worth closing a section of track for rehabilitation. Similar research has also been carried out in Australian alpine regions over recent years (Scherrer, 2001; Whinam et al., Chapter 15, this volume).

In many ecosystems, the most significant ecological impact of tourism and recreation is not localized trampling but the potential introduction of weeds and pathogens or disturbance to endangered animal species. For example, visitors can introduce new weeds (Buckley, 1981; Johnson and Pickering, 2001) or new water-borne pathogens (Buckley et al., 1998; Buckley and Warnken, 2003) into catchments or even countries where they were not previously present; and, if weeds or pathogens are able to establish and spread, the ecological consequences may be many orders of magnitude more serious than localized vegetation damage from trampling.

For animals, by far the most commonly studied indicator of visitor impacts is the human approach distance at which birds of various species take flight (e.g. Fitzpatrick and Bouchez, 1998; Buckley, 2001a). Shore birds and raptors have been studied most intensively. Distances flown before re-alighting have also been recorded for some species. More subtle pre-flight behavioural or physiological indicators of stress, however, have been studied for only a few species. Again, it is easy to walk towards a conspicuous bird in open country, note when it flies away and measure the distance by pacing or with a rangefinder. Measuring heart rates through remote telemetry, in contrast, requires specialist equipment, expertise and experimental design, which take a great deal more time and money (e.g. McArthur *et al.*, 1982a,b; Holmes *et al.*, 2001). Similarly, the population-level consequences of alarm disturbances, through, for example, effects on individual energy balances, effective reduction of available habitat area or predation of offspring, have been quantified for only a few species and circumstances. And, again, subtler impacts, such as the effects of passing hikers on foraging behaviour or territorial calls by rare and cryptic rainforest birds and small mammals, remain almost entirely unknown.

While detailed data on stress–response–recovery relationships for localized direct impacts, such as vegetation trampling or shore-bird alarm flights, are still restricted to a few ecosystems, species and circumstances, at least the impact mechanisms are identified and widely recognized. There are probably many other ecological impacts of tourism, however, which act through more complex indirect mechanisms whose existence may not even be identified. Even for pedestrian trampling, however, we have only a tiny proportion of the data which would be needed to predict the impacts of tramping at any intensity in any ecosystem worldwide (Cole, 1993; Liddle, 1997; Buckley, 2001a). The volume of research required to establish predictive eco-

logical models seems not to be generally appreciated by the tourism industry. There are perhaps several reasons for this. The first is that, compared with other industry sectors, which constantly rely on new technologies to locate or extract new resources or invent and manufacture new products, the tourism industry has seen itself as a service sector dealing only with people. It uses new technologies, from airline navigation systems to new polymers, infrared telescopes to internet booking systems, but it does not invent or manufacture them. In general, therefore, the tourism industry has little experience in commissioning or using scientific research.

Secondly, the tourism industry has only recently begun to acknowledge that it produces environmental impacts. This may be partly because the sector is relatively young, partly because it focuses more on consumption than on production and partly because many of its impacts are diffuse. Only large-scale tourism infrastructure developments, such as airports and integrated resorts, for example, are generally subject to formal EIA procedures (Warnken and Buckley, 1998).

The third likely reason is the much greater complexity of biological than physical systems, and the fourth is the relative youth of the ecological compared with the physical sciences. These reasons are of course common to all industry sectors, not only tourism. We can predict concentrations and speciation of chemical pollutants in a river downstream from a mine tailings discharge or in the sea around an ocean outfall with reasonable reliability; because physicists and chemists and their specialist cousins, such as hydrologists and geomorphologists, have carried out hundreds of thousands of scientific experiments over several centuries to understand how these physical systems behave. Even in these cases, we may have difficulty in predicting, for example, dispersion patterns in irregularly shaped tidal estuaries or speciation of complex organometallic ions. Our ability to predict the behaviour of these physical systems, however, is orders of magnitude more accurate than our ability to predict their effects on aquatic ecosystems. This is true even at the basic level of acute toxicity to individual species, and far more so at the level of chronic sublethal toxicity or secondary effects through interactions between species. Ecological systems are far more complicated than physical systems, and far less research effort has been devoted to them for a far shorter period of time. Our ability to predict ecological impacts, in any industry sector, is far less than our ability to predict physical impacts (Treweek, 1995). This applies for the impacts of tourism in protected areas as much as anywhere else.

Protected-area management agencies and environmental non-government organizations often number scientists among their staff and commonly recognize the complexity and significance of ecological impacts and the importance of good science in predicting and monitoring impacts. Rarely, however, do they have the resources to undertake or commission relevant research. Over the past decade, the authors have been asked repeatedly, by both community groups and parks agencies, to help design programmes to monitor the impacts of tourism on the natural environment. Not once, however, has the organization concerned acquired or allocated the resources to implement any monitoring plan more ambitious than direct human observation, expert or otherwise.

Indeed, for environmental parameters where the individual observations can be made with the naked human eye, and the most critical aspect of monitoring is a long-term series of observations at the same places, over many seasons and years, the recollections of an interested ranger are as reliable a method as any to determine the impacts of tourism and differentiate them from other anthropogenic impacts or natural sources of variation. Such indicators might include, for example, the spread of a particular weed species along a walking track; the arrival or disappearance of a particular bird species at a campground; or the years in which an endangered frog species could be heard calling at a particular waterhole. Each of these requires interest and attention to the issue concerned; accurate observations and recollections or field notes; and the field-naturalist skills to identify particular plant or animal species. They do not, however, require experimental design, statistical analysis or specialist equipment or instrumentation.

There are many other indicators, however, which generally cannot be detected by human senses alone. Such indicators include, for example: the presence and concentrations of water-borne pathogens or pollutants; noise regime; or the population structure of a cryptic animal species. For indicators such as these, the best advice is surely, 'Hire an ecologist.' People do not expect a home health manual to replace a medical doctor's diagnostic skills and equipment: why do they discount the lifetime training it takes to approach a similar level of understanding for ecological systems?

One major diagnostic tool for analysing impacts on any complex system is prior information on the types of impact known to occur and how common they are. This applies for the impacts of tourism on natural ecosystems as much as for the impacts of pathogens on the human body. As with any such information base, for different purposes it may be more useful to classify such information either: (i) by the source of impacts; (ii) by the type of impact; or (iii) by the system component affected. In the medical analogy, for example, these might include: (i) the symptoms of dengue fever or dislocation; (ii) the various causes of jaundice or fever; and (iii) the diseases of the leg or the liver.

For the impacts of tourism and recreation on the natural environment, examples include: (i) impacts from a specific source, such as hikers and helicopters; (ii) impacts of a specific type or mechanism, such as trampling or noise; and (iii) impacts on a specific ecosystem component or function, such as air quality or a particular plant or animal species. To illustrate these approaches, we have reviewed international published scientific literature for: (i) impacts of off-road vehicles (ORVs); (ii) impacts associated with jarrah dieback disease, *Phytophthora cinnamomi*; (iii) impacts on water quality; and (iv) impacts on wildlife. In each case we have tried to identify: (i) what is well established; (ii) what is new, little studied or less obvious; and (iii) what is missing.

Impacts of Off-road Vehicles

Recreational ORVs include four-wheel-drive (4WD) and 6WD cars and coaches, all-terrain vehicles (ATVs), trail and dirt bikes and snowmobiles. ORVs can have adverse environmental impacts on soils, vegetation, fauna and air (Buckley, 2001a,b; R. Buckley, 2004, submitted). ORVs compact soil at depth, which decreases infiltration rates while causing erosion near the surface and breaking up surface crusts (Eckert *et al.*, 1979; Iverson *et al.*, 1981; Anders and Leatherman, 1987; Wilson and Seney, 1994). Off-road vehicles cause a significant reduction in plant cover and diversity, with the most impacts generally experienced within the first few vehicle passes (Webb *et al.*, 1983; Yorks *et al.*, 1997; Kutiel *et al.*, 2000; Milchunas *et al.*, 2000), and can spread weeds and pathogens (Wace, 1977; Lonsdale and Lane, 1994). ORVs affect fauna through collisions and crushing, noise, displacement away from tracks, disturbance to feeding and social activities and habitat damage (Vollmer *et al.*, 1976; Brattstrom and Bondello, 1983; Dearden and Hall, 1983; Woolcott and Woolcott, 1984; Kuller, 1999). ORVs can have significant impacts on air quality and human health (Wilkinson, 1995).

ORV operators can minimize their environmental impacts by: using lightweight vehicles; avoiding easily damaged soils, marshes, wet trails, steep dunes and beaches above the high-tide mark; crossing dunes only on ramps or well worn tracks; minimizing creek crossings and, where necessary, crossing at existing fords or tracks or where it is possible to drive straight across; washing vehicles carefully before use; driving to reduce noise levels; slowing down in areas with wildlife or wildlife warning signs; and watching wildlife from a distance (Rickard and Brown, 1974; Buckley, 2001b). Land managers can minimize the environmental impacts of vehicles by: restricting vehicle use to a small number of heavily used, well-maintained tracks; signposting off-track areas; educating ORV operators and encouraging them to improve their minimal-impact driving skills; leaving road kills on roadsides; diverting ORVs away from critical wildlife habitat and warning operators of potential health risks; limiting

use of vehicles on beaches to wide sandy beaches at low tide during the day; and restricting vehicle numbers and warning operators where exhaust pollution may be detrimental to human health (R. Buckley, 2004, submitted).

Several of these impacts, such as deafening lizards (Brattstrom and Bondello, 1983) and crushing crabs (Woolcott and Woolcott, 1984), are not yet widely recognized by land managers or 4WD tour operators. Perhaps this is because the relevant scientific studies are few in number, even though they were carried out years or decades ago. Perhaps it is because the impacts are hidden rather than immediately visible. There would appear to be a range of potential impacts similar to these. For example, the study of ORV-induced hearing loss in desert lizards was for an off-road race, where noise levels are particularly high (Brattstrom and Bondello, 1983). What are the behavioural impacts of ORV noise at lower levels? For example, how do bettongs, potoroos or lyre-birds respond to the sound of 4WD vehicles on little-used forest tracks in Australia? And, if land managers upgrade 4WD tracks to reduce erosion or restrict the spread of jarrah dieback fungus (see below), does that make the track more of a barrier to local movements by small terrestrial and/or arboreal mammals and/or increase road kill (Turton and Goosem, 2001)? And how does track maintenance affect habitat for weeds, and how do weeds affect wildlife? All but the simplest questions remain unanswered.

Impacts through Dieback Disease

Tourism is now a highly significant factor in the spread of *P. cinnamomi* (jarrah dieback) in national parks and forests in several Australian states, especially in the temperate south (R. Buckley, N. King and T. Zubrinich, 2004, submitted). The broad-scale distribution history of *P. cinnamomi* remains problematic (Irwin *et al.*, 1995; Podger and Keane, 2000; Wilson *et al.*, 2000). At a local scale, susceptibility is high for vegetation on wet sandy soils, particular plant species and genotypes and individual plants stressed by drought, water-logging, fire, insects or other pathogens. Symptoms vary, but most heavily infected plants die within 3 years. Spores can be spread into previously uninfected areas in soil and water on machinery, vehicles, tyres, boots and camping equipment. Spores are spread along roads, tracks and trails by vehicles and pedestrians, and off-track by ORVs, mountain bikes, horses, hikers, waterflow and mycelial transmission between plants (Podger and Keane, 2000; Shearer and Smith, 2000; R. Buckley, N. King and T. Zubrinich, 2004, submitted). Chemical controls are ineffective and too expensive for broad-acre use. On flat dry ground, plant-to-plant transmission can sometimes be halted by clearing a broad bare barrier zone. Generally, however, once the pathogen has entered a catchment with susceptible soil and vegetation conditions, controls are largely ineffective (Cahill, 1999; Podger and Keane, 2000). The only effective control is mapping of infected areas and strict quarantine of uninfected areas. This may require restrictions on access, wash-down and other hygiene measures for vehicles, footwear and equipment; or a combination of these and other measures (R. Buckley, N. King and T. Zubrinich, 2004, submitted).

Dieback is more significant as a protected-area management issue in Australia than overseas, and more significant in states such as Western Australian and Tasmania than in the Northern Territory or Queensland. Different states have taken different management approaches, but their effectiveness is largely untested.

Impacts on Water Quality

Tourism can cause impacts on water bodies through increases in litter, fuels and oils, nutrients, toxins, turbidity and microbiota (King and Mace, 1974; Dickman and Dorais, 1977; R. Buckley, 2004, submitted). Any and all of these can endanger aquatic biota and ecosystems and reduce the appeal of water bodies for tourists. Tourists can drop litter on land or into water bodies. Fuel and oils enter water bodies from boat engines at all scales from jet-skis to cruise liners and also from runoff through storm-water drains (Nedohin and

Elefsiniotis, 1997; Mosisch and Arthington, 2001). Nutrients enter water bodies in sewage and storm-water runoff; in runoff from golf courses (Wan et al., 1996; Kunimatsu et al., 1999; Mallin and Wheeler, 2000); through human waste deposited near streams and lakes (Crabill et al., 1999); and through soil erosion (Robertson and Colletti, 1994). Storm-water runoff, municipal wastewater discharges, resorts and recreational boats can also contain biotoxic substances, ranging from industrial solvents, cleaning compounds and pesticides to antifouling agents, personal insect repellents and sunscreen residues. Recreational boating, soil erosion and nutrient-rich discharges can increase turbidity (Hilton and Phillips, 1982). Microbiota enter water bodies in sewage, disposal of human waste and potentially through water sports (Anderson et al., 1998; Cilimburg et al., 2000; Mallin and Wheeler, 2000).

All but the crudest water-quality parameters are expensive to monitor. To distinguish visitor impacts on concentrations of the intestinal bacteria Escherichia coli in a rainforest stream, for example, and differentiate them statistically from natural seasonal and rainfall-related variations required several thousand individual water samples and laboratory analyses over a 3-year period (Warnken, 1996). Even a basic presence–absence screening for the water-borne pathogenic protozoa Giardia and Cryptosporidium in remote protected areas required the development of new sampling technologies and research-standard microbiological laboratories (Buckley and Warnken, 2003). Testing the toxicity of specific pollutants, such as personal insect repellents, in confined aquatic ecosystems would require even more complex approaches.

Impacts on Wildlife

Recreational hunting, fishing (including catch-and-release) and collection of animals for souvenirs and artefacts (including medicines) all kill individual animals and disturb others. Whether this affects populations depends on population size, the various external and internal factors affecting survival and reproduction, how the population is managed and which animals are killed. Non-consumptive wildlife watching can also affect individuals and populations if infrastructure or human disturbance affect feeding, breeding, predation or disease, either directly or indirectly (Anderson and Keith, 1980; Ferguson and Keith, 1982; Gotmark and Ahlund, 1984; Ahlund and Gotmark, 1989; Goodrich and Berger, 1994; Liddle, 1997; Anderson, 1998; Shepherd and Boates, 1999; Au and Green, 2000; Green and Higginbottom, 2000). Approach distances for flight, alert behaviours, heart-rate increases, etc. have been quantified for a selection of species (McArthur *et al.*, 1982a,b; Knight, 1984; Au and Green, 2000), but population-scale impacts remain unknown for most watchable wildlife, except for heavily managed populations (Robert and Ralph, 1975; Belanger and Bedard, 1989; Green and Higginbottom, 2000). Wildlife may also be affected by other forms of tourism infrastructure, development and activity in or near their habitat areas, even where the wildlife themselves are not part of the tourism activity or attraction. Common impact mechanisms include: habitat destruction or modification; direct mortality of individuals through road kill, crushing of burrows, etc.; barriers to movement at large or small scales; direct disturbance through noise, sight or smell; health-related effects through contamination of soil, plants, water or air; effects on interspecies interactions through introduction of feral predators or competing herbivores or through changes to habitat or food supply that favour introduced species; introduction of stress-related increases in disease; and a wide range of more complex and indirect effects (Shepherd and Boates, 1999; Turton and Goosem, 2001). Even for relatively simple mechanisms, such as barriers caused by roads or fences, impacts depend on how different species respond and are not always easily predictable. More complex mechanisms, such as changes to energy balances through increased territorial interactions, noise impacts on bird-song displays, synergistic impacts of temperature changes and introduced species on endangered native fish, or cascaded predator–prey interactions where one species obtains a new food supply, may be recognized

but are rarely quantified. And no doubt there are many other impact mechanisms as yet unrecognized.

The impacts of tourism and recreation on wildlife are difficult to determine, for a number of reasons.

1. Many animal species, particularly those that are rare or endangered, may be difficult to observe because they are shy, cryptic or few in number.
2. Even where individual animals are easy to observe on occasions, behavioural or physiological responses to human disturbance may be difficult to detect and quantify without specialist equipment and expertise.
3. Even where immediate physiological or behavioural responses are easy to detect, the long-term effects on individual fitness and population size and structure may be difficult to determine.
4. Where population size and structure fluctuate markedly through natural causes, the effects of human disturbance are particularly difficult to differentiate.
5. Particularly for low levels of tourist activity, the disturbances caused by researchers may be similar to those caused by visitors.
6. Individual animals may adapt their behaviour in response to repeated disturbance either by tourists or researchers, whether through habituation or increased avoidance.
7. To determine the impacts of tourism and recreation with any confidence requires a set of undisturbed control populations, as well as a set of populations with visitor disturbance; and the dynamics of all these populations prior to disturbance needs to be known. This is rare.

As a result, the pioneering work of McArthur *et al.* (1982a,b), who used remote telemetry to monitor heart rate for bighorn sheep in Yellowstone National Park, and Bernard Stonehouse and his colleagues, who used dummy eggs to monitor the physiological responses of nesting penguins to disturbance by tourists (Giese and Riddle, 1999; Holmes *et al.*, 2001), are very much the exception rather than the rule in studies of tourist disturbance to wildlife. Similarly, the effects of tourist tracks and traffic on small terrestrial and arboreal mammals have as yet been examined in only a few ecosystems.

There are many other instances where a potential impact mechanism has been identified, but its significance has not been quantified. For example, snow grooming and over-snow vehicles may affect small mammals in the Australian alps by crushing their burrows under the snow and forcing them to spend more time on the surface, where they are vulnerable to predation (Green, 2000). In forest ecosystems such as those of eastern Australia, even little-used back-country tracks may provide a significant advantage for feral cats and foxes stalking small native mammals; but this has not yet been tested experimentally. Similarly, aggressive bird species seem to be particularly numerous and bold at many campsites, lookouts and other visitor attractions, presumably because food stolen from or provided by visitors provides a significant supplement to their food supply. Since these species also prey on the eggs and nestlings of other birds, it has been suggested that this may indirectly decrease the populations of smaller birds, including rarer species, around areas visited by tourists. And, in at least one park on Australia's central eastern coastline, park managers have had to construct fences to divert off-road vehicles on beaches around nesting colonies of an endangered tern species. But they still pass close by, and it seems likely that the disturbance increases predation on tern eggs and chicks by silver gulls.

Conclusions

The more direct and obvious impacts of tourism and recreation on the natural environment are widely recognized, and often mentioned in park management plans. Even for the most straightforward and heavily studied types of impacts, however, quantitative stress–response–recovery relationships are known for only a few ecosytems. More complex and less obvious impacts, particularly those which are indirect, diffuse or difficult to measure, have typically been identified in only a few isolated instances and analysed for even fewer. Reviews of published literature, such as those presented here, can help protected area managers to identify potential sources and mechanisms of impacts and, in some cases, to

assess their potential significance. Rarely, however, can results for one plant or animal species, community or ecosystem be applied directly for another (Dearden and Hall, 1983; Higham, 1998). Even for the simplest and most direct impacts, such as pedestrian trampling of ground-cover plants or visual disturbance of shoreline birds, where the same mechanisms apply in many different environments, the responses of different individual species and their significance for ecological integrity differ widely. And, for impacts which are more complex, indirect and potentially more significant ecologically, the impact mechanism itself may be specific to a particular species or ecosystem. If we are to manage the impacts of tourism and recreation in our protected areas and other land of high conservation value, we shall need a great deal more local and high-quality ecological research in addition to international reviews.

References

Ahlund, M. and Gotmark, F. (1989) Gull predation on eider ducklings, *Somateria mollissima*: effects of human disturbance. *Biological Conservation* 48, 115–127.

Anders, F.J. and Leatherman, S.P. (1987) Disturbance of beach sediment by off-road vehicles. *Environmental Geology and Water Sciences* 93, 183–189.

Anderson, D.W. and Keith, J.O. (1980) The human influence on seabird nesting success: conservation implications. *Biological Conservation* 18, 65–80.

Anderson, I. (1998) With people come plagues: tourists and scientists could be bringing deadly diseases to Antarctica's wildlife. *New Scientist* 159, 4.

Anderson, M.A., Stewart, M.H., Yates, M.V. and Gerba, C.P. (1998) Modelling the impact of body-contact recreation on pathogen concentrations in a source drinking water reservoir. *Water Research* 32, 3293–3306.

Au, W.W.L. and Green, M. (2000) Acoustic interaction of humpback whales and whale-watching boats. *Marine Environmental Research* 49, 469–481.

Belanger, L. and Bedard, J. (1989) Responses of staging greater snow geese to human disturbance. *Journal of Wildlife Management* 53, 713–719.

Brattstrom, S.P. and Bondello, M.C. (1983) Effects of off-road vehicle noise on desert vertebrates. In: Webb, R.H. and Wilshire, H.E. (eds) *Environmental Effects of Off-road Vehicles.* Springer, New York, pp. 167–206.

Buckley, R.C. (1981) Alien plants in central Australia. *Botanical Journal of the Linnean Society* 82, 369–379.

Buckley, R.C. (1994) A framework for ecotourism. *Annals of Tourism Research* 21, 661–669.

Buckley, R.C. (1998) Cumulative environmental impacts. In: Porter, A.L. and Fittipaldi, J.J. (eds) *Environment Methods Review.* AEPI, Tampa, Florida, pp. 95–99.

Buckley, R.C. (2000) Tourism in the most fragile environments. *Journal of Tourism Recreation Research* 25, 31–40.

Buckley, R.C. (2001a) Environmental impacts of ecotourism. In: Weaver, D. (ed.) *The Encyclopedia of Ecotourism.* CAB International, Wallingford, UK, pp. 379–394.

Buckley, R.C. (2001b) *Green Guide for 4WD and Off-road Tours.* CRC Tourism, Griffith University, Gold Coast.

Buckley, R.C. and Warnken, J. (1998) Triggering and technical quality of EIA: the tourism testbed. In: Porter, A.L. and Fittipaldi, J.J. (eds) *Environment Methods Review.* AEPI, Tampa, Florida, pp. 171–177.

Buckley, R.C. and Warnken, W. (2003) *Giardia* and *Cryptosporidium* in pristine Australian watercourses. *Ambio* 32, 84–86.

Buckley, R.C., Clough, L. and Warnken, W. (1998) *Plesiomonas shigelloides* in Australia. *Ambio* 27, 253.

Cahill, D. (1999) General biology and ecology of *Phytophthora* with special reference to *Phytophthora cinnamomi.* In: Gadek, P.A. (ed.) *Patch Deaths in Tropical Queensland Rainforests.* CRC Rainforest, Cairns, pp. 21–26.

Cilimburg, A., Monz, C. and Kehoe, S. (2000) Wildland recreation and human waste: a review of problems, practices and concerns. *Environmental Management* 25, 587–598.

Cole, D.N. (1993) Trampling effects on mountain vegetation in Washington, Colorado, New Hampshire and North Carolina. USDA Forest Services, Ogden, Utah. Research Paper INT-464, Intermountain Forest and Range Experimental Station.

Crabill, C., Donald, R., Snelling, J., Foust, R. and Southam, G. (1999) The impact of sediment fecal coliform reservoirs on seasonal water quality in Oak Creek, Arizona. *Water Research* 33, 2163–2171.

Dearden, P. and Hall, C. (1983) Non-consumptive recreation pressures and the case of the Vancouver Island marmot (*Marmota vancouverensis*). *Environmental Conservation* 10, 63–66.

Dickman, M. and Dorais, M. (1977) The impact of human trampling on phosphorus loading to a small lake in Gaitineau Park, Quebec, Canada. *Journal of Environmental Management* 5, 335–344.

Eckert, R.D., Jr, Wood, M.K., Blackburn, W.H. and Petersen, F.F. (1979) Impacts of off-road vehicles on infiltration and sediment production of two desert soils. *Journal of Range Management* 32, 294–397.

Ferguson, M.A.D. and Keith, L.B. (1982) Influence of Nordic skiing on distribution of moose and elk in Elk Island National Park, Alberta. *Canadian Field Naturalist* 96, 69–78.

Fitzpatrick, S. and Bouchez, B. (1998) Effects of recreational disturbance on the foraging behaviour of waders on a Rocky Beach. *Bird Study* 45, 157–171.

Giese, M. and Riddle, M. (1999) Disturbance of emperor penguin *Aptenodytes fosteri* chicks by helicopters. *Polar Biology* 22, 366–371.

Goodrich, J.M. and Berger J. (1994) Winter recreation and hibernating black bears *Ursus americanus. Biological Conservation* 67, 105–110.

Gotmark, F. and Ahlund, M. (1984) Do field observers attract nest predators and influence nesting success of common eiders? *Journal of Wildlife Management* 48, 381–387.

Green, K. (2000) Small mammal activity on snow surface. *Victorian Naturalist* 117, 230–234.

Green, R.J. and Higginbottom, K. (2000) The effects of non-consumptive wildlife tourism on free-ranging wildlife: a review. *Pacific Conservation Biology* 6, 183–197.

Higham, J.E.S. (1998) Tourists and albatrosses: the dynamics of tourism at the Northern Royal Albatross Colony, Taiaroa Head, New Zealand. *Tourism Management* 19, 521–531.

Hilton, J. and Phillips, G.L. (1982) The effect of boat activity on turbidity in a shallow Broadland river. *Journal of Applied Ecology* 19, 143–150.

Holmes, N., Giese, M. and Kriwoken, L. (2001) The effects of human activity on two penguin species on Macquarie Island: experimental methodology. In: Buckley, R.C. (ed.) *Abstracts, Nature Tourism and the Environment.* Australian Academy of Science, CRC Tourism and Griffith University, Gold Coast, p. 47.

Irwin, J.A.G., Cahill, D.M. and Drenth, A. (1995) *Phytophthora* in Australia. *Australian Journal of Agricultural Research* 46, 1311–1337.

Iverson, R.M., Hinckley, B.S., Webb, R.M. and Hallet, B. (1981) Physical effects of vehicular disturbances on arid landscapes. *Sciences* 212, 915–917.

Johnson, F. and Pickering, C.P. (2001) Alien plants in the Australian Alps. *Mountain Research and Development* 27, 284–291.

King, J.G. and Mace, A.C.J. (1974) Effect of recreation on water quality. *Journal of Water Pollution Control Federation* 46, 2453–2459.

Knight, R.L. (1984) Responses of wintering bald eagles to boating activity. *Journal of Wildlife Management* 48, 999–1004.

Kuller, Z. (1999) Current status and conservation of marine turtles on the Mediterranean coast of Israel. *Marine Turtle Newsletter* 86, 3–5.

Kunimatsu, T., Sudo, M. and Kawachi, T. (1999) Loading rates of nutrients discharging from a golf course and neighbouring forested basin. *Water Science and Technology* 39, 99–107.

Kutiel, P., Endenandy, E. and Zhevelev, Y. (2000) Effect of experimental trampling and off-road motorcycle traffic on soil and vegetation of stabilized coastal dunes, Israel. *Environmental Conservation* 27, 14–23.

Liddle, M.J. (1997) *Recreation Ecology.* Chapman & Hall, London, 639 pp.

Lonsdale, W.M. and Lane, A.M. (1994). Tourist vehicles as vectors of weed seeds in Kakadu National Park, northern Australia. *Biological Conservation* 69, 277–283.

McArthur, R.A., Geist, V. and Johnston, R.H. (1982a) Physiological correlates of social behaviour in bighorn sheep: a field study using electrocardiogram telemetry. *Journal of Zoological Society London* 196, 401–415.

McArthur, R.A., Geist, V. and Johnston, R.H. (1982b) Cardiac and behavioural responses of mountain sheep to human disturbance. *Journal of Wildlife Management* 46, 351–358.

Mallin, M.A. and Wheeler, T.L. (2000) Nutrient and fecal coliform discharge from coastal North Carolina golf courses. *Journal of Environmental Quality* 29, 515–524.

Manning, R.E. (1999) *Studies in Outdoor Recreation,* 2nd edn. Oregon State University Press, Corvallis.

Milchunas, D.G., Schultz, K.A. and Shaw, R.B. (2000) Plant community structure in relation to long-term disturbance by mechanized military maneuvers in a semiarid region. *Environmental Management* 25, 525–529.

Mosisch, T.D. and Arthington, A.H. (2001) Polycyclic aromatic hydrocarbon residues in the sediments of a dune lake as a result of power boating. *Lakes and Reservoirs: Research and Management* 6, 21–32.

Nedohin, D.N. and Elefsiniotis, P. (1997) The effects of motor boats on water quality in shallow lakes. *Toxicological and Environmental Chemistry* 61, 127–133.

Newsome, D., Moore, S.A. and Dowling, R.K. (2002) *Natural Area Tourism: Ecology, Impacts and Management.* Channel View, Clevedon, UK.

Podger, F.D. and Keane, P.J. (2000) Management of disease in native eucalypt woodlands. In: Keane, P.J., Kile, G.A., Podger, F.D. and Brown, B.N. (eds) *Diseases and Pathogens of Eucalypts.* CSIRO, Melbourne, pp. 455–475.

Rickard, W.E. and Brown, J. (1974) Effects of vehicles on Arctic tundra. *Environmental Conservation* 1, 55–62.

Robert, H.C. and Ralph, C.J. (1975) Effects of human disturbance on the breeding success of gulls. *Condor* 77, 495–499.

Robertson, R.A. and Colletti, J.P. (1994) Off-site impacts of soil erosion on recreation: the case of Lake Red Rock Reservoir in central Iowa. *Journal of Soil and Water Conservation* 49, 576–582.

Scherrer, P. (2001) The legacy of old tracks: a case study from the Kosciuszko alpine zone. In: Buckley, R.C. (ed.) *Abstracts, Nature Tourism and the Environment.* Australian Academy of Science, CRC Tourism and Griffith University, Gold Coast, p. 49.

Shearer, B.L. and Smith, I.W. (2000) Diseases of eucalypts caused by soil borne species of *Phytophthora* and *Pythium.* In: Keane, P.J., Kile, G.A., Podger, F.D. and Brown, B.N. (eds) *Diseases and Pathogens of Eucalypts.* CSIRO, Melbourne, pp. 259–291.

Shepherd, P.C.F. and Boates, J.S. (1999) Effects of a commercial baitworm harvest on semipalmated sandpipers and their prey in the Bay of Fundy Hemispheric Shorebird Reserve. *Conservation Biology* 13, 347–356.

Treweek, J. (1995) Ecological impact assessment. In: Vanclay, F. and Bronstein, D.A. (eds) *Environmental and Social Impact Assessment.* John Wiley & Sons, New York, pp. 171–192.

Turton, S.M. and Goosem, M.W. (2001) Environmental impacts of linear infrastructure and service corridors. In: Buckley, R.C. (ed.) *Abstracts, Nature Tourism and the Environment.* Australian Academy of

Science, CRC Tourism and Griffith University, Gold Coast, p. 28.

Vollmer, A.T., Maza, B.G., Medica, P.A., Turner, F.B. and Bamberg, S.A. (1976) The impact of off-road vehicles on a desert ecosystem. *Environmental Management* 1, 115–129.

Wace, N. (1977) Assessment of dispersal of plant species – the car-borne flora in Canberra. *Proceedings of the Ecological Society of Australia* 10, 167–186.

Wan, H.B., Wong, M.K. and Mok, C.Y. (1996) Pesticides in golf course waters associated with golf course runoff. *Bulletin of Environmental Contamination and Toxicology* 56, 205–209.

Warnken, J. and Buckley, R.C. (1998) Scientific quality of tourism EIA. *Journal of Applied Ecology* 35, 1–8.

Warnken, J. and Buckley, R.C. (2000) Monitoring diffuse impacts: Australian tourist development. *Journal of Environmental Management* 25, 453–461.

Warnken, W. (1996) Threshold detection of ecotourism impacts: microbiological and chemical indicators of recreational effects on water quality in a subtropical rainforest conservation reserve. PhD thesis, Griffith University, Gold Coast.

Webb, R.H., Wilshire, H.G. and Henry, M.A. (1983) Natural recovery of soils and vegetation following human disturbance. In: Webb, R.H. and Wilshire, H.G. (eds) *Environmental Effects of Off-road Vehicles: Impacts and Management in Arid Regions.* Springer, New York, pp. 279–302.

Wilkinson, T. (1995) Snowed under. *National Parks* 69, 32–36.

Wilson, B.A., Aberton, J.A. and Cahill, D.M. (2000) Relationships between site factors and distribution of *Phytophthora cinnamomi* in the Eastern Otway Ranges, Victoria. *Australian Journal of Botany* 48, 247–260.

Wilson, J.P. and Seney, J.P. (1994) Erosional impact of hikers, horses, motorcycles and off-road bicycles on mountain trails in Montana. *Research and Development* 14, 77–88.

Woolcott, T.G. and Woolcott, D.L. (1984) Impact of off-road vehicles on microinvertebrates of a mid-Atlantic beach. *Biological Conservation* 29, 217–240.

Yorks, T.P., West, N.E., Mueller, R.J. and Warren, S.D. (1997) Toleration of traffic by vegetation: life form conclusions and summary extracts from a comprehensive data base. *Environmental Management* 21, 121–131.

11

Small Recreational and Tourist Vessels in Inshore Coastal Areas: a Characterization of Types of Impacts

Jan Warnken and Troy Byrnes
School of Environmental and Applied Sciences, Griffith University, Queensland, Australia

---

Abstract

In most parts of the world, recreational boating activities are confined to sheltered near-shore coastal waters. Increased per capita leisure time and rising disposable incomes have kept growth rates of boat registrations at levels of 4% annually in most developed countries, including Australia. In many areas, this has led to increasing levels of congestion at popular anchor sites and launch facilities and to greater chances of producing significant impacts. This chapter examines two principal types of impacts associated with small recreational and tourist vessels and highlights current management strategies to mitigate adverse effects on the environment. Where possible, technical information and simplified models, rather than quantitative field data, were used to provide some estimates about pollution loads that can be emitted at crowded mooring sites.

Introduction

An increase in human population concentrated in coastal areas and, for most parts of the developed world, increased per capita leisure time as a result of our post-fordic society, together with higher disposable incomes, have resulted in a continuous growth of registrations of recreational boats and other pleasure craft. Over the last two decades, growth-rate estimates have averaged 4% in the USA and Queensland, Australia; 2% in New Zealand and 11% in France in 1999. According to US Coast Guard figures, the 50 states and territo-

ries of the USA alone have 12,740,000 registered boats, generating an estimated US$25 billion in retail expenditures (Beckett, 2001).

The predominant reason for using boats for recreational or tourism purpose is to enjoy parts of the natural environment. This includes anything from wave jumping on personal water crafts (PWCs) (or jet-skis), to whale-watching, fishing and dive trips. By their very nature, however, these pleasure craft cause disturbances to the environments in which they are used. Many of the disturbances produced by a single recreational vessel or pleasure craft are so small or infrequent that they are considered to be negligible or well within the range of natural events. Yet, where boats, particularly larger boats that provide sleeping facilities, aggregate in larger numbers, disturbances accumulate and are likely to cause impacts. Such impacts can arise from almost every aspect of boat use, leading to an equally wide range of impact types. This potential has long been recognized for commercial vessels. Accordingly, international, national and state organizations have responded by promulgating regulatory frameworks, such as the Australian and New Zealand Environment Conservation Council (ANZECC) Maritime Accidents and Pollution Strategy (MARPOL) and, at the state level, the *Transport Operation (Marine Pollution) Act* 1995 (Qld), for example.

Although smaller recreational vessels are often, though not always, included in these frameworks, their contribution to marine pollution and impacts on coastal environments is less well understood. This chapter examines two of the major types of impacts associated with recreational-boat usage and tries to illustrate the variability in the data published so far, in Australia as well as in other parts of the world. Searches for quantitative data published in peer-refereed journals or technical reports focused on antifouling agents and sewage-related impacts.

Antifouling

To date, the most concerning impacts arising from recreational vessels have been associated with the use of antifouling paints. Most hulls of recreational vessels that remain in the water when not in use need to be covered with a layer toxic to marine organisms that colonize submerged hard substrates. The biggest problem with antifouling agents, however, is their toxicity towards non-target organisms. Wherever large numbers of such antifouled hulls are exposed to a confined water body over an extended period of time, they cause significant effects on surrounding biota. Toxic components leach from these antifouling paints and accumulate in surrounding waters and sediments or filter-feeding organisms.

Tributyltin

Tributyltin (TBT) compounds have been the most effective but most toxic agents in these antifouling coatings (Goldberg, 1986). Modern copolymer paints have a high initial leach rate of TBT, which reaches a standard and constant value of approximately 4 μg TBT per cm^2 per day within days. The half-life of TBT in sea water is around 6 h (Batley, 1996); however, it rapidly partitions to suspended sediments or to the surface microlayer. In sediments, half-lives are estimated to range from 3.5 to 15 days (Seligman *et al.*, 1986; Hinga *et al.*, 1987) and, in laboratory experiments, from 330 days to several years for surficial and anaerobic layers, respectively (Dowson *et al.*, 1994). The toxicity of TBT is almost universal, thereby affecting a range of aquatic biota, including fish, macroalgae, molluscs and crustaceans and invertebrate communities of sea-grass beds (Evans *et al.*, 1995; Raffaelli and Hawkins, 1997).

The most pronounced effects of TBT, i.e. causing imposex, have been documented for the Pacific oyster, *Crassostrea gigas*, and the dog-whelk, *Nucella lapillus*, at sites close to marinas in France, Europe, Japan and the USA (Evans *et al.*, 1995; Stur-Lauridsen and Dahl, 1995; Dahl and Blanck, 1996; Ten Hallers-Tjabbes, 1997). Regulatory authorities reacted accordingly and banned the use of TBT-based antifouling paints for all vessels less than 25 m in length, first in France (1982), then in the UK (1987), in the USA (1988) and soon after in Canada, Japan, the European Union and in most states of Australia. Existing TBT deposits in sediments have been estimated to have a half-life of approximately 2.5 years (de Mora *et al.*, 1995). Therefore, TBT-related impacts from recreational vessels, most of which are smaller than 25 m, should phase out over the next decade and are not discussed in further detail.

Copper

Some of the oldest ingredients of metal-based antifouling coatings are lead and, more recently, copper (see discussions in Keen, 1991). Originally applied as metal sheets, copper is nowadays incorporated into ablative matrix or self-polishing copolymer paints that require replacement after 36 months (ablative matrix paints, etc.) or 5–7 years (TBT copolymers) (Nichols, 1988; Keen, 1991; Powell, 1995; Hunter, 1997). Copper-based antifouling paints are now widely used for recreational vessels not permanently moored on hard-stands or trailers, particularly since the ban of TBT. Estimates for actual leach rates of copper from submerged surfaces covered with modern antifouling paints range from 1.1–1.5 µg per cm^2 per day (Foerster *et al.*, 1999) to 18.6–21.6 µg per cm^2 per day (Thomas *et al.*, 2000) and 25–40 µg per cm^2 per day using standard methods adopted by the American Society of Testing Materials (ASTM). Accordingly, release rates of copper from antifouling paints have been set at 40 µg per cm^2 per day (Canada) or are considered to be set at that level (UK, USA, Australia) (see Champ, 2000).

Copper concentrations measured in environments utilized by recreational vessels have ranged from 20 µg per l in British estuarine waters (Matthiessen *et al.*, 1999) and 10–40 µg per l in two small marinas in the USA (Foerster *et al.*, 1999) to 79 mg per kg wet weight in marina sediments on the Gold Coast (AEC, 1988). This compares with 150 µg per l in untreated domestic sewage (Dojlido and Best, 1993) and approximately 1.5–4.5 µg per l of total copper in treated effluent (Donat *et al.*, 1994; Hall and Anderson, 1999). The actual effects of copper, however, are more difficult to determine. In low concentrations, copper ions are taken up by a large number of organisms as micronutrients. Many marine species are also known to develop community-induced tolerance to chronic copper exposure (Gustavson *et al.*, 1999). As a result, values causing acute toxicity in marine organisms vary from as low as 1.2 µg per l for some bivalves (e.g. *Villorita cyprinoides cochi*) to as high as 346,700 µg per l for mud crabs, *Scylla serrata*, which can withstand even these levels, sometimes without signs of any acute toxicity (Hall and Anderson, 1999). Based on a major review of all known copper-related toxic effects, a dissolved-copper acute toxicity 5th percentile value of 5.6 µg per l has been recommended for all marine waters in Europe (Hall and Anderson, 1999). Yet, as indicated earlier, concentrations of dissolved copper in marinas often exceed this threshold value by a factor of two to eight.

Other antifouling compounds

A variety of organic booster compounds have been developed to improve the antifouling capacity of respective coatings and to replace TBT. These include algicides, such as Irgarol 1051, general herbicides, such as Diuron, a major urea herbicide, and broad-spectrum biocides like Kathon 5287. Other biocides include Chlorothalonil, Dichlofluanid, Thiram and Ziram, and Maneb and Zineb (Voulvoulis *et al.*, 1999). The current lack of validated analytical methods, limited monitoring data and very little information about environmental half-lives prevent accurate risk assessments of the impacts associated with the use of these compounds in antifouling paints for recreational vessels.

Sewage

Boats with on-board facilities, such as toilets and kitchen or bathroom sinks, produce sewage and greywater. Apart from a few plastic items occasionally flushed down toilets (for example, plastic wrappings of sanitary items), all constituents of boat raw sewage are readily biodegradable. The major constituents of concern in untreated or raw sewage from use of toilets and sinks are nitrogen (N), phosphorus (P), faecal bacteria, protozoa and viruses – all at levels that can be several orders of magnitude higher than those of ocean and estuarine waters (e.g. Koot, 1974). They have no direct toxic effect and short half-lives in most environments. Despite attempts to regulate the release of such boat-sourced sewage in some areas, most sewage from boats is still released with little or no prior treatment (e.g. no enforcement of sewage provisions under the *Transport Operation (Marine Pollution)* Act 1995 (Qld)). Given the range of chemical and biological agents emitted with raw sewage, sewage released from boats has the potential to affect not only environmental health but human health as well.

Pathogens and Indicator Bacteria

Under normal circumstances, human recreational activities in coastal environments include no more than a few hours of direct contact with coastal waters. Such limited periods are usually too short to result in acute effects from exposure to toxins such as heavy metals or other organic compounds. In theory, though, a single pathogen ingested accidentally can trigger a major infection, and it is well known that many human diseases of the gastrointestinal tract are transmitted through water contaminated by faecal material.

Although there has been general agreement for some time that boats contribute to faecal contamination of water (Faust, 1982), demonstrating the exact magnitude and effect of such contamination proved to be less straightforward. The presence and extent of faecal pollution, as determined by indicator bacteria, have become an important factor in assessing the quality of a body of water and the best correlations between high boat numbers and increased concentrations of faecal coliform bacteria have been obtained for areas with low hydrological flushing during periods of peak usage (Fisher *et al.*, 1987; Gaines and Solow, 1990; Milliken and Lee, 1990). However, actual concentrations of indicator organisms have varied greatly due to differences in sampling protocols, methodology for detecting bacteria, background levels from terrestrial sources and seasonal variations. Earlier studies by Faust (1982) found that effects of boating were barely perceptible during summer in Chesapeake Bay, USA. Recent studies in the Broadwater area of the city of Gold Coast, Queensland, in central eastern Australia, have also suggested that tidal flushing, rain events and other terrestrial activities can mask the effect of boats on indicator signatures (Pratt, 2000).

Nutrients

In regard to impacts on the natural coastal environment, faecal bacteria and many other human pathogens seem to have little effect on local marine communities. Nutrients such as P and N are readily taken up by many marine organisms. Therefore, only larger quantities of sewage emitted continuously or over prolonged periods are likely to cause shifts in and consequently impacts on marine plant and animal communities. Sewage-related impacts from boating activities are therefore expected to be cumulative, i.e. in conjunction with land-based activities or in areas where boat-sourced nutrients are not readily dispersed. In other terms, the release of boat wastes is considered a problem primarily in enclosed inland waters and semi-enclosed coastal waters where flushing is minimal.

For coastal waters, excess N is believed to be the main factor that can cause significant changes to communities depending on low nutrient levels (Day *et al.*, 1989). Typical examples of these types of communities are coral reefs and sea-grass beds (Udy, 1997; Udy and Dennison, 1999), both of which are present in many protected areas along Australia's coastline. In the extreme, sea-grass beds can be replaced by algal assemblages (Walker *et al.*, 1999); therefore, levels of exogenous N introduced by large numbers of boats are of concern. At present, however, there are few data quantifying the overall amount of N and P released as a result of recreational boating activities, and no peer-reviewed publication in a scientific journal could be found that clearly demonstrated an effect of boat-sourced nutrients on local marine communities.

Estimating Impacts

In most developed nations, recreational boating activities are controlled by a complex set of regulations under nature conservation, pollution control and maritime safety legislation. As a result, most areas subject to high use intensities are nowadays covered by regional conservation and/or waterways management plans. In Australia, for example, such plans apply in Sydney Harbour, Moreton Bay, Port Phillip Bay and the Whitsunday Islands. These plans assign a type of zone with a defined set of management measures to a specific location based on local environmental settings and an assumed type and level of boating activities. Most of these zones have been assigned on the basis of broad-scale physical and environmental characteristics, rather than on the basis of quantitative data of actual use intensities or magnitudes of impact. In the light of increasing complexities of types and intensities of boat usage in coastal areas (e.g. emergence of PWCs and kite surfing), management measures for local sites need to be based on more realistic risk assessments or estimates of likely impacts.

Impacts associated with recreational vessels can be classified as: (i) continuous or regular; (ii) intermittent; or (iii) one-off and related to catastrophic events or accidents. Most category (i) and (iii) impacts are either confined to small local areas, such as antifouling agents released from vessels in busy marinas, or they are rare, such as major accidents resulting in larger oil or fuel spills (Warnken and Byrnes, 2000). Most other boating impacts originate from category (ii)-type disturbances. Typically these occur at anchor sites and include emissions of raw sewage and disturbance of bottom substrates by anchors.

Estimating pollutant loads from type (i) impacts is relatively straightforward. Daily inputs of antifouling agents into a marina can be calculated from occupancy figures for mooring sites, some algorithm that allows estimation of the submerged hull area (SHA) for a vessel based on its overall length and beam, and data for standard leaching rates of relevant compounds from antifouling paints. SHA can be approximated by treating the hull as a triangular prism with the beam equal to one-third of the length overall (LOA) and the draught equal to 0.3 x beam, less an adjustment of one-third of total calculated value to allow for the narrower areas around the bow and stern. This gives SHA = 0.26 $(LOA)^2$. Copper emission rates vary from 11 to 170 mg Cu^{2+} per m^2 per day (Foerster *et al.*, 1999; USEPA and Command NSS, 1999). Hence a typical 150–berth marina occupied to 80% by vessels with an assumed average LOA of 10 m would result in emissions between 34 kg and ~0.5 t of copper per day.

Predicting concentrations of boat-sourced pollutants in a marina requires additional information about volume, flushing rates and flow patterns of the marina basin. Small-scale spatial variations in concentrations of pollu-

tants require more extensive hydrological modelling (Heape, 1998). In theory, most of this information should be readily available for marinas approved subject to environmental-impact assessment (EIA). In practice, however, data in EIA documents are rarely detailed enough for hydrological modelling.

On the other hand, predicting type (iii) impacts originating from marine accidents is only possible at a very large scale and only with large error margins. Not all marine incidents are reported in searchable electronic format (Warnken and Byrnes, 2000). Indeed, many smaller incidents, particularly those that do not require assistance from coastguard or marine rescue vessels, are unlikely to be reported to the relevant authorities. Another limitation is the common lack of knowledge about the number of boat trips that affect a particular area over a year. Risk assessment is only possible where long-term accident data can be compared against growth rates of boat traffic in the area of interest.

The magnitude of typical category (ii) impacts generated by recreational boats depends largely on the number of boats in use and the number of people on board. Both frequencies of boat usage and the number of people on boats fluctuate depending on seasons and weather conditions. Boating activity in near-shore areas is highest during holidays or long weekends at times of calm and sunny weather, whereas stormy or rainy weather during midweek reduces usage of recreational boats to almost zero. As a result, type (ii) impacts are not only a function of boat size, boat numbers, people on board (sewage only) and area or volume of water affected, but also a function of local flushing rates, pollution inputs from terrestrial sources and the time between major boat-use events, i.e. time for recovery from disturbances. A conservative estimation of the number of faecal coliform (FCF) bacteria per day that can be emitted from an average-sized vessel with on-board facilities would equate to 11.38–22.75 × 10^8 FCF bacteria per day, assuming 2.5 people on board and an output of toilet wastes containing 4.55–9.1 × 10^8 FCF bacteria per person per day (Koot, 1974).

Based on these estimates, it requires 730–1520 m^3, or about twice the volume of a

25 m pool, to disperse these loads to levels of 150 FCF bacteria per 100 ml, as recommended for primary recreational contact by the Australian National Health and Medical Research Council (NHMRC).

Advances in Monitoring Impacts of Recreational Boats

In the past, most sampling programmes that tried to quantify concentrations of pollutants or sewage indicators had to rely on spot checks, i.e. a single or duplicated water sample collected in the field, which had to be transported into the laboratory for analysis. This methodology could only provide information about short time intervals, e.g. an hour or less. Extrapolation of overall loads, therefore, required longer-term monitoring to incorporate variations such as daily fluctuations in boat numbers, flow rates, tides, weather, etc. This involved more sophisticated sampling programmes with sufficient statistical power, i.e. frequent replication over time and space (see discussions in Warnken and Buckley, 2000), which in turn greatly increased the costs for such exercises.

To monitor pollution from antifouling agents and similar sources, one new approach involves the deployment of small diffusive gradients in thin film (DGT) probes (Zhang and Davidson, 1995; Denney *et al.*, 1999; Davidson *et al.*, 2000). This technology is based on two thin films. The outer one, the hydrogel, acts as a diffusion barrier with a distinct diffusion coefficient that is similar to that of an aqueous solution. The inner one, the binding gel, provides binding sites for the analyte of interest. Using Fick's law of diffusion, the exact length of time for deployment, the area of the hydrogel exposed to the water body of interest and the mass of the analyte bound to the binding gel allows calculation of a value for the concentration of the analyte integrated over the time that the probe was deployed. This technique is particularly useful for labile ionic analytes, such as Cu^+ and Cu^{2+} ions (Alfaro-De la Torre *et al.*, 2000), the principal biocide in many antifouling paints. DGT probes can be deployed for several days or even up to 2 weeks. The other advantage of DGT is that it pre-concentrates the analyte of interest and removes interference from high levels of sodium and chloride ions in estuarine and sea waters. This methodology is currently being tested at several sites in central eastern Australia.

In monitoring pollution from human sewage, one of the principal problems of standard bacteriological indicators is the lack of source specificity. Commonly used indicator organisms, such as FCF bacteria and *Escherichia coli*, can be found in faeces of warm-blooded animals, including pets and livestock, and also in marine sediments. Surface-water runoff and disturbance of sediments can also lead to increased concentrations of indicator organisms. This can mask the effect of boats or it can lead to overestimates of boating impacts where monitoring sites receive inputs of indicator organisms that are unrelated to boating. Alternatively, changes in water temperature and other environmental parameters can affect survival of coliform bacteria (Rhodes and Kator, 1988), which can cause a more rapid reduction in bacteria numbers, thereby leaving the impression that boats do not emit sewage quantities of concern.

Analysing the sterol fraction of organic compounds contained in sediments and the water column has been shown to provide a novel way for distinguishing between sources of faecal contamination (Green *et al.*, 1992; Chalaux *et al.*, 1995). The distribution of sterols found in faeces is caused by a combination of diet, an animal's ability to synthesize its own sterols and the intestinal microbiota in the digestive tract. In this aspect humans are no different. The principal human faecal sterol is coprostanol (5β(*H*)-cholestan-3β-ol), which is excreted in only trace amounts by birds and dogs, for example, and is not present in many herbivores, birds or fish (Leeming *et al.*, 1996). By analysing the sterol signature or fingerprint in a water or sediment sample, it is therefore possible to determine the contribution of faecal matter from different sources. In this way, sterol signatures are a lot less ambiguous than bacterial indicators, such as *E. coli*. Determining the sterol fingerprints of sediment and water samples has been used with great success to trace faecal contamination from sewage-treatment works for up to 20 km off the coast near Sydney (Nichols *et al.*, 1996). Similarly, small traces of faecal contamination have been detected along beaches in Antarctica about 150 m away from a treatment plant outlet that served a research station occupied by around 30 persons for most of the year (Green *et al.*, 1992).

The other advantage is that sterols are bio-organic compounds that can be assimilated by many organisms naturally occurring in the affected environments. Very low concentrations of coprostanol in the sediments several weeks after periods of high boating intensities would indicate that at least some of the components of faecal contamination are assimilated within carrying capacities of the natural environments. This technology is also being tested currently on the eastern Australian seaboard.

Management and the Need for More Accurate Data

Probably the most compelling argument for more accurate data about boating impacts stems from the difficulties with policing boating regulations. These difficulties are largely the result of the high costs involved in patrolling marine areas, the diverse range of pollution sources associated with boats and the 'out-of-sight out-of-mind' problem with many polluting substances. In practice, therefore, the role of legislative regulation is limited in regard to preventing impacts in the marine environment (Davis *et al.*, 1997). Another impediment to controlling pollution associated with small vessels is the unwavering opinion among several players in the Australian boating community that recreational and tourist activities cause negligible or no impacts (see comments in Byrnes and Warnken, Chapter 12, this book). In the past, sampling technology and the sampling design of many studies have not been able to demonstrate the overall contribution of small vessels to pollution in coastal environments. Without scientifically reliable demonstration of impacts and their relation to boating activities, there is little chance to educate the boating community and to effectively supplement legislative

regulations with alternative measures based on moral suasion and, consequently, industry or community self-regulation.

References

Alfaro-De la Torre, M.C., Yves Beaulieu, P. and Tessier, A. (2000) *In situ* measurements of trace metals in lakewater using the dialysis and DGT techniques. *Analytica Chimica Acta* 418, 53–68.

Australian Environment Council (AEC) (1988) *Impact of Marinas on Water Quality.* Australian Environment Council Report No. 24, Australian Government Publishing Service, Canberra.

Batley, G.E. (1996) Heavy metals and tributyltin in Australian coastal and estuarine waters. In: Zann, L.P. and Sutton, D.C. (eds) *State of the Marine Environment Report for Australia – Technical Annex 2: Pollution.* Ocean Rescue 2000 Program, Great Barrier Reef Marine Park Authority for the Department of Environment, Sport and Territories, Townsville, pp. 63–72.

Beckett, G. (2001) *US Market Overview.* National Marine Manufacturers Association, http://www.nmma-intl.org/bestofusa/bestofusa_overview.htm Last viewed 28 August 2001.

Chalaux, N., Takada, H. and Bayona, J. (1995) Molecular markers in Tokyo Bay sediments: sources and distribution. *Marine and Environmental Research* 40, 77–92.

Champ, M. (2000) A review of organotin regulatory strategies, pending actions, related costs and benefits. *Science of the Total Environment* 258(1–2), 21–71.

Dahl, B. and Blanck, H. (1996) Toxic effects of the antifouling agent irgarol 1051 on periphyton communities in coastal water microcosms. *Marine Pollution Bulletin* 32, 342.

Davidson, W., Fones, G., Harper, M., Teadsale, P. and Zhang, H. (2000) Dialysis, DET and DGT: *in situ* diffusional techniques for studying water, sediments and soils. In: Buffle, J. and Horvai, G. (eds) In situ *Monitoring of Aquatic Systems: Chemical Analysis and Speciation.* John Wiley & Sons, Chichester, pp. 496–569.

Davis, D., Banks, S., Birtles, A., Valentine, P. and Cuthill, M. (1997) Whale sharks in Ningaloo Marine Park: managing tourism in an Australian marine protected area. *Tourism Management* 18, 259–271.

Day, J.W., Hall, C.A., Kemp, W.M. and Yànez-Arancibia, M. (1989) *Estuarine Ecology.* John Wiley & Sons, New York, 576 pp.

de Mora, S.J., Stewart, C. and Phillips, D. (1995) Sources and rate of degradation of tri(*n*-butyl)tin in marine sediments near Auckland, New Zealand. *Marine Pollution Bulletin* 30(1), 50–57.

Denney, S., Sherwood, J. and Leyden, J. (1999) *in situ* measurements of labile Cu, Cd and Mn in river waters using DGT. In: *Science of the Total Environment*. Elsevier Science, Amsterdam, Netherlands, 239(1–3), 71–80.

Dojlido, J. and Best, G. (1993) Chemistry of water and water pollution. In: Winkler, M. (ed.) *Water and Wastewater Technology*. Ellis Horwood, Sydney, pp. 59–201.

Donat, J., Lao, K. and Bruland, K. (1994) Speciation of dissolved copper and nickel in south San Francisco Bay: a multi-method approach. *Analytica Chimica Acta* 284, 547–571.

Dowson, P., Bubb, J., Williams, T. and Lester, J. (1994) Degradation of tributyltin in freshwater and estuarine marine sediments. *Water Science Technology* 39, 483.

Evans, S.M., Leksono, T. and McKinnell, P.D. (1995) Tributyltin pollution: a diminishing problem following legislation limiting the use of TBT-based antifouling paints. *Marine Pollution Bulletin* 30(1), 14–21.

Faust, M.A. (1982) Contribution of pleasure boats to faecal bacteria concentrations in the Rhode River Estuary, Maryland, USA. *Science of the Total Environment* 25, 255–262.

Fisher, J.S., Perdue, R.R., Overton, M.F., Sobsey, M.D. and Sill, B.L. (1987) *Comparison of Water Quality at Two Recreational Marinas during Peak-use Periods*. Sea Grant Program, University of North Carolina, Raleigh, North Carolina.

Foerster, J., Lamontagne, R., Ewing, K. and Ervin, A. (1999) Copper circulation in two tidally influenced marinas studied with the use of a Nafion polymer probe. *Field Analytical Chemistry and Technology* 3(1), 3–18.

Gaines, A.G. and Solow, A.R. (1990) *The Distribution of Faecal Coliform Bacteria in Surface Waters of Edgartown Harbour Complex and Management Implications*. Woods Hole Oceanographic Institute, Woods Hole, Massachusetts.

Goldberg, E.D. (1986) TBT: an environmental dilemma. *Environment* 28, 17–44.

Green, G., Skerrat, J.H., Leeming, R. and Nichols, P.D. (1992) Hydrocarbon and coprostanol levels in seawater, sea-ice algae and sediments near Davies Station in eastern Antarctica: a regional survey and preliminary results for a field fuel spill experiment. *Marine Pollution Bulletin* 25, 293–302.

Gustavson, K., Peterson, S., Pedersen, B. and Stuer-Lauridsen, F. (1999) Pollution-induced community tolerance (PICT) in coastal phytoplankton communities exposure to copper. *Hydrobiologia* 416, 125–138.

Hall, L. and Anderson, R. (1999) A deterministic ecological risk assessment for copper in European saltwater environments. *Marine Pollution Bulletin* 38, 207–218.

Heape, D.A. (1998) Environmental problems in marinas. Masters thesis, University of Queensland, Brisbane, Australia.

Hinga, K.R., Adelman, D. and Pilson, M.E.Q. (1987) Radiolabeled butyltin studies in the MERL enclosed ecosystem. In: *Oceans '87, Proceedings of the International Organotin Symposium*, Vol. 4. Marine Technological Society, Washington, DC, pp. 1416–1419

Hunter, J. (1997) Antifouling coatings and the global environment debate. *Protective Coatings Europe* 2, 16.

Keen, R. (1991) Anti-foulings and the marine environment: past, present and a look to the future. *Marine Technology* 5, 19.

Koot, A.J.C. (1974) Van consument tot producent. *H₂O.* 7, 303–310.

Leeming, R., Ball, A., Ashbolt, N. and Nichols, P. (1996) Using faecal sterols from humans and animals to distinguish pollution in receiving waters. *Water Research* 30, 2893–2900.

Matthiessen, P., Reed, J. and Johnson, M. (1999) Sources and potential effects of copper and zinc concentrations in the estuarine waters of Essex and Suffolk, UK. *Marine Pollution Bulletin* 38, 908–920.

Milliken, A.S. and Lee, V. (1990) *Pollution Impacts from Recreational Boating: a Bibliography and Summary Review*. Rhode Island Sea Grant Publications, University of Rhode Island Bay Campus, Narrangansset, Rhode Island.

Nichols, J. (1988) Antifouling paints: use on boats in San Diego Bay and a way to minimize adverse impacts. *Journal of Environmental Management* 12, 243.

Nichols, P.D., Leeming, R., Latham, V. and Rayner, M. (1996) Detection of sewage pollution, including sources of, in inland and coastal Australian waters and sediments. In: *American Chemical Society National Meeting*, Vol. 36. Division of Environmental Chemistry, American Chemical Society, Orlando, Florida, pp. 175–79.

Powell, C. (1995) Copper–nickel sheathing and its use for ship hulls and offshore structures. *International Biodeterioration and Biodegradation* 34, 321.

Pratt, A. (2000) Quantitative determination of faecal

indicator bacteria in the Broadwater estuary and the effect of boating usage. Honours thesis, Griffith University, Gold Coast, Australia.

Raffaelli, D. and Hawkins, S. (1997) *Intertidal Ecology*. Chapman & Hall, Melbourne.

Rhodes, M.W. and Kator, H. (1988) Survival of *Escherichia coli* in estuarine environments. *Applied Environmental Microbiology* 54, 2902–2907.

Seligman, P.F., Valkirs, A.O. and Lee, R.F. (1986) Degradation of tributyltin in marine and estuarine waters. In: *Oceans '86, Proceedings of the International Organotin Symposium*, Vol. 4. Marine Technological Society, Washington, DC, pp. 1189–1195.

Stur-Lauridsen, F. and Dahl, B. (1995) Source of organotin at a marina water/sediment interface – a field study. *Chemosphere* 30, 831–845.

Ten Hallers-Tjabbes, C. (1997) Tributyltin and policies for antifouling. *Environmental Technology* 18, 1265.

Thomas, K., Blake, S. and Waldock, M. (2000) Antifouling paint booster biocide contamination in UK marine sediments. *Marine Pollution Bulletin* 40, 739–745.

Udy, J.W. (1997) Seagrass and sediment nutrient: growth and physiological responses of seagrass to elevated nutrients in Australia. PhD thesis, University of Queensland, Australia.

Udy, J.W. and Dennison, W.C. (1999) Growth and physiological responses of three seagrass species to elevated sediment nutrients in Moreton Bay, Australia. *Journal of Experimental Marine Biology and Ecology* 217, 253–257.

USEPA and Command NSS (1999) *Technical Development Report: Uniform Discharge Standards (UNDS) for Vessels of the Armed Forces*. US Department of the Navy and US Environmental Protection Agency, Washington, DC.

Voulvoulis, N., Scrimshaw, M.D. and Lester, J.N. (1999) Alternative antifouling biocides. *Applied Organometallic Chemistry* 13, 135–143.

Walker, D., Dennison, W. and Edgar, G. (1999) Status of Australian seagrass research and knowledge. In: Butler, A. and Jernakoff, P. (eds) *Seagrass in Australia*. CSIRO Publishing, Collingswood, Australia, pp. 1–24.

Warnken, J. and Buckley, R.C. (2000) Monitoring diffuse impacts: Australian tourism developments. *Environmental Management* 25, 453–461.

Warnken, J. and Byrnes, T.A. (2000) *Ship-sourced Pollution in the Brisbane River and Moreton Bay – Final Report*. South-east Queensland Regional Water Quality Management Strategy, Brisbane City Council, Brisbane.

Zhang, H. and Davidson, W. (1995) Performance characteristics of diffusion gradients in thin films for the *in situ* measurement of trace metals in aqueous solution. *Analytical Chemistry* 67, 3391.

12

Establishing Best-practice Environmental Management: Lessons from the Australian Tour-boat Industry

Troy Byrnes and Jan Warnken
School of Environmental and Applied Sciences, Griffith University, Queensland, Australia

---

Abstract

The environmental impacts of tour-boat operations are generally difficult to control through existing legislation and regulation alone. Policing the relevant provisions at a large scale usually becomes too costly to justify their expense in relation to their likely magnitude of impact. As an alternative to legislation and regulations imposed by government and management authorities, industry self-regulation has been promoted in Australia to minimize tour-boat-related impacts. The initial aims of this study were: (i) to assess the current level of use of formal, non-legislative environmental-management guidelines by Australian tour-boat operators (thereby allowing the identification of best practice in environmental-management measures); (ii) to try to establish what factors influence the level of compliance of tour-boat operators to formal, non-legislative environmental-management guidelines; and (iii) to gain an insight into the effect of the Australian tour-boat industry on the environment.

The methodology used was: (i) survey questionnaires administered during face-to-face personal interviews; and (ii) individual *in situ* boat audits carried out incognito. However, after almost 120 days in the field, nearly 1000 phone calls and investing considerable funds to become available to the operators, only 47 interviews and 32 individual boat audits were completed.

The problem pivotal to the study was the tour-boat operators. Most were generally very unwilling to cooperate in the survey for many reasons, including: survey fatigue; being too busy during the survey period; and a belief that they should not be answering the questionnaire – mostly because they could not see themselves as part of the tourism industry. Even when the operators did agree to participate in the survey, the majority were somewhat defensive and hostile.

Given this type of response, it would seem unlikely that industry self-regulation as it is currently implemented and promoted will be effective for the larger tour-boat operator industry sector. Inefficient or poor investment is seen as one of the major impediments to the successful implementation and adoption of industry self-regulation measures and hence the adoption of best-practice measures for environmental management.

Introduction

Besides a number of outstanding historical sites and areas with unique natural-heritage values, possibly the most sought-after mass-tourism destinations are located within the coastal zone. During the early days of mass tourism, the four Ss (sun, sand, surf and sex) were enough to make many tourism destinations competitive. As a result of increasing competition between destinations at the international and national levels, modern tourists generally expect a more diverse array of opportunities to satisfy their expectations. The coastal waters of various global destinations offer many potential activities to satisfy this demand, e.g. fishing, snorkelling, sailing, diving, cruising, boating, parasailing, etc. Most of the sites used for these activities are only accessible by boat (or some other form of marine transport, e.g. personnel water craft) and, as a result, the number of private and commercial vessels used for tourism and recreational purposes has increased in most parts of the world (see Warnken and Byrnes, Chapter 11, this book). However, with the number of sites or attractions around a seaside destination being limited, the increased demand for marine tours will inevitably lead to greater pressure on these often rare and fragile marine habitats.

In Australia, the natural environment forms a major attraction for overseas and domestic visitors, possibly to a greater degree than in other countries, due to a perceived lack in outstanding historic sites. The tourist industry dependent on these areas is economically significant for Australia. Marine-based tourism is a rapidly growing industry along its coastline and will assume even greater importance internationally as the quality of marine environments elsewhere in the world deteriorate (Zann, 1995).

Consequently, the demand to experience marine wildlife in its natural environment is growing rapidly, particularly in the case of marine animals such as dolphins and whales (Davis et al., 1997). For example, over 600,000 people participate in whale- and dolphin-watching activities in Australia each year, while approximately 100,000 visitors per annum interact with wild dolphins at Monkey

Mia in Western Australia (WA), and this trend is likely to increase (Davis et al., 1997). The only official figures for aquatic charter operators were published for WA and showed an increase of 337% over 7 years. 'A continued expansion at this rate would see approximately 1500 aquatic charter operators by the end of 2010. This rate of expansion is certainly not in decline, and may even be on the increase in some regions of WA' (TOFWGWA, 1998).

Tourism industries place a greater reliance on the use of natural resources than most other service industries, which can lead to these very resources becoming overused and degraded in the process (Butler, 1991; Garrod and Fyall, 1998). The increasing levels of pollution and habitat disturbance resulting from human activities, both commercial and recreational, experienced within the coastal zone over the last 20–30 years has led to major concerns over the environmental status of coastal and marine environments (RAC, 1993). These problems are not restricted to Australia alone. For example, in Canada, human-induced stresses, such as pollution, habitat degradation and resource depletion, continue to compromise the productivity and sustainability of coastal communities, resulting in the loss of potential income and ecological integrity (Ellsworth et al., 1997).

Boat operations have the potential to cause environmental impacts, including both the release of chemical pollutants and physical habitat disturbances (Chmura and Ross, 1978; San Francisco Estuary Project, 1995; Smith, 1995; Zann, 1995; Driml, 1996; Turner et al., 1997; Blanck and Dahl, 1998; Guillon-Cottard et al., 1998; Lambert and Lambert, 1998; Velander and Mocogni, 1998; Creed and Filho, 1999; Glasby, 1999; Scarlett et al., 1999a,b; Smethurst and Nietschmann, 1999). Furthermore, the marine and coastal areas used for boating operations are often ecologically sensitive areas that are inherently susceptible to pollution (Zann, 1995). There is growing concern that the cumulative effect of the increases in number and concentration of boats in coastal waters may have a significant impact on the marine environment. However, there is a lack of extensive information on all of the inputs resulting from human activities into the natural environment (Jacoby et al.,

1997), especially (in a quantitative sense) tour-boat operations in Australia.

Until the 1970s, international law regarding oceans had paid scant regard to marine pollution. However, it is now widely acknowledged that the ability of the ocean to absorb wastes is not infinite and that the freedom to allow the unrestricted introduction of pollutants into the sea can no longer be allowed (e.g. the Marine Accidents and Pollution Strategy (MARPOL), 1973–1978; Stephenson, 1992). Theoretically, there are three principal instruments that can be used to control shipping and, similarly, marine tour-operation impacts: (i) direct regulations (commonly referred to as command and control mechanisms, e.g. legislation and policy); (ii) economic instruments or price incentives, e.g. insurance premiums; and (iii) moral suasion, such as self-regulation (Common, 1996).

The use of command and control procedures (i.e. legislation and policy) will only work effectively in situations where relevant regulatory authorities are able to enforce these regulations through adequate policing. Difficulties arise in the regulation of boating operations in marine environments because of the vast area involved, the diverse range of pollution sources which may have an impact upon it and the problems associated with environmental monitoring in such an environment (Warnken and Buckley, 2000). Many pollutants are not readily observable: some sink and become part of the 'out-of-sight out-of-mind' problem, while others rapidly diffuse and become widely distributed due to the diluting capacity and currents of the ocean. Thus, in practical terms, the role of legislative regulation alone is extremely limited in the marine environment (e.g. Davis *et al.*, 1997).

An excellent example that illustrates the difficulties involved with policing legislation and regulations in the marine environment is provided by Australia's Great Barrier Reef Marine Park (GBRMP). This covers an area of approximately 350,000 km^2 and is policed by approximately 74 compliance boats (Bob Nankivell, Compliance Manager, GBRMP Authority, 19 June 2001, personal communication). This translates into about 4730 km^2 per boat, which would be equivalent to having only one police car monitoring the whole of the largest city in Queensland, the greater Brisbane area (4650 km^2), with an estimated population of over 3 million people.

Moral-suasion measures, such as self-regulation, are frequently promoted as an addition to institutional regulation by government authorities (Christensen and Handberg, 1996; Davis *et al.*, 1997; Ellsworth *et al.*, 1997; Jacoby *et al.*, 1997). Self-regulation is necessary for industry sectors not adequately covered by legislation, which are therefore ultimately responsible for regulating their own impact on the environment. Since the marine environment is the major asset of boat operators, self-regulation is clearly in their best interest. This is true not only for Australia, but for many other places around the world, wherever significant marine-tourism industries exist.

Formal adoption of environmental-management guidelines are a form of industry self-regulation. They represent a set of technical/operational guidelines that outline the most effective ways of avoiding or mitigating adverse effects of human activities on the natural environment. For the various sectors of the boating community these guidelines could be introduced through one or several industry associations, which could then adopt the guidelines and encourage their members to implement them. Marine tourism is probably the largest sector of the recreational boating industry and could serve as an ideal example of self-regulation through the adoption of such guidelines.

If authorities and industry bodies are to increasingly rely on the use of formal environmental-management guidelines as a workable supplement to legislative regulations, then there is a need for continuous monitoring to assess: (i) the level to which these guidelines are used; (ii) the factors that influence boat operators' decisions to adopt or alternatively to reject the practices outlined in such guidelines; and (iii) the extent to which they can actually reduce the adverse environmental effects of boat operations. Obviously, determining this question for all boat operators throughout Australia would prove to be an extremely difficult and time-consuming study. Therefore, this research examines a subsector of boat operators, i.e. commercial tour-boat operators at specific tourism 'hot spots' around Australia and their attitude towards and compliance with environmental best-practice standards. Commercial tour-boat operators were chosen as they use boats on a regular basis and thus should have a sound knowledge of the issues involved, their activities are usually concentrated in certain areas and they often conduct their tours in marine protected areas (where environmental impacts should be avoided altogether). However, it must be understood that the adverse effects of commercial tour-boat operations on the natural environment are not entirely unique to this sector of boat user. Therefore, it is hoped that results from this study will be used as a basis for boat users in general.

Aims

There were three major aims to this study. The first was to portray the current attitudes of tour-boat operators towards industry best

practice and environmental-management measures. The second was to assess the current level of adherence of Australian tour-boat operators to formal non-legislative environmental-management guidelines or, in cases where these were not implemented or available, best practice. The final aim of this study was to ascertain what factors influence the level of compliance of tour-boat operators to such guidelines.

Study Sites

The sites chosen for this study represent a selection of the major areas for marine tour-boat operations around the Australian coast. These were: Cairns; Whitsundays; Moreton Bay; Gold Coast; Melbourne; Broome; and Exmouth (Fig. 12.1). These areas represent two major tourism 'hot spots' (Cairns, Whitsundays), two isolated tourism 'hot spots' (Broome, Exmouth), a major coastal capital city (Melbourne), and the Gold Coast/Moreton

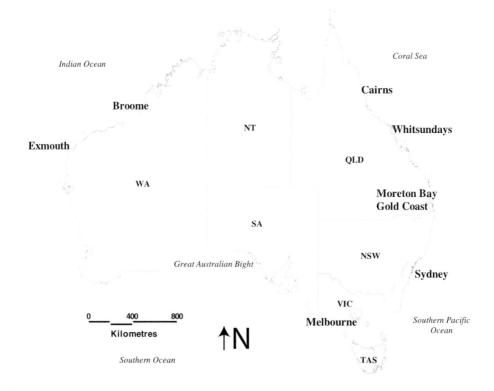

Fig. 12.1. Relative locations of study sites within Australia.

Bay area, Australia's second largest coastal tourism destination.

Methods

Information for this research was obtained using survey questionnaires administered during face-to-face personal interviews and incognito *in situ* field audits of individual tour-boat operators' environmental performance. Following consultation with experts in the field of social science/anthropology, it was decided that survey questionnaires would be administered during face-to-face personal interviews, rather than telephone or mail-out surveys, in an attempt to increase the survey response rate and the reliability of information obtained.

Due to the technical nature of many of the questions, respondents needed to have a sound understanding of the characteristics and the routine on-board procedures and practices of the vessel. This usually meant either the skipper of the vessel or a company director or manager who had a close association with the maintenance and operation of the vessel. Therefore, operators were phoned prior to the interview to arrange an appropriate time and place to meet the relevant personnel.

Preceding the completion of personal interviews at each of the study sites, randomly selected operators were assessed *in situ*. This involved the compilation of a check-list based on practices that could be physically observed during a boat trip. These included actions and measures related to waste disposal, sanitary arrangements, launching and operation of the boat and anchorage practices. Any other general observations regarding environmental impacts and management were also recorded. These inspections were done incognito so that the boat operators' typical practices could be observed and to ensure that no bias arose from the knowledge of their environmental-performance assessment.

Field trips to study sites were arranged to coincide with times relatively close to periods of peak tour-boat activity. This approach was chosen for four major reasons: (i) to ensure that most, if not all, operators would be present during the survey period at each of the study sites and thus allow the best chance of completing the highest number of survey questionnaires possible; (ii) to ensure that most boats would be operating on a regular basis and thus allow the best chance of any randomly chosen operator being available for an *in situ* field audit; (iii) to ensure that boats carried a large number of tourists, allowing field staff to remain anonymous and inconspicuous during *in situ* audits; and (iv) to avoid periods of maximum tour-boat activity and thus avoid potential conflict with extremely busy operators.

Results and Discussion

After spending almost 120 days in the field, making over 1000 phone calls and investing a considerable amount of funds to become available to tour-boat operators, a total of only 47 face-to-face survey questionnaires and 32 *in situ* field audits were completed. Such poor participation during personal interviews (i.e. only 47 face-to-face survey questionnaires completed from a randomly selected sample of 450 operators, approximately 30% of all operators considered active during the survey period) highlights one of the major difficulties in obtaining information from Australian tour-boat operators. Conversely, the number of completed environmental audits was limited by time and financial constraints, leaving too many different categories with insufficient replicates, thereby preventing in-depth statistical analysis. Consequently, results were based on qualitative observations rather than extensive analysis of quantitative data.

The apparent reluctance in collaboration was surprising in light of the fact that research into industry best practice and efficient environmental-management measures would be in the interest of the tour-boat operators themselves. The following is a preliminary review of both the results available and the notes taken before and after interviews and immediately following *in situ* audits. Characteristic statements or comments, together with some preliminary quantitative analyses, are provided to emphasize the general attitudes of the operators interviewed.

Observations during Interview Arrangements

The first major obstacle was to try to arrange a time and place to conduct interviews with the various operators randomly selected from each study area. Many different approaches were attempted to establish a first contact with the operator, each being met with equal lack of interest. For example, a small trial revealed that only one in 17 operators returned calls from messages left on answering machines. This was quite the opposite for arranging incognito *in situ* trips on boats to carry out environmental audits. Where required, several return phone calls were received until trip details were finalized.

Even where operators could be contacted directly, the next hurdle was to maintain their attention once they learnt the topic of the interview, i.e. environmental matters and industry self-regulation. More often than not they became elusive, defensive and occasionally hostile. Many tried to establish reasons as to why they should not be included in the survey or why they could not answer the questionnaire. The most common arguments included, but were not limited to, the following beliefs:

- having been called upon to answer far too many survey questionnaires already;
- not being in the area during the survey period;
- being far too busy during the survey period;
- not being part of the tour-boat operators industry sector;
- feeling ineligible, as only large companies should be answering the questionnaire.

Apart from these statements, several operators blatantly refused to participate in the survey, despite being told that they would be noted as 'unwilling to cooperate'.

Due to the large number of these types of responses and their potential to illustrate some of the issues regarding industry self-regulation for marine tour operators, it was considered necessary to investigate whether other factors could support these statements. Operators that did not hide their true intentions and blatant-ly refused to participate in the survey indicated their lack of interest in this research and perhaps in environmental issues altogether.

The perception that only large companies should be answering the questionnaire seems to indicate that smaller operators considered these companies as being responsible for most of the damage or impacts in the marine environment. For certain types of operations in particular areas, the market was dominated by a few large, high-profile companies. Prominent examples for reef tours included 'Quicksilver' and 'Great Adventures' in Cairns and 'Fantasea Tours' in the Whitsundays. Equivalent bareboat operators in the Whitsundays included 'Sunsail' and 'Whit-sunday Rent-A-Yacht'. However, most of their operations (including their reef pontoons) are closely monitored and subject to environmental-management plans and surveillance by relevant regulatory authorities (see Warnken and Buckley, 2000). Most other marine tours in Australia (i.e. fishing, diving, boating, etc.) were being conducted by an estimated 1500 small to medium-sized tour-boat operators (i.e. businesses operating one or two boats, based on advertisements in relevant telephone directories and telephone enquiries). Comments during this study indicated that most of the smaller operators were well aware of their competitors' impacts but were unable or unwilling to accept their undeniable potential for cumulative impacts.

Alternatively, operators who claimed that they were not part of the tour-boat operators industry sector (despite advertising their services as 'Tours' under 'Boat Charter Services' in the commercial sections of local telephone directories) seemed either to try to distance themselves from their involvement and responsibilities or genuinely believed that they were not associated with tourism operations. However, later observations revealed that almost 40% of the operators surveyed belonged to tourism-type industry associations, such as the Gold Coast Tourism Bureau or Tourism Victoria. This suggests a more widespread acceptance among tour-boat operators of their ties with the tourism industry.

Claims of not being in the area or being too busy as an argument for being unable to participate in an interview were more difficult to gauge. Several operators moved around during the year to capitalize on seasonally high demands for certain activities in tourism 'hot spots' and could have been legitimately unavailable when the principal location of their business was visited. Similarly, tourism activities are known to peak at certain times during the year and field trips were organized to capitalize on these periods of increased tour-boat activities. As indicated earlier, this survey strategy ensured that operators were visited when tours were likely to be run on a regular basis and close to capacity (i.e. as close as practical to peak seasons), thereby leaving the investigator less conspicuous during audits. During such peak periods, some operators increased the number and types of trips they ran. This made it more difficult to: (i) contact them directly; and (ii) arrange an interview. However, in some cases, operators could be contacted on several consecutive days, which did not seem to indicate that any of the above applied in their situation. Furthermore, the questionnaire was designed to be completed within 20 minutes without requiring any work (such as extracting data from files, etc.) from the operator, and the investigator was prepared to meet at a time and location that suited the person interviewed. Under these circumstances, it seemed unlikely that even busy operators were unable to allocate 20 minutes of their time to participate in the survey after hours.

The belief of having already answered too many questionnaires was probably the response that was most difficult to assess. Overexposure to survey questionnaires often results in survey fatigue. As with all research projects that wish to obtain views and opinions from an industry sector, generally, the only real tool available is the survey questionnaire, whether administered by telephone, through the post or during face-to-face personal interviews. When using survey questionnaires, there is always the very real possibility that the target research group has already been exposed to this technique of data acquisition and may fall victim to survey fatigue, i.e. being asked to answer too many surveys and hence becoming thoroughly weary, discouraged or even bored with completing them and therefore becoming

complacent about the importance of participating in other surveys. In some areas, e.g. Exmouth, Cairns, and the Gold Coast, operators were known to have been surveyed previously (e.g. Davis *et al.*, 1997; Peter Valentine, Senior Lecturer in Environmental Science, James Cook University, 21 April 1999, personal communication; David Taylor, PhD scholar, Southern Cross University, 2 October 2000, personal communication; respectively), making it quite possible that the same operators were indeed sampled more than once and were likely to be subject to survey fatigue.

Observations Made during Interviews and Audits

Observations during interviews

After overcoming the obstructions discussed above and finally meeting for an interview, operators became increasingly uneasy, defensive and in some cases even hostile. The worst-case scenario resulted in an interview that had to be terminated due to an operator's fascination with spaceships, being abusive and saying, 'It's all there on the survey, just read it!'

On more than one occasion, operators claimed that the questionnaire was a waste of time, both to them and to the research project, as they had already answered exactly the same questions for surveys being conducted by other researchers. However, only two projects were found to be operating at the same time (one in Cairns and one on the Gold Coast) and both were related to fish-stock assessment-type research and had nothing to do with the use of environmental-management guidelines for vessel-operation procedures. The response mentioned above was made immediately following the completion of this questionnaire and indicated a lack of understanding of the issues addressed by this study and quite possibly environmental issues in general.

Another common reply encountered during interviews was, 'Are you referring to my boat or other people's boats?' This was often followed by operators' highlighting the failings of other operators' environmental performance, presumably in an attempt to have attention focused away from themselves. This presents another issue with the tour-boat operators: they often failed to see themselves as a distinct industry group and viewed their operation as being isolated from other operators. Therefore, as mentioned earlier, they were likely to misjudge the true magnitude of their cumulative effect on the environment when focusing solely on their own activities.

On a larger scale, there was the ever-present rhetoric used by operators when pointing at other industry sectors and retaliating with the question, 'Why don't you just leave us alone and concentrate on someone or something else that has a far greater environmental impact than we do?' Although this may be a theoretically valid point in some cases, in reality the potential effects of any activity that has an impact on the environment cannot be ignored. Most impacts occur in aggregate, and even smaller impacts, if left unchecked, eventually increase in scope and magnitude, leading ultimately to more significant effects. For example, climate change leading to coral bleaching probably has a much greater impact; however, it cannot be changed immediately, and boating impacts, which can be changed more rapidly, can cause irreparable harm to already stressed coral communities. Again, this rhetoric demonstrated the apathy of at least some operators in regard to management of and responsibilities for the environmental assets that provide the basis of their income.

Observations during audits

Additional evidence highlighting the lack of attention of tour-boat operators to environmental-protection measures came from *in situ* audits. International regulations such as MARPOL and relevant federal and state legislation, for example the *Protection of the Sea (Prevention of Pollution from Ships) Act 1983 (Cth)*, prohibits disposal of unmodified solid wastes from any vessel while at sea. However, over half of the vessels audited had some type of solid waste thrown overboard by either crew members or clients. The main items to be thrown overboard included food scraps,

garbage and offcuts of fishing-line on approximately 43, 52 and 10% of vessels audited, respectively. The most common type of waste item to be thrown overboard was cigarette butts, of which 126 were thrown from approximately 38% of the vessels audited.

Another indicator of the above-mentioned indifference of tour-boat operators towards their environmental performance was the lack of any obviously observable evidence for the use of environmental-management guidelines or best-practice manuals during *in situ* audits, e.g. reference during briefings or presence of written materials. This was in spite of 45% of the 47% of operators surveyed claiming to be currently using some sort of formal guidelines on management practices that regulate the effect their vessel has on the environment. Seven of these operators used 'in-house' publications which were never available for inspection, while the environmental guidelines a further two operators claimed to be using turned out to be legislative regulations (e.g. Victorian Marine Board Regulations). Removing these from the total leaves only around one-quarter of operators that can claim to use guidelines for environmental-management practices aimed at reducing the impacts of their vessel on the environment. A review of management guidelines available in Australia revealed that these did not specifically target or cover all aspects of boating operations (Rainbow, 1999). The majority of operators not claiming to use guidelines stated during interviews that the main reason for this was that such guidelines were not made available to them.

Industry Self-regulation for Tour-boat Operators: Lessons from Australia

Comprehensive industry self-regulation can be a valuable and cost-effective management tool when used in association with existing legislation and regulations. However, from the observations made during this study, there seem to be at least three major impediments to the successful adoption and implementation of industry best-practice environmental-management standards for the tour-boat industry in Australia and perhaps other locations throughout the world.

First, most operators appeared to believe that they have no real impact on the environment and do not require regulation, or they consider their operation as being managed in a way that would cause only minimal impact and therefore they could not see the need for industry self-regulation. In other words, without a clear understanding about their impacts, there is little room for triggering self-motivated and operator-driven implementation of impact-mitigation measures.

Secondly, operators failed to see themselves as part of a distinct industry group and had a rather simplistic view of themselves operating in isolation. This leads to two separate problems:

1. It prevented the formation of a single, Australia-wide industry organization equivalent to other professional associations, such as among dental and medical practitioners (i.e. the Australian Dental Association (ADA) or the Australian Medical Association (AMA)), which could have drafted, promoted, disseminated and monitored industry best-practice standards.

2. Operators were probably unable to realize how many of them used the same resource and in what ways and that there was the potential for causing a significant cumulative impact.

Finally, the few guidelines that have been prepared by management agencies and industry bodies are often vague and not 'user-friendly' or comprehensive. This seems to have created resentment among operators to actually incorporate these into their daily activities.

Some of the above-mentioned impediments seemed to have resulted from a poor or perhaps biased investment in tour-boat operator education programmes. The fact that many tour-boat operators failed to recognize the potential magnitude of their impacts calls for more quantitative research into specific boat-related impacts to show the type and scale of boat-related impacts on the environment. Secondly, boat operators need to be specifically educated about their role in creating or preventing such impacts. Although

most regulatory authorities regularly disseminate leaflets and provide information on the World Wide Web, their emphasis is often on safety issues and not on environmental issues *per se*, which diverts attention from and reduces the status of the latter. It should also be noted here, however, that some further attention needs to be given to the appropriate methods for education, as it is generally only larger companies that have the available time and resources to attend and participate in regular workshops.

Furthermore, there has been little effort to consolidate the very many highly fragmented and often localized organizations that represented Australian tour-boat operators. The current landscape of boating-related organizations in Australia includes boat manufacturers, dive operations, recreational and commercial fishers, and yachting and powerboat clubs, each with its own specific scope and agenda. For example, boat manufacturers' interests are represented by relatively independent state chapters of the Boating Industry Association (BIA), dive operators are mostly organized under various international dive organizations, such as the Professional Association of Underwater Instructors (PADI) and National Association of Underwater Instructors (NAUI), not to mention the many local, regional and national fishing affiliations. Some have a very narrow focus, for example for dive operators licensing and safety issues, while others cover not only tour-boat operators but many other tour operators as well, e.g. Gold Coast Tourism Bureau, Victorian Tourism Operators Association. Given the current diversity of representative bodies for tourism operators, it would seem vitally important that regulatory authorities establish a forum that encourages all tour-boat operators to unite as a single group – before undertaking any further steps to promote industry self-regulation as an environmental-management tool.

Recapturing the attitude experienced during phone calls, interviews and audits through sets of 'objective' observations and numerical values, particularly for relatively small samples, requires caution when extrapolating these findings into other areas. However, several key aspects of industry self-regulation through environmental best-practice guidelines were highlighted by this study. Before considering industry self-regulation as a serious accompaniment to legislative regulations, the following requirements need to be addressed: (i) the structure and organization of the industry needs to be analysed in detail in the planning phase; and (ii) considerable initial investment in effectively educating the industry's individual members is required to build the moral foundation for embracing guidelines in the future. Finally, education and leading by example should not be limited only to tour-boat operators. For example, while auditing one vessel at Exmouth, two marine biologists were observed throwing their cigarette butts overboard into the sea. How can we expect tour-boat operators to become more environmentally aware when such disregard for the environment is shown by the so-called educated élite?

References

Blanck, H. and Dahl, B. (1998) Recovery of marine periphyton communities around a Swedish marina after the ban of TBT use in antifouling paint. *Marine Pollution Bulletin* 36(6), 437–442.

Butler, R.W. (1991) Tourism, environment, and sustainable development. *Environmental Conservation* 18, 201–209.

Chmura, G.L. and Ross, N.W. (1978) *The Environmental Impacts of Marinas and their Boats: a Literature Review with Management Considerations.* Marine Advisory Service, University of Rhode Island, Narragansett, 32 pp.

Christensen, P. and Handberg, S. (1996) Forces and incentives in the promotion of environmental protection and improved working conditions. *Environmental Management and Health* 7(3), 4–11.

Common, M. (1996) *Consumption and the Environment*: Background Paper, Environmental Economics Seminar Series, Department of the Environment, Sport and Territories, Canberra. www.ea.gov.au/pcd/economics/consumption/bgpaper.html Last viewed 23 October 2002.

Creed, J.C. and Filho, G.M.A. (1999) Disturbance and recovery of the macroflora of a seagrass (*Halodule wrightii* Ascherson) meadow in the Abrolhos Marine National Park, Brazil: an experimental evaluation of anchor damage. *Journal of Experimental Marine Biology and Ecology* 235(2), 285–306.

Davis, D., Banks, S., Birtles, A., Valentine, P. and Cuthill, M. (1997) Whale sharks in Ningaloo Marine Park: managing tourism in an Australian marine protected area. *Tourism Management* 18(5), 259–271.

Driml, S., (1996) Coastal and marine tourism and recreation. In: Zann, L.P. (ed.) *The State of the Marine Environment Report for Australia – Technical Summary.* Ocean Rescue 2000 Program, Great Barrier Reef Marine Park Authority for the Department of the Environment, Sport and Territories, Townsville, pp. 159–165.

Ellsworth, J.P., Hildebrand, L.P. and Glover, E.A. (1997) Canada's Atlantic Coastal Action Program: a community-based approach to collective governance. *Ocean and Coastal Management* 36(1–3), 121–142.

Garrod, B. and Fyall, A. (1998) Beyond the rhetoric of sustainable tourism? *Tourism Management* 19(3), 199–212.

Glasby, T.M. (1999) Effects of shading on subtidal epibiotic assemblages. *Journal of Experimental Marine Biology and Ecology* 234(2), 275–290.

Guillon-Cottard, I., Augier, H., Console, J.J. and Esmieu, O. (1998) Study of microbiological pollution of a pleasure boat harbour using mussels as bioindicators. *Marine Environmental Research* 45(3), 239–247.

Jacoby, C., Manning, C., Fritz, S. and Rose, L. (1997) Three recent initiatives for monitoring of Australian coasts by the community. *Ocean and Coastal Management* 36(1–3), 205–226.

Lambert, C.C. and Lambert, G. (1998) Non-indigenous ascidians in Southern California harbours and marinas. *Marine Biology* 130(4), 675–688.

MARPOL (1973–1978) *International Convention for the Prevention of Pollution from Ships.* International Maritime Organization, London.

RAC (1993) *Coastal Zone Inquiry: Final Report.* Resource Assessment Commission, Canberra, 520 pp.

Rainbow, J. (1999) Best practice environmental management for dive boat operators in southern Queensland and northern New South Wales. Honours thesis, Griffith University, Queensland, Australia.

San Francisco Estuary Project (1995) *How Boat Sewage Discharges Affect the Environment.* California Department of Boating and Waterways, Oakland, California, 3 pp.

Scarlett, A., Donkin, P., Fileman, T.W., Evans S.V. and Donkin, M.E. (1999a) Risk posed by the antifouling agent Irgarol 1051 to the seagrass,

Zostera marina. Aquatic Toxicology 45(2–3), 159–170.

Scarlett, A., Donkin, P., Fileman, T.W. and Morris, R.J. (1999b) Occurrence of the antifouling herbicide, Irgarol 1051, within coastal-water seagrasses from Queensland, Australia. *Marine Pollution Bulletin* 38(8), 687–691.

Smethurst, D. and Nietschmann, B. (1999) The distribution of manatees (*Trichechus manatus*) in the coastal waterways of Tortuguero, Costa Rica. *Biological Conservation* 89(3), 267–274.

Smith, H.D. (1995) The environmental management of shipping. *Marine Policy* 19(6), 503–508.

Stephenson, M.A. (1992) Vessel-source pollution under the Law of the Sea Convention – an analysis of the prescriptive standards. *University of Queensland Law Journal* 17(1), 117–134.

TOFWGWA (1998) *Future Management of the Aquatic Charter Industry in Western Australia.* Fisheries Management Paper No. 116, Tour Operators Fishing Working Group of Western Australia for Fisheries Western Australia, Perth.

www.fish.wa.gov.au/comm/broc/mp/mp116/f mp116.pdf Last viewed 23 October 2002.

Turner, S.J., Thrush, S.F., Cummings, V.J., Hewitt, J.E., Wilkinson, M.R., Williamson, R.B. and Lee, D.J. (1997) Changes in epifaunal assemblages in response to marina operations and boating activities. *Marine Environmental Research* 43(3), 181–199.

Velander, K.A. and Mocogni, M. (1998) Maritime litter and sewage contamination at Cramond Beach Edinburgh – a comparative study. *Marine Pollution Bulletin* 36(5), 385–389.

Warnken, J. and Buckley, R.C. (2000) Monitoring diffuse impacts: Australian tourism developments. *Environmental Management* 25(4), 453–461.

Zann, L.P. (ed.) (1995) *Our Sea, Our Future – Major Findings of the State of the Marine Environment Report for Australia.* Ocean Rescue 2000 Program, Great Barrier Reef Marine Park Authority for the Department of the Environment, Sport and Territories, Townsville, 112 pp.

13

Impacts of Nature Tourism on the Mount Kosciuszko Alpine Area, Australia

Catherine Pickering,[1] Stuart Johnston,[2] Ken Green[3] and Graeme Enders[3]

[1]School of Environmental and Applied Sciences, Griffith University, Queensland Australia; [2]School of Resources, Environment and Society, Australian National University, Canberra, Australia; [3]New South Wales National Parks Service, Snowy Mountains Region, Jindabyne, Australia

Abstract

The alpine area around continental Australia's highest mountain, Mt Kosciuszko, is an increasingly popular summer tourism destination. Estimated numbers of people visiting the area have risen in the last 25 years from 20,000 to 70,000 per year. Tourists in summer principally go on day walks in the area, with the summit of Mt Kosciuszko the major destination. Winter activities principally consist of cross-country skiing, snowboarding and snow- and ice-climbing. Tourism is causing a range of impacts on the soils, water quality, flora and fauna, through recreation activities, travel and transport and accommodation near or in the area. Summer tourism and its impacts are likely to increase with an increasing promotion of the area as a summer tourism destination. The types of impacts and effectiveness of current management responses are discussed. Further ecological and social research is required if tourism on the roof of Australia is to remain ecologically sustainable.

Introduction

Mountain tourism is increasingly popular worldwide as more people become aware of the attraction of high-altitude sites for both winter and summer tourism. Management of tourism in the Australian Alps faces similar challenges to those for mountain regions overseas (Buckley et al., 2000; Hill and Pickering, 2002; Worboys and Pickering, 2002a,b). There are changes in the timing and types of tourism activities in mountain regions around the world and in their impacts on the natural environment (Buckley et al., 2000; Hill and Pickering, 2002; Newsome et al., 2002; Worboys and Pickering, 2002b). Ecosystems in such regions are at particular risk from tourism activities, with vegetation highly susceptible to damage and slow to recover (Körner, 1999). Management challenges are similar for these regions, revolving around how best to ensure the ecological sustainability of mountain tourism while preserving the natural and cultural values that attract so many people to these environments (Buckley *et al.*, 2000; Worboys *et al.*, 2001; Hill and Pickering, 2002; Newsome *et al.*, 2002; Worboys and Pickering, 2002a,b).

Within Australia there is limited alpine vegetation, with Mt Kosciuszko (2228 m) and the associated peaks of the Main Range representing the most extensive alpine ecosystem (Green and Osborne, 1994; Fig. 13.1). Although the area is very small, 100 km² in

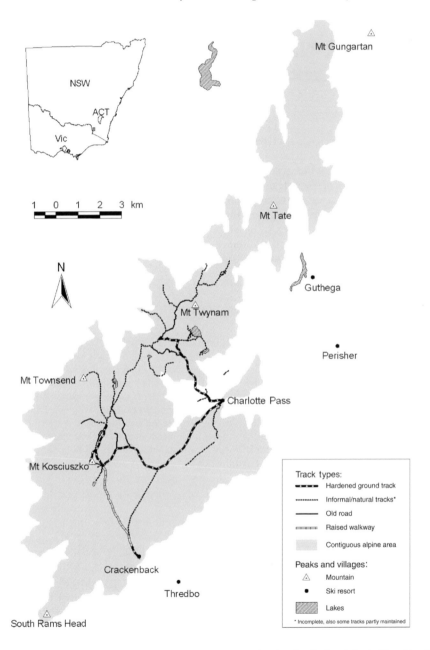

Fig. 13.1. Contiguous alpine area around Mt Kosciuszko, in Kosciuszko National Park, New South Wales, Australia including walking trails. Modified from Pascal Scherrer from data provided by the New South Wales National Parks and Wildlife Service.

total, it is of international biological and conservation significance, containing endemic and endangered species of animals and plants and unique ecosystems (Good, 1992; Green and Osborne, 1994; Costin *et al.*, 2000). Not surprisingly, it is a popular destination for outdoor enthusiasts and naturalists from Australia and overseas, who come to ascend Australia's highest mountain and see the unique landscape (Good, 1992; Arkle, 2000; Johnston, S.W. and Pickering, 2001; Worboys and Pickering, 2002a).

Previous human activities (notably grazing of cattle and sheep and associated regular burning) on the Main Range caused extensive damage, including vegetation loss and soil erosion (Costin, 1954, 1958; Clothier and Condon, 1968; Good, 1992). This required extensive and expensive rehabilitation, which itself produced impacts, including the introduction of alien plants (Bryant, 1971; Mallen-Cooper, 1990; Good, 1992; Scherrer and Pickering, 2001). Since 1944, the area has been protected, originally in the Kosciuszko State Park and since 1967 within Kosciuszko National Park. Human activities on the Main Range are generally restricted to recreation, tourism, conservation research and the management activities that support them (NSW NPWS, 1988; Good, 1992; Virtanen, 1993; Worboys and Pickering, 2002a).

The major focus of tourism within Kosciuszko National Park is winter activities, centred not in the alpine area but in the adjacent subalpine–alpine ski resorts (Good, 1992; Buckley *et al.*, 2000; Worboys and Pickering, 2002a). The environmental impacts of winter tourism and resorts are of concern (Buckley *et al.*, 2000; Pickering and Hill, Chapter 14, this volume), particularly for the New South Wales National Parks and Wildlife Service (NSW NPWS). This park agency is responsible for the management of the park and is required by legislation to protect the area's natural values (NSW NPWS, 1988). The effects of snow tourism on the alpine area are generally associated with the recreational 'footprint' of the resorts, the activities of backcountry skiing, snowboarding, camping in the snow and winter search-and-rescue operations (Buckley *et al.*, 2000; Pickering and Hill, Chapter 14, this volume). Such impacts include habitat frag-

mentation, vegetation damage associated with slope grooming, snow compaction, faecal/waste contamination of soil and water, littering and fire-scar formation under low snow conditions (Good and Grenier, 1994; Byrne, 1997; Pickering and Hill, Chapter 14, this volume; NSW NPWS, personal communication).

The increasing popularity of summer tourism in the region also has the potential to affect the alpine environment detrimentally unless effectively managed (Virtanen, 1993; Good and Grenier, 1994; Worboys *et al.*, 1995; Byrne, 1997; Arkle, 2000; Johnston, F. and Pickering, 2001; Worboys and Pickering, 2002a). Negative physical effects of summer tourism include informal track formation, braiding of tracks, vegetation damage leading to soil loss and/or compaction, hardening of existing tracks, littering and water pollution (Bryant, 1971; Edwards, 1977; Virtanen, 1993; Good and Grenier, 1994; Australia, Department of Tourism, 1997; Byrne, 1997; Johnston, S.W. and Pickering, 2001; Worboys and Pickering, 2002a). Biological impacts include damage and loss of vegetation, the modification or loss of animal habitat, disturbance to native animals and the spread of soil pathogens, weeds and feral animals (Bryant, 1971; Edwards, 1977; Virtanen, 1993; Good and Grenier, 1994; Australia, Department of Tourism, 1997; Byrne, 1997; Johnston, F. and Pickering, 2001; Worboys and Pickering, 2002a).

Potential and documented impacts of tourism on the alpine area of Australia are reviewed in this chapter to enhance ecologically suitable tourism. Recommendations for the management of the impacts of tourism are provided.

The Kosciuszko Alpine Area

The largest contiguous alpine ecosystem in Australia occurs in the Snowy Mountains along the Main Range, in the south-east of mainland Australia (Costin, 1989). Other areas of alpine ecosystem occur as smaller areas in Kosciuszko National Park (Fig. 13.1), as isolated areas centred on the higher peaks in Victoria, between Mt Hotham and Mt Bogong, and in the Central Highlands and higher peaks in Tasmania (Costin, 1989).

The alpine area of the Main Range extends from the upper limits of tree vegetation, at about 1830 m, to the top of Mt Kosciuszko, at 2228 m. The Main Range sector constitutes about 40% (100 km^2) of the total alpine area (250 km^2) in Kosciuszko National Park (Costin, 1989; Costin et al., 2000; Fig. 13.1). Unlike the steep sawtooth mountain ranges characteristic of some other alpine regions, the Main Range consists of an undulating plateau with a gradual stepped fall to the east and a very steep western face falling approximately 1500 m in elevation (Good, 1992).

Alpine humus soils completely cover all but a few rocky areas and support an almost complete vegetative cover (Costin, 1954, 1989; Good, 1996). The soils are substantially deeper than the organic soils found in high mountain areas elsewhere in the world, demonstrating a long, stable period of soil development. The soils of the Main Range are highly susceptible to erosion if vegetative cover is reduced below a critical threshold that provides insulation from frost and freezing of soil moisture (Costin and Wimbush, 1973; Johnston and Ryan, 2000).

The Main Range is also an important water catchment, with the headwaters of the Snowy River just below Mt Kosciuszko. In addition, the area contains glacial lakes and tarns (Cootapatamba, Albina, Club and Blue Lakes and Headley Tarn) and perennial groundwater-fed streams with distinctive ecology (Cullen, 1992; Good, 1992). Contamination of these waterways by sediment as a result of erosion and pathogens associated with human waste and feral animals is a concern (Cullen, 1992; Good, 1992; Good and Grenier, 1994).

The Main Range, along with the other alpine areas of the Australian Alps, is of enormous biological importance for Australia and internationally. The unique and distinctive biota contains endemic species of flora and fauna. Species under threat in the area include the Feldmark grass (*Erythranthera pumila*), the mountain pygmy possum (*Burramys parvus*) (once thought to be extinct) and the attractive broad-toothed rat (*Mastacomys fuscus*) (Good,

1992; Green and Osborne, 1994). The flora includes a high proportion of endemic and rare species, with 21 endemic species and 33 rare species out of around 212 species in total. This is one of the highest proportions of endemic and threatened species in the world (Smith, 1986; Good, 1992; Costin et al., 2000).

Tourism Activities

Kosciuszko National Park is within a day's drive of approximately 50% of the Australian population, with around 860,000 people visiting the park annually (Good, 1992; Worboys and Pickering, 2002b). Of these visitors, the majority visit during the winter season of June to October (Good, 1992). Most winter tourists visit ski resorts that are in the subalpine region adjacent to the alpine area. The majority participates in downhill skiing and snowboarding, with others engaging in cross-country skiing, either on fixed trails or in the extensive subalpine backcountry, and other activities (Good, 1992; Buckley et al., 2000). Some resort visitors do not engage in outdoor winter recreation activities but participate in the social life of the resorts. A relatively small proportion (~5%) of visitors go on to visit the alpine area in winter. They are primarily involved in snowboarding or ski-touring, either on day trips (often from resorts) or participating in overnight camping in snow caves and/or tents. A relative few engage in snow- and ice-climbing and snow-shoeing (Virtanen, 1993; NSW NPWS, personal communication; Table 13.1).

Summer tourism to the Australian Alps has increased significantly over the past 25 years, visitation to just the small alpine area of the Main Range having trebled during that period. A survey published in 1978 estimated 20,000 summer visitors to the alpine area (Worboys, 1978). By the early 1980s the number had increased to 36,000 people per summer (Murphy, 1985). The most recent estimate for the snow-free period of 1999/2000 is 70,000 people (Johnston, S.W., 2002, personal communication, ANU).

The main activities undertaken by the visitors are sightseeing, bushwalking, camping, mountain-biking, wildflower appreciation,

Table 13.1. Tourism and recreational activities associated with the alpine area of Kosciuszko National Park (data from: NSW NPWS, 1988; Good, 1992; Mackay and Nixon, 1995; Arkle, 2000; Johnston, S.W. and Pickering, 2001; Worboys and Pickering, 2002a).

Activity	Winter	Summer
Transport and travel		
To alpine	Private vehicles, commercial tours, commercial train (ski-tube), snow cats, skidoos, ski-lifts	Private vehicles, commercial tours, bikes
In alpine	Cross-country skis, snowshoes, snow cats and skidoos (rescue only)	Bush walking on and off trails, mountain bikes, four-wheel drives and quad bikes (management services only)
Accommodation and shelter		
Adjacent to alpine	Private lodges or public hotels/lodges in resorts	Private lodges or public hotels/lodges in resorts
	Private housing, hotels, youth hostels, etc. in local towns or areas	Private housing, hotels, youth hostels, etc. in local towns or areas
In alpine	Snow caves, tents (no official campground), huts	Tents (no official campground), huts
Recreation activity		
In alpine	Downhill skiing (barely in alpine), cross-country skiing, snow- and ice-climbing, snowshoeing, snowboarding	Backcountry camping, bushwalking, sightseeing, picnicking, wildflower viewing, climbing, swimming, running, mountain-biking, fishing, paragliding

climbing, photography and fishing (Good, 1992; Arkle, 2000; McMaster, 2000; Johnston, S.W. and Pickering, 2001; Worboys and Pickering, 2002a; Table 13.1). Nearly all tourism occurs within the 36 km^2 area between the top of the Thredbo chair-lift, Mt Kosciuszko, Blue Lake and Charlottes Pass (Arkle, 2000; Johnston, S.W. and Pickering, 2001; Worboys and Pickering, 2002a; Fig. 13.1). Because the area contains Australia's highest mainland peak, it is a Mecca for a high number of day walkers who wish to ascend the summit. Public holidays, such as Christmas and Easter, are the most popular times to visit the alpine area, with as many as 4500 people per day visiting the Main Range at these times (Arkle, 2000; Johnston, S.W. and Pickering, 2001).

Impacts of Tourism

The impacts of tourism on the alpine region of Kosciuszko National Park fall into three groups: (i) those associated with the travel and

transport of visitors to the alpine area; (ii) those associated with accommodation for tourists in and near the alpine area; and (iii) those associated with local travel and activities within the alpine area. Here we focus on the second and third of these, i.e. impacts in and around the alpine area itself.

Accommodation impacts

Accommodation in Kosciuszko National Park ranges from permanent accommodation, such as resort lodges and hotels, formal camping areas and huts through to temporary accommodation, such as snow caves and small tents (NSW NPWS, 1988; Good, 1992; Virtanen, 1993; Worboys and Pickering, 2002b; Table 13.2). In the Main Range area the only types of accommodation are two emergency shelters (huts), snow caves and informal camping. Impacts associated with permanent accommodation provided in the subalpine zone include vegetation clearance and disturbance and soil erosion and compaction (NSW

Table 13.2. Impact of tourism accommodation within the Kosciuszko alpine region (data from personal observations and from Edwards, 1977; Keane *et al.*, 1979; Mallen-Cooper, 1990; Good and Grenier, 1994; Good, 1995; Byrne, 1997; CDT, 1997; Johnston, 1997; Parr-Smith and Polley, 1998; AALC, 2000; Arkle, 2000; Buckley *et al.*, 2000; Green, 2000; Johnston, S.W. and Pickering, 2001; Scherrer and Pickering, 2001).

Type of impact	Huts	Tents	Snow caves
Flora			
Vegetation clearance or disturbance from			
Construction	•		
Use	•	•	
Trampling	•	•	
Introduction of weeds associated with			
Construction	•		
Use	•		
Trampling	•		
Habitat for weeds	•		
Fauna			
Compaction of subniveal space		•	•
Alteration to behaviour (feeding, reproduction, etc.) due to noise and human activity	•	•	•
Increased feral animal activity	•		
Geomorphology			
Soil erosion and/or compaction from			
Construction	•	•	•
Use	•	•	•
Nutrification	•	•	•
Modified drainage patterns	•	•	•
Pollution			
Visual impacts	•	•	
Litter	•	•	•
Human waste	•	•	•
Noise pollution	•	•	
Increased fire risk	•	•	

NPWS, 1988; Good, 1995; Buckley *et al.*, 2000). These impacts continue during use, as well as generating additional impacts. Impacts associated with use include disturbance and interruption to wildlife, the production of wastes, water pollution from effluent (Cullen and Norris, 1989; Cullen, 1992), the leaching of toxic materials (Johnston and Good, 2001), noise pollution, reduction of visual amenity and invasion of weeds and pathogens (Good, 1995, Table 13.2).

The temporary accommodation in the alpine area of the Main Range, such as tents and snow caves, also has environmental effects. Impacts such as solid waste, faecal contamination and nutrient enrichment of water (NSW NPWS, 1988; Cullen and Norris, 1989; Virtanen, 1993; Good and Grenier, 1994; Good, 1995; Byrne, 1997; AALC, 2000) are potentially greater per person in the alpine area than in resorts because of the absence of sewage-treatment plants. The sustainability of camping depends on the level of use and the capacity of the area to absorb impacts; however, carrying capacities are generally unknown or are not documented. For example, intensive summer and winter camping in the catchment areas around the alpine glacial lakes has led to erosion, soil compaction, loss of vegetation and faecal contamination of the glacial lakes (Cullen and Norris, 1989; Virtanen, 1993; Byrne, 1997; McLean, 2000). Camping in these catchments has now been banned.

Table 13.3. Impacts of local travel and recreational activities (references as for Table 13.2).

Type of impact	Over-snow vehicles	Backcountry skiing	Snow- and ice-climbing	Walking on tracks	Walking off tracks	Fishing	Mountain-biking	Rock-climbing
Flora								
Vegetation clearance or disturbance from								
Construction	•			•				
Use	•			•			•	
Trampling					•	•		•
Introduction of weeds								
Construction of tracks				•	•		•	
Use				•	•		•	
Trampling					•			
Habitat for weeds				•	•	•	•	•
Fauna								
Habitat fragmentation	•			•	•		•	•
Compaction of subniveal space	•	•						
Alteration to behaviour (feeding, reproductive, etc.) due to noise and human activity	•	•	•		•	•		•
Increased feral animal activity	•							
Damage to vegetation		•	•	•	•	•	•	•
Geomorphology								
Soil erosion and/compaction from								
Construction of tracks	•			•	•		•	
Use	•			•	•	•	•	•
Contamination – hydrocarbons	•				•		•	
Modified drainage patterns	•			•	•	•	•	
Nutrification	•			•	•	•	•	•
Pollution								
Visual impacts	•	•	•	•	•	•	•	•
Litter	•	•	•	•	•	•	•	•
Human waste	•	•	•	•	•	•	•	•
Noise pollution	•	•	•	•	•	•	•	•
Increased fire risk				•	•	•	•	•

Local travel and tourist activities

Most of the impacts associated with travel and transport occur outside the actual alpine area in the adjacent subalpine regions. The major impacts of local travel and activities within Kosciuszko National Park are summarized in Table 13.3.

Local travel can affect the natural environment through clearance and disturbance of vegetation, soil modification and erosion, soil compaction and soil and water nutrification, sedimentation and contamination with pathogens (Edwards, 1977; Keane et al., 1979; Hardie, 1993; Virtanen, 1993; Good and Grenier, 1994; Good, 1995; Australia, Department of Tourism, 1997; Parr-Smith and Polley, 1998; Arkle, 2000; Buckley et al., 2000). These impacts are usually most severe during the construction of facilities such as roads and trails (Virtanen, 1993; Good and Grenier, 1994; Australia, Department of Tourism, 1997; Parr-Smith and Polley, 1998; Buckley et al., 2000). Other impacts of transport and travel include wildlife disturbance, mortality and habitat destruction, air pollution, noise, increased fire risk and introduction of pathogens and weeds (Buckley et al., 2000 and references therein). These can occur both during construction of facilities and also in the use of the facilities (Keane et al., 1979; Hardie, 1993; Good, 1995; Byrne, 1997; Buckley et al., 2000). Impacts can accumulate over time, and all tend to amplify with increased usage of roads and trails, even if there is no new construction (Keane et al., 1979; Hardie, 1993; Arkle, 2000; Buckley et al., 2000; Newsome et al., 2002).

By far the most popular activity within the alpine area in summer is walking, with over 80% of visitors in summer going for a walk (Arkle, 2000; Johnston, S.W. and Pickering, 2001). The next most popular activity is sightseeing (10%), with only 2% of people camping. The most popular walk is to the summit of Australia's highest mainland mountain, Mt Kosciuszko, with people starting the walk from either Thredbo or Charlotte Pass along the existing hardened tracks (Arkle, 2000; Johnston, S.W. and Pickering, 2001; Fig. 13.1). Visitor numbers to the summit of Mt Kosciuszko vary from around 134 people per

day on non-school holidays to over 700 people on major public holidays. These visitors (average-size group 2.5 people) spend on average 26 minutes in the 100 m radius of the summit of Mt Kosciuszko (Arkle, 2000).

Summer tourism activities have a range of impacts, both as a direct result of activities and from the provision of infrastructure for activities, such as walking tracks (Table 13.3). The provision of formed tracks and walkways has reduced impacts, such as erosion and vegetation trampling, associated with informal tracks (Edwards, 1977; Virtanen, 1993; Australia, Department of Tourism, 1997). However, the formed tracks have their own impacts, including compaction of soil, clearing of vegetation, introduction of alien plants and leaching of nutrients into adjacent areas that changes the local soil chemistry (Virtanen, 1993, personal observation).

In addition to the hardening of surfaces for walking, other tourism management methods may be required, particularly for the most popular destination. A recent visitor survey found that 47% of tourists walking to Mt Kosciuszko arrive at the summit during lunchtime (Arkle, 2000). As a result, overcrowding, especially during the peak periods, has occurred. This has not only detracted from the quality of the experience for visitors, but also caused damage to areas of revegetation next to the paths and to the adjacent native vegetation. Because of the overcrowding, people spread out from the central hardened area on to surrounding vegetated areas (Arkle, 2000).

Mountain-biking is currently permitted only along the old summit road from Charlotte Pass (Fig. 13.1) to Rawson Pass. However, bike riding in other areas does occur (personal observation). While fishing is popular in many other areas of the park, only limited numbers of anglers make their way into the alpine zone. However, the rainbow and brown trout, introduced for recreational fishing, have had negative effects on stream ecosystems, including exclusion of the native fish *Galaxias olidus* from many waterways (Green and Osborne, 1994).

Winter tourism activities have fewer impacts than summer tourism (Table 13.3). This is in part due to the lower numbers of visitors to the alpine area when there is snow cover and partly because the snow itself provides some protection from direct mechanical impacts (Table 13.3). Where the snow is compacted, impacts on vegetation and soils can occur (Pickering and Hill, Chapter 14, this volume). Other impacts involve human waste, litter, visual impacts and noise pollution (Buckley *et al.*, 2000).

The degree of physical and biological impact of the tourism activities vary with the level of use, type of recreational activity, site-specific conditions (such as specific vegetation, edaphic factors, slope, etc.) and how these factors interact (Virtanen, 1993; Arkle, 2000). It has been demonstrated for alpine soils that impacts have been amplified with increasing recreation/tourism use up to a threshold level of disturbance. Beyond the threshold, damage is permanent without restoration, even if tourism numbers decline (Arkle, 2000; Johnston *et al.*, 2002). For example, if trampling and associated impacts remove vegetation cover beyond a threshold value, erosion of the organic layers of the alpine soils results until a stable rock pavement is formed or bedrock reached. Although further walking impacts would be unlikely to erode the new surface further, reducing those impacts would not result in restoration of the soils and vegetation. This has occurred on some sections of informal paths within the alpine zone, particularly where entrenched drainage lines have developed (Virtanen, 1993; personal observation). Restoration of these areas is now dependent on human intervention, which may not be effective.

Management Response

Recreation in the alpine zone is likely to be causing impacts above the natural recovery rate of the ecosystem (Tables 13.2 and 13.3). The more obvious physical damage and public-health issues have long been recognized by management authorities. Education programmes have been established to increase awareness of visitor impacts and to define codes of practice to minimize them (AALC, 1993a,b; Virtanen, 1993; Mackay and Nixon, 1995; Byrne, 1997; McMaster, 2000). In addi-

tion, regulations prohibiting the use of wood fires in the alpine area and camping in the catchments of the glacial lakes have been implemented (AALC, 1993a,b; Virtanen, 1993). A revegetation programme for eroded areas and hardening of high-usage tracks has also been undertaken at a cost of more than Aus$3 million (Byrne, 1997; CDT, 1997; NSW NPWS, personal communication).

Management of tourism and recreation activities in the alpine area has, until recently, been guided by a principle of providing public facilities at the edges of the alpine region rather than within it (NSW NPWS, 1988; Virtanen, 1993). Currently it is considered best practice to conduct surveys of visitor use and analyse patterns of use prior to developing or modifying facilities/access (AALC, 1999; McMaster, 2000; Johnston, S.W. and Pickering, 2001; Worboys and Pickering, 2002a). Kosciuszko National Park managers have done some monitoring of tourism use of the area and have begun to explore the potential for restricting visitor numbers at times of peak visitation, for example by issuing camping permits for public use of the area and licensing commercial tours (Virtanen, 1993; Byrne, 1997; McMaster, 2000; Johnston, S.W. and Pickering, 2001; Worboys and Pickering, 2002a,b).

Recent upgrading of the surface of tracks has been undertaken in order to protect the vegetation and soil from further deterioration under the physical impacts of visitor use (CDT, 1997; Johnston, 1997; Worboys and Pickering, 2002a). This remedial work is being undertaken, but the way it has been undertaken does not appear to have considered research into impacts of current visitor use, impacts of different track types or visitor preferences for different types of tracks (Johnston, S.W. and Pickering, 2001; Worboys and Pickering, 2002a). It is important that research into ecological impacts and use patterns is undertaken to confirm the directions of management and its assumptions about the visitors and their effects on the ecosystem (Virtanen, 1993; Johnston, S.W. and Pickering, 2001; Worboys *et al.*, 2001; Worboys and Pickering, 2002a). The response of park managers to the more subtle tourism impacts on vegetation, fauna, soil and water will increasingly rely on research to identify recovery thresholds for affected ecosystems (Worboys *et al.*, 2001; Newsome *et al.*, 2002).

Priorities for impact management

The information reviewed leads us to suggest associated priority areas of research for the alpine area of Kosciuszko National Park. These are:

1. Ecological research into impact thresholds for the different native vegetation communities in the alpine area. Existing research has identified thresholds for grazing on the tall alpine herbfield. This could be extended to identify the thresholds for various tourism activities, including trampling damage associated with camping and walking tracks.
2. Monitoring of water quality, including pathogens in waterways such as lakes near camping sites (e.g. below Snowy River Bridge, Blue Lake and Club Lake Creek, etc.), is also required for effective management of camping.
3. Ecological and social research into the impacts of different track types. There are clearly ecological issues associated with the different types of tracks that have been used in the alpine area, including the dispersal of weeds and potential for calcium leaching into the surrounding environment (personal observation). A clear preference for some track types, such as existing raised metal walkways, was found in a survey of 1126 people (Johnston, S.W. and Pickering, 2001).
4. Regular visitor monitoring will help parks services to identify changing demands and social and ecological impacts that are developing with the high numbers of summer visitors already in the area. Recent visitor monitoring has already provided key management information (Johnston, S.W. and Pickering, 2001; Worboys and Pickering, 2002a). As a result of monitoring, the number of tourists accessing the summit of Mt Kosciuszko at peak times has been recognized as a critical management issue (Arkle, 2000; Johnston, S.W. and Pickering, 2001).
5. There is also a need to review the effectiveness of interpretation of the alpine environment and of safety issues for tourists (McMaster, 2000; Johnston, S.W. and Pickering, 2001). Current interpretation may be inadequate, and more research is required (McMaster, 2000). The aforementioned survey of 1126 visitors identified a visitor preference for more short loop tracks with interpretative signs at access points to the alpine area (Johnston, S.W. and Pickering, 2001).

Trends in Visitor Use and Impacts

The impacts of tourism on the alpine environment are likely to become more severe in the future, particularly if climate change leads to shorter or intermittent periods of snow cover (König, 1998; Whetton, 1998). For example, the ski industry is likely to substitute other activities if decreased snow cover and higher temperatures reduce the length of the ski season. Resort operators are already placing more emphasis on developing summer activities to maintain economic viability, including the use of ski-lifts to facilitate sightseeing. Recent recommendations for mountain-resort viability are based on year-round tourism and include conference, educational, adventure and health tourism (König, 1998). These changes in tourism activities and their timing and intensity are likely to increase the range and intensity of ecological impacts. Attempting to manage both the impacts of climate change and increasing numbers and diversification of tourism activities will require detailed information about how these processes will affect the alpine ecosystem and an assessment of how they are likely to interact (Worboys and Pickering, 2002a,b).

Acknowledgements

We thank Pascal Scherrer for providing the map in Fig. 13.1 and NSW NPWS for providing the original data. The Cooperative Research Centre for Sustainable Tourism and NSW NPWS provided support for several of the research studies used in formulating management recommendations in this chapter.

References

AALC (1993a) *Bushwalking Code.* Australian Alps Liaison Committee, Canberra, Australia.

AALC (1993b) *Snow Camping Code.* Australian Alps Liaison Committee, Canberra, Australia.

AALC (1999) *Recreation Strategy – All Management Units Summary Report for the Australian Alps National Parks.* Commissioned from Missing Link Tourism Consultants, Sydney by the Australian Alps Liaison Committee, Canberra, Australia.

AALC (2000) *Australian Alps Best Practice Human Waste Management Workshop Papers and Presentations.* Australian Alps Liaison Committee, Canberra, Australia.

Arkle, P. (2000) *Tourism in the summit area of Mt Kosciuszko: an assessment of tourist interaction and impact.* Honours thesis, Australian National University, Canberra, Australia.

Australia, Department of Tourism (1997) *Repairing the Roof of Australia – Ecotourism Infrastructure in Kosciuszko National Park.* Australia, Commonwealth Department of Tourism, Canberra, Australia.

Bryant, W.G. (1971) Deterioration of vegetation and erosion in the Guthega catchment area, Snowy Mountains, NSW. *Journal of the Soil Conservation Service of New South Wales* 27, 62–81.

Buckley, R.C., Pickering, C.M. and Warnken, J. (2000) Environmental management for alpine tourism and resorts in Australia. In: Goode, P.M., Price, M.F. and Zimmermann, F.M. (eds) *Tourism and Development in Mountain Regions.* CAB International, Wallingford, UK, pp. 27–46.

Byrne, N. (1997) Recreation impacts in the Australian Alps. *Trees and Natural Resources* 39, 17–19.

CDT (1997) *Repairing the Roof of Australia – Ecotourism Infrastructure in Kosciuszko National Park.* Commonwealth Department of Tourism, Canberra.

Clothier, D.P. and Condon, R.W. (1968) Soil conservation in alpine catchments. *Journal of the Soil Conservation Service of New South Wales* 24, 96–113.

Costin, A.B. (1954) *A Study of the Ecosystems of the Monaro Region of New South Wales with Special Reference to Soil Erosion.* Soil Conservation Service of New South Wales, Sydney, Australia.

Costin, A.B. (1958) *The Grazing Factor and the Maintenance of Catchment Values in the Australian Alps.* Commonwealth Scientific and Industrial Research Organization (CSIRO), Melbourne, Australia.

Costin, A.B. (1989) The Alps in a global perspective. In: Good, R. (ed.) *The Scientific Significance of the Australian Alps.* Australian Alps Liaison Committee, Canberra, Australia, pp. 7–19.

Costin, A.B. and Wimbush, D.J. (1973) Frost cracks and earth hummocks at Kosciuszko, Snowy Mountains, Australia. *Arctic and Alpine Research* 5, 111–120.

Costin, A.B., Gray, C.J., Totterdell, C. and Wimbush, D.J. (2000) *Kosciuszko Alpine Flora.* Collins, Melbourne.

Cullen, P. (1992) Management of water quality in the Australian Alps. In: Good, R. and Grenier, P. (eds) *The Australian Alps.* Revue de Géographie Alpine, Institut de Géographie Alpine, Grenoble, France, pp. 425–449.

Cullen, P. and Norris, R. (1989) Significance of lakes and rivers in the Australian mainland Alps. In: Good, R. (ed.) *The Scientific Significance of the Australian Alps.* Australian Alps Liaison Committee, Canberra, Australia.

Edwards, I.J. (1977) The ecological impact of pedestrian traffic on alpine vegetation in Kosciuszko National Park. *Australian Forestry* 40, 108–120.

Good, R.B. (1992) *Kosciuszko Heritage: the Conservation Significance of the Kosciuszko National Park.* National Parks and Wildlife Service of New South Wales, Sydney, Australia.

Good, R.B. (1995) Ecologically sustainable development in the Australian Alps. *Mountain Research and Development* 15, 251–258.

Good, R.B. (1996) Conflict in the Australian Alps: grazing and protected areas. In: Ralston, M.M., Hughey, K.F.D. and O'Connor, K.F. (eds) *Mountains of East Asia and Pacific.* Centre for Mountain Studies, Lincoln University, Canterbury, New Zealand, pp. 58–64.

Good, R.B. and Grenier, P. (1994) Some environmental impacts of recreation in the Australian Alps. *Australian Parks and Recreation* Summer, 20–26.

Green, K. (2000) Small mammal activity on snow surface. *Victorian Naturalist* 117, 230–234.

Green, K. and Osborne, W.S. (1994) *Wildlife of the Australian Snow-Country.* Reed, Sydney.

Hardie, M. (1993) *Measuring Bushwalking and Camping Impacts – Mount Bogong Victoria.* National Parks and Public Land Division, Department of Conservation and Natural Resources, Melbourne, Australia.

Hill, W. and Pickering, C.M. (2002) *Regulation of*

Summer Tourism in Mountain Conservation Reserves in Australia. Mountain Tourism Research Report No. 2, Cooperative Research Centre for Sustainable Tourism, Griffith University, Gold Coast, Australia.

Johnston, F. and Pickering, C.M. (2001) Alien plants in the Australian Alps. *Mountain Research and Development* 21, 284–291.

Johnston, S.W. (1997) *Snowy River Borrow Pit: Report on Works*. New South Wales National Park and Wildlife Service Report, Jindabyne, Australia.

Johnston, S.W. and Good, R.G. (2001) The management of zinc toxicity during and following revegetation of eroded alpine lands. In: Worboys, G., Lockwood, M. and DeLacy, T. (eds) *Protected Area Management: Principles and Practice*. Oxford University Press, Melbourne, Australia.

Johnston, S.W. and Pickering, C.M. (2001) Visitor monitoring and social expectations for track planning: a case study of the Kosciuszko alpine area. In: *Proceedings of the Mountain Walking Track Management Conference, March 2001*. Australian Alps Liaison Committee, Canberra, Australia, pp. 167–172.

Johnston, S.W. and Ryan, M. (2000) Occurrence of arbuscular mycorrhizal fungi across a range of alpine humus soil conditions in Kosciuszko National Park, Australia. *Arctic, Antarctic and Alpine Research* 32, 255–261.

Johnston, S., Greene, R., Banks, J. and Good, R. (2002) Function and sustainability of Australian alpine ecosystems: studies in the tall alpine herbfield community, Kosciuszko National Park, Australia. In: *Proceeding of the Ecological and Earth Sciences in Mountain Areas, Banff, Canada, 6–10 September 2002*.

Keane, P.A., Wild, A.E.R. and Rogers, J.H. (1979) Trampling and erosion in alpine country. *Journal of the Soil Conservation Service of New South Wales* 35, 7–12.

König, U. (1998) Climate change and the Australian ski industry. In: Green, K. (ed.) *Snow, a Natural History: an Uncertain Future*. Australian Alps Liaison Committee, Canberra, Australia, pp. 207–223.

Körner, C. (1999) *Alpine Plant Life: Functional Plant Ecology of High Mountain Ecosystems*. Springer, Berlin, Germany.

Mackay, J. and Nixon, A. (1995) *Australian Alps National Parks Back-country Recreation Strategy*. Australian Alps Liaison Committee, Canberra, Australia.

McLean, P. (2000) The impact of tourism on Blue Lake. Unpublished Report, University of Western Sydney, Sydney, Australia.

McMaster, K. (2000) Interpretation for summer recreation in the Kosciuszko alpine area. Honours thesis, Australian National University, Canberra, Australia.

Mallen-Cooper, J. (1990) Introduced plants in the high altitude environments of Kosciuszko National Park, south eastern Australia. PhD thesis, Australian National University, Canberra, Australia.

Murphy, P.J. (1985) Recreation impact on Blue Lake, Kosciuszko National Park. Honours thesis, University of New South Wales, Sydney, Australia.

Newsome, D., Moore, S. and Dowling, R.K. (2002) *Natural Area Tourism: Ecology, Impacts and Management*. Channel View Publications, Sydney, Australia.

NSW NPWS (1988) *Kosciuszko National Park – Plan of Management*, 2nd edn. New South Wales National Parks and Wildlife Service, Sydney, Australia.

Parr-Smith, G. and Polley, V. (1998) *Alpine Rehabilitation Manual for Alpine and Sub-Alpine Environments in the Australian Alps – Working Draft*. Australian Alps Liaison Committee, Melbourne, Australia.

Scherrer, P. and Pickering, C.M. (2001) Effects of grazing, tourism and climate change on the alpine vegetation of Kosciuszko National Park. *Victorian Naturalist* 118, 93–99.

Smith, J.M.B. (1986) Origins of the Australasian tropical pine and alpine floras. In: Barlow, B.A. (ed.) *Flora and Fauna of Alpine Australasia: Ages and Origins*. Commonwealth Scientific and Industrial Research Organization (CSIRO), Melbourne, Australia.

Virtanen, S. (1993) *Toward Conservation and Recreation Management of Kosciuszko Alpine Area*. New South Wales National Parks and Wildlife Service Report, Jindabyne, Australia.

Whetton, P. (1998) Climate change impacts on the spatial extent of snow-cover in the Australian Alps. In: Green, K. (ed.) *Snow, a Natural History: an Uncertain Future*. Australian Alps Liaison Committee, Canberra, Australia, pp. 195–206.

Worboys, G. (1978) *The Mount Kosciuszko Outstanding Natural Area Plan of Management*. New South Wales National Parks and Wildlife Service, Jindabyne, Australia.

Worboys, G. and Pickering, C.M. (2002a) *Managing the Kosciuszko Alpine Area: Conservation*

Milestones and Future Challenges. Mountain Tourism Research Report No. 3, Cooperative Research Centre for Sustainable Tourism, Griffith University, Gold Coast, Australia.

Worboys, G. and Pickering, C.M. (2002b) Tourism and recreation values of Kosciuszko National Park. In: *An Assessment of the Values of Kosciuszko National Park*. Interim Report of the Independent Scientific Committee for the New Plan of Management for Kosciuszko National Park, New South Wales National Parks and Wildlife Service, Queanbeyan, Australia.

Worboys, G.L., Pulsford, I. and Mackay, J. (1995) Conservation gains, setbacks and opportunities. In: *IUCN Transboundary Mountain Protected Areas Workshop*. Australian Alps Liaison Committee, Canberra, Australia.

Worboys, G., Lockwood, M. and De Lacy, T. (2001) *Protected Area Management: Principles and Practice*. Oxford University Press, Melbourne, Australia.

14

Ecological Change as a Result of Winter Tourism: Snow Manipulation in the Australian Alps

Catherine Pickering and Wendy Hill
*School of Environmental and Applied Sciences, Griffith University, Queensland,
Australia*

Abstract

This study examines potential direct and indirect effects of snow manipulation (e.g. slope grooming, snow grooming, snow making, snow harvesting and snow fences) on vegetation in the Australian Alps. The extent of snow manipulation has increased substantially over the last decade, in order to maintain the economic viability of ski resorts. In Australia, little research has been done on the resulting environmental impacts. This is despite the high conservation value of the Australian Alps, with resorts located either in or adjacent to national parks.

Overseas research indicates that snow manipulation results in a cascade of changes that can negatively affect native flora. Slope grooming can involve extensive modification of the environment, including removal of native vegetation and reformation of slope topography, and this results in changes to hydrological patterns. Snow grooming not only physically damages plants but also compacts the snow, increasing its density and reducing porosity and permeability. This limits the ability of the snow pack to slow water runoff, thus increasing the risk of erosion, and can retard spring snowmelt. Snow compaction affects plants by increasing the risk of physical damage from freezing. However, the range of indirect impacts on plants can be extensive, and includes impacts due to lower soil temperatures, greater depth of soil freezing, depleted soil nutrients and higher soil pH. Biological effects of snow compaction and other snow manipulation techniques have been studied less, but include changes in soil biota, herbivory, animal activity, predation, insect activity, seed dispersal and the composition of plant communities. This study highlights the need for research into environmental impacts of tourism, to ensure that winter ski tourism in Australia is not just economically but also environmentally sustainable.

Introduction

Winter tourism in the Australian Alps principally consists of resort-based skiing (Buckley *et al.*, 2000). It is a rapidly expanding multi-million-dollar industry, estimated to be worth over Aus$50 million per annum (Buckby *et al.*, 1993; KPMG Management Consulting, 1994, cited in Digance and Norris, 1999). This type of adventure tourism occurs in or near national parks in Australia, and has clear negative impacts on these protected areas and potentially on other tourism activities in these areas (Buckley et al., 2000). As successful conservation of the areas requires the management of any type of tourism that affects such environments (McKercher, 1996), ski tourism will be treated as a type of nature tourism for the purposes of this review.

There is strong competition among ski resorts for customers. With increasing temperatures and less consistent snow conditions in the Australian Alps, a resort's success is influenced by the quality of the snow cover it can provide (Keage, 1990; PBPL, 1997; König, 1998a). This has resulted in the expenditure of considerable effort and money on improving the quality and extent of snow cover at resorts (PBPL, 1997; NSW NPWS, 1998a,b). Snow-manipulation practices used by resorts to improve snow cover, as with other tourism activities and infrastructure, can have serious direct and indirect negative effects on the natural environment. The long-term ecological changes associated with such impacts are not always recognized, even by parks agencies regulating and monitoring such tourism activities in or adjacent to national parks. This chapter hopes to highlight the issue, by documenting the extensive reported and potential impacts of manipulation of a natural resource – snow. This activity is carried out to facilitate the economic sustainability of the tourism industry, potentially at the expense of its environmental sustainability.

Characteristics of Australian Alps Ski Resorts

There are 12 ski resorts operating in the Australian Alps: four in New South Wales (NSW), seven in Victoria and one in the Australian Capital Territory (ACT) (Table 14.1). Resorts in NSW operate within the subalpine areas of Kosciuszko National Park through site leases administered by the NSW National Parks and Wildlife Service (NPWS) (NSW NPWS, 1998b). Resorts in Victoria differ from those in NSW. They are more dispersed, corresponding to the scattered areas of snow country in that state. Also, all the Victorian

resorts (except Mt Buffalo) are located adjacent to national parks rather than within them. Two Victorian resorts (Lake Mountain and Mt Stirling) are dedicated to cross-country skiing and do not provide accommodation. The only resort in the ACT, Corin Forest, is small and orientated to day visitors, with unreliable natural snow cover and only one lift (Table 14.1).

In order to attract visitors, resorts depend on providing reliable and adequate snow conditions. To do this, they use a variety of snow-manipulation techniques to increase the quality and area of skiable snow, thereby improving the skier experience (PBPL, 1997; König, 1998a,b).

Snow Manipulation in Australian Alps Ski Resorts

Ski-slope development and super-grooming

Ski resorts manipulate snow conditions by altering ski slopes, and this includes extensive changes to soils and natural vegetation communities. Most of the area utilized by resorts was originally subalpine woodlands dominated by snow gums (Eucalyptus niphophila), native heaths, grasslands, bogs and sod-tussock grasslands (Kosciuszko Thredbo Pty Ltd, 1988; PBPL, 1997). Resorts have altered the landscape to enhance the quality and durability of the winter snow pack. Low-level slope grooming in summer can involve the selective removal of trees and any large rocks that could protrude above the snow in winter. More extensive grooming can involve the removal of nearly all rocks protruding above the soil surface and either removal or extensive pruning of shrubs. The most extensive slope modification (super-grooming) can involve the complete removal of native vegetation, blasting of rocks and importation and compaction of soil and fill material using heavy earth-moving equipment. The slope is then seeded with a grass mix containing native and alien species (the alpine mix) (PBPL, 1997). Additionally, creeks may be rerouted and slopes drained to reduce water accumulation. Super-grooming can achieve an even, well-drained, lightly vegetated surface, free of rocks and heath. This

Table 14.1. Increase and extent of snow manipulation in ski resorts in Australia, 1991–2001 (sources: websites for each of the resorts and personal communication with resort snow managers, June 2001).

Resort	Altitude max (m)	Artificial snow area (ha)		Downhill ski area (ha)		Capacity per skiers per h (× 1000)		Cross-country trails (km)		No. snow groomers	Downhill area groomed	
		1991	2001	1991	2001	1991	2001	1991	2001	2001	max (ha) 2001	% total
New South Wales												
Perisher Blue[a]	2054	34.5	35	1114	1250	46.8	53.9	105	100	19	600	48
Thredbo	2037	55	120	163	480	17.1	18	–	12	6	100	21
Charlotte Pass	1980	–	0.5	45	50	2	2.5	–	1.8v	2	8	100
Selwyn Snowfields	1601	5	36	22	45	9.5	9.5	35	45	4	45	100
Total NSW		94.5	191.5	1344	1825	75.4	83.9	140	158.8	31	753	67.25
Victoria												
Mt Buller	1790	10	61.5	162	180	38.5	40	11	12	8	80	57
Falls Creek	1780	10	100	145	450	23	19.4	20	32.8	10	145	32
Mt Hotham	1563	–	10	43	245	11.7	24.5	22	35	8	245	28
Mt Baw Baw	1563	–	3	25	35	6	9	16	10	2	35	100
Mt Buffalo	1595	3.5	3.5	27	30	10	45	14.5	14.5	2	7	70
Lake Mountain[b]	1520	–	0.03	–	–	–	–	27	37	–	–	–
Mount Stirling[b]	1747	–	–	–	–	–	–	65	70	–	–	–
Total Victoria		23.5	178.03	402	940	89.2	137.9	175.5	211.3	30	512	57.4
ACT												
Corin Forest	1200	–	12	–	12	–	–	–	–	1	12	–
Total for all resorts		118	381.53	1746	2777	164.6	221.80	315.5	370.01	62	1277	62

a Perisher Blue Resort was formed by the merger of Perisher-Smiggins and Blue Cow-Guthega Resorts in 1995.
b No accommodation, no downhill ski facilities.

type of slope requires much less snow cover to achieve a skiable surface and is the optimal slope for the deposition of artificial snow (PBPL, 1997). Generally, resort staff groom only their most highly used slopes to this standard.

Snow grooming

Resorts also alter the snow cover in winter, using specialized over-snow vehicles (known generically as 'snow groomers') to compact the snow pack and scarify (cut grooves on) the surface. The aim is to achieve even snow cover and improve skier safety. Snow groomers work for up to 8 h per night in winter to achieve the desired cover and finish. Smaller, more manoeuvrable machines, such as 'snow cats', are used for steep terrain and cross-country tracks. Grooming compacts the snow pack, by mechanically altering snow grain structure and removing air from between ice crystals. This increases snow durability, while decreasing wear on the snow pack and snow loss (Keage, 1990).

Snow grooming is extensively practised at all ski resorts (Table 14.1). Depending on the prevailing weather conditions, around 50% of the total skiable area can be groomed each night. The downhill skiable area of Victorian resorts has almost doubled since 1991, with a corresponding increase in the area of groomed snow. The skiable area of NSW resorts has grown less since 1991, although the existing groomed area is 50% (153 ha) larger than in Victoria (512 ha). In addition, the area of groomed slopes in NSW is likely to increase if plans to expand and upgrade facilities at Perisher Blue Resort are approved (PBPL, 1997).

Snow harvesting using snow fences

A further method used to improve snow cover and depth is the redistribution of snow that naturally accumulates in sheltered sites. It is moved to high-use sites or areas with patchy natural snow cover (PBPL, 1997). Snow loss due to wind scour is also reduced by snow fences at some resorts. The snow that builds up against the fences is then used on location or transported to other high-use areas (Keage, 1990).

Artificial snow making

Artificial snow making allows the ski season to be extended by 2–3 weeks prior to its 'natural' start, improves snow cover when the natural cover is thin, and extends the end of the season (O'Brien and Shepherd, 1985; PBPL, 1997; König, 1998b). It is expensive, in terms of both energy and water (NSW NPWS, 1990; PBPL, 1997; König, 1998b), but is now extensively used in most resorts. There are two

Table 14.2. Direct physical impacts of snow manipulation. (Australian sources: Keane *et al.*, 1980; Keage, 1990; Green and Osborne, 1994; Cousins, 1998; Green, 1998; Growcock, 1999; McDougall and Appleby, 2000. Overseas sources: Wanek, 1971; Neumann and Merriam, 1972; Masyk, 1973; Rickard and Brown, 1974; Gersper and Challinor, 1975; Keddy *et al.*, 1979; Mosimann, 1985; Price, 1985; Watson, 1985; Tsuyuzaki, 1990; Racine and Ahlstrand, 1991; Felix *et al.*, 1992; Forbes, 1992; Pignatti, 1993; Tsuyuzaki and Hokkaido, 1994; Emers *et al.*, 1995; Kevan *et al.*, 1995; Fahey and Wardle, 1998, 1999a,b; Ruth-Balaganskaya, 2000.)

Direct physical effects	Slope grooming	Snow compaction	Snow making	Snow harvesting	Snow fences
Change in snow conditions	*	*	*	*	*
Change in amount of snow	*		*	*	*
Compaction of snow	*	*	*		
Reduction in subniveal space	*	*		*	
Mechanical damage to vegetation	*	*		*	
Compaction of soil	*	*		*	
Introduction of contaminates	*	*	*	*	

snow-making systems in use: fixed-air pressurized installations and non-pressurized mobile fans (snow guns) (Keage, 1990). Both systems atomize water pumped from storage pools. Water is broken into very small droplets and cooled. It may be nucleated with a protein from the bacterium *Pseudomonas syringae*. This protein attracts water molecules and facilitates ice-crystal formation (Brown, 1997), thus increasing the efficiency of artificial snow making and reducing the amount of water required (NSW NPWS, 1990).

There has been a major increase in the area covered by artificial snow in the last 10 years (Table 14.1). In NSW this has increased the skiable area from 7% to 9%, with further areas proposed. In Victoria the use of artificial snow has increased from 6% to 19%, with the two largest Victorian resorts having 34% (Mt Buller) and 68% (Falls Creek) of their skiable area serviced by artificial snow making (Table 14.1).

Impacts of Snow Manipulation

In this review we summarize what is known about the impacts of snow manipulation on vegetation and soils. Then, basing our predictions on overseas studies and on the limited Australian research in this area (see Cousins, 1998; Cole and Hallam, 1999; Growcock, 1999), we describe how snow manipulation may affect the vegetation and soils of the Australian Alps.

Impacts of ski-slope development and summer slope grooming

Environmental degradation as a result of ski-slope development has been clearly demonstrated overseas. Impacts of particular concern include soil erosion, changes in plant-community composition, changes in soil structure, changes in soil biota and hydrology and contamination of ski areas with pathogens and weed propagules (Baiderin, 1983; Kattelmann, 1985; Mosimann, 1985; Watson, 1985; Tsuyuzaki, 1990, 1991; Tsuyuzaki and Hokkaido, 1994; Urbanska, *et al.*, 1999; Ruth-Balaganskaya, 2000).

There are obvious impacts from the physical alteration of the terrain during ski-slope development (see Table 14.2). This alteration

Table 14.3. Likely physical changes and resultant impacts associated with removal of dominant vegetation type as part of slope grooming. (Australian sources: Good, 1995, 1998; Costin *et al.*, 2000; McDougall and Appleby, 2000. Overseas sources: Schrind, 1971; Gersper and Challinor, 1975; Baiderin, 1980, 1983; Hamilton, 1981, cited in Fahey and Wardle, 1998; Illich and Haslett, 1994; Emers *et al.*, 1995; Fahey and Wardle, 1998.)

Change	Impact	Extent of grooming		
		Limited	Moderate	Total
Increased light	Increased biomass in understorey	*	*	*
	Increased soil temperature	*	*	
	Drier conditions in summer	*	*	
Change in winter temperature	Range of effects	*	*	*
Faster snowmelt	Increased frost damage	*	*	*
	Drier conditions in summer	*	*	*
	Longer growing season	*	*	*
Increased wind speeds	Increased evapotranspiration	*	*	
	Direct damage by wind	*	*	

* Indicates increasing effect compared with previous state, e.g. natural to limited, limited to moderate, moderate to total. Limited = removal of trees and large rocks. Moderate = in addition to removal used in limited, shrubs are either removed or slashed, and most rocks removed. Total = removal of all trees and shrubs, physical manipulation of slope shape, importation of new substrate, seeding of area with mix of native and introduced plants.

Table 14.4. Biological impacts as a result of changes in vegetation as part of slope grooming. (Overseas sources: Rickard and Brown, 1974; Keddy *et al.*, 1979; Felix and Raynolds, 1989; Tappeiner and Cernusca, 1989; Tsuyuzaki, 1991; Felix *et al.*, 1992; Forbes, 1992; Holaus and Parti, 1993; Illich and Haslett, 1994; Emers *et al.*, 1995; Fahey and Wardle, 1998.)

	Extent of grooming		
Specific biological impacts	Limited	Moderate	Total
Change in species composition	*	*	*
Reduced native biodiversity	*	*	*
Increased weed diversity and abundance			*
Change in soil biota	*	*	*
Change in root zone	*	*	*
Change in nutrient cycling	*	*	*
Change in native herbivory	*	*	*
Change in pest herbivory (rabbits, etc.)	*	*	*
Change in insect abundance, diversity and activity	*	*	*

* Indicates increasing effect compared with previous state, e.g. natural to limited, limited to moderate, moderate to total. Limited = removal of trees and large rocks. Moderate = in addition to removal used in limited, shrubs are either removed or slashed, and most rocks removed. Total = removal of all trees and shrubs, physical manipulation of slope shape, importation of new substrate, seeding of area with mix of native and introduced plants.

includes clearing of vegetation, removal of rocks, installation of drainage systems, importation of soil and seeding of areas. Environmental-impact statements for Australian ski resorts list a series of direct impacts of slope development and summer slope maintenance. These include changes in natural appearance, soil compaction, soil erosion, and changes in plant-species composition and hydrology (groundwater and surface-water regimes). The most severe impacts are found on slopes that have been subjected to the most intensive grooming regimes (Keane *et al.*, 1980; Good and Grenier, 1994; Good, 1995).

A number of secondary negative environmental impacts of ski-slope development and use have been identified (Tables 14.3 and 14.4). For example, the removal of natural vegetation decreases the water-holding capacity of the soil. This can result in more extensive runoff during rain events and lower soil moisture at other times. Changes in soil moisture can dramatically influence vegetation on the slope as well as in surrounding areas, such as the valley floors, and this leads to changes in plant-community composition (Mosimann, 1985; Watson, 1985). Other secondary impacts include increased growth of the understorey (on super-groomed slopes, often a mixture of exotic and native plants), increased

soil and air temperatures in summer, decreased temperatures in spring and autumn, drier conditions in summer, longer growing seasons and changes in soil biota, including mycorrhiza (Mosimann, 1985; Watson, 1985; Tables 14.3 and 14.4). Even minimal slope grooming that involves trimming and removing trees can affect the ecology of the understorey. For example, decreasing the tree canopy increases the amount of light reaching the understorey, which in turn influences the composition of plant communities (Keane *et al.*, 1980; Tappeiner and Cernusca, 1989; Tables 14.3 and 14.4).

Impacts of snow grooming on vegetation and soil

Direct and indirect impacts of over-snow vehicles and snow-grooming machines have been documented, with snow grooming found to cause significant environmental degradation in ski resorts (Fahey and Wardle, 1998). Impacts may be considered in two categories: (i) those resulting from physical damage by vehicles to the vegetation and soils; and (ii) those resulting from snow compaction and redistribution.

Most studies have examined the impacts of over-snow vehicles on vegetation (Watson *et al.,* 1970; Wanek, 1971; Greller *et al.,* 1974; Baiderin, 1980; Felix and Raynolds, 1989; Emers *et al.,* 1995; Kevan *et al.,* 1995), with damage to vegetation particularly severe when little or no snow cover is present (i.e. at the beginning or end of the season). When snow cover is thin, there is increased mechanical damage to vegetation, greater compaction of vegetation and soil and decreased water infiltration rates into the soil. These changes can result in increased bare ground and the risk of soil erosion (Watson *et al.,* 1970; Wanek, 1971; Greller *et al.,* 1974; Baiderin, 1980; Felix and Raynolds, 1989). Changes to soil chemistry have also been found as a result of use of over-snow vehicles. These include higher soil pH, depleted C, K and P and increased levels of NO_3 and NH_4 (Kevan *et al.,* 1995). High levels of disturbance can result in changes in species composition, such as the replacement of mosses with sedges and of prostrate shrubs with grasses. However, even low levels of disturbance can result in decreased vegetation cover (Emers *et al.,* 1995).

Snow compaction, with increased density and hardness of the snow pack, is a major objective of snow grooming (e.g. Wanek, 1971; Neumann and Merriam, 1972; Baiderin, 1980, 1983; Kattelmann, 1985; Racine and Ahlstrand, 1991; Fahey and Wardle, 1999a,b; Table 14.2). This compaction can directly damage plant species that have tissue in the snow pack. As a result, woody, erect species such as shrubs and low trees are among the most susceptible to direct damage from snow compaction (Felix *et al.,* 1992; Forbes, 1992; Emers *et al.,* 1995). Herbs and grasses, in contrast, commonly die back in winter, with buds often protected at or below the surface (Greller *et al.,* 1974). Therefore they are less likely to experience direct mechanical damage associated with compaction of snow.

Changes in the snow pack as a result of snow compaction also cause an array of secondary impacts (Table 14.5). Compaction increases the snow's thermal conductivity and reduces its heat-insulation capacity. This can result in reductions in soil temperatures and increased frost penetration of the soil (Wanek, 1971). Such changes in soil temperature can be dramatic. Five- to sevenfold reductions in soil temperature and seven- to 11-fold increases in penetration of frost into the soil beneath compacted snow have been reported (Baiderin, 1980, 1983). Where flower and vegetative buds occur along branches within the snow pack, such as in many woody shrubs, direct damage to the plant tissue can occur as a result of these lower temperatures in the compacted snow. Freezing soils and changes in snowmelt patterns in the spring can also adversely affect lower-growing plants such as herbs. Secondary impacts of snow compaction include a decrease in the rate of decomposition of organic material, due to the reduced temperatures (Neumann and Merriam, 1972; Meyer, 1993). There can also be reductions in

Table 14.5. Effect of snow manipulation on snow-pack characteristics. (Australian sources: Growcock, 1999. Overseas sources: Schrind, 1971; Neumann and Merriam, 1972; Baiderin, 1980, 1983; Kattelmann, 1985; Newesely *et al.,* 1993; Fahey and Wardle, 1998, 1999a,b.)

Effect on snow pack	Snow grooming	Snow making	Snow harvesting	Snow fences
Increased snow density and hardness	*	*		*
Decreased water-holding capacity	*			
Formation of ice layers at the soil surface	*			
Decreased snow permeability	*		*	
Reduced porosity (faster snowmelt)	*		*	
Increased thermal energy transfer – so soils under snow pack colder, frost penetration into soil deeper	*		*	
Increased snow-pack retention in spring	*	*		*
Faster runoff in spring.	*			
Loss/decrease of subniveal space	*			

the number of soil bacteria and fungi involved in nutrient cycling and even oxygen deficiency in the soil (Neumann and Merriam, 1972; Meyer, 1993; Newesely et al., 1993).

Changes in snow-pack characteristics can result in a later snowmelt in spring, thus decreasing the length of the growing season (Neumann and Merriam, 1972; Keddy et al., 1979; Table 14.6). For example, snow retention can delay the onset of flowering, resulting in a shortened flowering season for populations (Baiderin, 1983). This can cause changes in the composition of plant communities, with the proportions of spring- and summer-flowering species declining, while autumn-flowering species increase (Baiderin, 1980). Delayed snowmelt has been shown to change soil carbon : nitrogen ratios (Walsh et al., 1997). Changes of this kind differentially affect plant growth characteristics and can alter the composition of plant communities (Neumann and Merriam, 1972; Masyk, 1973; Felix et al., 1992; Forbes, 1992; Körner, 1999). The compaction of snow also eliminates the subniveal space (natural space between the soil surface and bottom layer of the snow pack), restricting the movement of small mammals under the snow (Baiderin, 1983). Changes in fauna activity can then affect the vegetation by changing herbivory and other impacts (Green and Osborne, 1994; Körner, 1999).

Impacts of snow harvesting and artificial snow on vegetation and soil

Snow depth is changed by snow harvesting, i.e. the stockpiling and redistribution of snow (Table 14.6). This can have a range of impacts on vegetation. For example, if snow depth is increased, the amount of light that penetrates the snow may be decreased, with resultant delays in seed germination and flowering of plants, and growth retardation (Richardson and Salisbury, 1977; Körner, 1999). Increased snow depth has been found to delay the onset of snowmelt. The results of this can include changes in soil conditions, such as reduced organic content, water content, nitrogen and phosphorus and increased acidity of soil (Stanton et al., 1994). Because changes in snow depth differentially affect plant species, the composition of communities may be modified (Richardson and Salisbury, 1977; Körner 1999). For example, species richness and total vegetation cover can be decreased in sites with later snowmelt (Stanton et al., 1994).

There have been very few studies on the

Table 14.6. Range of secondary biological impacts likely on vegetation as a result of changes in timing of snowmelt associated with snow manipulation. (Overseas sources: as for Table 14.3. Plus Richardson and Salisbury, 1977; Tappeiner and Cernusca, 1989; Holaus and Parti, 1993; Illich and Haslett, 1994; Stanton et al., 1994; Jones and Devarennes, 1995; Walsh et al., 1997; Fahey and Wardle, 1998; Urbanska et al., 1999.)

Physical change and biological effect	Slope grooming	Snow compression	Snow making	Snow harvesting
Later snowmelt[a]				
Shorter growing season	*	*		*
More water in spring	*	*		*
Colder soils in spring	*	*		*
Longer protection from frosts	*	*		*
Change in soil biota	*	*		*
Earlier snowmelt[a]				
Longer growing season			*	*
Less water in spring			*	*
Warmer soils in spring			*	*
Less insulation from frosts			*	*
Drought in summer			*	*
Change in soil biota			*	*

[a] Snowmelt might be earlier or later depending on the effect of the change in snow conditions due to snow manipulation.

environmental effects of artificial snow on the natural environment. The few such studies, however, indicate that artificial snow can affect vegetation. For example, the chemical composition of artificial-snow melt water may differentially affect growth characteristics of ground-cover plants (Holaus and Parti, 1993; Jones and Devarennes, 1995). Some plant species have also been observed to be more abundant adjacent to natural-snow melt water, while others prefer artificial-snow melt water (Holaus and Parti, 1993; Jones and Devarennes, 1995).

Impacts of slope grooming and snow grooming in Australia

There has been little empirical research in Australia examining the effects of snow manipulation on vegetation. In two of the few studies in Australia, ski-slope construction, slope grooming and snow grooming at Perisher Valley have been found to have altered soil structure and composition (Cousins, 1998; Growcock, 1999). The super-groomed, revegetated ski slopes had thin mineral soils with minimal organic content, compared with the deep peat soils found on undeveloped sites. Vegetation on the ski slopes was dominated by sedges (*Carex* sp.) and introduced plant species, with few areas of mosses (*Sphagnum*), in contrast to undeveloped sites. The hydrology of the ski slopes was altered, resulting in increased infiltration rates but lower water-holding capacity (Growcock, 1999). This increased the potential for erosion during snowmelt on the developed ski slopes (Growcock, 1999).

Many indirect impacts of snow grooming do not seem to have been examined in Australia. This is surprising since grooming occurs over large areas of resorts and secondary environmental impacts have adversely affected vegetation in ski resorts overseas.

Impacts of artificial snow making in Australia

While it has been suggested that snow making will result in unacceptable changes to flora

and water quality in Australia (Good and Grenier, 1994; Good, 1995), as far as the authors are aware only one study has specifically investigated this activity. Cole and Hallam (1999) examined some effects of artificial snow, made using the additive 'Snomax', on alpine vegetation, soil and water. The study was largely limited to an examination of microbial differences between leaf surfaces following cover with natural and artificial snow. While the study concluded that no changes in microbial damage to vegetation occurred, some of the conclusions do not appear to be supported by their data (McDougall, 2000). The authors did not examine impacts on any other vegetation characteristics.

Predicted Impacts of Snow Manipulation on Flora in the Australian Alps

Although there is little Australian research on impacts of snow manipulation, some predictions can be made, based on evidence from overseas studies on snow manipulation, combined with research on other land-use impacts on vegetation in the Australian Alps. For example, it is likely that groundwater communities such as bogs, fens and sod-tussock grasslands would be highly susceptible to the changes in hydrology associated with snow manipulation in Australia. We have already described how slope grooming, snow grooming, artificial snow making and snow harvesting can all affect the hydrology of a site. In the Australian Alps, changes in drainage patterns associated with previous land use have had clear negative impacts on these communities, some of which are still recovering (Wimbush and Costin, 1985; Good and Grenier, 1994).

Australian woody shrubs, such as yellow bottlebrush (*Callistemon sieberi*), yellow kunzea (*Kunzea muelleri*), alpine baeckea (*Baeckea gunniana*) and alpine heaths (*Epacris* spp.), appear likely to be susceptible to the types of direct physical damage from groomers and over-snow vehicles that have been described in plants with a similar form overseas. Other heath species, such as ovate phebalium (*Phebalium ovatifolium*), the alpine and royal grevilleas (*Grevillea australis* and *Grevillea victoriae*), alpine orites (*Orites lancifolia*), alpine mint bush (*Prostantha cuneata*) and native peas (*Hovea* spp., *Oxylobium* spp. and *Bossiaea* spp.), are also at risk. These shrubs are likely to be directly affected not only by physical damage from snow compaction, but also by freezing damage to floral buds and growing points on the branches caused by likely changes in the thermal properties of the snow pack.

Direct damage caused by snow grooming to species with high conservation status, such as old snow gums (*E. niphophila*) and mountain plum pine (*Podocarpus lawrencei*), has also been recorded (Gen Wright, NPWS, personal communication; personal observation).

Conclusions

Despite the high conservation values of the receding alpine habitat in and around ski resorts in Australia and the increased utilization of these lands for 'non-consumptive' activities, such as ecotourism, there are limited field data directly addressing the impact of snow manipulation. This is despite clear evidence from overseas of the significant impact of snow manipulation on vegetation and soils. In particular, impacts arising from physical changes, such as compaction of the snow pack and variation in its depth and duration, are well known. The continuing demand for snow manipulation, and in particular increased snow making, makes it vital that research is conducted to help us understand better the potential impacts of this activity on areas of high conservation value in the Australian Alps.

Acknowledgements

Financial support from the Cooperative Research Centre for Sustainable Tourism for this research is gratefully acknowledged. We thank the two independent anonymous reviewers of this research and Editing Matters (Darri Adamson) for comments on the manuscript.

References

Baiderin, V.V. (1980) Experimental modelling of ecological consequences of winter recreations. *Soviet Journal of Ecology* 11, 140–146.

Baiderin, V.V. (1983) Winter recreation and subnivean plant development. *Soviet Journal of Ecology* 13, 287–291.

Brown, R. (1997) Man made snow. *Scientific American.* http://www.sciam.com/0197issue 0197working.html Viewed March 2002.

Buckby, M., Burgan, B. and Molloy, J. (1993) *The Economic Significance of the Alpine Resorts.* Centre for South Australian Economic Studies, University of Adelaide, Adelaide, Australia.

Buckley, R.C., Pickering, C.M. and Warnken, J. (2000) Environmental management for alpine tourism and resorts in Australia. In: Goode, P.M., Price, M.F. and Zimmermann, F.M. (eds) *Tourism and Development in Mountain Regions.* CAB International, Wallingford, UK, pp. 27–46.

Cole, F.M. and Hallam, N.D. (1999) *A Report on the Effect of Artificial Snow Making on the Vegetation, Soil and Water of Thredbo and Perisher Valley, NSW, 1999–2000.* Report to the New South Wales National Parks and Wildlife Service, Jindabyne.

Costin, A.B., Gray, M., Totterdell, C.J. and Wimbush, D.J. (2000) Kosciuszko Alpine Flora. Jointly published by the Commonwealth Scientific and Industrial Research Organization and Collins, Sydney, Australia.

Cousins, K. (1998) An assessment of soil disturbance in two catchments, located in the region of Kosciuszko National Park, through the identification and comparison of organic horizon characteristics. Honours thesis, Australian National University, Canberra, Australia.

Digance, J. and Norris, R. (1999) Environmental impacts of tourism in the Australian Alps: Thredbo River Valley. *Pacific Tourism Review* 3, 37–48.

Emers, M., Jorgenson, J.C. and Raynolds, M.K. (1995) Response of arctic tundra plant communities to winter vehicle disturbance. *Canadian Journal of Botany* 73, 905–917.

Fahey, B. and Wardle, K. (1998) *Likely Impacts of Snow Grooming and Related Activities in the West Otago Ski Fields.* Department of Conservation, Wellington, New Zealand.

Fahey, B. and Wardle, K. (1999a) Environmental effects associated with snow grooming and skiing at the Treble Cone ski field. Part I. Vegetation and soil disturbance. *Science for Conservation* 120, 1–48.

Fahey, B. and Wardle, K. (1999b) Environmental

effects associated with snow grooming and skiing at the Treble Cone ski field. Part 2. Snow properties on groomed and ungroomed slopes. *Science for Conservation* 120, 49–62.

Felix, N.A. and Raynolds, M.K. (1989) The effects of winter seismic trails on tundra vegetation in north-eastern Alaska, USA. *Arctic and Alpine Research* 21, 188–202.

Felix, N.A., Raynolds, M.K., Jorgenson, J.C. and DuBois, K.E. (1992) Resistance and resilience of tundra plant communities to disturbance by winter seismic vehicles. *Arctic and Alpine Research* 24, 69–77.

Forbes, B.C. (1992) Tundra disturbance studies, I: Long term effects of vehicle disturbance on species richness and biomass. *Environmental Conservation* 19, 48–58.

Gersper, P.L. and Challinor, J.L. (1975) Vehicle perturbation effects upon a tundra soil–plant system: I. Effects on morphological and physical environmental properties of the soil. *Proceedings of the Soil Science Society of America* 39, 737–746.

Good, R. (1995) Ecologically sustainable development in the Australian Alps. *Mountain Research and Development* 15, 251–258.

Good, R. (1998) Changing snow regimes and the distribution of alpine vegetation. In: Green, K. (ed.) *Snow: a Natural History and Uncertain Future.* Australian Alps Liaison Committee, Canberra, Australia, pp. 98–112.

Good, R. and Grenier, P. (1994) Some environmental impacts of recreation in the Australian Alps. *Australian Parks and Recreation* Summer, 20–26.

Green, K. (1998) A winter niche: the subnivean space. In: Green, K. (ed.) *Snow: a Natural History and Uncertain Future.* Australian Alps Liaison Committee, Canberra, Australia. pp. 125–140.

Green, K. and Osborne, W.S. (1994) *Wildlife of the Australian Snow-Country.* Reed, Sydney.

Greller, A.M., Goldstein, M. and Marcus, L. (1974) Snowmobile impact on three alpine tundra plant communities. *Environmental Conservation* 1(2), 101–110.

Grenier, P. (1992) Skiing in the Australian Alps: development and conflict. In: Good, R. (ed.) *The Australian Alps.* Revue de Géographie Alpine, Grenoble, France, pp. 227–275.

Growcock, A. (1999) Ski industry development in Kosciuszko National Park: a comparison of slope hydrology. Graduate Diploma thesis, Australian National University, Canberra, Australia.

Hamilton, E.H. (1981) The alpine vegetation of Marmot Basin, Jasper National Park, Alberta,

and the impact of ski activities upon It. Masters thesis, University of Alberta, Edmonton, Alberta, Canada.

Holaus, K. and Parti, C. (1993) Artificial snow covering of permanent meadows: effects of plant composition, biomass accumulation and soil structure. *Verhandlungen – Gesellschaft für Ökologie* 23, 269–276.

Illich, I.P. and Haslett, J.R. (1994) Responses of assemblages of orthoptera to management and use of ski slopes on upper sub-alpine meadows in the Austrian Alps. *Oecologia* 97(4), 470–474.

Jones, H.G. and Devarennes, G. (1995) The chemistry of artificial snow and its influence on germination of mountain flora. *Biogeochemistry of Seasonally Snow Covered Catchments* 228, 355–360.

Kattelmann, R. (1985) Snow management at ski areas: hydrological effects. In: *Watershed Management in the Eighties.* Proceedings of a symposium of the American Society of Civil Engineers, Colorado, USA.

Keage, P. (1990) Skiing in the greenhouse. *Trees and Natural Resources* 32, 15–18.

Keane, P.A., Wild, A.E.R. and Rogers, J.H. (1980) Soil conservation on the ski slopes. *Journal of the Soil Conservation Services of New South Wales* 36, 6–15.

Keddy, P.A., Spavold, A.J. and Keddy, C.J. (1979) Snowmobile impact on old field and marsh vegetation in Nova Scotia, Canada: an experimental study. *Environmental Management* 3, 409–414.

Kevan, P.G., Forbes, B.C., Kevan, S.M. and Behan-Pelleiter, V. (1995) Vehicle tracks on high Arctic tundra: their effects on the soil, vegetation, and soil arthropods. *Journal of Applied Ecology* 32, 655–667.

König, U. (1998a) Climate change and tourism: investigations into the decision making process of skiers in the Australian ski fields. *Pacific Tourism Review* 2, 83–90.

König, U. (1998b) Climate change and the Australian ski industry. In: Green, K. (ed.) *Snow: a Natural History and Uncertain Future.* Australian Alps Liaison Committee, Canberra, Australia, pp. 207–223.

Körner, C. (1999) *Alpine Plant Life: Functional Plant Ecology of High Mountain Ecosystems.* Springer, Berlin, Germany.

Kosciuszko Thredbo Pty Ltd (1988) *Thredbo Village Master Plan.* Prepared for KTPL by Rice Daubney in Association with Margules and Partners and Sinclair Knight and Partners, Jindabyne, Australia.

KPMG Management Consulting (1994) *NSW Alpine*

Industry: Economic Impact Study. Report prepared on behalf of the Australian Ski Industry Association, Sydney, Australia.

McDougall, K. (2000) *Comments on 'A Report on the Effect of Artificial Snow Making on the Alpine Vegetation, Soil and Water of Thredbo and Perisher Valley, NSW 1999–2000' by Cole and Hallam.* New South Wales National Parks and Wildlife Service, Jindabyne, Australia.

McDougall, K.L. and Appleby, M.L. (2000) Plant invasions in the high mountains of north-eastern Victoria. *The Victorian Naturalist* 117, 52–59.

McKercher, B. (1996) Differences between tourism and recreation in national parks. *Annals of Tourism Research* 23(3), 563–575.

Masyk, W.J. (1973) *The Snowmobile, a Recreational Technology in Banff National Park: Environmental Impact and Decision Making.* Studies in Landuse History and Landscape Change, National Park Series No. 5, University of Calgary, Calgary, Alberta, Canada.

Meyer, E. (1993) The impact of summer and winter tourism on the fauna of alpine soils in western Austria (Oetztal Alps, Ratikon). *Revue Suisse de Zoologie* 100, 519–517.

Mosimann, T. (1985) Geo-ecological impacts of ski piste construction in the Swiss Alps. *Applied Geography* 5, 29–37.

Neumann, P.W. and Merriam, H.G. (1972) Ecological effects of snowmobiles. *Canadian Field Naturalist* 86, 207–212.

Newesely, C., Cernusca, A. and Bodner, M. (1993) Origin and effects of oxygen deficiency on differently prepared ski slopes. *Verhandlungen – Gesellschaft fur Okologie* 23, 277–282.

New South Wales National Parks and Wildlife Service (NSW NPWS) (1990) *Ski 2000.* Discussion Paper, NSW NPWS, Sydney, Australia.

New South Wales National Parks and Wildlife Service (NSW NPWS) (1998a) *Final Submission to the Commission of Inquiry into the Perisher Range Village Master Plan/Environmental Impact Statement.* For the NSW NPWS, June 1998, Sydney, Australia.

New South Wales National Parks and Wildlife Service (NSW NPWS) (1998b) *Proposed Perisher Range Resort Area Village Centre Master Plan.* Report to the Minister for Urban Affairs and Planning and the Minister for Housing by the NSW NPWS, November 1998, Sydney, Australia.

O'Brien, P. and Shepherd, T. (1985) *Blue Cow Ski Resort Snow Making System: Review of Environmental Factors.* For the New South Wales National Parks and Wildlife Service, Jindabyne, Australia.

Perisher Blue Pty Ltd (PBPL) (1997) *Perisher Blue Ski Resort Draft Mountain Master Plan. An Overview of the Main Elements of the Perisher Blue Ski Slope Plan.* PBPL, David Hogg Pty Ltd and Design Workshop, Inc., Sydney, Australia.

Pignatti, S. (1993) Impacts of tourism on the mountain landscape of central Italy. *Landscape and Urban Planning* 24, 49–53.

Price, M.F. (1985) Impacts of recreational activities on alpine vegetation in western North America. *Mountain Research and Development* 5, 263–277.

Racine, C.H. and Ahlstrand, G.M. (1991) Thaw response of tussock shrub tundra to experimental all-terrain vehicle disturbances in south-central Alaska. *Arctic* 44, 31–37.

Richardson, S.G. and Salisbury, F.B. (1977) Plant responses to the light penetrating snow. *Ecology* 58, 1152–1158.

Rickard, W.E. and Brown, J. (1974) Effects of vehicles on Arctic tundra. *Environmental Conservation* 1, 55–61.

Ruth-Balaganskaya, E. (2000) Soil nutrient status and revegetation practices of downhill skiing areas in Finnish Lapland: a case study of Mt Yllas. *Landscape and Urban Planning* 50, 259–268.

Schrind, W.D. (1971) Modification of subniveal microclimate by snowmobiles. In: Haugen, A.O. (ed.) *Proceedings, Symposium on Snow and Ice in Relation to Wildlife and Recreation.* Iowa State University Press, Ames, Iowa, USA.

Stanton, M.L., Rejmanek, M. and Galen, C. (1994) Changes in vegetation and soil fertility along a predictable snowmelt gradient in the Mosquito Range, Colorado, USA. *Arctic and Alpine Research* 26, 364–374.

Tappeiner, U. and Cernusca, A. (1989) Canopy structure and light climate of different alpine plant communities: analysis by means of a model. *Theoretical and Applied Climatology* 40, 81–92.

Tsuyuzaki, S. (1990) Species composition and soil erosion on a ski area in Hokkaido, northern Japan. *Environmental Management* 14, 203–207.

Tsuyuzaki, S. (1991) Present condition and regeneration of ski ground vegetation in Hokkaido: ski grounds which have received modification. *Japanese Journal of Ecology* 41, 83–91. Abstract only available in English.

Tsuyuzaki, S. and Hokkaido, S. (1994) Environmental deterioration resulting from ski-resort construction in Japan. *Environmental Conservation* 21, 121–125.

Urbanska, K.M., Fattorini, M., Theiel, K. and Pflugshaupt, K. (1999) Seed rain on alpine ski runs in Switzerland. *Botanica Helvetica* 109, 199–216.

Walsh, N.E., McCabe, T.R., Welker, J.M. and Parsons, A.N. (1997) Experimental manipulation of snow-depth: effects on nutrient content of caribou forage. *Global Climate Change* 3, 158–164.

Wanek, I.W.J. (1971) Snowmobile impacts on vegetation, temperature and soil microbes. In: Chubb, M. (ed.) *Proceedings of the 1971 Snowmobile and Off-road Vehicle Symposium in Michigan State University.* Technical Report No. 8, Department of Parks and Recreation Resources, Michigan State University, East Lansing, USA.

Watson, A. (1985) Soil erosion and vegetation damage near ski lifts at Cairn Gorm, Scotland. *Biological Conservation* 33, 363–381.

Watson, A., Bayfield, N. and Moyes, S.M. (1970) Research on human pressures on Scottish tundra, soil and animals. In: Fuller, W.A. and Kevan, P.G. (eds) *Productivity and Conservation in Northern Circumpolar Lands.* Paper No. 27. New Series 16, pp. 256–266.

Wimbush, D. and Costin, A.B. (1985) Trends in drainage characteristics in the subalpine zone at Kosciuszko. *Proceeding of the Ecological Society of Australia* 12, 143–154.

15

A Method for Calculating Environmental Sensitivity to Walker Trampling in the Tasmanian Wilderness World Heritage Area

Jennie Whinam, Nicole Chilcott, Roger Ling and Phil Wyatt
Department of Primary Industries, Water and Environment, Hobart, Australia

Abstract

A walking-track management strategy has been prepared as a framework to manage the impacts of walkers in the Tasmanian Wilderness World Heritage Area, Australia. The main components of the strategy include: a system of categorizing tracks, based on the zoning of the area and the level of track infrastructure; an education campaign; monitoring impacts on existing tracks; and research into the impacts of walkers in various environments.

This chapter examines how sustainable carrying capacities might be calculated for walking areas in the Tasmanian wilderness, based on walking-track monitoring, walker-impact trampling trials and sensitivity mapping. This information can be used to estimate at what level user quotas may need to be set, or intensive management measures applied, to maintain ecological sustainability of specific areas.

Experimental trials have been established to examine the effects of different trampling intensities and the effects of spreading walker traffic over different time periods. These trials have been established at sites of varying altitude, slope, aspect, bedrock geology, soils and vegetation communities. The areas represent typical montane and alpine walking environments in the Tasmanian Wilderness World Heritage Area. Over a period of 5 years, data have been collected on impacts on vegetation and soils and subsequent recovery, to provide an environmental framework for management decisions. From these data it is possible to assess the sensitivity of vegetation communities to trampling impacts, and to extrapolate recovery data for the different plant life-forms present. The geographical information system (GIS) mapping programs MapInfo Professional and Vertical Mapper provide an efficient means of geographically representing likely impacts at various usage levels over large areas.

Introduction

The Tasmanian Wilderness World Heritage Area (WHA) is one of the largest conservation reserves in Australia. With a total area of 1.38 million ha, the WHA occupies approximately 20% of the island State of Tasmania. The WHA contains outstanding geological, biological, aesthetic and cultural features. The area is also highly valued for recreation and tourism based on its natural and scenic qualities. The management objectives of the WHA are to identify, protect, conserve and rehabilitate the natural and cultural values (Parks and Wildlife Service, 1999). The balance between protecting natural and cultural resources in wilderness recreational areas while providing quality visitor experiences is made more challenging because of increasing visitation, cumulative resource impacts and shrinking budgets (Wang et al., 2000).

The *Walking Track Management Strategy for the Tasmanian Wilderness World Heritage Area* (Parks and Wildlife Service, 1994) was prepared as a framework for managing the impacts of recreational walkers in the Tasmanian Wilderness WHA. The strategy details the recreational opportunities available, classifies all tracks into a seven-tiered classification system, sets priorities for future upgrading and reconstruction and suggests new approaches to walking-track management. Recommendations for regulation, works, education, monitoring and research are all detailed and take into account issues across the entire WHA. The strategy also recognizes that no single technique can manage all impacts and that combinations of techniques will apply in different recreational settings.

The strategy moves away from intensive works in small areas to a more holistic, wide-area approach to management. This includes extensive erosion control works, more emphasis on investigating and implementing rerouting of tracks to more resilient areas and more appropriate grades, closure of some tracks and upgrading works appropriate for the track classification.

An intensive education programme, with brochures, videos and travelling displays, advises walkers of current management practices and highlights problems with past management techniques. It also seeks support from the bushwalking community in accepting new management initiatives. The programme highlights the need to regulate use in areas where impacts are high and where other management techniques may cause displacement of walkers and changes to the recreational opportunities.

The final focus of the strategy is a detailed monitoring and research programme to study the impacts of bushwalkers on vegetation, the rate of track development and the measuring of rates of change in track conditions. Over 500 monitoring sites have been established in representative areas to sample impacts on the track network. It is from this extensive monitoring programme that the experimental walker-impact trials were initiated, to quantify walker impacts.

The aim of this chapter is to present two examples from Western Tasmania that illustrate how a variety of different data can be combined to visually display the environmental limitations of an area when planning new tracks and campsites or when assessing options in managing recreational impacts.

This case study examines how sustainable carrying capacities (i.e. numbers of walkers that can visit an area each year before degradation occurs) might be calculated for walking areas in the Tasmanian wilderness. This study is based on walking-track monitoring, walker-impact trampling trials and vegetation and sensitivity mapping. This information may then be used to estimate at what level quotas for the number of walkers may need to be set or intensive management applied to ensure long-term sustainability of walking tracks.

To address issues of user demand and user impacts, a series of recreation resource management innovations have been developed, including the recreation opportunity spectrum (ROS) planning system and the limits of acceptable change (LAC) system for wilderness planning (Cole and McCool, 1998; Wang et al., 2000).

Key thresholds in walking-track development are likely to be at two stages and usage levels: (i) when untracked areas develop pads, i.e. visibly trampled routes with living vegetation mostly intact; and (ii) when pads turn into tracks, i.e. visibly trampled routes with green vegetation removed from the track surface. Thresholds acceptable to managers and users are likely to be influenced by whether the site is at the 'primitive' or 'urban' end of the ROS (Buist and Hoots, 1982). Research data from untracked country on the levels of use at which pads and tracks develop can assist in

Fig. 15.1. Location of study sites in the Tasmanian Wilderness World Heritage Area.

the development of indicators when setting LAC in various recreational settings.

In addition to monitoring existing tracks, experimental walker trials have been established to examine the effect of different trampling intensities in typical Tasmanian alpine and montane bushwalking environments, as well as the effect of spreading walker traffic over different time periods. These trials have been established at sites of varying altitude, slope, aspect, soils, bedrock geology and vegetation communities, to represent typical

Table 15.1. Environmental site data for experimental trampling trial sites and modelling sites.

	Experimental trampling trial sites			Modelling sites	
	Central Plateau	Western Arthur Range	Tim Shea	Anne Range	Dennison Range
Altitude (m a.s.l.)	1000–1420	300–1160	950–1000	300–1425	400–1280
Rainfall (mm per annum)	800–3000	Up to 3000	Up to 2000	2000–2500	2000–2500
Geology	Jurassic dolerite and Tertiary basalt	Precambrian quartzite and schist	Precambrian quartzite and schist	Precambrian quartzite and Jurassic dolerite	Ordovician conglomerate and sandstone

a.s.l., above sea level.

montane and alpine environments in the Tasmanian Wilderness WHA. Over a period of 5 years, surface profiles and changes in vegetation cover at different intensities of trampling have been recorded. In the Western Arthur Range subsequent recovery rates are also being monitored. From these data it is possible to identify the sensitivity of life-forms in these vegetation communities to trampling impacts, and hence to predict sustainable carrying capacities. This information can then be displayed geographically to show likely impacts at various usage levels over large areas.

Methods

Trampling trials were established in three representative vegetation communities, topographies, geologies and climatic settings, namely the Western Arthur Range, Tim Shea Range and Central Plateau (Fig. 15.1, Table 15.1). Incorporating data from these trials, the sensitivity of vegetation communities to trampling impact was modelled for two further areas, the Anne Range (Fig. 15.2) and the Denison Range (Fig 15.3).

Fig. 15.2. Mt Anne (left) from above Spanner Lake, Anne Range, Tasmania.   Photograph: Grant Dixon.

Fig. 15.3. Northern Denison Range from above Lake Rhona. Photograph: Parks and Wildlife Service, Tasmania.

Site descriptions

The Western Arthur Range study area was selected for experimental trampling because it is typical of many of the quartzitic alpine environments in Tasmania in which the main recreational activity is bushwalking, both on and off marked tracks. The range is subject to prevailing westerly winds, cool to mild temperatures (mean annual maximum 10°C), low evaporation and high relative humidity. It is estimated that peat formation in this environment is of the order of 1–2 cm every 1000 years (M. Pemberton, personal communication). The subalpine vegetation on the Western Arthur Range comprises bolster heath (various cushion-plant species with some grasses and sedges) and heath to scrub in sheltered depressions. Fjaeldmark and bolster heath are typical in exposed alpine areas. Extensive descriptions of this region can be found in Kirkpatrick (1980) and Pemberton (1989).

The Tim Shea Range is subject to extreme westerly winds and is typical of the quartzitic montane buttongrass environments that dominate much of montane western Tasmania, where recreational activity is primarily bushwalking, both on and off marked trails.

The Central Plateau of Tasmania is a continuous sheet of Jurassic dolerite, several hundred metres thick, with some overlying outcrops of Tertiary and Triassic rocks (Banks, 1973). In contrast to the mountain ranges of western Tasmania, the alpine/subalpine Central Plateau of Tasmania has a history of disturbance by human activity. The combination of livestock grazing (excluded 1989), burning (prohibited 1989) and burrowing and grazing by introduced rabbits (myxomatosis introduced in 1952) has resulted in widespread and severe sheet erosion (Jackson, 1973; Pemberton, 1986; Richley, 1986; Jetson, 1989). The Central Plateau includes the most severely eroded alpine and subalpine ecosystems in Australia (Cullen, 1995). The subalpine and alpine plant communities of the Central Plateau have been described by Jackson (1973) and Kirkpatrick (1983, 1986, 1997). The vegetation includes one of the largest remaining tracts of native grasslands in Tasmania, and several rare and unreserved species (Kirkpatrick *et al.*, 1988). *Grevillea australis* is dominant in the understorey of the shrublands. The grasslands are dominated by tussock grasses (*Poa labillardierei, Poa gunnii*). Bolster heath is dominated by the cushion plant, *Abrotanella forsteroides*. Detailed soil and vegetation descriptions of the shrubland, grassland, fen and bolster heath sites are given in Whinam *et al.* (1994).

The Anne Range varies in topography from a flat plateau to slopes of up to 30°, and there is a dramatic change in vegetation as a response to the boundary between the dolerite and quartzite areas. As altitude increases, the open scrub is replaced by open heath and then bolster moorland and herbfield, with islands of closed heath. Revegetation and erosion of disturbed sites may be hampered by frost heave (Pemberton, 1989).

The Denison Range is dominated by prominent ridges and peaks of siliceous Ordovician conglomerate and sandstone. Soil formation on higher slopes has been restricted by soil slippage due to steeply dipping bedrock. Slope varies from 5° on crests and ridges up to 80° on the upper slopes (Pemberton, 1989). The vegetation ranges from closed heath and sedgeland on slopes, crests and ridges to heath and sedgeland on higher slopes (Pemberton, 1989).

Experimental trampling

Experimental trampling trials were established in three locations: the Western Arthur and Tim Shea Ranges in south-west Tasmania, and the Central Plateau. These sites encompass nine vegetation communities of differing geology, soil type, slope and aspect. In the Western Arthur and Tim Shea Ranges, trampling treatments were applied in steep, sloping and flat alpine herbfields and sloping montane buttongrass. On the Central Plateau, treatments were applied in grassland, fen, cushion and shrubland. The duration of the experimental periods for these trials ranged from 1 to 5 years.

Trampling was conducted in randomly allocated lanes by volunteers ranging in weight (59–96 kg) and bushwalking experience. All volunteer walkers carried overnight packs weighing between 12 and 21 kg. Due to logistic considerations associated with the remote location of the sites, all trampling was conducted on a single day (cf. Hylgaard and Liddle, 1981; Cole, 1987; Cole and Bayfield, 1993) and midway through the growing season (Cole, 1993) when peak recreational walking occurs in the Tasmanian Wilderness

WHA (S. Rundle, unpublished data, 1998). Other experimental trampling trials have found little or no difference between the impacts of trampling carried out all at once, as compared with the same amount of trampling spread out over a longer period (Hylgaard and Liddle, 1981; Price, 1985; Cole, 1987; Cole and Bayfield, 1993). Treatment levels applied were 0 passes per annum (control), 30 passes per annum (low intensity), 100 passes per annum (medium) and 500 (Western Arthur Range/Tim Shea) or 700 (Central Plateau) passes per annum (high). Sites were retrampled annually at the Western Arthur Range sites for 3 years, with the exception of the 500-pass treatments, which were rested for the second year due to concerns over continuing degradation and erosion.

Measurements were recorded prior to and immediately after trampling, and at 6 weeks, 6 months and 1 year after trampling. In the Western Arthur Range, sites were monitored at this frequency for the first 3 years of the trial and then annually for the following 2 years.

Data were collected for change in vegetation cover using 50 cm × 50 cm quadrat squares (Whinam and Chilcott, 1999, 2003). Species data were aggregated to life-form level for analysis, because of the low percentage cover of some species. Soil/vegetation surface profiles (Whinam and Comfort, 1996; Whinam and Chilcott, 1999) were measured at each site to quantify soil and vegetation loss, as well as compaction and churning resulting from trampling. Broken plant material was collected from all trampling lanes following impact. Broken material was dried and weighed. Comparisons of results for each life-form were made to determine the susceptibility of life-forms to breakage resulting from trampling impact.

Vegetation data were analysed for each set of trampling trials as change in percentage cover or change in relative vegetation cover (Bayfield, 1979; Cole and Bayfield, 1993). Loss of vegetation/soil from surface profiles was calculated as total loss from treatments or by comparison of medians (McPherson, 1990). Impact and recovery were quantified for all sites and treatment levels.

Sensitivity mapping

Trampling sensitivity maps were produced for the Anne and Denison Ranges using data from the experimental trampling trials in the other three sites. Maps were produced using the desktop geographical information system (GIS) software program MapInfo Professional, together with a plug-in Vertical Mapper. Map layers used to build all maps were obtained from existing files or created using standard GIS techniques.

Digital elevation models (DEMs) were first constructed for the two case-study areas in the Anne and Denison Ranges. These DEMs, which use a raster-based coverage commonly termed a 'grid', were constructed from existing contour data using Vertical Mapper's triangular irregular network (TIN) interpolation method. A cell size of 10 m was chosen. The DEM was coloured to distinguish between lowland, montane and alpine areas using the height histogram, with other vector data, including lakes, creeks, roads and tracks, draped on top. Three-dimensional (3D) models were created using Vertical Mapper's 3D viewing and drape function. Parameters such as vertical exaggeration (1.75), azimuth, viewing location, distance from location, location of the sun and the angle of viewing were toggled to produce the final views. These final 3D views were then exported to bitmap raster files. A more comprehensive digital 3D model was also constructed for the Anne Range, allowing a virtual 360° bird's-eye view of the Anne Range. This is accessible at our website www.parks.tas.gov.au

A number of different approaches are available for preparing trampling-sensitivity models. The method described below was selected as it was able to overcome spatial inconsistencies in the existing vegetation data and known limitations of Vertical Mapper's analysis of DEM.

In this model, trampling sensitivity was determined by two parameters: the trampling sensitivity of various vegetation communities, based on the results of the trampling trials described above; and the slope of the landscape. Slope was simplified to three categories, 'gentle' ($< 8°$), 'moderate' ($8°–18°$) and 'steep' ($> 18°$). A slope DEM of the study area was created using the TIN interpolation method (20 m). Vector polygons were then created for each of the slope categories.

Vegetation mapping is commonly based on community classification, which may not be easily interpreted in terms of trampling sensitivity. The results of our trampling trials support other findings that show that life-form and plant size affect resistance and resilience (Cole and Trull, 1992; Cole, 1993; Sun and Liddle, 1993; Cole and Landres, 1996). Ecological interpretation of vegetation communities for particular areas is required to categorize trampling sensitivity more accurately. For example, tall graminoid tussocks are much more susceptible to trampling damage than small graminoid tussocks. Vegetation mapping will not necessarily distinguish between the sizes of the same life-form. Scale is again relevant where, for example, sensitive vegetation is interspersed between boulders and rock slabs that are extremely resistant to trampling. The vegetation mapping used in this case study is at a scale of 1 : 25,000.

The classification of plant groups into mapping units is based on a structural/floristic system described by Kirkpatrick (1989), which uses vegetation units known as synusiae. Each synusia, which is represented by a single symbol, must be recognizable in the field from its structure and key species and also on 1 : 25,000 air photos. Each community is described in structural layers (Kirkpatrick, 1989), with the components of each layer specified in order of abundance. This system was developed principally for alpine areas, but has been extended to produce synusia-based vegetation-mapping data from a broader vegetation-mapping project for the Tasmania Western Wilderness WHA (Sib Corbett, unpublished data). The latter was used to provide the base vegetation data for this model. In this form of vegetation mapping, a synusia is used to describe one mappable vegetation unit with consistent characteristics. Each synusia is recognized by one or more species which are present consistently. Vegetation polygons are described by a string of synusiae arranged in structural layers, from tallest to shortest; and within each layer in order of abundance. For example:

Ac-As/C Alpine conifer open canopy over
        alpine shrubs with minor cushion
        plants

Ah/Ag/As Alpine herbfield interspersed with
        alpine grass tussocks and alpine
        shrubs

The sensitivity assigned to each different vegetation community was determined by allocating a sensitivity class to the dominant life-form, based on the results of the experimental trampling trials (Whinam and Chilcott, 1999, 2003) and base vegetation data for the area as above. For example, trampling sensitivity class 1 (highest sensitivity) was allocated to cushion plants, class 2 to buttongrass and alpine heath; class 3 to rocky patches interspersed with alpine rainforest and/or graminoid heath, and class 4 to *Poa* grasslands and bare ground. To allow for the environmental impacts of slope observed during the trampling trials, all 'steep' slopes were upgraded to the next level of sensitivity except for buttongrass communities, which were upgraded one level of sensitivity on moderate slopes and two levels of sensitivity on steep slopes. Where areas of vegetation contained plant lifeforms known to be particularly sensitive to trampling (e.g. *Sphagnum* moss), then that community was allocated to sensitivity class 1. Similarly if the vegetation classification included a particularly resilient vegetation type (e.g. *Poa* grassland), then the community was allocated to sensitivity class 4. Based on earlier findings on the sensitivity of Tasmania's cool temperate rainforest to horse trampling (Whinam and Comfort, 1996), and taking into account the particular conservation values of the conifer forests, vegetation communities with *Athrotaxis selaginoides* and *Athrotaxis cupressoides* were classified as sensitivity class 1. As trampling trials have not been conducted in rainforest or eucalyptus forests, sensitivity codes have not been allocated to these vegetation communities.

Vegetation polygons were tagged with their assigned sensitivity classes: class 1 (fewer than 30 passes per annum), class 2 (30–100 passes per annum), class 3 (100–500 passes per annum) and class 4 (greater than 500 passes per annum). Each vegetation polygon had a separate sensitivity class for each of the three slope categories (gentle, moderate, steep). Each vegetation polygon (with its attached sensitivity attributes) was matched with the generated slope polygons to produce a model of trampling sensitivity.

Vertical Mapper's region-to-grid utility enabled the vegetation polygons to be converted into a grid for each of the slope categories defined for each polygon. For each vegetation slope grid, further grids were created for each trampling class (1, 2, 3 or 4). As there were three vegetation slope grids and a maximum of four classes in each of those grids, the maximum number of vegetation slope grids for each trampling class was 12. Each of these grids was then converted into polygons.

Up to this point all analysis of the vegetation coverage was slope-independent. Each of the vegetation-class polygon layers was then matched against the existing slope polygons created earlier. Where there was an overlap, that part of the vegetation-class polygon was erased (or 'cookie-cut') by the appropriate slope polygons. Each of the vegetation-class layers was shaded and joined with other base layers to form the final maps.

Results

Experimental trampling trials

Results from experimental trampling trials in Tasmania's Western Wilderness WHA and Central Plateau indicate the following:

- Vegetation in western Tasmania is more sensitive to trampling impact than that on the Central Plateau.
- Plant death peaked between 6 and 9 months after initial trampling treatment.
- The greatest loss of vegetation cover occurred in the third year of trampling, after continued trampling impact, at all trampling intensities.
- Recovery from trampling impact to pre-trampling cover abundance is very slow in all vegetation communities (i.e. between 3 and 5 years), with the exception of the Central Plateau grasslands, which proved resilient to trampling impact.

- Slopes greater than 18° show much greater trampling impacts than gentler slopes.
- Shrubs, tall tussock graminoids and cushions are most susceptible to damage.
- Organosoils are much more sensitive to trampling impact than mineral soils.
- Alpine and subalpine areas adjacent to lakes and tarns (representative of many campsites) are susceptible to damage at more than 200 passes per annum.

In terms of life-forms, trampling trials have demonstrated that immediate impact was greatest in prostrate plants due to breakage (Rogova, 1976; Whinam and Chilcott, 1999, 2003). Life-forms with delicate leaves were highly susceptible to impact at medium and high trampling levels. Tall tussock graminoids were also susceptible to more impact than the lower-growing tufted graminoids and grasses. These findings are supported by other trampling trials (Cole and Landres, 1996), where short stature, rosette, creeping or caespitose growth form, flexible stems and leaves that are small, thick and flexible (able to fold under pressure) contributed to trampling resistance. It seems that resilience is conferred by lifeforms that protect perennating tissues.

In summary, the results of trampling trials in Tasmania indicate that, in general:

- no impacts were visible from trampling levels of less than 30 passes per annum;
- the formation of pads occurred at 30–100 passes per annum;
- the development of tracks occurred at 100–500 passes per annum;
- degradation of developed tracks occurred at trampling levels greater than 500 passes per annum, and as low as 250 passes per annum in some situations.

Trampling-sensitivity mapping

The 3D model of the Anne Range (Fig. 15.4) gives an indication of slope and topography, with current walking tracks and routes superimposed. The highest point on the range is Mt Anne at 1425 m. Trampling sensitivity for the Anne Range is shown in Fig. 15.5. This illustrates that much of the existing track network and pad formation has developed in areas of sensitive vegetation. However, the topography illustrated in the 3D model indicates the practical difficulties of avoiding these sensitive areas.

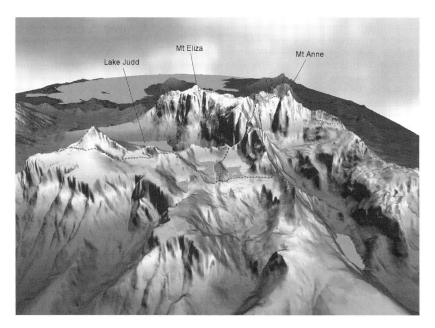

Fig. 15.4. A three-dimensional view of the Anne Range.

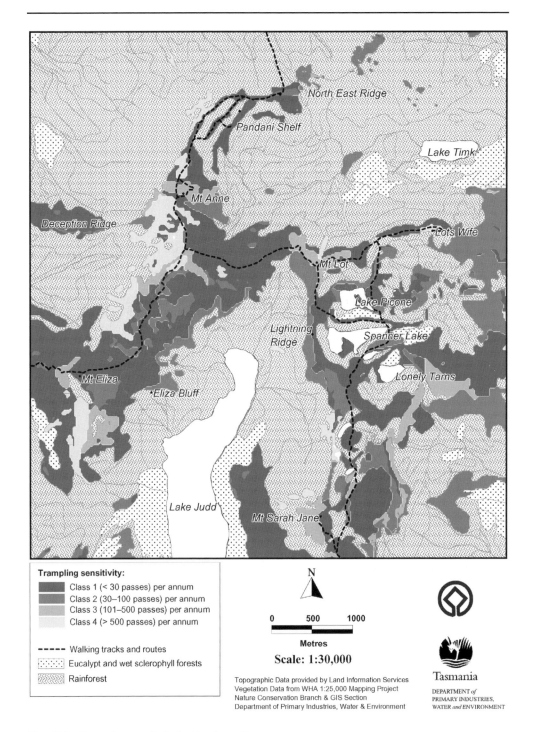

Fig. 15.5. Trampling sensitivity for the Anne Range.

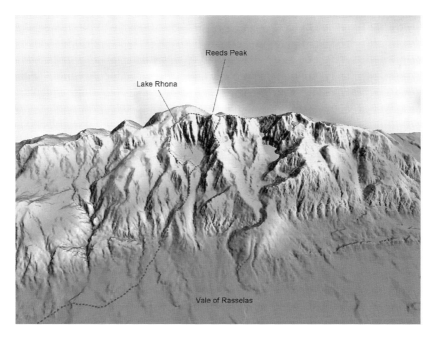

Lake Rhona

Reeds Peak

Vale of Rasselas

Fig. 15.6. A three-dimensional view of the Denison Range.

Figure 15.6 shows the slope and topography of the Denison Range with the existing track network superimposed. Trampling sensitivity for the Denison Range is shown in Fig. 15.7. The Denison Range is not as high as the Anne Range. Reeds Peak is the highest point at 1280 m. Glacial cirques on the Denison Range, however, restrict the number of walking routes.

Management Applications

Recreational use and its management have been identified as one of the most significant threats to wilderness ecosystems (Cole and Landres, 1996). As many wilderness areas are located at high elevations, they are naturally stressed ecosystems that are not highly resilient (Cole and Landres, 1996). Research is recognized as critical to meeting the challenge of preserving wilderness resources for future generations, particularly in relation to a better understanding of natural conditions (Cole and Landres, 1996; Cole *et al.*, 2000). A crucial management question is how much trampling is tolerable in wilderness (Landres *et al.*, 2000).

Managers need practical indicators and techniques for assessing conditions, as well as predicting and monitoring deviation from natural or acceptable conditions (Cole *et al.*, 2000). The necessity and difficulty of describing natural or desired conditions at large spatial and temporal scales have been recognized (Cole and Landres, 1996).

The mapping of areas sensitive to trampling allows the presentation of complex scientific data in a user-friendly format. However, there are several points to bear in mind when looking at the applicability of mapped sensitivity to impacts. A limitation to its widespread use is the need for a variety of data to be available, such as vegetation mapping, electronic cartographic features and data on carrying capacity in untracked country of the different vegetation types at a relevant scale. The better and more accurate the quality of the data, the more the sensitivity mapping will reflect the actual on-ground conditions. Whatever data are available, the assigning of sensitivity classes must be supported by ground-testing.

The scale of the data available will also affect the application of the sensitivity map-

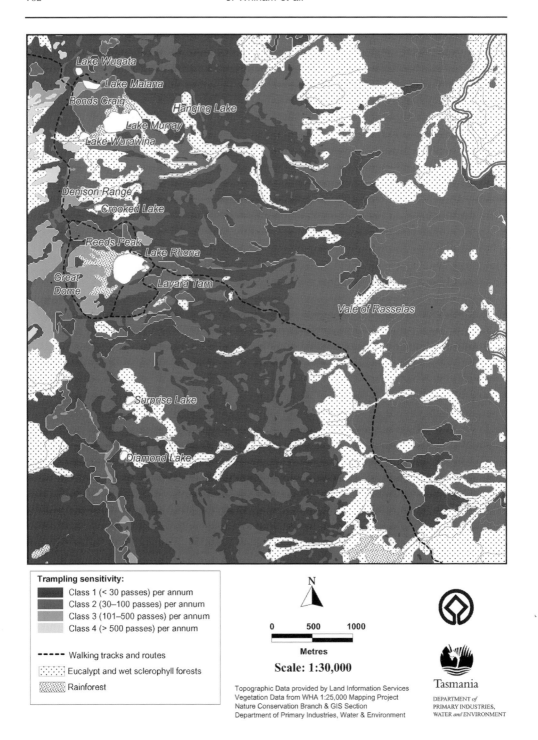

Trampling sensitivity:

- Class 1 (< 30 passes) per annum
- Class 2 (30–100 passes) per annum
- Class 3 (101–500 passes) per annum
- Class 4 (> 500 passes) per annum

- - - - - Walking tracks and routes

Eucalypt and wet sclerophyll forests

Rainforest

N

0   500   1000

Metres

Scale: 1:30,000

Topographic Data provided by Land Information Services
Vegetation Data from WHA 1:25,000 Mapping Project
Nature Conservation Branch & GIS Section
Department of Primary Industries, Water & Environment

Tasmania
DEPARTMENT *of*
PRIMARY INDUSTRIES,
WATER *and* ENVIRONMENT

Fig. 15.7. Trampling sensitivity for the Denison Range.

ping, by limiting the degree of resolution for planning and management decisions. For example, slope characteristics and vegetation mapping may be based on data on a 1 : 25,000 scale, while sections of track may be substantially steeper or flatter than the general landscape and contain vegetation that differs from the surrounding slopes. Therefore, while sensitivity mapping on a 1 : 25,000 scale is useful for regional planning, a finer resolution (e.g. 1 : 5000) would be more useful for specific area planning. Also, other environmental parameters that significantly affect local trampling sensitivity, such as drainage, are difficult to superimpose on the sensitivity map, because of small-scale variability. Conservation values of particular species or communities may also need to be considered.

Generally, areas that receive heavy recreation use are allocated the most wilderness management resources (people, time, information and money). However, it has been argued (Cole, 1997) that more resources should be allocated to lightly used wilderness areas because these are the places that are in most natural condition, most vulnerable and most responsive to management. This viewpoint, combined with the extremely slow recovery rates recorded (J. Whinam and N. Chilcott, unpublished data, 2002), supports the need to plan and manage recreational use in untracked alpine wilderness areas.

The sensitivity mapping presented could be a useful planning and management tool when assessing the range of options for new track and campsite developments on a regional level, by highlighting sensitive areas that would be best avoided. It can contribute to the database from which LAC (Stankey and Wood, 1982) can be formulated. However, once pads develop into tracks in sensitive areas, as the case studies illustrate, other management options need to be considered, such as track hardening or track closure.

Acknowledgements

Topographic data provided by Land Information Services, Department of Primary Industries, Water and Environment (DPIWE), Tasmania. Vegetation data extracted from WHA 1 : 25,000 Mapping Project, Nature Conservation Branch and GIS Sections, Resource Management and Conservation, DPIWE. Michael Pemberton provided information on geology. Grant Dixon and an anonymous referee provided helpful comments. This project was supported by the Tasmanian Wilderness WHA Program.

References

Banks, M.R. (1973) *General Geology.* Symposium conducted by the Royal Society of Tasmania, Launceston.

Bayfield, N.G. (1979) Recovery of four montane heath communities on Cairngorm, Scotland, from disturbance by trampling. *Biological Conservation* 15, 165–179.

Buist, J.L. and Hoots, T.A. (1982) Recreational opportunity spectrum approach to resource planning. *Journal of Forestry* 80, 84–86.

Cole, D.N. (1987) Effects of three seasons of experimental trampling on five montane forest communities and a grassland in western Montana, USA. *Biological Conservation* 40, 219–244.

Cole, D.N. (1993) Experimental trampling of vegetation. II. Predictors of resistance and resilience. *Journal of Applied Ecology* 32(1), 215–224.

Cole, D.N. (1997) Recreation management priorities are misplaced – allocate more resources to low-use wilderness. *International Journal of Wilderness* 3(4), 4–8.

Cole, D.N. and Bayfield, N.G. (1993) Recreational trampling of vegetation: standard experimental procedures. *Biological Conservation* 63, 209–215.

Cole, D.N. and Landres, P.B. (1996) Threats to wilderness ecosystems: impacts and research needs. *Ecological Applications* 6(1), 168–183.

Cole, D.N. and McCool, S.F. (1998) Limits of acceptable change and natural resources planning: when is LAC useful, when is it not? In: McCool, S.F. and Cole, D.N. (eds) *Proceedings of Limits of Acceptable Change and Related Planning Processes: Progress and Future Directions, 20–22 May 1997, Missoula, Montana.* General Technical Report INT-GTR-371, Forest Service, US Department of Agriculture, Rocky Mountain Research Station, Ogden, Utah.

Cole, D.N. and Trull, S.J. (1992) Quantifying vegetation response to recreational disturbance in the North Cascades, Washington. *Northwest Science* 66, 229–236.

Cole, D.N., McCool, S.F., Parsons, D.J. and Brown, P.J. (2000) Wilderness science in a time of change: a conference. In: Cole, D.N., McCool, S.F., Freimeund, W.A. and O'Laughlin, J. (eds) *Proceedings of Wilderness Science in a Time of Change*, Vol. 1, *Changing Perspectives and Future Directions, 23–27 May 1999, Missoula, Montana*. Rocky Mountain Research Station, Forest Service, US Department of Agriculture, Ogden, Utah.

Cullen, P. (1995) *Land Degradation on the Central Plateau, Tasmania: the Legacy of 170 Years of Exploitation*. Tasmanian Parks and Wildlife Service, Hobart.

Hylgaard, T. and Liddle, M.J. (1981) The effect of human trampling on a sand dune ecosystem dominated by *Empetrum nigrum*. *Journal of Applied Ecology* 18, 559–569.

Jackson, W.D. (1973) *Vegetation*. Symposium conducted by the Royal Society of Tasmania, Foot and Playstead, Launceston.

Jetson, T. (1989) *The Roof of Tasmania: a History of the Central Plateau*. Pelion Press, Launceston.

Kirkpatrick, J.B. (1980) Tasmanian high mountain vegetation. I. A reconnaissance survey of the Eastern Arthur Range and Mt. Picton. *Papers and Proceedings of the Royal Society of Tasmania* 114, 1–20.

Kirkpatrick, J.B. (1983) Treeless plant communities of the Tasmanian High Country. *Proceedings of the Ecological Society of Australia* 12, 61–77.

Kirkpatrick, J.B. (1986) Conservation of plant species, alliances and associations of the treeless high country of Tasmania, Australia. *Biological Conservation* 37, 43–57.

Kirkpatrick, J.B. (1989) A synusia-based vegetation mapping system for the conservation management of natural vegetation, with an example from Tasmania, Australia. *Biological Conservation* 32, 613–629.

Kirkpatrick, J.B. (1997) *Alpine Tasmania: an Illustrated Field Guide to the Flora and Vegetation*. Oxford University Press, Melbourne, 196 pp.

Kirkpatrick, J.B., Gilfedder, L. and Fensham, R. (1988) *City Parks and Cemeteries, Tasmania's Remnant Grasslands and Grassy Woodlands*. Tasmanian Conservation Trust, Hobart.

Landres, P.B., Brunson, M.W., Merigliano, L., Sydoriak, C. and Morton, S. (2000) Naturalness and wildness: the dilemma and irony of managing wilderness. In: Cole, D.N., McCool, S.F., Freimeund, W.A. and O'Laughlin, J. (eds) In: *Proceedings of Wilderness Science in a Time of Change*, Vol. 5, *Changing Perspectives and Future Directions, 23–27 May 1999, Missoula, Montana*. Rocky Mountain Research Station, Forest Service, US Department of Agriculture, Ogden, Utah.

McPherson, G. (1990) *Statistics in Scientific Investigation: Its Basis, Application and Interpretation*. Springer-Verlag, New York, 666 pp.

Parks and Wildlife Service (1994) *Walking Track Management Strategy for the Tasmanian Wilderness World Heritage Area*. Tasmanian Parks and Wildlife Service, Hobart.

Parks and Wildlife Service (1999) *Tasmanian Wilderness World Heritage Area Management Plan*. Parks and Wildlife Service, Hobart.

Pemberton, M. (1986) *Land Systems of Tasmania Region 5 – Central Plateau*. Department of Agriculture, Hobart.

Pemberton, M. (1989) *Land Systems of Tasmania Region 7 – South West*. Department of Agriculture, Hobart.

Price, M.F. (1985) *A Review of Research into the Impacts of Recreation on Alpine Vegetation in Western North America*. In: Bayfeild, N.G. and Barrow, G.C. (eds) The Impacts of Outdoor Recreation on Mountain Areas in Europe and North America. *Recreation Ecology Research Group Report No. 9*.

Richley, L.R. (1986) *Report on the Degradation of Crown Land Used for Grazing on the Central Plateau*. Department of Agriculture, Tasmania.

Rogova, T.V. (1976) Influence of trampling on vegetation of forest meadow and whortleberry-moss pine forest cenoses. *Soviet Journal of Ecology* 7, 356–359.

Stankey, G.H. and Wood, J. (1982) The recreation opportunity spectrum: an introduction. *Australian Parks and Recreation* February, 6–15.

Sun, D. and Liddle, M.J. (1993) Plant morphological characteristics and resistance to simulated trampling. *Environmental Management* 17, 511–521.

Wang, T.L., Anderson, D.H. and Lime, D.W. (2000) Protecting resources and visitor opportunities: a decision process to help managers maintain the quality of park resources and visitor experiences. *Park Science* 20(2), 23–27.

Whinam, J. and Chilcott, N. (1999) Impacts of trampling on alpine environments in central Tasmania. *Journal of Environmental Management* 57(3), 205–220.

Whinam, J. and Chilcott, N. (2003) Impacts after four years of experimental trampling on alpine environments in western Tasmania. *Journal of Environmental Management* (in press).

Whinam, J. and Comfort, M. (1996) The impact of commercial horse riding on sub-alpine environments at Cradle Mountain, Tasmania, Australia. *Journal of Environmental Management* 47, 61–70.

Whinam, J., Cannell, E.J., Kirkpatrick, J.B. and Comfort, M. (1994) Studies on the potential impact of recreational horseriding on some alpine environments of the Central Plateau, Tasmania. *Journal of Environmental Management* 40, 103–117.

16

Modelling Potential for Nature-based Tourism

Colin Arrowsmith

Department of Geospatial Science, RMIT University, Melbourne, Victoria, Australia

Abstract

A spatial tourism-potential model has been developed that combines the outputs from an environmental-resiliency model developed using multivariate analysis, with a tourism-attractiveness model, using geographical information systems (GIS). The model is tested and applied to a popular conservation reserve, Grampians National Park (GNP) in the south-east of Australia. Currently tourism is heavily concentrated in the northern Grampians. This has resulted in adverse impacts on the environment, which could potentially diminish the overall tourism experience of the region. It is anticipated that using the tourism-potential model will help to identify new opportunities for tourism growth in the region, particularly in the south of the park. The model has particular application in planning for nature-based tourism and will assist in identifying locations that are attractive, environmentally resilient and can form part of an interesting and diverse series of nature-based tourist attractions in close proximity to each other.

Introduction

Grampians National Park (GNP) lies 260 km north-west of Melbourne in the State of Victoria in south-eastern Australia. With a total area of 167,000 ha, it is known particularly for granite mountain ranges and spring wildflowers and is a popular tourist destination. It supports a high diversity of birds, including threatened species, such as powerful owl, over 40 native mammal species and 800 indigenous plant species, of which 20 are locally endemic. There are eight vegetation communities within the park, many subject to frequent fires. These range from subalpine to eucalyptus scrubs and woodlands and wetland communities.

An environmental-resiliency model for the GNP has been developed previously by Arrowsmith and Inbakaran (2001). In this chapter we describe an extension of that model to include tourism access and attractiveness, so as to yield a tourism-potential model.

Using principal-components analysis, the environmental-resiliency model shows that, for the study area, susceptibility to environmental damage decreases with increasing

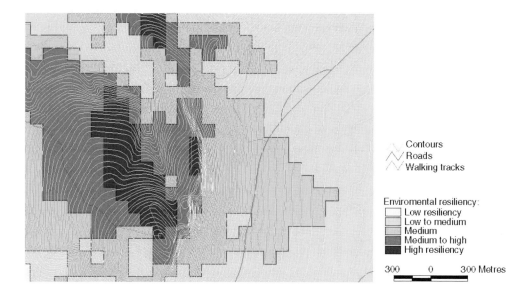

Contours
Roads
Walking tracks

Enviromental resiliency:
Low resiliency
Low to medium
Medium
Medium to high
High resiliency

300   0   300 Metres

Fig. 16.1 Resiliency polygons for part of the study area.

elevation (Fig. 16.1). In general, walking tracks through the region commence at lower altitudes and tend to traverse erodible sandy soils before climbing on to more resilient rocky outcrops, with typically scenic outlooks. In addition, most of the current tourism activity is concentrated in a limited area. Arrowsmith and Inbakaran (2001) concluded that there are opportunities to accommodate increasing tourist numbers via multi-path tracks through less resilient areas and by seeking tourism potential in currently less popular areas.

In addition to outputs from the environmental-resiliency model, the tourism-potential model described here also incorporates indices of tourism attractiveness, based on tourism features, their relative attractiveness and importance and their accessibility, as well as the diversity of attractions within a specified geographical area.

This model provides a basis for future tourism planning. It provides opportunities to identify locations for dissipation of tourism activity. Forman and Godron (1986, p. 500) note that:

If the management objective is to maintain or restore the natural landscape, the survey of landscape elements must focus on their

sensitivity to human influence . . . [and] . . . human activities must be dispersed, low in intensity, and inversely proportional to the sensitivity of each landscape element.

Tourism is a social activity that is highly subjective. The scope of this chapter prevents an in-depth assessment of the myriad cognitive processes that lead to differential appreciation of tourism attractions (for example, see Lowenthal and Prince, 1965). The approach adopted here is to seek individual preferences, aggregate these and then determine an average or 'collective' preference for the various tourist attractions throughout the study area. Tourists usually visit particular locations because of some attraction. This chapter sets out a method for determining and quantifying what tourists collectively perceive as attractive and therefore consider worthwhile visiting. To determine levels of perceived attractiveness, a questionnaire was administered to 120 tourists and visitors to the region. From the evaluation of the questionnaires, measures of attractiveness throughout the region were then determined as part of the developed tourism-attractiveness index discussed below.

Using a geographical information system

(GIS), attractiveness indices are derived across the study area and converted into attractiveness polygons. These polygons are then spatially intersected with the environmental-resiliency polygons derived from the environmental-resiliency model (Arrowsmith and Inbakaran, 2001). The result is a combined spatial model (that is, a map) of tourism attractiveness and environmental resiliency. Against this map, a diversity index is also generated, based on the range of different tourist-attraction types found in close proximity to each other. So that comparisons between subregions within the study area could be made, the study area is spatially segmented approximating the 1 : 25,000 topographic map-sheet boundaries. This resulted in 116 quadrats or map sheets, each 5 km by 6 km. Initial results showed high attractiveness and diversity in the northern sector. However, in the central southern and central western sectors of the GNP, there was also evidence of highly attractive and diverse locations that could be found on highly resilient topography. Tourists are unlikely to consider individual attractions in their own right, but rather a collection of attractions. For example, in an analysis of waterfalls as a recreational and tourism resource, Hudson (1998) notes that visitors come mainly for other reasons than the attraction of waterfalls. Those areas where a diversity of attraction types are greatest would presumably be more attractive for tourist visitation, and the 5 km by 6 km map sheets could be expected to be reasonably managed on a 1-day excursion.

It is recognized at the outset that working by map sheet to determine tourism potential has its limitations. Summation of resilient and attractive areas by map sheet limits geographical location only to the map-sheet boundary rather than to specific geographical sites. In addition, arbitrary delineation of map-sheet boundaries may result in segmentation of clustered diverse and attractive tourist locations. However, keeping these limitations in mind, future opportunities for dispersing tourism throughout the GNP can be based on relative attractiveness, diversity and spatial distribution, as well as biophysical environmental resilience. The resultant model has been termed the 'tourism-potential model'.

Tourism Attraction

Attractiveness is subjective and may vary according to an individual's gender, cultural and ethnic background, socio-economic status, educational level, family situation, health, disability and age. In a study by Abello and Bernaldez (1986), for example, findings confirmed previous studies that a correlation exists between personality and landscape preference. DeLucio and Mugica (1994), in assessing landscape preferences and behaviour of visitors to Spanish national parks, noted that different visitor types exhibit differing degrees of interest, knowledge and dedication to their visits. Tourist attractions are the basic elements on which tourism is developed (Lew, 1987). In their study, Mackay and Fesenmaier (1997) use principal-component analysis in an investigation into image formation. The first component (or factor) Mackay and Fesenmaier (1997) labelled 'attractiveness'. Variables such as excitement, fun, 'lots to do' and enjoyable, are highly correlated with this component. They recognized this component as an activity dimension where interaction with the environment is occurring. This chapter concentrates on the human impact on fragile environments and therefore all potential visitation nodes must be considered as tourist attractions. Tourist attractions encourage visitation and therefore act as nodes for potential environmental impact.

Tourist attractions primarily fall into one of two categories. Nature-based attractions include rivers, scenic vistas, waterfalls, flora and fauna and interesting geomorphology. Historic sites, important buildings and entertainment centres could be considered as cultural attractions. Recreational attractions, however, may fall within either category. For example, golf-courses, tennis-courts, boating facilities, picnic and barbecue areas, as well as scenic lookouts, could all be considered cultural as they have involved human intervention in their establishment, whereas beaches and rock climbing are recreational attractions relating to the natural environment. The infrastructure that supports these attractions must also be seen as a tourist attraction in its own right. Lew (1987, p. 557) regards these attractions as the 'nature–human interface' attractions. Toilets, shops and kiosks, information centres, walking tracks and picnic and camping grounds, for example, could be considered infrastructure supporting primary tourist attractions. While in themselves they may not act as attractions, they will nevertheless encourage human visitation and, therefore, potential environmental impact and hence are considered in this study as attractions.

Quantifying Attractiveness

Tourist preferences for attractions in the GNP were obtained using a questionnaire administered to visitors over a 2-week period. As well as questionnaires being filled in *in situ*, questionnaires were left at five key tourist-information centres located within the vicinity of the national park. A total of 120 completed questionnaires were received.

Key findings from the responses were as follows:

- Most respondents visit the GNP for its natural beauty and see this as its greatest attraction.
- Of the natural attractions, scenic views, waterfalls, walking tracks and geological formations are the most important.
- Infrastructure such as information centres and public facilities are not considered to be important attractions.
- Specialized tourist pursuits, such as rock climbing and boating, are not considered to be important by most visitors to the region.
- Many tourists, particularly interstate and international visitors, were unfamiliar with attractions except in the most heavily visited areas.
- While tourist infrastructure is not recognized as an important attraction in its own right, it does add to the comfort and therefore the experience of the tourist.

Wall (1997) identifies three feature-type tourist attractions, each with varying capacities to withstand large numbers of tourists. Using this as a basis for categorizing tourist attractions, they were broken down into areal, lineal or point feature types for input into the

GIS on the basis of each attraction's spatial shape and areal coverage.

Point feature attractions for this study included those attractions that take up an area of less than one grid cell of 100 m × 100 m (that is, 1 ha) in the GIS. The majority of tourist attractions fall under this feature type. They include: scenic lookouts, picnic spots, camping sites, waterfalls, geological formations, rock-climbing sites, boating facilities (jetties, etc.), European historic sites, Aboriginal historic sites, tourist-information centres, key accommodation centres, caves, mines and monuments.

According to Wall (1997), point attractions serve to concentrate tourism activity in a small area. While catering for tourists can be efficiently conducted, it does result in dangers associated with 'congestion, over-commercialisation, reduction in the quality of visitor experience, and occasional destruction of the resource' (Wall, 1997, p. 241). This can be seen, for example, in the closure of a standing platform at one site in GNP, because of vandalism and overuse of the holding rails.

Lineal attractions comprised walking tracks and rivers and streams. It should be noted that, while a number of geomorphological features could be considered as lineal features, for example escarpments, these were considered to comprise point attractions for lookouts and lineal attractions for walking tracks.

Areal attractions cover a wider area than point-feature-type attractions. Vegetation was considered an areal feature. Using photographs of each of the ecological vegetation classes in the analysis, respondents were asked to identify those communities of greatest or least attractiveness. Riverside, swamp scrub and subalpine were ranked with highest attractiveness, open forest, stringbark forest and heathland intermediate and heath woodland and rocky woodland as least attractive.

It should be noted that, while the intention was to measure response to vegetation class alone, ranks given may also be affected by the actual situation or setting of the questionnaire and/or photograph, the objects found within each photograph and external factors, such as weather conditions and camera settings. Approaches using simulated environments (Bishop *et al.*, 2001; Johnson *et al.*, Chapter 9, this volume) are also available but were not used in this instance.

The Land Conservation Council of Victoria (LCC) has produced a report that lists the historic and cultural features for south-west Victoria, including the GNP (LCC, 1997). In the report, recommendations are made regarding site preservation and/or changes to existing land use. The report acknowledges the tourism potential of the many and varied historic places throughout the region. Each site is graded according to its level of significance. Category A places are assessed to be of State significance, while categories B and C have regional and local significance, respectively. All places identified in this report for the study area have been included in the tourism-potential model.

The 1:25,000 topographic map sheets published by the former Division of Survey and Mapping in 1985 provided a number of cultural and historic site locations (including old ruins, Aboriginal sites, hotels and motels and camping and picnic grounds). As well as cultural and historic features, natural features, including geomorphological structures, waterfalls, rock outcrops, rivers and streams, access roads and walking trails, could be located on these map sheets. Additional information was acquired from publications by Thomas (1995), Tourism Victoria (undated, *c.* 1995), the National Parks Service (1996) and Parks Victoria (1997, 1998a,b) and from field assessments.

Constructing a Tourism-potential Model

Constructing the tourism-potential model involves nine steps, as follows. Each attraction was first assigned an attractiveness ranking, AT_i, from 1 (least attractive) to 4 (most attractive). For example, major waterfalls and lookouts were ranked 4, whereas minor unnamed waterfalls were ranked 2.

Scenic views present a particular problem in determining relative attractiveness. There has been considerable research (for example, Hull and Buhyoff, 1983; Hammitt *et al.*, 1994;

Miller *et al.*, 1994) in landscape evaluation and measurement of attractiveness of landscapes from viewpoints. In this study, the relative attractiveness of scenic views was defined by the size of the viewshed.

To determine the scenic-view catchment areas or viewsheds, a visibility analysis was conducted on key lookout locations across the study area. Rock outcrops, tree-canopy heights and curvature and refraction corrections were made to the ground digital elevation model. Output consisted of a grid showing areal extents of what could and could not be seen from each viewpoint. Each scenic viewshed was then intersected with topographical features, such as water bodies, vegetation types and elevation and slopes, factors deemed important in discriminating good and poor views (Hull and Buhyoff, 1983; Hammitt *et al.*, 1994; Bishop, 1996; Nova Scotia Museum of Natural History, 1996). On the basis of scenic-view composition and area within the viewshed, an attractiveness level was then assigned to each scenic viewpoint.

The second step was to assign each attraction an accessibility weighting, AC_i, according to distance from access points, such as roads and walking tracks. These weights ranged from 1 (easiest access) through to 4 (impossible to reach). The third step was to assign preference ranks, P_i, based on the visitor questionnaires described earlier. Respondents were asked to assign a rank from 1 to 14 to a range of tourist attractions. Averaged ranks ranged from 2.49 for scenic views to 12.33 for boating facilities.

For each attraction, a weighted rank, W_i, was calculated as $W_i = AT_i/AC_i$ and an overall attractiveness index, $AI_i = W_i/P_i$. These became the fourth and fifth steps, respectively. These attractiveness indices, AI_i, apply to individual attractions. In many instances, however, there are several independent attractions at a single location. For each 100 m × 100 m cell across the study area, therefore, an aggregate spatial attractiveness index was calculated by adding the indices for individual attractions within that cell. Aggregate indices ranged from 0.1 to 2.0. These were reclassified, as part of step six, into four standardized ranks, with ranks of 1 (low), 2 (medium) and 3 (high attractiveness) assigned for aggregate indices of 0.1–0.3, 0.4–0.6 and 0.7–1.0, respectively, and rank 4 (very high attractiveness) for aggregate indices more than 1.0.

In the seventh step, these tourist-attractiveness ranks (1–4) were then combined with environmental-resiliency ranks (1–5) from the model of Arrowsmith and Inbarakan (2001) to yield an index of tourism appropriateness. Areas with low or medium attractiveness (ranks 1 or 2) were assigned a low appropriateness index, irrespective of resiliency. Areas of high and very high attractiveness (ranks 3 and 4) and low resiliency (ranks 1–3) were assigned moderate appropriateness, and those with high to very high attractiveness and high resiliency (ranks 4 or 5) were assigned high tourism appropriateness. Note that, in ascertaining tourism appropriateness, attractiveness was determined as being a function of both attractiveness and accessibility. This model therefore assesses tourism potential in the light of current accessibility, without further development. In some instances (for example, certain lookouts and caves), access is currently almost impossible due to severe topographical and physical accessibility restrictions.

To assist in the analysis, 116 map sheets, each 5 km wide (east–west) and 6 km long (north–south), covering the entire study area (Fig. 16.2) were superimposed over the resultant tourism-appropriateness polygons. This became step eight in the development of the tourism-potential model. It was also considered that a visitor could reasonably traverse a 5 km by 6 km area within a single day visit. Areas of environmental resiliency, attractiveness and tourism potential were summed for each map sheet. Map sheets were then ranked into quartiles according to the amount of summed area classified by environmental resiliency, attractiveness and tourism potential. This resulted in the ability to spatially locate concentrations of tourism potential.

Because diversity of attractions is considered important, a diversity index was generated for each of the 116 map sheets. For each map sheet (Fig. 16.2), a diversity index was calculated such that: $DI_i = n_i / N$, where DI_i = diversity index for the i_{th} map sheet, n_i = number of different attraction types for the

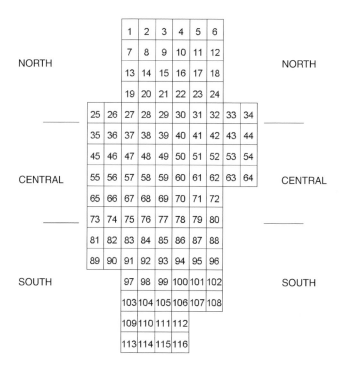

Fig. 16.2. Map-sheet numbers for the study area.

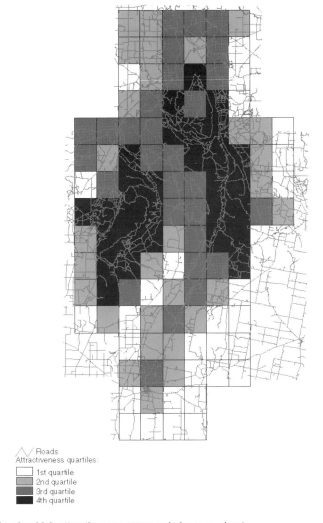

Roads
Attractiveness quartiles:

☐ 1st quartile
▨ 2nd quartile
▧ 3rd quartile
■ 4th quartile

Fig. 16.3. Map showing high-attractiveness areas only by map sheet.

i_{th} mapsheet, and N = total number of different attraction types across the study area. The final result yields the tourism-potential model.

The final, ninth, step was to generate a series of three maps showing map sheets ranked by quartile. These are shown in Figs 16.3, 16.4 and 16.5. Figure 16.3 shows map sheets shaded according to total summed areas of highly attractive polygons – that is, those polygons where attractiveness levels are 3 or 4. Shading is based on quartiles, where the top 25% of the number of map sheets with the highest total areas of high attractiveness are shaded dark grey, down to the lowest 25% shaded light grey.

Figure 16.4 combines high-resiliency map sheets with attractiveness. This shows shaded map sheets according to summed areas of highly attractive and highly resilient areas. Again, the top 25% of map sheets with the highest summed areas are shaded dark grey.

Diversity within each map sheet is shown in Fig. 16.5, again by quartile. The top 25% of map sheets containing the highest diversity of tourist attractions are shaded dark grey.

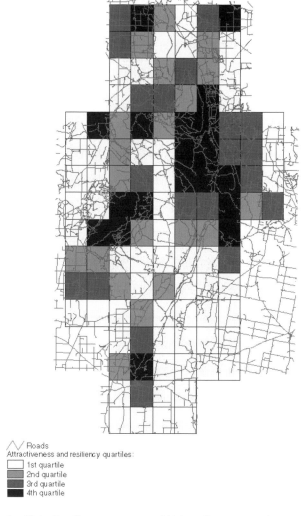

Fig. 16.4. Map showing high-attractiveness areas and high-resiliency areas by map sheet.

Using attractions across the GNP as a mechanism for dispersing tourism

For descriptive purposes, divisions have been made separating the northern, central and southern sections of the park. These are shown in Fig. 16.3 and tabulated according to the proportion of map sheets falling within quartile classifications in Table 16.1.

From Fig. 16.3 and Table 16.1 it can be seen that there are marked differences between the northern, central and southern sectors in terms of attractiveness. For example, while the central sector has more than 47% of

its map sheets ranked as highly attractive, the southern sector has less than 3% (one of the 36 map sheets), with the northern sector at just over 17%.

Concentrations of highly attractive areas can be seen throughout the central region, where there is a distinct division between the central east (map-sheet numbers 29–31, 40–42, 51, 52, 61, 62 and 72) and the central west (map sheets 37, 47, 48, 56–58, 66–68, 74, 75 and 82) (Fig. 16.2).

If we include environmental resilience into the analysis, it can be seen from Fig. 16.4 that the total number of map sheets ranked as

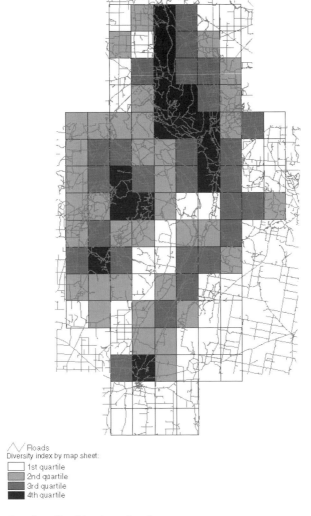

Roads
Diversity index by map sheet:
  1st quartile
  2nd quartile
  3rd quartile
  4th quartile

Fig. 16.5. Map showing diversity of tourism attractions.

highly attractive is reduced. There is still a central-sector tendency for highly attractive locations, and the divide between the central east and central west can still be seen. However, the region in the extreme south around the township of Dunkeld (map-sheet number 104) shows high attractiveness on resilient ground. Where the central sector had more than 47% of its map sheets ranked as highly attractive, this drops to slightly less than 24%, while the northern sector actually increases from 17.64% to 20.59% when environmental resiliency is taken into account.

Diversity concentration can be found throughout the north, central east and central west sectors and in one map sheet surrounding the township of Dunkeld to the south.

Further examination of spatial relationships and configurations of individual map sheets can be undertaken using spatial association or fragmentation within each quartile classification. Measures of spatial autocorrelation, using 'normalized join counts' where the actual number of similarly classified joined (or adjacent) map sheets can be compared with what might be expected by chance, can be

Table 16.1. Counts of map sheets by quartile rank.

Quartile rank	Number in northern sector	Percentage in northern sector	Number in central sector	Percentage in central sector	Number in southern sector	Percentage in southern sector
Fig. 16.3. High-attractiveness (only) areas						
Low	$^{5}/_{34}$	14.71	$^{4}/_{46}$	8.70	$^{20}/_{36}$	55.55
Medium low	$^{10}/_{34}$	29.41	$^{8}/_{46}$	17.39	$^{11}/_{36}$	30.56
Medium high	$^{13}/_{34}$	38.24	$^{12}/_{46}$	26.09	$^{4}/_{36}$	11.11
High	$^{6}/_{34}$	17.64	$^{22}/_{46}$	47.82	$^{1}/_{36}$	2.78
Fig. 16.4. High-attractiveness and high-resiliency areas						
Low	$^{11}/_{34}$	32.35	$^{19}/_{46}$	41.30	$^{27}/_{36}$	75.00
Medium low	$^{8}/_{34}$	23.53	$^{8}/_{46}$	17.39	$^{4}/_{36}$	11.11
Medium high	$^{8}/_{34}$	23.53	$^{8}/_{46}$	17.39	$^{4}/_{36}$	11.11
High	$^{7}/_{34}$	20.59	$^{11}/_{46}$	23.92	$^{1}/_{36}$	2.78
Fig. 16.5. Diversity of attractions						
Low	$^{8}/_{34}$	23.53	$^{9}/_{46}$	19.57	$^{22}/_{36}$	61.11
Medium low	$^{11}/_{34}$	32.35	$^{15}/_{46}$	32.61	$^{10}/_{36}$	27.78
Medium high	$^{7}/_{34}$	20.59	$^{16}/_{46}$	34.78	$^{3}/_{36}$	8.33
High	$^{8}/_{34}$	23.53	$^{6}/_{46}$	13.04	$^{1}/_{36}$	2.78

undertaken. This approach is well documented by Unwin (1981).

Spatial correlations between highly attractive, environmentally resilient and diverse tourist-attraction map sheets will yield locations that could offer potential tourism sites. Table 16.2 combines Figs 16.4 and 16.5, yielding tourism potential. This is shown in Fig. 16.6. It should be noted that no attempt has been made to combine both attractiveness and diversity into one index, but rather these two components are looked at individually.

Analysis and Discussion

Map sheets categorized both highly attractive and resilient are spatially autocorrelated. Rather than attractive and resilient areas being scattered throughout the study area, they are found close together. Diversity of attractions is also spatially autocorrelated and there are concentrations of diversity of tourist attractions throughout the study area.

Figure 16.6 shows that, for a number of map sheets ranked highly as tourist attractions, there are significant areas of environmentally resilient ground that offer a diversity of attrac-

Table 16.2. Tourism potential by map sheet for the Grampians National Park.

Tourism potential	Categories	Map-sheet number
Excellent	High attractiveness, high resiliency and high diversity	23, 30, 31, 40, 41, 51, 52, 57, 58, 104
Very good	High attractiveness, high resiliency and medium high diversity	26, 50, 62, 66, 67, 72
Good	High attractiveness, high resiliency and medium low or low diversity	2, 6, 28
Very good	Medium high attractiveness, high resiliency and high diversity	21, 33, 42
Good	Medium high attractiveness, high resiliency and medium high diversity	16, 20, 48, 98
Worth considering	Medium high attractiveness, high resiliency and medium low or low diversity	1, 5, 7, 32, 43, 53, 60, 61, 64, 80, 81, 82, 110

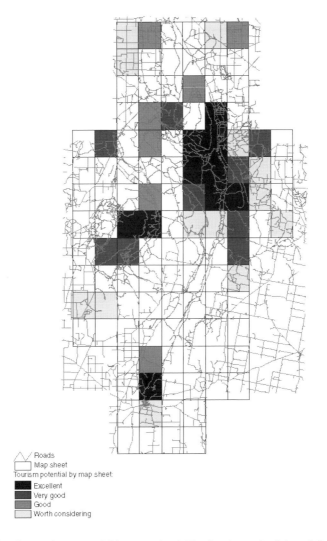

Fig. 16.6. Map showing tourism potential by map sheet. The 'tourism-potential model'.

tions. These are considered as offering excellent tourism potential (refer to Table 16.2).

Map sheets exhibiting the most tourism potential, not surprisingly, dominate the popular regions around Halls Gap in the north-east sector (map-sheet 31). The township supports the largest number of accommodation centres and acts as the 'hub' of tourist activity in the park. However, the tourism-potential model enables new opportunities, in particular to the west and south, for the more popular tourist sites to be examined for tourism potential. map sheet 104 in the south and map-sheets 57, 58,

66 and 67 all offer very good to excellent tourism potential. We need to examine these map-sheet locations in more detail to identify particular opportunities. However, the benefits from supporting tourism identified in these alternative locations are fivefold:

- by offering potential recreational opportunities in environmentally resilient locations;
- by offering a diverse range of attractions to sustain the interest of potential tourists;
- by offering a range of attractions that

could be feasibly explored in one-half to one day;

- by offering the opportunity for tourists to get away from heavily concentrated tourist spots, enabling social carrying capacities to be maintained and yet increasing overall numbers to the region;
- by offering potential economic benefits to the townships of Dunkeld in the south and Cavendish in the south-west without having to develop accommodation centres inside the park boundaries. New-five star accommodation has already been built in Dunkeld.

Conclusions

This chapter has demonstrated a spatial model developed using GIS to assess relative sub-areas within a tourist destination for tourism potential and appropriateness. This model has been founded upon, first, one of the principles of environmental sustainability, namely minimizing environmental degradation, and, secondly, maximizing the tourist satisfaction experience based on tourist dissipation and diversity of high-appeal attractions. While the approach is a positivist one, using a predefined questionnaire administered to visitors, it does offer an objective and repeatable assessment. Tourism planners and park managers can use the developed tourism-potential model to take proactive measures to control nature-based tourism in environmentally fragile tourist destinations.

However, there are a number of limitations with this approach to determining tourism potential. First, it will be necessary to investigate more carefully the actual tourist sites on each map sheet to ascertain how environmentally resilient actual tourist point features are. The model will give only summed areas that have been found environmentally resilient and attractive. In reality it might be that the actual tourist site is vulnerable to tourism impact. Secondly, the arbitrary delineation of map-sheet boundaries may cut across highly diverse and attractive tourist locations. The result is that each map sheet may then incorporate only a small section of what is a larger potential tourist site and be overlooked

as a potential location. Finally, the entire process has been predicated on responses to questionnaires administered to a sample set of visitors to the region. Attractiveness is subjective. Preferences for the various vegetation types were based on ecological vegetation classes and were ascertained using photographs within the questionnaire. While an attempt has been made to measure response to vegetation class alone, the actual situation or setting of the questionnaire and/or photograph, the objects found within each photograph, as well as external factors, such as weather conditions, camera settings, etc., could all influence the ranks given. It was noted that adopting a simulated environment, used by Bishop *et al.* (2001), would enable external factors to be controlled. In addition, there has been no attempt to accommodate or analyse responses from people with varying gender, cultural and ethnic background, socio-economic status, educational level, family situation, health, disability and age. This must form part of future research.

References

Abello, R. and Bernaldez, F. (1986) Landscape preference and personality. *Landscape and Urban Planning* 13, 19–28.

Arrowsmith, C.A. and Inbakaran, R. (2001) Estimating environmental resiliency for the Grampians National Park. *Tourism Management* 23(3), 295–309.

Bishop, I. (1996) Comparing regression and neural net based approaches to modelling of scenic beauty. *Landscape and Urban Planning* 34(2), 125–134.

Bishop, I.J., Wherrett, J.R. and Millar, D. (2001) Assessment of path choices on a country walk using a virtual environment. *Landscape and Urban Planning* 52, 227–239.

DeLucio, J.V. and Mugica, M. (1994) Landscape preferences and behaviour of visitors to Spanish national parks. *Landscape and Urban Planning* 29, 145–160.

Forman, R. and Godron, M. (1986) *Landscape Ecology*. John Wiley & Sons, New York.

Hammitt, W.E., Patterson, M.E. and Noe, F.P. (1994) Identifying and predicting visual preference of southern Appalachian forest recreation vistas. *Landscape and Urban Planning* 29, 171–183.

Hudson, B.J. (1998) Waterfalls: resources for tourism. *Annals of Tourism Research* 25(4), 958–973.

Hull, R.B. and Buhyoff, G.J. (1983) Distance and scenic beauty. *Environment and Behavior* 15(1), 77–91.

Land Conservation Council of Victoria (LCC) (1997) *Historic Places Special Investigation South-western Victoria Final Recommendations.* Land Conservation Council of Victoria, Melbourne.

Lew, A. (1987) A framework of attraction research. *Annals of Tourism Research* 14, 553–575.

Lowenthal, D. and Prince, H.C. (1965) English landscape tastes. *Geographical Review* 55, 186–222.

Mackay, K. and Fesenmaier, D. (1997) Pictorial element of destination in image formation. *Annals of Tourism Research* 24(3), 537–565.

Miller, D.R., Morrice, J.G., Horne, P.L. and Aspinall, R.J. (1994) Use of GIS for analysis of scenery in the Cairngorm mountains of Scotland. In: Price, M.F. and Heywood, D.I. (eds) *Mountain Environments and Geographic Information Systems.* Taylor and Francis, London, pp. 119–132.

National Parks Service (1996) *Grampians National Park: Touring Guide.* Department of Natural Resources and Environment, East Melbourne, 39 pp.

Nova Scotia Museum of Natural History (1996) *Introduction to the Natural History of Nova Scotia.* http://museum.gov.ns.ca/mnh/nature/nhns/index.htm Accessed on 6 June 2001. Halifax, Nova Scotia, Nova Scotia Museum of Natural History.

Parks Victoria (1997) *Northern Grampians Walks.* Parks Victoria, Melbourne.

Parks Victoria (1998a) *Wonderland Walks.* Parks Victoria, Melbourne.

Parks Victoria (1998b) *Southern Grampians Walks.* Parks Victoria, Melbourne.

Thomas, T. (1995) *Fifty Walks in the Grampians: with Outdoor Tourist Attractions.* Hill of Content Publishing Company, Melbourne.

Tourism Victoria (undated, *c.* 1995) *The Grampians, Victoria, Australia.* Tourism Victoria, Melbourne, 58 pp.

Unwin, D. (1981) *Introductory Spatial Analysis.* Methuen, London.

Wall, G. (1997) Tourism attractions: points, lines and areas. *Annals of Tourism Research* 24(1), 240–243.

17

Contributions of Non-consumptive Wildlife Tourism to Conservation

Karen Higginbottom,[1] Andrew Tribe[2] and Rosemary Booth[2]
[1]School of Environmental and Applied Sciences, Griffith University, Queensland, Australia; [2]School of Animal Studies, University of Queensland, Gatton, Queensland, Australia

Abstract

Wildlife tourism has the potential to contribute to conservation through a variety of mechanisms. This chapter presents a preliminary assessment of the extent to which this potential is currently being realised, comparing tourism based on viewing of animals in captive settings (with a focus on federated zoos) with that in free-ranging situations (wildlife watching). The key mechanisms involved are: direct wildlife management and research; use of income derived from wildlife tourism to fund conservation; education of visitors to behave in a more conservation-friendly manner; political lobbying in support of conservation; and provision of a socio-economic incentive for conservation. All of these occur in at least some zoos and wildlife-watching situations, and collectively the contribution of non-consumptive wildlife tourism to conservation is significant, though impossible to quantify. The key strengths of the zoo sector in this regard are its inputs into captive breeding and its potential to educate large numbers of people. In contrast, wildlife watching provides significant socio-economic incentives for conservation of natural habitats. There seem to be significant opportunities for expanding the role of non-consumptive wildlife tourism in conservation.

Introduction

Tourism can have positive, neutral or negative effects on the natural environment (Budowski, 1976). In wildlife tourism, encounters with wild (non-domesticated) animals are a focus of the visitor experience. It is thus crucial, not only to the conservation of the animals but to the sustainability of the tourism businesses concerned, that the net effects of tourism on wildlife are neutral or preferably positive. Moreover, there is increasing consensus that nature-based or wildlife tourism should create a mutualistic relationship between tourism and nature conservation (e.g. WZO, 1993; Commonwealth Department of Tourism, 1994; Young *et al.*, 1996; van Oosterzee, 2000; Ecotourism Association of Australia, 2001).

The net effects of wildlife tourism on wildlife are a result of the balance between any negative impacts of the tourism-related activities on the animals and any – generally indirect – positive contributions to their conservation. While the potential negative effects have been reviewed in detail elsewhere (e.g. Liddle, 1997; Green and Higginbottom, 2001), there has been little attempt to systematically review the positive effects. Given a lack of adequate quantitative data, objective quantification of contributions of wildlife tourism to conservation is not yet possible, but this review represents a first step in this direction and provides a framework for future research. It is important to bear in mind, however, that a balanced assessment requires simultaneous consideration of both negative and positive effects.

This review focuses on so-called 'non-consumptive' wildlife tourism (i.e. excluding hunting and fishing). While many of the issues covered in this chapter are also applicable to consumptive wildlife tourism, the latter raises some additional issues that are beyond the scope of the present review. This chapter provides a new perspective by comparing the contributions of two sectors of non-consumptive wildlife tourism: captive wildlife tourism (carried out by institutions that are henceforth described as 'zoos') and non-consumptive wildlife tourism based on free-ranging animals (referred to henceforth as 'wildlife watching'). Nowadays there is a continuum ranging from situations where the animals are confined in small cages through to those where they are able to range freely without any barriers to movement. However, in practice, the distinction remains useful, as the types of organizations, the associated literature and the philosophies that have arisen around the two sectors remain largely distinct.

Ultimately, conservation of wildlife involves what people do (or do not do) to wild animals or their habitats that directly increases the chances of long-term persistence of wild populations. For convenience we refer to deliberate manipulations of wild animals or their habitats to achieve conservation goals as 'direct wildlife management'. Such management in turn nearly always requires funding and political support. The behaviour of the public sometimes directly influences animal populations and can be modified by education. However, the main way in which education is likely to lead to enhanced wildlife management is through increasing public con-

cern for conservation issues, which in turn translates into enhanced funding and political support, particularly through political pressure. Education can also lead to enhanced funding through facilitation of voluntary donations. Some tourism operators may be motivated to contribute to conservation because of their personal ethics and/or because tourism is linked to activities that were set up with conservation objectives in mind. Even where this is not the case, engaging in wildlife tourism can provide a political or economic incentive for engaging in conservation-enhancing behaviour.

Thus we can classify the ways in which wildlife tourism is potentially associated with conservation benefits into the following categories:

1. Direct wildlife management and supporting research.
2. Providing funding for conservation.
3. Providing education about conservation.
4. Political lobbying in support of conservation.
5. Providing socio-economic incentives for conservation.

In this chapter we review what is known of the nature, magnitude and effectiveness of each of these contributions for each sector, pointing out gaps in existing knowledge. We then use this information to draw general conclusions about the scope and magnitude of contributions to conservation by non-consumptive wildlife tourism; compare the situation for captive and non-captive sectors; and propose key steps that should be taken to enhance contributions to conservation. To provide the necessary context, we begin by introducing the zoo and wildlife-watching sectors, providing a brief overview of each sector and its approach to conservation.

Given a lack of systematic research aimed at quantifying such contributions, our review is necessarily mainly qualitative. While our scope is international, the review is applicable especially to more developed countries than to less developed countries, especially in the case of zoos. Where available, we use Australian examples to illustrate our points and, whenever not stated otherwise, the wildlife-tourism sites or activities we refer to are in Australia. The present chapter draws heavily on a report by Higginbottom *et al.* (2001a), which provides further details on some of the issues covered in this chapter.

Zoos and their role in conservation

Zoos can be defined as institutions that confine, manage and exhibit collections of living wild animals. The World Zoo Conservation Strategy (WZO, 1993) estimates that there may be well over 10,000 zoos worldwide, of which approximately 1000 participate in national or international zoo federations. This report focuses on these federated zoos, because membership requires a commitment to work together towards joint conservation goals.

Zoos today see themselves as important conservators of nature. Despite their claims, they are still seen by some as being superficial, expensive and ineffective (ANZFAS, 1996; Hewitt, 2001). Consequently, as Larcombe (1995a) explains, zoos must not only contribute to conservation but must also be seen to be doing so. As Bartos and Kelly (1998) argue, 'a summary of measurable contributions by zoos in the areas of education, conservation, research and tourism is of critical importance in demonstrating their contribution to the whole community'.

Wildlife watching and its role in conservation

Wildlife watching is a subset of nature-based tourism and comprises a diversity of forms, based on tours, attractions or accommodation. Although called 'watching' here for convenience, this form of tourism can also involve listening, photography, feeding, live-trapping or any other form of interaction that does not kill the animal. Further information on the scope of activities involved is given by Higginbottom *et al.* (2001b).

There have been a number of claims that wildlife watching, like nature-based tourism in general, can be good for conservation (e.g. Roe *et al.*, 1997; National Watchable Wildlife Program, 2001; International Association of Fish and Wildlife Agencies, 2002), especially

because of associated economic incentives and education. Further, in policy statements and in popular terminology, wildlife watching is often seen as a form of ecotourism. According to some definitions of the latter term, this necessarily means that the tourism is associated with conservation-related education and other localized conservation benefits (Weaver, 2001). Promotion of this concept of ecotourism by governments and industry associations in more developed countries, such as Australia and the USA, has helped to provide an impetus to attempts to maximize the conservation benefits of wildlife watching.

Methods

Information for this review was obtained from the following main sources:

- A review of the relevant literature, both published and unpublished.
- Semi-structured telephone interviews with key staff of Australian conservation agencies.
- Informal conversations with selected wildlife-watching tour operators.
- A review of the conservation objectives and achievements of zoos, through face-to-face interviews with key individuals and stakeholders at a selection of zoos and through their relevant professional associations. These concentrated on the UK and Australia, which were chosen as being representative of federated zoos throughout the world.

Direct Wildlife Management and Supporting Research

Zoos

The involvement of zoos in conservation is chiefly *ex situ* (outside the natural habitat), but recently some zoos have also become involved with *in situ* (inside the natural habitat) conservation initiatives.

The desire of zoos to contribute to wildlife conservation is demonstrated in the way they manage their collections. Nowadays, this is via cooperative species-management pro-grammes, in which the genetic diversity, population size and origin of the founders are all accounted for. This greatly enhances the reintroduction potential of captive-bred popu-lations (Mitchell, 1991). Such genetic management is facilitated regionally through the zoo federations and globally through the International Species Inventory System (ISIS), with the aim of having self-sustaining captive collections as insurance for wild populations. ISIS data indicate that 92% of zoo mammals and 71% of birds are now captive-bred.

Zoos are also involved in captive breed-ing for reintroduction. For instance, Australian zoos participate in at least 35 such pro-grammes (de Koff, 1998) and, over the past 10 years, have refined their captive management to cooperate with government authorities in the process of recovering threatened species. Consequently, Craig *et al.* (1999) claim that Australian zoos now have a well-defined role in the conservation of endangered wildlife.

Nevertheless, captive breeding of endan-gered species is limited for two main reasons: the lack of captive space available (Seal, 1991; Bartos and Kelly, 1998; Conway, 1999a) and the high cost of producing animals. For instance, in Australia each native animal pro-duced for reintroduction costs on average Aus$6546 (Perth Zoo, 2000). Similarly, Alibhai and Jewell (1994) estimate that it is 16 times more expensive to maintain a black rhi-noceros in captivity than to protect enough wild habitat to support it. Thus Dixon and Travers (1994) and Hewitt (2001) argue that zoos are not the best targets for limited con-servation funds.

Many zoos actively cooperate with research organizations. Zoo-based collabora-tive research is usually concerned *ex situ* with improving captive management through stud-ies of nutrition, growth, infectious disease, environmental toxins, reproduction, reintro-duction biology, stress and behaviour (Mitchell, 1991).

However, zoo research can also have an important role in linking *in situ* and *ex situ* conservation activities. There is a flow of information from zoo researchers to field sci-entists that can assist in species reintroduction and management, while, reciprocally, data

collected in the field can enhance captive breeding. Ryder and Feistner (1995) have reviewed new research initiatives being under-taken by zoos and found that reproductive and genetic technologies have particular signifi-cance for conservation of threatened species. They conclude that this role needs to be expanded and developed as wildlife popula-tions and biological diversity continue to decline.

An increasing number of zoos now rec-ognize the importance of promoting the interface between captive breeding and in-country conservation efforts (Durrell and Mallinson, 1998; Mallinson, 1998). For instance, in 1992 fewer than 325 *in situ* con-servation projects were being supported by American Zoological Association zoos, while by 1999 the number had increased to over 650 (Conway, 1999a). Similarly, federated zoos in the UK supported 177 *in situ* projects in 2000, an increase of 61% since 1995 (Federation of Zoological Gardens of Great Britain and Ireland, 2001). If this trend continues, Conway (1999a) believes that zoos could become the primary non-government field-conservation organizations.

In Australia, zoos have traditionally been more involved with captive breeding pro-grammes for native species, but recently some have established partnerships to support *in situ* projects. Examples of such work are Adelaide Zoo's participation in the rescue and health screening of the endangered Seychelles mag-pie robin (Adelaide Zoo, 2000), Melbourne Zoo's contribution to the restoration of the Calperum Biosphere Reserve (Melbourne Zoo, 2000) and the establishment of a 150 ha predator-free sanctuary by Western Plains Zoo (David Blyde, Manager, Life Sciences, Western Plains Zoo, Dubbo, New South Wales, 6 February 2002, personal communication).

Wildlife watching

In contrast to zoos, direct wildlife management associated with wildlife watching is nearly always *in situ*, and covers a wider range of activities, such as reintroduction, control of exotic predators, patrolling for poachers, tree planting and weed control. There has been very little research to indicate the effectiveness of any of these initiatives in contributing to conservation. Whether a wildlife-watching operation is involved in conservation appears to be very much dependent on the philosophy and objectives of the individual operator, in contrast to the more institutionalized approach of the larger zoos. One exception – at least in principle – is operators who have obtained certification from a marketing programme that recognizes contributions to conservation, with Australia's Nature and Ecotourism Accreditation Program (NEAP II) as a leading example (NEAPWG, 2000).

Wildlife-watching operators who participate in conservation-related wildlife management include government organizations (e.g. Landscope Expeditions, Western Australia), non-profit organizations set up mainly for conservation reasons (e.g. Australian Koala Foundation) and commercial tourism operators. Even the latter make significant contributions to conservation in some cases. Operators of private game reserves in South Africa have reintroduced a range of animal species that had become locally extirpated, including some that are endangered (James and Goodman, 2000). Earth Sanctuaries Ltd is a publicly listed Australian company established with a conservation mission, but with the explicit intention of using tourism to help achieve this mission (Earth Sanctuaries, 2002). The company undertakes its own captive breeding, combined with acquisition of animals from elsewhere, and carries out reintroductions into a network of private reserves.

In addition to deliberately undertaking activities that assist conservation, wildlife tour operators in some cases contribute indirectly by acting as deterrents to the disturbance or killing of wildlife by people. The Zaire Gorilla Conservation Project provided surveillance for a large area of a park inhabited by endangered mountain gorillas, with four of the largest families being monitored daily. This has been demonstrated to have helped reduce poaching of gorillas (Aveling and Aveling, 1989; McNeilage, 1996).

Some larger wildlife-watching attractions make a significant contribution to wildlife research. Tourism income derived from Phillip

Island Penguin Reserve (Australia) has funded research and monitoring that has greatly increased knowledge of the biology of the little penguin, other fauna of the region, and related conservation management issues (Rowley, 1992; Phillip Island Nature Park Board of Management, 1998; Ray Leivers, General Manager, Phillip Island Nature Park, Cowes, Phillip Island, Victoria, 25 September 2001, personal communication). A number of smaller Australian operators, listed by Higginbottom *et al.* (2001a), combine commercial objectives with participation in conservation research.

In the wildlife-watching sector, in contrast to zoos, tourists as well as operators are sometimes involved in direct wildlife management or research. There are small but growing numbers of organizations internationally that specialize in activities where tourists assist in conservation-related field research, monitoring or conservation work (IRG, 1992; Preece and van Oosterzee, 1997). Major examples of such organizations operating in Australia are Landscope Expeditions, Earthwatch, Conservation Volunteers Australia and Operation Raleigh (see Higginbottom *et al.*, 2001a, for further details).

Providing Funding for Conservation

Zoos

Zoos invest considerable amounts of money in pursuit of their conservation objectives. For instance, in 1995 UK federated zoos contributed approximately Aus$4.5 million to *in situ* conservation and more than Aus$15 million in 2000. In addition, specific campaigns since 1996 have raised a further Aus$1 million (Federation of Zoological Gardens of Great Britain and Ireland, 2001).

Unfortunately, in most cases it is not possible to calculate the amount spent specifically on conservation, because the costs involved are bound up with the running expenses of the zoo. This is particularly true for *ex situ* projects, where staff time, equipment and facilities come out of routine operational budgets. Thus, in Australia, while the total income derived from the zoo industry was Aus$142 million in

1996/97 (ABS, 1998), it is not known how much was used to fund conservation. As an indication, Perth Zoo, in their 1998/99 annual report, calculated the total cost of producing seven threatened species for reintroduction as Aus$1,066,951, representing 18% of its gross income (Perth Zoo, 1999).

Most zoos have difficulty finding enough resources to become involved in conservation (Mitchell, 1994). As Larcombe (1995b) explains, they must strike balances between the allocation of scarce resources for exhibits and the demands of conservation. He maintains that the costs of maintaining Melbourne Zoo's collection doubled during the period from 1992 to 1995 due to their greater involvement in conservation.

Wildlife watching

There is a range of government charges on commercial nature-based tourism operators and tourists that are intended to contribute to the costs of management associated with tourism activities. Most of these fees relate to the use of protected areas (where most wildlife watching probably occurs). Less common is the practice of requiring permits (with associated fees) for tourism operators who offer close encounters with particular species of wildlife that are of conservation concern, even if outside protected areas. For instance, in Western Australia (WA), operators who provide encounters with whale sharks must pay for a special interaction licence (Doug Coughran, Supervising Wildlife Officer, Department of Conservation and Land Management, WA, 25 September 2001, personal communication).

Although revenues from parks around the world are generally not sufficient to fully offset their operating costs (Goodwin et al., 1998), let alone to provide net funding for conservation, there are some exceptions. User fees at some parks or in some regions provide revenues that not only support their own operations but provide funding for conservation measures (Lindberg et al., 1996; FPTF, 2000; IUCN, 2000; GBRMPA, 2001). Most of the cases reported in the literature where government charges relating to wildlife tourism have raised funding for conservation involve big-game hunting. One of the few published cases involving wildlife watching is tourism based on mountain gorillas in East Africa. Income from tourism has been used to pay for habitat conservation and anti-poaching measures, which have apparently been crucial to conservation of this endangered species (McNeilage, 1996; Butynski and Kalina, 1998). Although application of the 'user-pays' principle is becoming increasingly widespread (Goodwin et al., 1998; IUCN, 2000), there are various philosophical, political and practical constraints on the use of this mechanism to fund conservation (e.g. Butynski and Kalina, 1998; Buckley, 2000a; IUCN, 2000; Lindberg, 2001).

Some developed attractions based on wildlife watching provide significant revenue for conservation. Net income to the Phillip Island Penguin Reserve in Victoria in 1992/93 was estimated to be Aus$690,000 (Meek et al., 1994). Revenue generated from turtle-viewing tourism at Mon Repos Conservation Park in Queensland, Australia, is invested in sea-turtle research, patrolling nesting beaches and predator-control measures (Tisdell and Wilson, 2000). Many authors suggest that the revenue-generating potential of some nature-based tourism products (both private and public) is not being realized, particularly where the funds are seen to contribute to conservation (Lindberg, 1991; Pearce, 1995; Laarman and Gregersen, 1996). A recent study at Mon Repos Conservation Park (Australia) indicated that tourists would be willing to pay more than double the existing fee (Tisdell and Wilson, 2000). Recent in-house research at Phillip Island Penguin Reserve similarly established that entrance prices could be raised well above their levels at the time (Ray Leivers, General Manager, Phillip Island Nature Park, Cowes, Phillip Island, 25 September 2001, personal communication). It is important to caution, however, that such indications of willingness do not necessarily translate into action.

Like zoos, some wildlife-watching enterprises donate at least some of their profits to conservation initiatives or provide opportunities for their guests to make financial contributions to conservation through donations or sponsorships (see examples in

Lindberg, 1991; IRG, 1992; Higginbottom *et al.*, 2001a). Earth Sanctuaries Ltd explicitly uses tourism as a source of revenue for its conservation and education programmes. There seems to be scope for expanded use of donations by visitors (Lindberg, 1991; IUCN, 2000; Higginbottom *et al.*, 2001a).

Providing Education about Conservation

Overview

It is often stated that visitors, as part of their wildlife- or nature-based tourism experience, can be educated to increase their conservation awareness and to behave in ways that have positive consequences for wildlife and/or their habitats (e.g. Duff, 1993; NBTAC, 1994; Parks and Wildlife Commission Northern Territory, n.d.). Education of wildlife tourists can occur through changes in attitudes and/or increased knowledge, which in turn may promote:

- more responsible behaviour towards wildlife and the natural environment, both in terms of minimizing negative effects in the area where tourism occurs and more broadly;
- subsequent involvement in wildlife conservation or research;
- increased donations of money towards conservation;
- increased political pressure on governments to achieve conservation objectives;
- more satisfied customers and therefore more successful businesses.

Zoos

The development of zoos as educational establishments has mirrored their change from menageries to conservation parks. Contemporary zoos strive to display their animals as part of the overall environment and to utilize them in a variety of both formal and informal educational roles (Woollard, 1998).

Formal education involves structured programmes for schools and an increasing involvement in tertiary education. For instance, in a review of zoo education in the UK and Ireland, Woollard (1999) found that 71% of zoos had an education department and 73% taught visiting school pupils, with more than 750,000 pupils visiting these zoos. In Australia, many zoos also have a significant commitment to formal education. The Melbourne Zoo Education Service, for instance, has 12 full-time teachers, with more than 120,000 children utilizing the service each year (Melbourne Zoo, 1999).

Most zoos also attempt to communicate a conservation message through the informal education of their visitors. However, assessing these activities is difficult (Bartos and Kelly, 1998), and critics suggest that their effectiveness is unclear (Ollason, 1993; Jamieson, 1995; Scott, 2001). On the one hand, several studies have found that exposure to captive wildlife in combination with some form of interpretation was associated with increased support for conservation (Broad, 1996; Tarrant *et al.*, 1997; Moscardo *et al.*, 2001). On the other hand, Mazur (1995) has questioned this effectiveness by concluding that, while visitors exhibit an awareness of endangered species and habitat destruction, it is not clear that they have gained this from their zoo experience. She maintains that for zoos to fulfil their education potential, they should critically evaluate their current activities and provide more tangible information about conservation threats and measures used to combat them.

Wildlife watching

Many wildlife- and nature-based tourism operators, whether from the private or the public sector, incorporate environmental interpretation and education components. For many non-profit organizations involved in wildlife tourism, raising public awareness of environmental issues is the primary purpose (IRG, 1992; see Australian examples in Higginbottom *et al.*, 2001a). Government conservation agencies around the world also make varying levels of commitment to providing environmental interpretation, mainly in protected areas. For most commercial operators, commitment to education is a personal or business decision of the individual operator.

However, operators accredited under Australia's NEAP II (NEAPWG, 2000) are required to ensure that customers have access to well-planned interpretation, accurate information and trained staff that have an understanding of nature and conservation issues. The recent development of a related accreditation system for nature guides (Crabtree and Black, 2000), initiated by the Ecotourism Association of Australia, is a further step to facilitate improvement of the standard of interpretation in nature-based tourism products in Australia.

There is little published research on the effectiveness of wildlife interpretation in free-ranging settings, in contrast to the situation in zoos. Two Australian studies of visitors' responses in relation to sea-turtle viewing at Mon Repos Conservation Park showed that exposure to interpretation resulted in attitudes indicating increased support for conservation of these turtles (Howard, 1999; Tisdell and Wilson, 2000). Other positive effects on conservation-related attitudes have been noted for the dolphin interpretation programme at Tangalooma, Australia (Orams, 1995). A number of key informants interviewed by Moscardo et al. (2001) and Higginbottom et al. (2001a) felt that the quality of wildlife interpretation available in Australia needs to be improved in order to realize much of its educational potential, and this situation is probably common worldwide.

Political Lobbying in Support of Conservation

Zoos

Apart from their role in conservation education, zoos are rarely involved in lobbying for conservation and, where this has occurred, it has usually been through their federations. For instance, the European Association of Zoos and Aquaria has recently launched a substantial public campaign against the bushmeat trade in Africa (EAZA, 2000). This lack of involvement apparently stems from both a belief that this is not a core role of zoos and a reluctance to be seen as being political (Ed MacAllister, Director, Adelaide Zoo, South

Australia, and President, Australasian Regional Association of Zoological Parks and Aquaria (ARAZPA), 12 October 2001, personal communication).

Wildlife watching

There are a number of situations in which wildlife-watching operators have lobbied for conservation of the natural resources on which they depend financially. In Tasmania, many wildlife-tourism operators lobbied the government in opposition to both the proposed damming of the Franklin River and the process of clearfell logging in areas where wildlife operations occur (Nick Mooney, Wildlife Management Officer, Tasmanian Department of Environment and Land Management, Tasmania, 31 March 2000, personal communication). Purportedly as a result of lobbying from Great Barrier Reef tourism operators, the Australian government recently allocated additional funds into research on the crown-of-thorns starfish, which is detrimentally affecting the Reef. However, a number of authors (e.g. Buckley, 2000a; van Oosterzee, 2000) have noted that, unlike other commercial interest groups that depend on natural resources, the tourism industry generally seems to lack awareness of its dependence on natural resources and could be doing much more to lobby for conservation.

Providing Socio-economic Incentives for Conservation

Zoos

Contemporary zoos not only have a self-imposed commitment to conservation, but they are subject to a sociopolitical imperative to contribute to conservation, enforced by the relevant zoo legislation. For instance, the Secretary of State's revised Standards of Modern Zoo Practice in the UK and the European Union's Zoos Directive both state that in future zoos will have to satisfy conservation requirements to be relicensed (Department of Environment, Transport and the Regions, 2000). Similar legislative requirements have been introduced in Australia (Department of Natural Resources and Environment, Victoria, 1998). These requirements reflect a view of society that keeping animals in captivity must be justified on conservation grounds (Conway, 1999b; Tribe, 2000).

In general, however, zoos do not appear to view the need to attract customers as an economic incentive for conservation. Indeed, there is little information about the expectation or satisfaction of visitors with the role of zoos in conservation (Ed MacAllister, Director, Adelaide Zoo, South Australia, and President, ARAZPA, 12 October 2001, personal communication). In the absence of evidence, some zoos seem reluctant to fully embrace their conservation potential, apparently believing that money spent on conservation will not be compensated for by increased visitor revenue (Ed MacAllister, Director, Adelaide Zoo, South Australia, and President, ARAZPA, 12 October 2001, personal communication, cf. Cherfas, 1984). In so doing, such zoos may in fact be missing out on important marketing and fundraising opportunities. Gipps (1993) suggests that the problem with zoo management is its lack of awareness that 'conservation can sell tickets', and, if zoos are to attract visitors and financial support, then they will have to work harder at promoting their conservation activities. For an industry committed to supporting wildlife conservation, it is clear that more information is needed about the role that conservation can play in supporting the industry.

Wildlife watching

Since wildlife watching, unlike zoos, is dependent directly on the existence of natural populations of wildlife, the existence of this form of tourism can provide operators and/or host communities who benefit from this tourism with a vital incentive for conservation (cf. Buckley 2000b; van Oosterzee, 2000).

In many countries, expected revenue from nature-based tourism has been reported to have provided an economic and political incentive for the creation of government-owned protected areas (Young *et al.*, 1996; Preece and van Oosterzee, 1997; Goodwin *et*

al., 1998). In many cases, the principal attraction involved is wildlife (see EWG, 1995; Isaacs, 2000; Higginbottom *et al.*, 2001a). In the USA, a major increase in participation in non-consumptive wildlife recreation is reported to have helped motivate interest in the protection of natural areas for the benefit of tourism (Vickerman, 1988).

There are also several published examples of wildlife tourism creating an economic incentive for conservation of private lands (see also Higginbottom *et al.*, 2001a). In a survey of 27 private game-reserve managers in South Africa, 48% said that if [wildlife] tourism had not been a commercial option, they would have continued to farm cattle (which is generally considered to be a less sustainable land use in such areas) (James and Goodman, 2000). Across South Africa more generally, successful reintroduction programmes on hundreds of private game reserves and small state reserves are reported to have been motivated largely by the economic incentive provided by wildlife tourism, especially wildlife watching (Stuart Pimm, Professor, University of Tenessee, Knoxville, USA, 10 July 2001, personal communication).

The introduction of wildlife tourism may also provide an economic incentive leading to conservation-orientated changes in wildlife-management practices. This is likely to be of most conservation significance in cases where the wildlife are hunted or taken for live trade for subsistence or commercial purposes. The mountain gorilla is a classic case of a highly endangered species, threatened by poaching, for which it is widely thought that the introduction of tourism has allowed continued survival, largely because of a socio-economic incentive (McNeilage, 1996; Vieta, 1999). A similar argument may apply in more developed countries, where it is most likely to apply to species normally considered to be pests, particularly to agriculture (e.g. Brooke, 1996).

Several international examples (mostly from less developed countries) illustrate links between the implementation of wildlife tourism and increased support for wildlife conservation from local communities, who benefit through income and/or employment. These include political support for a ban on hunting (Parsler, 1997) and apparent increased support for the protection of wildlife (Groom et al., 1991; Shackley, 1995; Gillingham and Lee, 1999; Higginbottom et al., 2001a). Despite numerous anecdotes, evidence for changes in local attitudes as a result of nature-based tourism is mostly of poor quality (see Higginbottom et al., 2001a, for more details).

As for zoos, a final socio-economic incentive for wildlife-tourism operators to contribute to conservation is that this may assist them in

Table 17.1. Summary of contributions of non-consumptive wildlife tourism to conservation.

Type of contribution	Wildlife watching (free-ranging wildlife)	Zoos (captive wildlife in federated zoos)
Direct wildlife management and research:		
in situ	• Significant numbers of mostly small-scale contributions, though minority of operators	• Minority of operators with mostly small-scale contributions, but growing
ex situ	• Very rare; a few cases involving captive breeding and reintroduction	• A major formal objective and the primary way in which zoos contribute to conservation; occurs in all cases
Providing funding for conservation	• Government charges provide contributions in a minority of cases • Significant numbers, though a minority, of operators provide contributions • Donations provided by tourists in a minority of cases; probable unmet potential • Contributions are generally to *in situ* conservation, often by other organizations	• Government charges do not provide contributions • All operators provide contributions • Donations provided by tourists in all cases • Contributions are generally to *ex situ* conservation, within the zoo
Providing education about conservation	• Highly variable in quantity and quality between operators • Potential to reach large numbers of people, limited mainly to interpretative displays and signs in protected areas	• A major formal objective; significant efforts in all cases • Potential to reach very large numbers of people; far from fully realized
Political lobbying in support of conservation	• Small minority of cases	• Small minority of cases
Providing socio-economic incentives for conservation	• Major contribution in terms of protected-area creation, especially in less developed countries • Significant contribution in terms of private land conservation, though opportunities for increase in some regions • Minor but growing incentive associated with marketing • No strong sociopolitical imperative for conservation	• Possible incentive associated with marketing, but little recognized • Strong sociopolitical incentive for conservation in some countries

attracting tourists. Some commercial nature-based tourism operators who make contributions to conservation are at least partially motivated to do so by their perception that this will help them to attract environmentally aware clients, and they incorporate this into their advertising (EWG, 1995; Higginbottom *et al.*, 2001a). Accreditation schemes like Australia's NEAP II (NEAPWG, 2000) are based on the premise that operators will be able to use accreditation (which, at the advanced level, signifies that the operator makes contributions to conservation) to help market themselves. However, there has been no convincing research confirming the validity of this assumption.

Conclusions

There is clearly a wide range of mechanisms through which non-consumptive wildlife tourism currently contributes to conservation, as summarized in Table 17.1. It is not possible to quantify these contributions, although an indication of their probable scale is given. Further quantitative research is recommended in order to refine the conclusions and recommendations given here. It is, however, clear that, within each sector and collectively, the contributions of non-consumptive wildlife tourism to conservation are significant and probably growing. There also seems to be considerable unrealized potential.

The key strength in relation to conservation potential that is particular to wildlife watching is the economic incentive that this can create for the conservation of natural environments. Such links could be strengthened by wider quantification and publicizing of the financial benefits derived from protected areas and from an increase in government support to private landowners considering implementation of nature-based tourism. The key strengths of zoos lie in their contributions to *ex situ* wildlife management and to intensive education of large numbers of people. However, the extent to which these mechanisms are effective is yet to be established, and it has been argued that the former is an inefficient use of conservation funding. The coordinated approach to conservation efforts

that applies to federated zoos should also help facilitate more efficient channelling of conservation efforts than generally occurs in the free-ranging sector. Efforts by governments and industry associations (such as Australia's NEAP) to achieve greater coordination with and between nature-based tourism operators should be encouraged, although this is difficult since operators are diverse, numerous and typically small. There is considerable common ground between the two sectors in feasible mechanisms for contributing to conservation, suggesting that there may be benefits in zoos collaborating with wildlife-watching operators to learn from each others' experience and achieve greater efficiencies in achieving joint conservation objectives.

While there may be potential for increasing the contributions of non-consumptive wildlife tourism to conservation, there are a number of serious constraints on this potential. The most obvious is the limited capacity of tourists and operators to divert finances and time into conservation. Significant increases in contributions thus depend to a large extent on increasing the tourism income obtained by wildlife-tourism operators and using the existing potential more effectively. However, this will still be constrained by the primarily commercial orientation of some wildlife-watching operators. Another major constraint is the lack of research in this area, particularly in terms of assessing effectiveness of existing mechanisms (especially education) in making a real difference to conservation and in determining the relationship between participation of operators in conservation and their ability to attract customers. Specific actions that can be taken to enhance the contributions of wildlife tourism to conservation are given by Tribe (2000) and Higginbottom *et al.* (2001a). These should occur in the context of a strategic and coordinated approach, involving cooperation between different types of wildlife-tourism operators and other conservation stakeholders. Such an approach should allow wildlife tourism to more fully realize its apparently substantial potential to contribute to conservation.

Acknowledgements

This research was financially supported by the Cooperative Research Centre for Sustainable Tourism and Hermon Slade Fund. We are grateful to Chelsea Northrope for assisting with the preparation of the manuscript.

References

Adelaide Zoo (2000) Annual Report, 1999–2000. Zoological Board of South Australia, Adelaide.

Alibhai, S.K. and Jewell, Z.C. (1994) Saving the last rhino: *in-situ* conservation or captive breeding. In: Olney, P.J.S., Mace, G.M. and Feistner, A.T.C. (eds) *Creative Conservation: Interactive Management of Wild and Captive Populations.* Chapman & Hall, London, pp. 123–133.

Australian and New Zealand Federation of Animal Societies (ANZFAS) (1996) *Policy Compendium.* Australian and New Zealand Federation of Animal Societies, Collingwood, Victoria.

Australian Bureau of Statistics (ABS) (1998) *Zoos, Parks and Gardens Industry.* Australian Bureau of Statistics Publication No. 8699.0, ABS, Canberra.

Aveling, C. and Aveling, R. (1989) Gorilla conservation in Zaire. *Oryx* 23(2), 64–70.

Bartos, J.M. and Kelly, J.D. (1998) Towards best practice in the zoo industry: developing key performance indicators as benchmarks for progress. *International Zoo Yearbook* 36, 143–157.

Broad, G. (1996) Visitor profile and evaluation of informal education at Jersey Zoo. *Dodo: Journal of the Jersey Wildlife Preservation Trusts* 32, 166–192.

Brooke, J. (1996) Yellowstone wolves get an ally in tourist trade. *New York Times* 11 February.

Buckley, R.C. (2000a) Tourism in the most fragile environments. *Tourism Recreation Research* 25(1), 31–40.

Buckley, R.C. (2000b) Tourism and wilderness: dancing with the messy monster. In: McCool, S.F., Cole, D.N., Borrie, W.T. and O'Loughlin, J. (eds) *Proceedings of Wilderness Science in a Time of Change Conference,* Vol. 2, *Wilderness Within the Context of Larger Systems, 23–27 May 1999, Missoula, Montana.* Rocky Mountain Research Station, Forest Service, USDA, Ogden, Utah, pp. 1–4.

Budowski, G. (1976) Tourism and environmental conservation: conflict, coexistence or symbiosis. *Environmental Conservation* 3, 27–31.

Butynski, T.M. and Kalina, J. (1998) Gorilla tourism: a critical look. In: Milner-Gulland, E.J. and Mace, R. (eds) *Conservation of Biological Resources.* Blackwell Science, London.

Cherfas, J. (1984) *Zoo 2000: a Look Beyond the Bars.* British Broadcasting Corporation (BBC), London.

Commonwealth Department of Tourism (1994) *National Ecotourism Strategy.* Commonwealth of Australia, Canberra, Australian Capital Territory.

Conway, W. (1999a) Linking zoo and field, and keeping promises to dodos. In: *Proceedings of the 7th World Conference on Breeding Endangered Species.* Cincinnati Zoo and Botanical Garden, Cincinnati, pp. 5–11.

Conway, W. (1999b) The changing role of zoos in the 21st century. In: *Proceedings of the Annual Conference of the World Zoo Organization, South Africa.* World Zoo Organization, Cape Town, pp. 1–8.

Crabtree, A.E. and Black, R.S. (2000) *EcoGuide Program: Guide Workbook.* Ecotourism Association of Australia, Brisbane, Queensland.

Craig, M., Barlow, S., Wilcken, J., Hopkins, C. and Less, C. (1999) Zoo Involvement in the Australasian species recovery process. In: *Proceedings of the 7th World Conference on Breeding Endangered Species.* Cincinnati Zoo and Botanical Garden, Cincinnati, pp. 215–225

de Koff, G. (1998) *Conservation efforts of Australasian zoos: a review.* Unpublished report for Australasian Regional Association of Zoological Parks and Aquaria (ARAZPA).

Department of Environment, Transport and the Regions (2000) *Revised Version of the Secretary of State's Standards of Modern Zoo Practice.* Department of Environment, Transport and the Regions, London.

Department of Natural Resources and Environment, Victoria (DNRE, Victoria) (1998) *A Guide to Laws Relating to Keeping Wildlife for Commercial Purposes in Victoria.* Game and Wildlife Licensing Unit, Department of Natural Resources and Environment, East Melbourne, Victoria.

Dixon, A. and Travers, W. (1994) *The Zoo Inquiry.* World Society for the Protection of Animals and the Born Free Foundation, London.

Duff, L. (1993) Ecotourism in national parks: impacts and benefits. *National Parks Journal* June, 18–20.

Durrell, L. and Mallinson, J.J.C. (1998) The impact of an institutional review: a change of emphasis towards field conservation programmes. *International Zoo Yearbook* 36, 1–8.

Earth Sanctuaries (2002) Earth Sanctuaries: a sustainable solution. http://www.esl.com.au/solution.htm Last viewed 23 October 2002.

Ecotourism Association of Australia (2001) About the Ecotourism Association of Australia. http://www.ecotourism.org.au/abouteaa.cfm Last viewed 23 October 2002.

Ecotourism Working Group (EWG) (1995) *Ecotourism as a Conservation Instrument? Making Conservation Projects More Attractive.* Research Report of the Federal Ministry for Economic Cooperation and Development, Germany, Hurst, London.

European Association of Zoos and Aquaria (EAZA) (2000) *Guidelines on How to Participate in the EAZA Bushmeat Campaign, 2000–2001.* European Association of Zoos and Aquaria, Amsterdam.

Federation of Zoological Gardens of Great Britain and Ireland (2001) in situ *Conservation Projects, 2000.* Internal Report for Members of the Federation of Zoological Gardens of Great Britain and Ireland, May.

Financing Protected Areas Task Force of the WCPA of IUCN/Economics Unit of IUCN (FPTF) (2000) *Financing Protected Areas: Guidelines for Protected Area Managers.* IUCN, Gland, Switzerland.

Gillingham, S. and Lee, P.C. (1999) The impact of wildlife-related benefits on the conservation attitudes of local people around the Selous Game Reserve, Tanzania. *Environmental Conservation* 26, 218–228.

Gipps, J. (1993) Zoo survival. *Independent*, 19 November.

Goodwin, H., Kent, I., Parker, K. and Walpole, M. (1998) *Tourism, Conservation and Sustainable Development: Case Studies from Asia and Africa.* IIED Wildlife and Development Series No. 12, December, International Institute for Environment and Development, London.

Great Barrier Reef Marine Park Authority (GBRMPA) (2001) Environment management charge. http://www.gbrmpa.gov.au/corp_site/permits/emc.html Last viewed 23 October 2002.

Green, R.J. and Higginbottom, K. (2001) *Negative Effects of Wildlife Tourism on Wildlife.* Wildlife Tourism Research Report No. 5, Status Assessment of Wildlife Tourism in Australia Series, CRC for Sustainable Tourism, Gold Coast, Queensland.

Groom, M.J., Podolsky, R.D. and Munn, C.A. (1991) Tourism as a sustained use of wildlife: a case study of Madre de Dios, Southeastern Peru. In: Robinson, J.G. and Redford, K.H. (eds) *Neotropical Wildlife Use and Conservation.*

University of Chicago Press, Chicago, pp. 339–412.

Hewitt, N. (2001) Action stations: zoo check is go! *Wildlife Times* Winter, 17.

Higginbottom, K., Northrope, C.L. and Green, R.J. (2001a) *Positive Effects of Wildlife Tourism on Wildlife.* Wildlife Tourism Research Report No. 6, Status Assessment of Wildlife Tourism in Australia Series, CRC for Sustainable Tourism, Gold Coast, Queensland.

Higginbottom, K., Rann, K., Moscardo, G., Davis, D. and Muloin, S. (2001b) *Wildlife Tourism in Australia Overview.* Wildlife Tourism Research Report No. 1, Status Assessment of Wildlife Tourism in Australia Series, CRC for Sustainable Tourism, Gold Coast, Queensland.

Howard, J. (1999) *Mon Repos Conservation Park Visitor Survey.* Report No. 114, Johnstone Centre of Parks, Recreation and Heritage, Charles Sturt University, Albury, New South Wales.

International Association of Fish and Wildlife Agencies (2002) Teaming with wildlife: why do we need teaming with wildlife? http://www.teaming.com/site/about_tww.cfm Last viewed 29 October 2002.

International Resources Group (IRG) (1992) *Ecotourism: a Viable Alternative for Sustainable Management of Natural Resources in Africa.* Agency for International Development Bureau of Africa, Washington, DC.

Isaacs, J.C. (2000) The limited potential of ecotourism to contribute to wildlife conservation. *Wildlife Society Bulletin* 28(1), 61–69.

IUCN (2000) *Financing Protected Areas: Guidelines for Protected Area Managers.* IUCN, Gland, Switzerland.

James, B.M. and Goodman, P.S. (2000) *Nature Tourism and Conservation: a World Bank Research Project – Ecological Study.* Brousse-James and Associates, Pietermeritzburg.

Jamieson, D. (1995) Zoos revisited. In: Norton, B.G., Hutchins, M., Stevens, E.F. and Maple, T.L. (eds) *Ethics of the Ark: Zoos, Animal Welfare and Wildlife Conservation.* Smithsonian Institution Press, Washington, DC, pp. 52–65.

Laarman, J.G. and Gregersen, H.M. (1996) Pricing policy in nature-based tourism. *Tourism Management* 17(4), 247–254.

Larcombe, C. (1995a) Building or burning bridges. a proactive approach towards zoo critics. In: *Proceedings of the ARAZPA/ASZK Conference, Perth, Western Australia*, ARAZPA, Sydney, pp. 91–93.

Larcombe, C. (1995b) Sustainable development of zoological parks and aquaria. *Melbourne Zoo News* 15(1), 10–12.

Liddle, M.J. (1997) *Recreation Ecology: the Ecological Impact of Outdoor Recreation and Ecotourism.* Chapman & Hall, London.

Lindberg, K. (1991) *Policies for Maximizing Nature Tourism's Ecological and Economic Benefits.* World Resources Institute, Washington, DC.

Lindberg, K. (2001) Economic impacts. In: Weaver, D. (ed.) *The Encyclopedia of Ecotourism.* CAB International, Wallingford, pp. 363–377.

Lindberg, K., Enriquez, J. and Sproule, K. (1996) Ecotourism questioned: case studies from Belize. *Annals of Tourism Research* 23(3), 543–562.

McNeilage, A. (1996) Ecotourism and mountain gorillas in the Virunga Volcanoes. In: Taylor, V.J. and Dunstone, N. (eds) *The Exploitation of Mammal Populations.* Chapman & Hall, London, pp. 334–344.

Mallinson, J.C. (1998) The diverse role of zoos in a changing world: from zoological parks to conservation centres. In: Proceedings of the ARAZPA/ASZK *Conference, Sydney, New South Wales,* ARAZPA, Sydney, pp. 10–19.

Mazur, N. (1995) Perceptions of the role of zoos in conservation: an Australian case study. In: *Proceedings of the ARAZPA/ASZK Conference, Perth, Western Australia,* ARAZPA, Sydney, pp. 102–109.

Meek, I., Willis, A., Weir, I. and Frey, J. (1994) *Proceedings of the ANZECC 6th Australasian Regional Seminar on National Parks and Wildlife Management, Australian Alps, 13–27 March 1994.* ANZECC, Canberra, Australian Capital Territory.

Melbourne Zoo (1999) *Annual Report, 1998-1999.* Royal Melbourne Zoological Gardens, Zoological Parks and Gardens Board, Victoria.

Melbourne Zoo (2000) Annual Report, 1999-2000. Royal Melbourne Zoological Gardens, Zoological Parks and Gardens Board, Victoria.

Mitchell, G.F. (1991) Conserving biological diversity: a view from the zoo. *Today's Life Sciences* 3, 10–18.

Mitchell, G.F. (1994) A perspective of zoos in a changing environment. *Australian Academy of Technological Sciences and Engineering – Focus 81* (March/April), 23–25.

Moscardo, G., Woods, B. and Greenwood, T. (2001) *Understanding Visitor Perspectives on Wildlife Tourism.* Wildlife Tourism Research Report No. 2, Status Assessment of Wildlife Tourism in Australia Series, CRC for Sustainable Tourism, Gold Coast, Queensland.

National Watchable Wildlife Program (2001) Watchable Wildlife Inc – helping communities and wildlife prosper: what is Watchable Wildlife? http://www.watchablewildlife.org/

what_is_ww.htm Last viewed 29 October 2002.

Nature and Ecotourism Accreditation Program Working Group (NEAPWG) (2000) *Nature and Ecotourism Accreditation Program,* 2nd edn. NEAP, Brisbane, Queensland.

Nature Based Tourism Advisory Committee (NBTAC) (1994) *Towards a Nature Based Tourism Strategy for Western Australia.* Discussion Paper, Western Australian Tourism Commission, Perth, Western Australia.

Ollason, R.J. (1993) Getting the message across. Proceedings of the 11th IZE Congress. *Journal of the International Association of Zoo Educators, Taronga Zoo* 29, 186.

Orams, M. (1995) Managing interaction between wild dolphins and tourists at a dolphin feeding program, Tangalooma, Australia. PhD thesis, University of Queensland, Brisbane.

Parks and Wildlife Commission, Northern Territory (n.d.) *Northern Territory Parks Masterplan.* Parks and Wildlife Commission Northern Territory, Darwin, Northern Territory.

Parsler, J. (1997) Tourism and the environment in Madagascar. In: Stabler, M.J. (ed.) *Tourism and Sustainability: Principles to Practice.* CAB International, Wallingford, pp. 347–355.

Pearce, F. (1995) Selling wildlife short. *New Scientist* September, 28–31.

Perth Zoo (1999) *Annual Report, 1998–1999.* Zoological Board of Western Australia, Perth, Western Australia.

Perth Zoo (2000) *Annual Report, 1999–2000.* Zoological Board of Western Australia, Perth, Western Australia.

Phillip Island Nature Park Board of Management (1998) *Phillip Island Nature Park Draft Management Plan, October 1998.* Biosis Research, Port Melbourne, Victoria.

Preece, N. and van Oosterzee, P. (1997) *Biodiversity Conservation and Ecotourism: an Investigation of the Linkages, Mutual Benefits and Future Opportunities.* Paper No. 5, Biodiversity Series, Biodiversity Unit, Department of the Environment Sport and Territories, Canberra, Australian Capital Territory.

Roe, D., Leader-Williams, N. and Dalal-Clayton, B. (1997) *Take Only Photographs, Leave Only Footprints: the Environmental Impacts of Wildlife Tourism.* International Institute for Environment and Development, London.

Rowley, I.C.R. (ed.) (1992) Little penguin supplement [special issue]. *Emu* 91(5), 261–408.

Ryder, O.A. and Feistner, A.T.C. (1995) Research in zoos: a growth area in conservation. *Biodiversity and Conservation* 4, 671–677.

Scott, S. (2001) Captive breeding. In: Jordan, B. (ed.)

Who Cares For Planet Earth? The Con In Conservation. Alpha Press, Brighton, UK, pp. 50–63.

Seal, U.S. (1991) The role of captive breeding in conserving wildlife. *Proceedings of a Symposium of the Zoological Society of London* 62, 145–163.

Shackley, M.L. (1995) The future of gorilla tourism in Rwanda. *Journal of Sustainable Tourism* 3(2), 1–12.

Tarrant, M.A., Bright, A.D. and Cordell, H.K. (1997) Attitudes toward wildlife species protection: assessing, moderating and mediating effects in the value-attitude relationship. *Human Dimensions of Wildlife* 2(2), 1–20.

Tisdell, C. and Wilson, C. (2000) *Economic, Educational and Conservation Benefits of Sea Turtle Based Ecotourism: a Study Focused on Mon Repos.* Wildlife Tourism Research Report No. 20, Status Assessment of Wildlife Tourism in Australia Series, CRC for Sustainable Tourism, Gold Coast, Queensland.

Tribe, A. (2000) *Captive Wildlife Tourism in Australia.* Wildlife Tourism Research Report No. 14, Status Assessment of Wildlife Tourism in Australia Series, CRC for Sustainable Tourism, Gold Coast, Queensland.

van Oosterzee, P. (2000) Ecotourism and biodiversity conservation: two-way track. *Pacific Conservation Biology* 6(2), 89–93.

Vickerman, S. (1988) Stimulating tourism and eco-nomic growth by featuring new wildlife recreation opportunities. *Proceedings of Transactions of the 53rd North American Wildlife and Natural Resources Conference (1988).* Wildlife Management Institute, Washington, DC, pp. 414–423.

Vieta, F.E. (1999) Ecotourism propels development. Africa Recovery Online. http://www.un.org/ecosocdev/geninfo/afrec/vol13no1/tourism.htm Last viewed 24 October 2002.

Weaver, D. (2001) *Ecotourism.* John Wiley & Sons Australia, Milton, Queensland.

Woollard, S.P. (1998) The development of zoo education. *International Zoo News* 45(7), 422–426.

Woollard, S.P. (1999) A review of zoo education in the United Kingdom and Ireland. *International Zoo News* 46(1), 20–24.

World Zoo Organisation (WZO) (1993) *The World Zoo Conservation Strategy: the Role of Zoos and Aquaria of the World in Global Conservation.* Chicago Zoological Society, Chicago.

Young, M.D., Gunningham, N., Elix, J., Lambert, J., Howard, B., Grabosky, P. and McCrone, E. (1996) *Reimbursing the Future: an Evaluation of Motivational, Voluntary, Price-Based, Property-Right, and Regulatory Incentives for the Conservation of Biodiversity.* Paper No. 9, Biodiversity Series, Biodiversity Unit, Canberra.

18

Balancing Conservation and Visitation in Protected Areas

Robyn Bushell
School of Environment and Agriculture, University of Western Sydney,
New South Wales, Australia

Abstract

Many protected-area managers are encountering difficulties balancing the demands of conservation and visitors. An essential component for sound management planning is having objective data on appropriate use, visitor-use impacts and visitor needs. Visitor-impact management in protected areas poses several difficulties because systems of management and control are not equipped to predict or monitor often complex, subtle and cumulative impacts on biological diversity or cultural heritage in either the short or long term; and different stakeholders have diverse views on what constitutes appropriate use. Additionally, the environmental costs of tourism development are typically externalized by tourism operators and visitors wanting access to the resource, often placing unreasonable expectations on natural-resource management agencies which have very limited funding.

Introduction

Nature-based recreation and tourism are directly dependent on natural resources in a relatively undeveloped state. These often focus on parks and other protected areas, and the levels of visitation to these biologically valuable sites are growing dramatically. Successful nature-based tourism depends on high levels of environmental quality and suitable levels of consumer service, though the latter leads to issues of appropriate use and questions of resource allocation (Eagles, 1999; Bushell *et al.*, 2002).

Globally, the land area dedicated as parks and protected areas has increased significant-ly in the past 30 years. In 1996 there were 30,361 parks in 225 countries, with a total area of 13.2 million km^2 or 8.84% of the total land area of the planet (Green and Paine, 1997). The establishment, maintenance and support for a worldwide system of protected areas mark a long history of changing attitudes towards nature (Halvorson, 1996).

In many parts of the world, protected areas are nevertheless seen by governments as marginal to other areas of policy, such as economic development. Tourism is increasingly viewed as a source of revenue that can replace public funding. Protected-area managers are therefore encountering increased difficulties in balancing the demands of conservation work and visitor management. The World Commission for Protected Areas (WCPA) identified effective management of visitor use in protected areas as a key future challenge (Sheppard, 1999).

Australia, for example, contributed some 60 million ha or 7.9% of its terrestrial landmass and 3.5% of its marine 'exclusive economic zone' to the global conservation estate in 1999 (Worboys et al., 2001). In the State of New South Wales (NSW), the protected-area system covers nearly 5.5 million ha or nearly 6.7% of the State. This includes some 607 protected areas, 500 within the NSW National Parks and Wildlife Service (NPWS) system. Of these, 29 are within the Sydney region (Brown, 2001; B. Gilligan and C. Allen, 2001, unpublished), which also has Australia's largest urban population and is the State's premier tourist destination and gateway for international visitors.

The Australian situation is important because Australia is the only developed-country member of the world's 12 megadiverse nations which together support 75% of the earth's biodiversity (Mott and Bridgewater, 1999). Australia therefore, has a particularly significant responsibility to ensure that its natural environment is well managed and protected. At the same time, the country's national and state tourism authorities are marketing Australia very actively as a nature-based tourism destination, with special emphasis on the nation's many national parks and its 14 World Heritage Areas (WHAs).

Visitation to Natural Areas

Increasing visitation to protected areas is a global phenomenon. Worldwide, parks are being identified as major attractions for visitors, both domestic and international. In the USA, between 10 and 24% of all visitation in 1995 was directly related to protected areas (TWAC, 1996). Protected areas throughout Australia receive more than 60 million visitors per year, making national parks the country's single largest category of tourist attraction (Worboys et al., 2001). In NSW, some 26.5 million people visited national parks, reserves and state forests in 1999, an increase of 1.9%

over the previous year. Eighty-four per cent of the nature-tourism market in NSW, which includes visitation to protected areas, crownland, public beaches and natural areas on private land, consists of domestic visitors. Some 30% of all domestic visitors to NSW in 1999 took part in nature-tourism activities (Missing Link, 2001), while 50% of international visitors to Australia in 1995 went to a national park during their stay (Blamey, 1995). Most of these come for recreational activities, including bushwalking, camping, cycling, picnicking, scenic drives, community and family gatherings, swimming and other water sports, adventure activities such as abseiling, and photography, painting and meditation. Increasing numbers arrive as part of commercial tours or school excursions or for guided walks (Peter Kennedy, NSW NPWS, 2001, personal communication).

As the shortfalls in government support for protected-area conservation become increasingly severe, support from non-government sources, such as local communities, private landowners, land-users and non-governmental organizations (NGOs), becomes more important (McNeely, 1994). Key to this is identifying and communicating the many values and benefits that protected areas offer society (D. Sheppard, 1999, unpublished). The relationship between tourism and protected areas can be useful in this process.

Visitor Impacts and Appropriate Use

Many residents of urban regions are increasingly alienated from nature. Consequently, the quality of their lives is diminished, they have little understanding of the benefits of natural areas and they may be less likely to provide political support for conservation. Many are afraid of wildlife and wilderness (Finger, 1993). Appreciation of nature is more likely to be achieved through outdoor recreation than through classroom environmental education. Without direct experience of nature, teaching environmental issues can even breed cynicism about the environment (Trzyna, 2001). Visitation to protected areas may hence be valuable, not only in a direct economic sense, but also to foster environmental awareness and a conservation ethic. However, visitation itself generates environmental impacts and issues, so tourism and visitor use must be planned carefully if they are not to destroy the natural resource on which they depend.

Visitor-impact management in many protected areas poses particular difficulties because: (i) systems of management and control are not equipped or resourced to predict and monitor complex, subtle and cumulative impacts on biological diversity or cultural heritage, in either the short or long term; and (ii) different stakeholders may have highly diverse views on what constitutes appropriate use. Additionally, the environmental costs of tourism development are commonly externalized by operators and visitors wanting access to the resource, and in consequence they place unreasonable expectations on natural-resource management agencies that have very limited funding (Bushell, 1999a).

While there are plenty of examples of good practice, there are many examples around the world of excessive or inappropriate tourist use of protected areas, coupled with poor planning, which have caused significant environmental impact (D. Sheppard, 1999, unpublished). Tourism as a complex global activity requires planning and management, with consideration for ecological impacts as well as the economic, political and social realities of the host destination and its source markets. Ensuring sufficient protection for the natural environment, even in protected areas, can prove to be very difficult in the face of such factors (Robertson, cited in Figgis, 1999, p. 13). Successful planning requires far greater research into the needs of protected-area systems, their managers and their visitors, with increased dialogue and cooperation between resource-management agencies and the tourism industry. The building of broader constituencies for protected areas is seen as a priority by many conservation agencies. Leadership and firm policies are needed to ensure that the tourism industry recognizes and respects the primacy of the conservation role of protected areas.

According to Figgis (1999) a combination of various motivations in the 1980s saw changes to Australian community attitudes to protected-area management. Tourism gained some support from conservation groups, as an acceptable alternative employment strategy, in the battle against the extractive industries of mining and logging; and as an incentive for rural and indigenous communities to conserve rather than exploit their natural resources. A report of the Australian Tourist Commission confirmed that the natural environment was the main attraction of Australia for international visitors. The subsequent commitment of Aus$10 million for a National Ecotourism Strategy and the following state-based strategies for eco- and nature-based tourism encouraged the tourism industry to demand increasing access to protected areas. Concurrent reductions in federal-government budget allocations to conservation led to increased dependence on external sources of funding. Hence governments and natural-resource management agencies have increasingly looked to tourism to generate funds through entry fees, licences, concessions, levies and development rights (see Buckley *et al.*, Chapter 7, this volume). This in turn creates pressure for higher visitation and the granting of more concessions and licences.

An Australian International Union for the Conservation of Nature (IUCN) review of a few years ago (Figgis, 1999) drew attention to two concerns: the increasing commercialization of nature and culture; and the increasing distortion of protected-area management, with the needs of tourism, visitors and economic rationalist thinking (tourism-centred planning) taking precedence over conservation priorities (nature-centred planning). Figgis and other prominent conservationists see the trend for commercial tourism developments in protected areas as one of the major threats of ecotourism. They see the ecotourism label as a 'cloak of green' with ecological, aesthetic and cultural impacts ignored due to economic benefits (Figgis, 1999).

The major sources of environmental impacts associated with visitors in national parks differ according to the features of the site and prevailing conditions, as well as the types of activity. Buckley and Pannell (1990) broadly summarized the types of impacts as: damage to tracks and off-road due to vehicles; trampling; damage to river-banks; firewood collection; water pollution and depletion; human waste; litter; noise; disturbance to wildlife; vandalism; and visual impact due to visitor infrastructure. Additional impacts relate to: soil compaction and erosion; damage to flora and habitat; removal of plants and seed sources; introduction of exotic species, weeds and pests; and loss of biodiversity (see also Buckley and King, Chapter 10, this volume).

Many authors, including Brandon *et al.* (1998), Figgis (1999) and Honey (1999), have raised concern at the eagerness of governments and the tourism industry worldwide to confer environmental awards on high-impact developments within and around national parks. Such awards set precedents for similar developments elsewhere. The trend towards commercial development in Australia is the opposite of that in the USA, where some 50% of parks are 'regreening' after years of commercial development, by closing down roads and food and lodging facilities (Figgis, 1999). The USA, it seems, has recognized the high impacts such infrastructure and facilities commonly have on conservation in parks. Similarly, in the UK a 1995 parliamentary inquiry (UK, House of Commons, 1995) recognized damage due to overvisitation in England's national parks and recommended: the closure of certain roads and vehicle-access points; limiting car-parking spaces and introducing restrictive car-park pricing mechanisms; levying a charge for entry to sensitive sites; and increased investment in visitor management. Australia, it seems, has not yet learnt these lessons. The UK report points to the paradox that the better the protection and conservation, the more attractive the site becomes; but the more visitors it receives, the more impacts continue to increase (Evans, 2001).

New Approaches and Attitudes to Park Management

'Gone are the days of the *Forstmeister*, when local resource managers dictated management activities according to straightforward guidelines. Natural resource issues are increasingly complex from administrative, political, legal and social perspectives' (Harmon, 1994, cited

in Peterson, 1996). There is no question that natural-resource management is now inherently a social science, heavily influenced not only by scientific knowledge but by political priorities, policy settings and social values (Lockie *et al.*, 2001). Managers also need effective communications and partnerships with the wider community.

So, while many conservationists are concerned about the significant increases in visitation and the potential for visitor needs to compromise conservation priorities, it must also be noted that many visitors are locals. As well as benefiting from its parks, the local community also often makes contributions to its local national park and supports the park service in many other ways. For example, the Lane Cove National Park in Sydney is only 600 ha but has a perimeter of 70 km and over 2000 neighbours. It receives over 1 million visitors each year, making it one of the most popular national parks in Australia. Most visitors arrive by car. The critical issues for such a site are mostly off-site and include water and air quality, exotic species and use of adjacent land. Following severe bushfires in 1994, the NSW NPWS received a grant of Aus$330,000 to support the 'Friends of Lane Cove National Park', a community-based bush-regeneration programme. In 3 years the 'Friends' have contributed over 10,000 hours of labour and the prospect of a sound future for the park by tapping into the local community to convey conservation messages. The partnership has led to much greater appreciation of the values and vulnerability of 'their' park, in turn leading to positive behaviour, such as restraining pets, not dumping garden waste, controlling invasive garden plants and refraining from the use of fertilizers. The community support also influences local governance policy. In this case, local councils are donating additional adjoining lands (Brown, 2001).

Reconciling Conservation Values and Broader Social and Cultural Values

While the involvement of a broad range of stakeholders in planning for sustainable use is commendable, and examples such as 'The

Friends of Lane Cove National Park' demonstrate a very productive partnership, working with multiple stakeholders is anything but straightforward. Processes of consultation allowing for a wide cross-section of groups and interests and encouraging participation are recognized as necessary. Consultation with local-community and other stakeholders, however, is rarely simple or cheap, nor is it guaranteed to achieve sustainable-use objectives. Indeed, some of the most vocal lobby groups, especially those which champion human use over nature conservation, have quite specific agendas. These include industries, such as mining and logging, and recreational groups, such as hunting and off-road vehicle enthusiasts, who demand access to exploit resources in parks purely for human profit or enjoyment. Some of these believe strongly that all areas should be available for unconstrained human activity (Figgis, 1999). Such groups are often highly organized politically and can dominate attempts to include public participation in decision-making and planning processes. Such issues add to the challenge of protected-area management, especially since the social sciences are not the usual province of natural-resource managers.

Land managers now need to understand cultural as well as biophysical landscapes. Cultural landscape is a term used to integrate the cultural and natural values of a place (Lee, 2000). It was first used in heritage conservation to describe places where the sociocultural context, i.e. the cultural, symbolic, spiritual and physical interrelationships in the landscape, is more significant to the people living in those landscapes than any single cultural icon or monument (Taylor and Tallents, 1996). A variety of cultural and ethical issues surround the identification, evaluation and management of cultural landscapes, particularly those associated with the history of indigenous people and the associated issues of territory, dislocation, secret knowledge, lost language and sacredness. In Australia, the focus of heritage-conservation efforts on precontact sites, relics and history has meant that contemporary indigenous social values have been neglected or devalued (English, 2000). This includes issues of traditional use of biological resources, land rights and own-

ership. The rights of indigenous people form a difficult and complex area, particularly for colonized peoples who have been dislocated and have contested identity, relationships and rights within their own communities. The issues of indigenous people are often oversimplified and romanticized. Debates over appropriate use of protected areas and models of management have been linked to efforts to restore and address the land rights of indigenous peoples. Now recognized as extremely important, indigenous knowledge is tied to concepts of sustainable land use. The 1992 IUCN Caracas declaration called upon governments and appropriate organizations to: 'Support the development of national protected area policies which are sensitive to customs and traditions [and] safeguard the interests of indigenous people' (Kempf, 1993).

Consideration of the rights of indigenous peoples to 'protected areas' reinforces the concept of 'nature' as a social construct. 'The idea of wilderness as untamed land is mostly a view of urbanised people, far removed from their natural environment' (Gomez-Pompa and Kaus, 1992, p. 273). Even the concept of 'wilderness' is contested. 'The vision of empty bushland is both baffling and insulting' to indigenous people who have lived as a part of these landscapes for centuries (Strang, 1996). A vast 'undisturbed' scenic area is the typical popular image associated with protected areas, but these same places represent different values to different people. What may be regarded by a conservationist as important habitat or by a botanist as having exceptional scientific merit may be seen by a forester as having high economic value, by a hunter as a perfect place for shooting (Gomez-Pompa and Kaus, 1992) or by a tourism entrepreneur as an ideal site for an 'ecolodge'.

Protected areas are social spaces, conceived by people as deserving preservation (Ghimire and Pimbert, 1997, p. 5). This construction of nature varies in time across cultural, political and social beliefs and economic status. This influences what values are placed on nature; what are regarded as priorities for protection; and what is considered as acceptable use (Bushell, 1999b; Figgis, 1999; Staiff *et al.*, 2002).

Appreciating how different groups of people value nature is essential to managing visitor use. Tourism and recreation are seen as a priority objective of the IUCN protected-area management categories – II (national parks), III (natural monuments) and V (protected landscape/seascapes) (IUCN, 1994). However, visitor use must be compatible with other uses and with the social, cultural, legal, institutional and geographical context. Compatibility among users is important to financial success and effective management of protected areas. Incompatible user groups can lead to conflict, loss of support and wasted investment (FPATF, 2000). Overuse can lead to destruction of the asset.

The designation of certain areas as being 'of outstanding natural beauty and heritage' aims to preserve their distinctive character while providing opportunities for their enjoyment. 'In reality this relationship between conservation and recreation has proved somewhat conflicting, and the popularity of national parks, as a visitor resource, is currently threatening the continuing protection of their unique qualities' (Evans, 2001, p. 77).

One of the social realities is the economic value placed on nature. Tourism based on protected areas is increasingly important because of its economic potential, but this is not without problems. For example, Machu Picchu World Heritage Site has outstanding cultural and agrarian values as a 500-year-old Inca city. For many it is a sacred site. It is also the most visited site in Peru and one of the most important tourist destinations in Latin America. The number of visitors rose from 55,000 per annum in the early 1990s to over 400,000 per annum by 1999, with a 30% increase between 1998 and 1999 and doubling by 2002. These visitors bring in some US$5 million for the sanctuary, plus other large-scale economic activities associated with the site, including rail, bus and helicopter transport, accommodation and the souvenir trade. But, along with economic success, the high rate of visitation has generated an environmental and social crisis. There are approximately 1600 urban and 1000 rural inhabitants in the area. Problems include ecosystem degradation and loss of biodiversity, due to the presence of both locals and visitors, from uncontrolled development of tourism infrastructure and waste manage-

ment. From an ethical position the local people, who are among the poorest in the world, are not compensated for the opportunity cost of the sanctuary (including restricted access to scarce arable land) or for the tourism activity that increasingly diminishes their available fuel and water and has many different impacts on their quality of life and normal routine. External travel businesses and national bureaucracies receive the majority of the economic benefit (Andrade, 2000). The attitude of the local people to this sacred site presumably remains reverent. Their attitude is one of considerable resentment and confusion towards the system that declared it 'protected', removed them from their land and then encouraged hundreds of thousands of visitors, generating vast income, while the asset is degraded, both spiritually and ecologically, and they experience loss of basic necessities of food and water.

Nature-based Tourism as a Mechanism to Fund Conservation

The challenge is to derive economic benefit without the degradation of other values. The impetus to achieve this is considerable because the economic benefits of park-based tourism can far exceed government expenditure to manage these sites (Driml and Common, 1995; Taskforce on Economic Benefits, 1998), yielding substantial net support for national economies. The Wet Tropics WHA of Australia currently has over 200 commercial operators utilizing some 200 designated visitor sites within the WHA and over 4 million visitors per annum. A study in 1997 estimated that tourism in the WHA contributed over Aus$170 million directly to the regional economy (R. Watkinson, 2000, unpublished). However, unless the activity is managed for minimal impact and unless a significant proportion of the economic benefits is captured to protect the resource, the scenario is exploitative and non-sustainable. Economic benefit should also support local people, so that the local people continue to support conservation and the protected area.

In the State of NSW, Australia, the NSW NPWS has completed a number of studies on socio-economic issues surrounding nature conservation, designed to foster better relationships with local government, community groups, other agencies and individuals to ensure the well-being of rural and regional areas. In assessing the economic benefits of protected areas to regional economies, input–output analyses have been used to measure the contribution of protected areas to gross regional output (business turnover), gross regional product (value-added activity), household income and employment. The economic contribution from national parks to these different elements occurs in two main ways. First, the park-management agency itself contributes directly: by employing local residents; by buying local goods and services, which stimulates local businesses and trade; and through consumer spending by park staff and their families. Secondly, the national park acts as a magnet to attract visitors to a region. The flow-on effect of these visitors is through the purchasing of accommodation, food and beverages, transport, motor-vehicle services, shopping and other related activities within communities surrounding the park (Conner, 1999). Local people must have some equity in these businesses if they are to receive financial benefits, though there are other multiplier effects and locals need to be made aware of such benefits. In Budderoo National Park on the southern coast of NSW, for example, the construction of visitor facilities increased visitor numbers from 72,000 in 1992 to 140,000 in 1995. Regional economic benefits from these visitors have been estimated at Aus$1.4 million (US$0.7 million) in additional household income and Aus$4.1 million (US$2.1 million) in additional regional economic product (Gillespie, 1997; Conner, 1999).

If protected areas are to be valued and managed for their economic potential, protected-area managers need to service both their public and private customers and to receive a fair return from both through appropriate financial mechanisms. As noted in the WCPA guidelines on *Financing Protected Areas* (FPATF, 2000), protected areas supply a range of goods and services providing both use and non-use benefits. To capture economic return from use benefits, it is necessary to determine the nature of the uses and the ben-

eficiaries and whether they are public or private in nature or hybrid. A public good can be any good or service for which provision is non-excludable and non-divisible: that is, once provided, it is available to the general public. A private good, on the other hand, is excludable and divisible. Once provided for someone, it is not available to others. In relation to protected areas, watershed services and carbon sequestering provide examples of public goods, while private goods include fishing and camping. Once a fish is caught or a camping permit allocated, they are no longer available to anyone else. Certain private goods, such as controlled entry to protected areas, may be excludable but not divisible. These are termed 'toll goods'. There are also 'common pool goods', which are divisible but not excludable. For these, access is open to anyone, but the goods can only be used once. An example is picking flowers in a forest (FPATF, 2000).

The public-good aspects of protected areas usually require grant funding, from government or overseas development or foundation support. Private aspects and 'toll goods' from protected areas are more easily commercialized and can be funded by private sources of finance, such as tourism charges, gate fees or licence fees. Commercial customers of a protected area are those who derive direct use (economic) benefits from the area, such as tour operators. Innovation is often required to capture the values that these customers derive from the protected area. Gate fees and user fees are two of the more traditional means. Donation boxes, equipment hire, specialized tours and provision of park guides are among alternative ways of capturing visitor-generated funds (FPATF, 2000).

Visitation Supporting Conservation?

Most of the world's individual protected areas currently charge low or zero entry and user fees. Many of the opportunities to capture funds, however, are at the individual site level, as people are more motivated to pay or donate when they see either a tangible return or benefit. Often this is a user fee. 'User fees' cover several possible services including: entry fees;

admission fees for special attractions or fea-tures; parking and camping fees; fees for picnic facilities, such as gas barbecues; fees from concessionaires who profit from operating lodging, food and beverage, guiding or other operations within the protected area; and boat-ing fees. User fees can be collected by protected-area staff or by concessionaires, who pay for the right to run their business. The benefit of collecting fees directly is that rev-enue is more likely to stay on site and benefit the site. However, many fee-generating activ-ities also involve costs and may require specialist services and skills, so they can be more efficiently and effectively run by private profit-based businesses (FPATF, 2000). The challenge is to ensure that tourism becomes a tool of conservation management rather than national parks simply being used as sites of tourism business (Bushell, 1999b).

In most parks, these various fees cover only a small portion of the cost of protecting and providing the features on which park vis-itation depends (Van Sickle and Eagles, 1998; Eagles, 1999). Many pricing policies for pro-tected areas were developed when the 'public good' of protecting nature was considered a benefit to society and therefore paid for by society through public taxes (Eagles, 1999). Increasingly, however, private operators are making their businesses out of guided trips to parks and governments worldwide are with-drawing from public funding and looking to greater cost recovery, forcing parks to use vis-itors as a source of conservation revenue (Eagles, 1995; Staiff et al., 2002). In Australia the practice of charging fees varies consider-ably. Buckley et al. (2001) identified the variation that occurs from park to park between and within the States, depending on size, type and access at different parks. For example, in NSW entrance fees apply to only 44 of some 500 parks and reserves. Visitors may purchase a single entry, a day pass or an annual pass. Fees are charged per vehicle and are also charged for boat trailers and camp-ing. There are also variations in method of payment, including prepaid passes, staffed entry stations, honour collection boxes and pay-and-display ticket-vending machines; and in revenue-distribution mechanisms and rates of retention (Buckley et al., 2001).

The more protected-area managers have to rely on visitor-based funding, the more like-ly is it that compromises will favour tourism rather than conservation priorities (Figgis, 1999). Parks often supply the most important component of a nature-based tourism experi-ence, but frequently capture little of the economic return (Driml and Common, 1995; Wells, 1997; Van Sickle and Eagles, 1998). In the past 6 years the NSW protected-area estate has increased by 35%, while state government expenditure has more than doubled, from Aus\$15 to 35 (US\$8 to 18) per ha. The great-est proportion of this is spent on providing visitor facilities and services. Implementing user-pays policies while maintaining equity of access is an increasingly important challenge (B. Gilligan and C. Allen, 2001, unpublished). Setting appropriate fees is a complex task. Low entry and use fees are often the result of many factors, both social and political. These include: the existence of centralized budget-allocation processes; issues of equity and access for all; political concern about increas-es in park fees upsetting local constituencies; issues relating to the continued belief that soci-ety generally should pay for protected areas; pressure from conservation groups to keep vis-itation low; lack of planning for levels of visitation; lack of research into appropriate methods of determining reasonable pricing policies; lack of partnerships between private operators and parks agencies; and varying lev-els of visitor services and infrastructure (Eagles, 1999). Additionally, the emergence of private-sector conservation enterprises that utilize visitation to fund their conservation efforts, such as Conservation Corporation Africa (Carlisle, Chapter 4, this volume) or Earth Sanctuaries in Australia, raises other equity issues, such as competitive neutrality (B. Gilligan and C. Allen, 2001, unpublished).

Access and Equity

Associated with park fees is the issue of equi-ty. In a study by Gurran (2001) in two rural towns in northern NSW, the nearby parks were identified as very important to local people. Both towns are adjacent to national parks that enjoy high levels of visitation; the local communities are regular visitors and consider the neighbouring park to be an important place for social gatherings, especially to take visitors for walks and picnics. Some 70% of the people interviewed from both towns understood the conservation value of parks. These resident groups strongly identified with and valued the protected area. Aesthetic beauty and access were the highest valued benefits. Economic benefits were regarded as very important to 21% of respondents in one of the two towns, who saw flow-on benefits to business from park visitors. Only 2% of respondents in both towns cited visitor-related impacts as a disadvantage of living near a national park. However, they all expressed strong vocal opposition to park-user fees.

Should local taxpayers pay an entrance fee? If they pay, should it be the same as visitors from elsewhere? This is a contentious issue, especially when a park or reserve has only recently been gazetted as a protected area and locals may already feel alienated from land that either traditionally or historically had been considered a freely available community resource. Local communities frequently put political pressure on policy makers to oppose recommendations when either the introduction of fees or increases in park fees are otherwise justified. The equity issue of entry fees has numerous aspects. A large differential between fees charged for locals and visitors can create tensions for local tour operators. Arguments can also be made that parks increase the land values for neighbours, especially in urban areas, and that such real estate is much sought after. Woven into the equity issue is the belief that society generally and not just users should pay for protected areas since everyone derives many benefits.

Modern economic studies of the value of natural areas and ecosystems emphasize the importance of total economic valuation, moving beyond just direct use benefits and tangible benefits. However, controversy surrounds the estimation of these different values (Tisdell, 1999). The value of protected areas to society can be summarized as a contribution to biodiversity conservation and from this a flow of ecosystem services that benefits nature conservation, health, agriculture, industry and foreign affairs. These include: the provision of

clean water; contributions to watershed protection; assistance with natural resources and water-supply management; assistance with storm protection and reduction in natural disaster damage; the provision of a major asset for the tourism industry and consequent economic regional and local development; contribution to a local amenity that supports local government in the provision of healthy environments; and open spaces and recreational opportunity. All contribute to quality of life and public health through spiritual, mental and physical well-being. The provision of forest products supports forestry, local communities and economic development. Soil conservation assists agriculture and natural-resource management. The provision of large areas for carbon sequestration contributes to energy policy and foreign affairs. The provision of research and education facilities and field stations contributes to the advancement of science, knowledge and education at all levels. The maintenance of cultural values contributes to community health, well-being and sense of place (adapted from Phillips, 1998, in D. Sheppard, 1999, unpublished, FPATF, 2000).

Protected areas also assist with an ethical responsibility to respect nature and create opportunities for the wider community to learn about nature and the environment (Lee, 2000). The principles of the Caracas Declaration remind us that nature has intrinsic worth and warrants respect regardless of its usefulness to society (Lucas, 1992).

Another aspect of equity is ensuring that everyone is able to enjoy regular access to natural areas. As with other areas of public policy, such as health and education, there are many issues about the user-pays approach, which can deny access to many in lower socio-economic groups. In order to address equity issues for a wide range of user groups, such as locals, senior citizens, pensioners, schoolchildren, family groups and members of parks associations, some parks services have established such complex pricing structures that parks staff find it unmanageable. These and other factors mean that park fees continue to be kept below the level that would enable management agencies to meet visitor demands for infrastructure, or even to maintain existing infrastructure, such as wooden walkways, paths, signs, seating and toilets. This makes the task of visitor-impact management even more demanding (Peter Kennedy, NSW NPWS, 2001, personal communication).

The Need to Better Understand Visitor Management

To improve economic return and manage visitation effectively involves understanding both the patterns of visitation and the nature of the impacts. It is also important to understand that visitor impacts are dynamic, as is nature. Strategic approaches must have both a short- and a long-term focus, with a view to managing over time, using a wide range of performance indicators (Gilligan and Allen, 2001). NSW NPWS management, for example, acknowledges that information on visitation is currently lacking. Issues requiring research include: the role and effectiveness of conservation education and interpretation, including multicultural dimensions; comprehensive information on visitor numbers, source markets and demography; visitation patterns, including repeat visitation and length of stay; and visitor satisfaction and motivations (B. Gilligan and C. Allen, 2001, unpublished).

Visitor satisfaction and service quality can suffer when financial return from visitors is not tied directly to financial operation of a park. Market pricing and a competitive environment are considered important, not only for creating a more commercially viable operation and releasing funds for non-commercial conservation, but also for providing managers and other stakeholders with incentives to improve their performance and that of the park as a whole (Taskforce on Economic Benefits, 1998). Central budgeting also denies park managers flexibility to manage and run the operation as a business and to be commercially competitive. Lack of data on the economic contributions of protected areas and conservation leads to severe under-representation of its importance relative to other economic activities, such as forestry (Eagles, 1999). Instead of proactively determining appropriate use and levels of visitation, the process is reactive, responding to problems and issues as they

arise or as they are perceived. This is unlikely to result in optimal conservation outcomes or visitor satisfaction (Bushell, 1999a).

Experience throughout the world tends to indicate that negative impacts of tourism on park resources are influenced more by inadequate visitor planning, management and staffing than by actual visitor numbers. Concern also stems from a lack of visitor-management skills among parks staff. The majority of parks agencies are strong in scientific natural-resource management. Most are weaker in tourism and visitor-related competencies and learn these skills on the job. The concept of 'carrying capacity', despite never being operationalized successfully, has tended to spawn the belief that there is a direct relationship between numbers and impacts. However, parks that are competently managed and properly resourced with suitable infrastructure have been shown to be capable of creating high levels of economic return with minimal environmental impact (Eagles, 1999).

Many parks-service staff remain divided on the concept of allowing a site manager to operate under commercially competitive conditions. Conservation organizations, generally, are also very cautious about the effects of encouraging natural-resource managers to think like business people. However, research shows that, by using the concept of total economic value, it is possible to identify the goods and services or 'products' protected areas offer, which are suitable for raising revenue for the conservation of protected areas. With proper management the 'products' can be sold repeatedly without diminishing the value of the protected area. Managers need to have business plans for assessing and realizing the potential benefits to ensure the long-term financial sustainability of protected areas in their care (Taskforce on Economic Benefits, 1998; FPATF, 2000).

Sound planning needs reliable information and appropriate methods to determine pricing policies and social carrying capacity and to monitor ecological impacts and the effectiveness of various interpretation strategies and approaches. If one primary purpose of increasing visitation to parks is to encourage the development of a robust conservation constituency within society at large, then it is imperative to evaluate the effects of conservation messages on park users. To date, considerable research has been conducted to determine the most effective types of sign and the most utilitarian approach in reaching audiences of different ages, but little effort has been devoted to understanding the different ways in which people construct and relate to nature and how this understanding could inform approaches to interpretation and education programmes (Staiff *et al.*, 2002).

Conclusion

Protected-area managers are encountering difficulties in balancing the demands of conservation work and visitor management. Essential components for sound management planning include more objective data on visitor use, impacts and needs; and the ability to undertake informed longitudinal cost/benefit analyses so as to make sound long- and short-term management decisions.

References

Andrade, G.I. (2000) The non-material values of Machu Picchu World Heritage Site, from acknowledgement to action. *Parks* 10(2), 49–62.

Blamey, R. (1995) *The Nature of Ecotourism*. BTR Occasional Paper No. 21, Bureau of Tourism Research, Canberra.

Brandon, K., Redford, K.H. and Sanderson, S.E. (1998) *Parks in Peril*. Island Press, Washington.

Brown, I.R. (2001) Lane Cove: national park in a city. *Parks* 11(3), 21–27.

Buckley, R. and Pannell, J. (1990) Environmental impacts of tourism and recreation in national parks and conservation reserves. *Journal of Tourism Studies* 1(1), 24–32.

Buckley, R., Witting, N. and Guest, M. (2001) *Managing People in Australian Parks. 1. Visitor Entrance and Camping Fees*. CRC Sustainable Tourism, Australia.

Bushell, R. (1999a) *Development of Approaches and Practice for Sustainable Use of Biological Resources – Tourism*. Policy Recommendation for the International Union for the Conservation of Nature (IUCN) for the Fourth Meeting of the Subsidiary Body on Scientific, Technical and Technological Advice,

Convention on Biological Diversity, Montreal.

Bushell, R. (1999b) Global issues for protected areas and nature-based tourism: case studies of partnerships in Australia addressing some of these issues. Representing the Task Force on Tourism and Protected Areas of WCPA, IUCN, at the International Expert Workshop Sustainable Use of Biodiversity – the Example of Tourism, 11–14 November, Federal Agency for Nature Conservation, Isle of Vilm, Germany.

Bushell, R., Staiff, R. and Conner, N. (2002) The role of nature-based tourism in the contribution of protected areas to quality of life in rural and regional communities in Australia. *Journal of Hospitality and Tourism Management* 9(1), 24–36.

Conner, N. (1999) *The Contribution of National Parks to Sustainable Rural and Regional Development*. NSW NPWS Environmental Economic Series, NSW National Parks and Wildlife Service, Sydney.

Driml, S. and Common, M. (1995) Economic and financial benefits of tourism in major protected areas. *Australian Journal of Environmental Management* 2(2), 19–39.

Eagles, P.F.J. (1995) Tourism and Canadian parks: fiscal relationships. *Managing Leisure* 1(1), 16–27.

Eagles, P.F.J. (1999) International trends in park tourism and ecotourism. Background paper for the Mediterranean Protected Areas: Status, Adequacy, Management and Training Needs Workshop, Cilento, Italy.

English, A. (2000) An emu in the hole: exploring the link between biodiversity and Aboriginal cultural heritage in NSW, Australia. *Parks* 10(2), 13–25.

Evans, S. (2001) Community forestry: countering excess visitor demands in England's national parks. In: McCool, S.E. and Moisey, R.N. (eds) *Tourism, Recreation and Sustainability*, CAB International, Wallingford, pp. 77–90.

Figgis, P.J. (1999) *Australia's National Parks and Protected Areas: Future Directions* Occasional Paper No. 8, Australian Committee for IUCN, Sydney.

Financing Protected Areas Task Force (FPATF) of the World Commission for Protected Areas in Collaboration with the Economics Unit of IUCN (2000) *Financing Protected Areas*. IUCN, Gland, Switzerland, and Cambridge.

Finger, M. (1993) *Environmental Adult Learning in Switzerland*. Centre for Adult Learning Teachers College, Columbia University, New York.

Ghimire, K.B. and Pimbert, M.P. (eds) (1997) *Social Change and Conservation*. Earthscan, UK.

Gillespie, R. (1997) *Economic Value and Regional Economic Impact of Minnamurra Rainforest Centre, Budderoo National Park*. NSW National Parks and Wildlife Service, Sydney.

Gomez-Pompa, A. and Kaus, A. (1992) Taming the wilderness myth. *Bioscience* 42(4), 271–279.

Green, M.J.B. and Paine, J. (1997) State of the world's protected areas at the end of the 20th century. Paper presented to the World Commission for Protected Areas Symposium, Protected Areas in the 21st Century: From Islands to Networks, Albany, Western Australia.

Gurran, N. (2001) *Planning for Park Communities*. Interim Report No. 3. Department of Architecture, Planning and Allied Arts, University of Sydney, Sydney.

Halvorson, W.L. (1996) Changes in landscape values and expectations: what do we want? And how do we measure it? In: Wright, R.G. (ed.) *National Parks and Protected Areas: their Role in Environmental Protection*. Blackwell Science, Massachusetts, pp. 15–30

Honey, M. (1999) *Ecotourism and Sustainable Development: Who Owns Paradise?* Island Press, Washington.

International Union for the Conservation of Nature (IUCN) (1994) *Guidelines for Protected Area Management Categories*. IUCN, Gland, Switzerland.

Kempf, E. (ed.) (1993) *The Law of the Mother: Protecting Indigenous People in Protected Areas*. Sierra Book Club, San Francisco.

Lee, E. (2000) Cultural connections to the land – a Canadian example. *Parks* 10(2), 3–12.

Lockie, S., Higgins, V. and Lawrence, G. (2001) What's social about natural resources and why do we need to theorise it? In: Lawrence, G., Higgins, V. and Lockie, S. (eds) *Environment, Society and Natural Resource Management: Theoretical Perspectives from Australasia and the Americas*. Edward Elgar, Cheltenham.

Lucas, B. (1992) The Caracas Declaration. *Parks* 3(2), 7–8.

McNeely, J.A. (1994) Protected areas for the twenty first century: working to provide benefits to society. *Unasylva* 176(46), 3–8.

Missing Link (2001) NSW *Nature Tourism Discussion Paper*. Tourism NSW, Sydney.

Mott, J.J. and Bridgewater, P.B. (1999) Biodiversity, conservation and ecologically sustainable development. *Search* 23(9), 284–287.

Peterson, D.L. (1996) Research in parks and protected areas: forging the links between science and management. In: Wright, R.G. (ed.) *National Parks and Protected Areas: Their Role in Environmental Protection*. Blackwell Science, Massachusetts.

Staiff, R., Bushell, R. and Kennedy, P. (2002) Interpretation in national parks: some critical questions. *Journal of Sustainable Tourism* 10(2), 97–113.

Strang, V. (1996) Sustaining tourism in far north Queensland. In: Price, M. (ed.) *People and Tourism in Fragile Environments*. Royal Geographical Society and John Wiley & Sons, Chichester.

Taskforce on Economic Benefits of Protected Areas of the World Commission on Protected Areas of IUCN, in collaboration with the Economic Service Unit of IUCN (1998) *Economic Values of Protected Areas: Guidelines for Protected Area Managers*. IUCN, Gland, Switzerland, and Cambridge.

Taylor, K. and Tallents, C. (1996) Cultural landscapes protection in Australia. *International Journal of Heritage Studies* 2(3), 133–144.

Tisdell, C. (1999) *Biodiversity, Conservation and Sustainable Development: New Horizons in Environmental Economics*. Edward Elgar, Cheltenham.

Tourism Works for America Council (TWAC) (1996) *Annual Report*. TWAC, Washington, DC.

Trzyna, T. (2001) California's protected areas: progress despite daunting pressure. *Parks* 11(3), 4–15.

UK, House of Commons (1995) *The Environmental Impact of Leisure Activities*. Environment Committee, House of Commons, London.

Van Sickle, K. and Eagles, P.F.J. (1998) User fees and pricing policies in Canadian senior park agencies. *Tourism Management* 19(3), 225–235.

Wells, M.P. (1997) *Economic Perspectives on Nature Tourism, Conservation and Development*. Paper No. 55, Environment Department, Pollution and Environment Economics Division, World Bank, Washington, DC.

Worboys, G., Lockwood, M. and De Lacy, T. (2001) *Protected Area Management: Principles and Practice*. Oxford University Press, South Melbourne.

19

Conclusions

Ralf Buckley

International Centre for Ecotourism Research, Griffith University, Queensland, Australia

---

This book was compiled and edited during the International Year of Ecotourism (IYE) and completed in December 2002 as IYE drew to a close. During 2002, public and government attention focused on many of the issues addressed in these chapters and contributions. The significance of ecotourism as a tool in poverty alleviation has been recognized at the World Summit on Sustainable Development.

In the short term, private-sector tour operators and government tourism-promotion agencies are currently most concerned about the influence of terrorism and commercial weaknesses in the airline industry. In the longer term, however, the links between nature tourism and land management, addressed in this volume and summarized below, are likely to assume increasing importance for both.

Nature tourism is a major management component for protected areas, heritage sites and other public and private lands worldwide and is continuing to increase in scale.

Protected-area management agencies in particular face a 'triple pinch': more visitors, less wilderness, less money. There are two main management approaches to the triple pinch. The first is to move visitors to different areas, by: making new land available for recre-

ation and tourism; quotas and other regulatory restrictions in particular areas; or marketing and demarketing.

The second is to reduce the per capita impacts of visitors through site hardening, regulations (including zoning) or education. In particular, concentrating visitors in hardened front-country sacrifice areas, as commonly occurs with large-scale tourism in parks, can reduce the per capita impacts of those visitors; but it can also increase impacts by: increasing total visitor numbers; attracting higher-impact visitors to parks; and displacing wilderness visitors into back country areas.

Scientific knowledge of tourist and visitor impacts in protected areas and other relatively undisturbed natural areas in most countries is rather poor, and land-management decisions are commonly made in the absence of good science. Ecological studies need ecological expertise, and there are rather few recreation ecologists worldwide.

There is a continuing tension between managing parks for conservation and managing them for recreation. Visitor management is a major component of protected-area management. In most countries, however, the general public does not think that parks should be run as tourism businesses. Public participation in visitor and tourist planning, management and infrastructure is hence a valuable approach.

Parks agencies worldwide face similar issues in regard to user fees and permits, even though specific fee structures are very different. There could be advantages in improved coordination.

Parks and forests agencies can raise revenue from tourism and recreation in a variety of ways, including: (i) through 'pay-to-play' user fees; (ii) by conducting commercial tourism operations themselves; (iii) by forming commercial partnerships with individual tourism businesses; (iv) by forming political partnerships with tourism portfolios to lobby for increased government funding; (v) potentially, by buying and selling land around park boundaries; and (vi) potentially, by trading land within their overall estate: e.g. by selling some of the lands allocated by public processes and buying private land of higher conservation value.

Partnerships between tourism interests and parks agencies can be valuable in some circumstances – for example, where parks agencies have historic buildings or other heavily visited natural or cultural visitor attractions to manage. Such partnerships will generally only be applicable for small areas and for management of visitors and facilities rather than natural resources and environment. Tourism operators in parks should provide a significant return for the parks agency, reflecting all components of management costs for areas used by tourists.

Parks agencies can use marketing and demarketing tools as well as regulations. Marketing costs money, however, and has to have clear goals to be effective. Parks agen-

cies can regulate the use of parks materials, including both images and information, by private tour operators.

The commodification of recreation and promotion of adventure lifestyles are leading to increased demand for high-impact recreational opportunities, especially those using motorized recreational vehicles and watercraft. These, however, may require sacrificial sites and should generally not be in higher-order protected areas such as national parks. Likewise, visitor facilities do not have to be inside parks, even if built by the parks agency for public use: the agency can lease or buy adjacent land.

Public forests contribute more to most economies through tourism and recreation than through timber production, and tourism facilities developed in public forests by forestry agencies can generate significant revenues.

Private land can be profitable for tourism and conservation if landowners can provide exclusive access to a tourism attraction, such as wildlife or scenery – for example, through individual ownership of wildlife.

Private land adjacent to publicly owned national parks is particularly valuable. Indeed, in some regions, tourism in parks is a transitional phase. Once parks become well known, amenity migration and real-estate development around park margins become far more significant than tourism, both economically and socially. These external forces must be taken into account in protected-area planning and management, as they can subsequently exercise a significant influence over the ability of protected areas to sustain a healthy natural environment and to provide high-quality visitor experiences.

Index

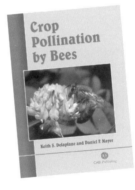
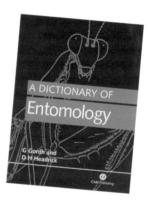
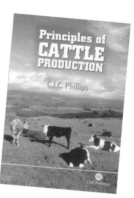